For Gabby Hobson

CONTENTS

List of figures		page ix
List of tables		x
Acknowledgments		xi
1	Introduction: constructing Eurocentrism and international theory as Eurocentric construct	1
I	**1760–1914: Manifest Eurocentrism and scientific racism in international theory**	**31**
2	Eurocentric imperialism: liberalism and Marxism, c. 1830–1914	33
3	Eurocentric anti-imperialism: liberalism, c. 1760–1800	59
4	Racist anti-imperialism: classical liberalism and cultural-realism, c. 1850–1914	84
5	Racist imperialism: racist-realism, liberalism and socialism, 1860–1914	106
II	**1914–1945: The high tide of manifest Eurocentrism and the climax of scientific racism**	**131**
6	Anti-imperialism and the myths of 1919: Marxist Eurocentrism and racist cultural-realism, 1914–1945	133
7	Racist and Eurocentric imperialism: racist-realism, racist-liberalism and 'progressive' Eurocentric liberalism/Fabianism, 1919–1945	150
III	**1945–1989: Subliminal Eurocentrism in international theory**	**183**
8	Orthodox subliminal Eurocentrism: from classical realism to neorealism, 1945–1989	185

9	Orthodox subliminal Eurocentrism: neoliberal institutionalism and the English School, c. 1966–1989	214
10	Critical subliminal Eurocentrism: Gramscianism and world-systems theory, c. 1967–1989	234
IV	**1989–2010: Back to the future of manifest 'Eurocentrism' in mainstream international theory**	255
11	Imperialist and anti-imperialist Eurocentrism: post-1989 'Western realism' and the spiritual return to post-1889 racist-realism	257
12	Imperialist Eurocentrism: post-1989 'Western-liberalism' and the return to post-1830 liberal paternalist Eurocentrism	285
V	**Conclusion: Mapping the promiscuous architecture of Eurocentrism in international theory, 1760–2010**	311
13	Constructing civilization: global hierarchy, 'gradated sovereignty' and globalization in international theory, 1760–2010	313
	References	345
	Index	376

FIGURES

1.1	The definitional continuum of imperialism, past and present	page 24
2.1	Paternalist Eurocentrism and the imperial civilizing mission, c. 1830–1913	34
3.1	Anti-paternalist Eurocentrism and the critique of imperialism, c. 1760–1800	61
4.1	Defensive racism and the critique of empire, c. 1850–1914	85
5.1	Offensive racist conceptions of imperialism, 1889–1914	109
6.1	Defensive racism and critical subliminal Eurocentrism in the critique of imperialism, 1914–45	137
7.1	Racist-realist conceptions of imperialist world politics, 1889–1945	152
7.2	Offensive racist and paternalist Eurocentrism in liberal and Fabian interwar 'international imperialism', c. 1900–45	153
8.1	Subliminal Eurocentrism in classical realism and neorealism, c. 1945–89	187
9.1	Subliminal Eurocentrism in liberal international theory, post-1945	215
10.1	Subliminal anti-paternalist Eurocentrism in neo-Marxist IR theory, c. 1967–2010	235
11.1	Post-1989 IR theory as promoter and defender of Western civilization	260
13.1	The conventional ahistorical 'great narrative' of liberal international theory	328
13.2	Alternative 'polymorphous/protean' career of anti-imperialist liberalism	329
13.3	Alternative 'polymorphous/protean' career of paternalist-imperial liberalism	330
13.4	Alternative 'polymorphous/protean' career of realism	332
13.5	Alternative 'polymorphous/protean' career of Marxism	333
13.6	Civilizational hierarchies and gradated sovereignties in the Eurocentric and scientific racist mirrors	336

TABLES

1.1 Alternative conceptions of Orientalism/Eurocentrism *page* 4
1.2 The four variants of generic Eurocentrism in international theory 5
11.1 Back to the future of post-1889 racist-realism/racist cultural-realism 259
12.1 Back to the future of post-1830 paternalist-Eurocentrism 286
13.1 Mapping the changing architecture of 'Eurocentrism' in international theory, 1760–2010 314

ACKNOWLEDGMENTS

As I explain in Chapter 1, undertaking the research for this book has often felt like an odyssey that led me through a vast and lonely underground complex of dank corridors and barely-lit chambers as I explored the dark underside of international theory. Happily, serendipity intervened as I occasionally bumped into a few kindly souls who were also wandering down there and who shone some light at various moments to help guide my way. I am most grateful to five souls in particular. Luke Ashworth and Brian Schmidt, who provided numerous suggestions for the interwar period, as well as Beate Jahn, whose suggestions led me to revise a great deal of the manuscript in more ways than even she would have anticipated. Bob Vitalis came to my rescue on a good number of occasions and provided some key suggestions on the pre-1945 research that not only helped improve the manuscript in countless ways, but also saved me from making one or two embarrassing howlers. And equally, Martin Hall shared some of the early part of the journey with me, the product of which was mostly published in our joint 2010 article in *International Theory* (Hall and Hobson 2010).

There were also a number of people who very kindly commented on various parts of the manuscript and who offered precious pointers: Duncan Bell, Brett Bowden, Ben de Carvalho, Roger Kanet, Halvard Leira, Naeem Inayatullah, George Lawson, David Long, Xavier Mathieu, Jeanne Morefield, Liliana Riga, Matthew Watson and my Kantian colleague here at Sheffield, Garrett Brown, with whom I have had many enjoyable discussions both in private and public. I also thank those people who made suggestions at various talks and workshops where I tried out certain parts of the book; notably CSGR/POLSIS at the University of Warwick (2009), organized by Len Seabrooke; the Liberal International Theory workshop hosted by Tim Dunne, Marjo Koivisto and Trine Flockhart, at the British Academy (2010); the Department of International Relations at the University of Sussex (2010); and last, but not least, various Sheffield Politics departmental talks to colleagues though mainly postgraduate students, of whom I would like to thank especially Adrian Gallagher, Chris Kitchen and Eddie Tembo. Thanks too must go to David Farrow for his frequently called upon computer skills and to John Haslam at Cambridge University Press (CUP) for his patience, efforts and incisive advice throughout; and thanks too go to the super-efficient production team at CUP including Gillian Dadd, Abigail Jones and my copy-editor, Louise Staples. And, last but not least, deepest thanks go to my family for putting up with my abbreviated space-time presence, especially in what turned out to be a major re-write phase from January to June, 2011. I shall dedicate this book to my daughter, Gabby, in the possibly forlorn hope that one day she might find it in her warm heart to forgive me for the precious time we lost.

THE EUROCENTRIC CONCEPTION
OF WORLD POLITICS

John Hobson claims that throughout its history most international theory has been embedded within various forms of Eurocentrism. Rather than producing value-free and universalist theories of inter-state relations, international theory instead provides provincial analyses that celebrate and defend Western civilization as the subject of, and ideal normative referent in, world politics. Hobson also provides a sympathetic critique of Edward Said's conception of Eurocentrism and Orientalism, revealing how Eurocentrism takes different forms, which can be imperialist or anti-imperialist, and showing how these have played out in international theory since 1760. The book thus speaks to scholars of International Relations, but also to all those interested in understanding Eurocentrism in the disciplines of political science/political theory, political economy/international political economy, geography, cultural and literary studies, sociology and, not least, anthropology.

JOHN M. HOBSON is Professor of Politics and International Relations at the University of Sheffield. His publications include *Everyday Politics of the World Economy* (2007), co-edited with Leonard Seabrooke; *The Eastern Origins of Western Civilisation* (2004); *Historical Sociology of International Relations* (2002), co-edited with Steve Hobden and *The State and International Relations* (2000).

THE EUROCENTRIC CONCEPTION OF WORLD POLITICS

Western International Theory, 1760–2010

JOHN M. HOBSON

CAMBRIDGE
UNIVERSITY PRESS

University Printing House, Cambridge CB2 8BS, United Kingdom
One Liberty Plaza, 20th Floor, New York, NY 10006, USA
477 Williamstown Road, Port Melbourne, VIC 3207, Australia
4843/24, 2nd Floor, Ansari Road, Daryaganj, Delhi - 110002, India
79 Anson Road, #06-04/06, Singapore 079906

Cambridge University Press is part of the University of Cambridge.

It furthers the University's mission by disseminating knowledge in the pursuit of education, learning and research at the highest international levels of excellence.

www.cambridge.org
Information on this title: www.cambridge.org/9781107604544

© John M. Hobson 2012

This publication is in copyright. Subject to statutory exception and to the provisions of relevant collective licensing agreements, no reproduction of any part may take place without the written permission of Cambridge University Press.

First published 2012

A catalogue record for this publication is available from the British Library

ISBN 978-1-107-02020-7 Hardback
ISBN 978-1-107-60454-4 Paperback

Cambridge University Press has no responsibility for the persistence or accuracy of URLs for external or third-party internet websites referred to in this publication, and does not guarantee that any content on such websites is, or will remain, accurate or appropriate.

1

Introduction: Constructing Eurocentrism and international theory as Eurocentric construct

Introduction: international theory as defender of Western civilization

This book produces a twin-revisionist narrative of Eurocentrism and international theory. While the first narrative provides an alternative understanding of Eurocentrism/Orientalism to the reductive conception that was bequeathed by the late, pioneering Edward Said (1978/2003), the second argues that international theory, which has developed both inside and outside of the discipline of International Relations in the last quarter-millennium is, for the most part, a Eurocentric construct. Or to put it more accurately, international theory largely constructs a series of Eurocentric conceptions of world politics. I state this in the plural because I argue that Eurocentrism is a polymorphous, multivalent discourse that crystallizes in a variety of forms. And this leads on to one of my central claims: that international theory does not so much explain international politics in an objective, positivist and universalist manner but seeks, rather, to parochially celebrate and defend or promote the West as the proactive subject of, and as the highest or ideal normative referent in, world politics.

Of course, my reader will assume immediately that in portraying much of international theory as Eurocentric so I will necessarily (re)view it in an imperialist light. But one of the major claims I make in this book is that 'Eurocentrism' not only takes different forms, but that some of these are anti-imperialist while others are imperialist. Such a move, of course, problematizes in an immediate way Said's inherently imperialist definition of Eurocentrism/Orientalism. Of course, I realize that breaking the Gordian Knot between Eurocentrism and imperialism would most likely be viewed within postcolonial circles as a heretical move. But, as I shall argue in this book, an anti-imperialist politics is often as politically fraught as is its so-called imperialist 'Other'. For my claim is that the conventional binary that differentiates a Eurocentric or racist conception of imperialism from a *tolerant* cultural-pluralist conception of anti-imperialism often turns out to be more imaginary than real.

Accordingly, this book will speak to a variety of disciplines: to International Relations, of course, but also to those who have an interest in understanding Eurocentrism/Orientalism. For since the publication of Edward Said's seminal book, *Orientalism* in 1978, the idea and critique of Eurocentrism or Orientalism has spread right across the Social Sciences and Humanities permeating a series of conceptually-based disciplines such as Politics, Political Theory and International Relations (IR), Political Economy/ International Political Economy (IPE), Political Geography, Sociology, Literary/Cultural Studies and, not least, Anthropology. And given my belief that Eurocentrism infects significant swathes of these disciplines so the need to learn more about it should be a matter of concern for such disciplinary practitioners, if not of some urgency. Nevertheless, many potential non-IR readers might still be put off from reading a book that deals with international theorists, most of whom reside within the discipline of IR.

Here, it is important to understand that I do not simply treat international theory as the pure subject of interest for it also doubles up as a vehicle, or repository, of the various Eurocentric metanarratives. In this way, then, international theory is to this book what Western literature is to Edward Said's, *Orientalism*; a book that people read even if they do not reside within cultural or literary studies. And in any case, given Said's claim that Eurocentrism has a clear link with international politics – in his case imperialism – then international theory should logically constitute the ultimate litmus test for revealing this discourse in Western academic thought. Accordingly, this book can be read by two separate audiences in two separate but complementary ways: by a non-IR readership that is interested in learning more about Eurocentrism – the multiple forms it has taken and how its architecture changes over time – and by an IR readership that is interested in understanding the Eurocentric foundations of international theory. It is also for this reason that I ask for the IR reader's forbearance at particular times given that I discuss various thinkers who are not conventionally associated with IR – for example, Karl Pearson, Benjamin Kidd, David Starr Jordan and Lothrop Stoddard.

In order to prepare the reader for the journey ahead, this chapter introduces three major areas, the first of which spells out some of the key conceptual moves that my alternative vision of Eurocentrism entails. I then deconstruct six of IR's cardinal axioms in the light of the argument made in this book, before closing the chapter by setting out my own definitions of imperialism and anti-imperialism within international theory.

Re-visioning 'Eurocentrism' as a multivalent, promiscuous discourse

Unpacking the four generic variants of 'Orientalism'

It should be noted that the focus of Chapters 2–12 zooms in on the core properties that I outline on the right-hand side of Table 1.1. That is, each chapter reveals the specific metanarrative that underpins each international theory; the particulars of the 'standard of civilization' deployed; the degree of agency it ascribes to East and West; its position with respect to imperialism or anti-imperialism; and its particular 'sensibility'. The key point, of course, is that my pluralistic or multivalent conception of 'Orientalism' differs from that of Said's monochromatic definition on the grounds that mine builds in a strong degree of contingency on all the key dimensions (barring the shared agreement concerning the centrality of the standard of civilization that underpins all 'Orientalist' theories).

The source of Said's double-reductive conception of Eurocentrism/Orientalism is, in the first instance, that it conflates what I call Eurocentric institutionalism with scientific racism, and then in the second conflates Orientalism with a purely imperialist politics. Of the many examples that could be used the following two seem to be as good as any. For when discussing the prevalence of Orientalism in nineteenth-century Europe, Said believes it to be 'correct that every European, in what he could say about the Orient, was ... a racist, an imperialist, and almost totally ethnocentric' (Said 1978/2003: 203–4). Or again: '[t]o say that Orientalism was a rationalization of colonial rule is to ignore the extent to which colonial rule was justified in advance by Orientalism, rather than after the fact' (Said 1978/2003: 39). My own alternative non-reductive conception is laid out in Table 1.2, which presents a four-field matrix that reveals the four key dimensions of 'generic' Eurocentrism that existed in the period 1760–1945.

To counter Said's double-reductive move I begin by breaking down his concept of Orientalism into two component parts – scientific racism and Eurocentric institutionalism – and then subdividing these categories into their imperialist and anti-imperialist components. Eurocentric institutionalism, which began to appear in infant form after the 'discovery' of America by the Spanish,[1] took off during the eighteenth-century European Enlightenment and was consolidated

---

[1] See especially Jahn (2000); Inayatullah and Blaney (2004); Anghie (2005); Bowden (2009); cf. Pagden (1995).

Table 1.1 *Alternative conceptions of Orientalism/Eurocentrism*

	Said's reductive conception of Orientalism	'Non-reductive' conception of Eurocentric institutionalism & scientific racism
Relationship of Orientalism and Scientific Racism	**Inherent** Racism, especially social Darwinism and Eugenics, is merely the highest expression of imperialist-Orientalism	**Contingent** Racism and Eurocentric institutionalism are analytically differentiated even if they share various overlaps
The centrality of the 'standard of civilization'	Yes	Yes
Agency is the monopoly of the West	**Inherent** The West has hyper-agency, the East has none	**Contingent** The West always has pioneering agency, while the East ranges from high to low levels of agency; but where these are high they are deemed to be regressive or barbaric
Propensity for imperialism	**Inherent**	**Contingent** Can be imperialist and anti-imperialist
Sensibility (Propensity for Western triumphalism)	**Inherent**	**Contingent** Racism is often highly defensive and reflects Western anxiety. Some racist thought and much of Eurocentric institutionalism exhibits Western self-confidence, if not triumphalism

during the nineteenth century.[2] Reduced to its essence this discourse locates difference in institutional/cultural factors rather than genetic/biological ones. Critically, for the overwhelming part, Eurocentric

[2] Cf. Said (1978/2003); Amin (1989); Bernal (1991).

Table 1.2 *The four variants of generic Eurocentrism in international theory*

	Pro-imperialist	Anti-imperialist
Eurocentric institutionalism	(A) Paternalist	(B) Anti-paternalist
Scientific racism	(C) Offensive	(D) Defensive

institutionalists believed that *all* humans and *all* societies have recourse to universal reason and that *all* are capable of progressing from savagery/ barbarism into civilization. This is not, however, to say that climate and environment played no part within Eurocentric institutionalism. For some such as Friedrich List and Baron de Montesquieu, climate ultimately trumped culture and institutions. But these were very much the exceptions and to the extent that climate played a role in this genre it was at most an intervening variable.[3]

---

[3] Thus, for example, while climatic arguments hover in the very distant background of Karl Marx's theory of history, with the claim that aridity might have played a role in creating the 'Oriental despotic' state in Asia, nevertheless its negative impact on economic progress could be transcended by the European civilizing mission and the delivery of progressive institutions. Georg Hegel, by contrast, is considered by some to be a climatic determinist. Undoubtedly he accorded climate far more ontological weighting than did Marx, declaring that '[i]n the Frigid and in the Torrid Zone the locality of World-historical peoples cannot be found. ... The true theatre of History is therefore the temperate zone' (Hegel 1837/2001: 97). But even here Hegel followed this statement with the immediate qualification that '[n]ature should not be rated too high nor too low'. List and Montesquieu were the clear exceptions. List argued that Europe was advanced because industry flourishes only in the temperate zone. Critically, while he argued that European colonization could certainly bring economic benefits to the countries of the torrid zone (List 1841/1909: ch. 22), nevertheless the effects of a tropical climate are such that those 'which are at present dependent colonies can hardly ever liberate themselves from that condition' (List 1841/1909: 217). Unlike in Marx's formulation, even the benefits that were delivered to the East via the civilizing mission were ultimately insufficient to overcome the regressive grip of the torrid climate. It is also noteworthy that the argument which emphasizes the climatic origins of Oriental despotism – which was fully developed by the Marxist, Karl Wittfogel (1963) – had already emerged in the work of Montesquieu. So heavy was his emphasis on climate that at times Montesquieu draws close to morphing into a racist position (e.g., Montesquieu 1748/1900: 221–34). These exceptional cases point to the possibility that a thin interstitial (permeable) zone might well reside between Eurocentric institutionalism and scientific racism in Table 1.2.

Nevertheless, while it is conventionally assumed that this discourse is inherently imperialist – both inside and outside postcolonial circles – I identify within it two subdivisions, one imperialist the other anti-imperialist. The former I call 'paternalist Eurocentrism', which awards Western societies a *pioneering agency* such that they can auto-generate or auto-develop into modernity while conversely, Eastern societies are granted *conditional agency* and are unable to auto-generate or self-develop. In this paternalist imaginary it is incumbent upon the West to engage in an imperial civilizing mission in order to deliver the necessary rational institutions to the Eastern societies so as to bring to the surface their latent reason, thereby kick-starting their progressive development into modernity.

By contrast, the anti-imperialist variant takes the form of *anti-paternalist* Eurocentrism. While much of postcolonialism assumes that Eurocentrism in general rejects the proposition that the Eastern peoples are capable of self-generation or auto-development, I claim that this particular genre argues specifically that non-European peoples will evolve naturally and spontaneously – or 'auto-develop' – into civilization. This entails what I call Eastern *derivative agency* wherein such societies will develop but only by following the 'naturalized Western path' that had been pioneered by the Europeans through their 'exceptional institutional genius'. That is, the West remains the original pioneer of development such that its *particular* path is reified as the universal or *natural* one that the non-Western societies will automatically follow. Overall, this means not merely that there is no need for a Western civilizing mission to kick-start non-Western development, but also that imperialism is viewed as a hindrance to the developmental prospects of Eastern – as well as Western – societies.

While scientific racism places a strong degree of emphasis on genetics and biology as underpinning difference, this was often accompanied by a deep emphasis on climate and physical environment. For some, the causal pendulum of race behaviour swings towards the climatic/environmental pole, whereas for others it swings more towards the genetic pole. This multivalent archipelago of discourses was far more heterogeneous than Eurocentric institutionalism and was fractured into all sorts of subdiscourses, including Social Darwinism, Eugenics, Weismann's germ-plasm theory, Mendelianism and, not least Lamarckianism, some of which were complementary while others conflicted.[4] One of the most common misconceptions of the popular

---

[4] Thus August Weismann's germ-plasm theory, which emerged in the 1880s, rejected Lamarck's assumption that acquired use characteristics could be passed on to subsequent

received view is that scientific racism posited the fixity or immutability of the genetic properties of the various races. While this is certainly true of Eugenics, it ignores Lamarckianism (see esp. Stocking 1982). This is vitally important to appreciate because Lamarckianism factors social practice into the mix and because it was embraced, albeit in varying degrees, by many scientific racist international theorists. It is, therefore, worth exploring a little further.

In his seminal book *Zoological Philosophy* (1809/2011) Jean-Baptiste Lamarck argued that culture and social practices were partially autonomous determinants of race behaviour, as much as genetics and environment attained a partial autonomy in shaping behaviour. Moreover, these multiple determinants of race behaviour are then transmitted to subsequent generations through acquired hereditary characteristics. Typical examples of this are found in Robert Bean's explanation of the Jewish nose, which is viewed as the hereditary product of an habitual expression of indignation; or that a workman performing manual labour develops large hands that are then inherited by the subsequent generation. And to use the most well-known example, the giraffe acquired its long neck as an hereditary characteristic of its ancestors' practice of straining to reach up into the tops of trees in order to acquire food within an arid environment. Essentially, this approach is open to the point that changes in social behaviour and social environment can, over a succession of generations, lead on to changes in hereditary characteristics.

The critical take-home point is that Lamarckianism assumes that racial characteristics are not fixed and immutable but can change, evolve and not infrequently progress over time. Thus, if 'rational' institutions can be transmitted to the backward races via the civilizing mission, so over time these can effect 'progressive' change as the ability to act rationally eventually becomes embedded within the receiving race's gene pool. No less important is the point that neo-Lamarckianism could be deployed to produce a very wide variety of conceptions of domestic and world politics incorporating

> imperialists who spoke of the 'white man's burden' ... reformers who spoke of lifting up 'the backward races' ... Southerners who were erecting the framework of Jim Crow legislation, and ... those who saw the progress of the Negro race in terms of the gradualism of Booker T. Washington (Stocking 1982: 253).

generations. The exact formulation was that changes in the *soma* (body tissue) did not effect the *germ plasm* (the reproductive tissue). Much later on, germ plasm was relabelled DNA. Similarly Lamarckianism was challenged around the turn of the twentieth century by the rediscovery of Mendel's laws regarding genetic heredity.

8 CHAPTER 1: INTRODUCTION

And to this list I would add the anti-imperialism of Spencer's, as well as the violent racist-imperialism of Lester Ward's, Lamarckian social Darwinism.

Turning to scientific racism's stance on world politics I divide the literature into two generic categories – imperialist 'offensive racism' and anti-imperialist 'defensive racism'. Nevertheless, it is equally important to note that there are a large variety of positions within each of these two headlining categories. For example, taking defensive racism first, I argue that one strand is found in the likes of Herbert Spencer and William Graham Sumner; an approach which views imperialism as serving only to undermine the natural progress that all societies will inevitably make. Crucially, then, imperialism would be a regressive step, hindering spontaneous black and yellow racial development while simultaneously leading to the 'rebarbarization of (white) civilization'. By contrast, the relativist racism of the likes of James Blair and David Starr Jordan fundamentally denied the Eastern races any developmental agency by insisting that non-white development was impossible, thereby rendering the civilizing mission as all but futile since the non-white races were simply incapable of becoming civilized. Moreover, an important strand of defensive racism emphasized the 'yellow barbaric peril' as constituting a massive existential threat to white racial supremacy, and thereby awarded the yellow and sometimes brown races extremely high levels of agency, albeit of a regressive/barbaric nature (most notably Charles Pearson and Lothrop Stoddard). All in all, the lowest common denominator of defensive racism is the belief that the white race must avoid coming into contact with the non-white races for fear of racial contamination (especially through miscegenation or blood-mixing). This meant avoiding imperialism while at the same time putting up strong barriers to non-white immigration (the conception of the 'besieged Western citadel battening down the hatches'). That is, in seeking to *distance* the white West from the non-European races so they constructed various 'racial apartheid conceptions of world politics'.

In turn defensive racism is differentiated from imperialist-racism or what I term *offensive racism*. This found its expression in racist thinkers of liberal and socialist persuasions, some of whom even went so far as to embrace some form of exterminist racist imperialism, as in for example, Lester Ward, Benjamin Kidd and Karl Pearson. Racism also found its expression in 'racist-realism' (b. 1889, d. 1945). Significantly, racist-realism was no monolith but constituted a microcosm of scientific racism given that it expressed different types of racism and thereby yielded multiple conceptions of imperialism. Some were anxious about the coming 'yellow peril', awarding the yellow races high levels of, albeit regressive/predatory, agency such that they posed a direct threat to white civilization and therefore required imperial containment (e.g., Halford Mackinder and Alfred Mahan). Equally, as I explain in Chapter 7, other offensive racists were not so much worried that the 'barbarians are coming!' but were gripped by extreme levels of racial anxiety that derived from their perception that the 'barbarians are already here in our midst!' (e.g., Adolf Hitler and Houston Stewart Chamberlain). In Hitler's imperialist formulation, of course, the solution was to exterminate the barbaric threat – especially the alien Jew but also the unfit white German – who served only to contaminate and thereby undermine the vitality of the Aryan race. Nevertheless, there were also those who were far less pessimistic about such threats (e.g., Theodore Roosevelt and Henry Cabot Lodge), and in granting the Eastern races very little agency proclaimed in triumphant fashion a glorious future for the white race and its noble mission in spreading civilization across the global frontier.

To close this discussion I discern four primary variants of Orientalism or 'generic Eurocentrism' within which international theory was embedded prior to 1945, while noting important differences within each of them. Concerning the lowest common denominator, all of these variants analytically separate out East from West, purging the latter of all 'negative' features and transposing them onto the former.[5] In this way, the West is imbued with purely virtuous and/or progressive properties that in turn lead it to pioneer all that is progressive in world politics. Conversely, the East is always deemed to be less progressive than the pioneering West. At times the East was deemed, at worst, to be the repository of barbarous or savage regressivism that posed a threat to civilization and world order or, at best, was destined to be exterminated either by the actions of the superior civilized white race or by the 'merciful' hands of Nature. And in all cases, these variants invoke an *ahistorical* conception of world politics and of economic/political development, summarized by the trope of 'first the West and then elsewhere' (Chakrabarty 2000: esp. 4–11); or, if I may be permitted some interpretative licence here, 'first the West, then the Rest'. The one caveat of note here, though, is the point that a good number of scientific racists believed that the black and red savages would never develop even under the

---

[5] And for a deeper discussion of this see the poignant analyses in Nandy (1983) and Todorov (1984).

'exceptional tutelage' of the Western Empire. For such thinkers the trope of 'first the West, then the Rest' becomes transformed into 'only once, and only in the West'.

Of course, while many a reader might see little wrong with the notion of 'first the West, then the Rest' – for, after all, this appeals to the 'eminently reasonable' and 'common-sense' view of (Eurocentric) history – it should, however, be noted that I counter this at various points in Part III of this book with my non-Eurocentric idiom that 'without the Rest there might be no West'. By this I am referring to the point that the West was not an early- but a late-developer, and owes its breakthrough to modernity in large, though by no means exclusive, part to the East from which it borrowed all manner of technologies, institutions and ideas throughout its long developmental period between 800 and 1800 (see also Hobson 2004, 2007, 2011b).

As far as the post-1945 era is concerned, scientific racism disappears from IR theory (even if Eugenics programmes remained a feature of the domestic politics of various countries including the United States and Scandinavia for several more decades). And manifest Eurocentrism took on a *subliminal* form during the era of decolonization and the Cold War. I differentiate 'subliminal' from 'manifest' Eurocentrism on the basis that the former reproduces many of the aspects of the latter but that its Eurocentric properties are hidden from immediate view.[6] Thus, for example, all *explicit* talk of imperialism is dropped, with imperialism often going by a term that dares not speak its name – as in, for example, neorealist discussions of American or British *hegemony* (see Chapter 8). Equally, *explicit* talk of 'civilization versus barbarism' is largely dropped in favour of its equivalent 'sanitized' terms: 'modernity versus tradition' and 'core versus periphery'. This discourse underpins classical realism and neorealism (see Chapter 8), neoliberal institutionalism and classical pluralist English School theory (see Chapter 9), as well as much of neo-Marxism (see Chapter 10). After 1989, however, subliminal Eurocentric institutionalism recedes mainly into significant parts of critical IR theory and takes a back-seat to the revival of manifest Eurocentric institutionalism within mainstream IR theory. Thus what I call post-1989 'Western-realism' goes back to the future of post-1889 imperialist racist-realism, while post-1989 'Western-liberalism' returns us back to post-1830 paternalist-Eurocentrism.

---

[6] Though this distinction should not be confused with Said's contrast between what he calls Manifest and Latent Orientalism (Said 1978/2003: ch. 3).

Locating my approach within the wider literature on scientific racism and Eurocentrism

Despite the fact that my heuristic builds in a large amount of complexity, given that each of the four generic categories exhibits a wide range of positions, there might still be those – most probably historians – who feel that my sociological position is over-simplified, or equally those – most probably postcolonial-inspired social scientists – who view it as overly complex. In response to the criticism of over-simplification, I should point out that while I indeed recognize that my sociological enterprise risks various intellectual dangers I do, however, feel that if we abandon it then we are left by default in a quagmire of 'particularism' – or 'particularist-particularism' as it were – which, in refusing to try and untangle the complexity of the literature and thereby outlawing any kind of analytical overview or purchase, causes a number of distinct problems. This inherent predisposition towards 'particularism' is, of course, a function of the fact that this area is one that has been plied largely by historians – though this is in no way to denigrate the quite brilliant secondary historical literature on scientific racism,[7] which provides for a much thicker reading to that supplied by Said. Indeed, no one who reads these books can fail to be impressed by the levels and sheer depth of research.

But the first problem I encountered with this historical literature is its oft-conflation of Eurocentric institutionalism with scientific racism, thereby not ironically preventing the deeper picture that I am interested in unearthing from coming to light. Second, failure to distinguish these two generic variants means that we can make little sense of post-1945 international theory, which embodies Eurocentric-institutionalism rather than scientific racism. Both these problems merge in the point that it is the bigger picture that, by definition, interests me given that I am exploring the 1760–2010 era. Accordingly, a reification of the micro-historical picture denies us the capacity to understand how the discourses of Eurocentric institutionalism and scientific racism have changed through time.

---

[7] Though in fairness many of the books zoom in on only one type of racism – usually social Darwinism and sometimes Eugenics – thus making such a task superfluous. Primary among these books are: Gossett (1963/1997); Hofstadter (1944/1992); Kelly (1971); Gasman (1971/2004); Banton (1977); Bannister (1979); Jones (1980); Stocking (1982); Hunt (1987); Kevles (1985); Pick (1989); Gould (1992); Pieterse (1992); Crook (1994); Hannaford (1996); Hawkins (1997).

A third, albeit incidental, problem with this historical literature is its surprising lack of focus on the relationship between scientific racism and international politics, given that it is often much more interested in tracing the highly complex issues concerning the nature of evolutionism, the processes of hereditary transmission, and so forth.[8] This is surprising given that social Darwinism is conventionally held to be the prime incarnation of imperialist thought. But it turns out that '[i]n fact there is a dearth of detailed investigations of the role of social Darwinism in imperialist thought and practice' (Hawkins 1997: 203). It was partly for this reason that I found that I had little choice but to plough through a vast swathe of primary scientific racist texts, and partly because the very few secondary source books that consider the relationship of scientific racism and international politics usually fail to bring to light its anti-imperialist dimensions.[9]

However, if we turn away from the Humanities to explore the Social Sciences we encounter a growing and equally impressive secondary literature that focuses on the relationship between Eurocentrism and international theory. This literature resides within the vortex of a number of disciplines, most notably Political Theory, Political Geography, Sociology, International Law, International Relations and IPE.[10] Although I learned much from many of these pioneering and inspiring sources, the particular problem I encountered here was that much of this literature tends to black-box Eurocentrism, thereby glossing over the very internal differences and complexities that I am interested in unearthing.[11] Indeed, it sometimes felt to me that the modus operandi was to scan for any sign of an imperialist argument in a particular writer's work in order to prove the existence of an underlying

---

[8] The key exceptions here are found in the important books by Gossett (1963/1997); Pieterse (1992); Crook (1994); Weikart (2004); Lake and Reynolds (2008).

[9] Paul Crook's extraordinarily impressive historical text, however, remains the key exception (Crook 1994).

[10] In Political Theory see: Tully (1995); Pagden (1995); Tuck (1999); Mehta (1999); Parekh (1997); Hindess (2001); Pateman and Mills (2007). In International Law see: Grovogui (1996); Anghie (2005). In IR and International Political Theory see: Tinker (1977); Schmidt (1998a); Vitalis (2000, 2002, 2005, 2010); Salter (2002); Banton (2002); Inayatullah and Blaney (2004); Long and Schmidt (2005a); Keene (2005); Bowden (2009); Adib-Moghaddam (2011: esp. 179–194). In IPE see: McCarthy (2009); Blaney and Inayatullah (2010). In Political Geography see most notably Livingstone (1992). For the key sociological contributions, see the references in footnote 12.

[11] Nevertheless some of these scholars locate different dimensions to Eurocentrism; see especially Salter (2002), and above all Vitalis (2000, 2002, 2005, 2010).

Eurocentric metanarrative. My preference has been, by contrast, to zoom in specifically on the nature of the Eurocentric and racist metanarrative that a particular writer deploys from which I tease out its imperialist or anti-imperialist properties.

Nevertheless, by the same token it is highly possible that many of these scholars would find my heuristic too complex, and might well object to my claims that Eurocentrism and racism can be anti-imperialist on the one hand, and should be analytically differentiated on the other. Indeed the latter point in particular would be objected to by 'critical race' theorists, who view modern Eurocentrism as racism-in-disguise;[12] (though I reserve my more detailed response to this objection for Chapter 13 – see pp. 322–4). To respond here by reiterating my claim that the Saidian conception of 'Eurocentrism' that these literatures deploy is often too reductive would, of course, merely beg the question as to why such a reductive approach is problematic in the first place. Still, it seems to me that obscuring the dimensions that I reveal in this book means that the widely-used Saidian conception of Orientalism has to perform a great deal of leg-movement beneath the waterline in order to keep it afloat. But rather than abandon Said's conceptual ship my task in this book is to ply an alternative stream – to deepen and extend the Saidian/postcolonial understanding of Eurocentrism such that it is capable of reading the many nuances that exist within Eurocentric international theory, or equally to reveal similar complex nuances that exist within any comparable conceptually-oriented discipline. In the process I seek to transcend the conventional static reading of Orientalism/Eurocentrism by revealing its *changing forms* or *promiscuous properties* through time. This is necessary not only so as to better understand Eurocentrism, but also because if we were to apply the reductive conception of Eurocentrism to international theory – or equally to any other Social Science discipline for that matter – then logically it would require us to shoehorn all of it in its many nuances into a single Orientalist-imperial boot, notwithstanding the point that a large amount of IR theory exhibits, either explicitly or subconsciously, a commitment to imperialism in one form or another.

To close this particular discussion it is worth noting that because this literature tends to black-box Eurocentrism, so I was once again forced to go back to the drawing board and plough through a very large range

---

[12] Barker (1981); Hunt (1987); Balibar (1991); Miles (1993); Malik (1996); Füredi (1998a); MacMaster (2001); Perry (2007); also McCarthy (2009).

of primary Eurocentric institutionalist texts in order to tease out the differences and complexities that they embody. Here it is important to understand that because my approach tacks between the Scylla of complexity and the Charybdis of homogeneity so I was unable to afford the luxury of being able to focus in great depth on only a minimal number of thinkers, as is the preference of many political theorists,[13] but nor could I choose to focus on a very large number.[14] For the very nature of my enterprise demands that each chapter should provide just enough thinkers to support my claim that in aggregate they represent one type or genre of 'Eurocentrism', but not too many that the depth of analysis is lost.

Finally, I readily concede that my take on international theory is merely one among a range of possibilities. For this is not to deny that other 'metanarratives' find their place within international theory, most notably that of patriarchy.[15] Here it is noteworthy that the discourses of 'patriarchy' and 'Eurocentrism' overlap in manifold ways, though with the exception of some notable interventions,[16] this has yet to be fully explored by feminist IR scholars. At present this avenue of research is one that has been explored mainly by non-IR feminists.[17] Either way, though, the key issue at stake now concerns how my analysis of Eurocentrism/racism reconfigures some of the conventional axioms of the discipline of International Relations.

Six Eurocentric myths of IR: the moral purpose of IR as defender and promoter of Western civilization

In order to summarize by way of introduction my alternative take on IR theory and the core rationale of the discipline I shall, albeit heretically, deconstruct six of the key disciplinary axioms that are presently revered as self-evident truths and (re)present them as largely Eurocentric myths.

---

[13] See for example: Tuck (1999); Mehta (1999); Muthu (2003); Pitts (2005); Morefield (2005).
[14] As found in the enormously impressive works of Schmidt (1998a) and Bowden (2009).
[15] Most especially Tickner (1992, 2001).
[16] See the excellent and pioneering analyses in Ling (2002), Chowdhry and Nair (2002); Agathangelou and Ling (2009); Tickner (2011); Hutchings (2011).
[17] See the superb works of Harding (1998); Trivedi (1984); Amos and Parmar (1984); Mohanty (1986, 2003); Loomba (1998); Bulbeck (1998).

1. The 'noble identity/foundationist myth' of the discipline

Naturally a key facet of this volume is to engage in an intellectual history/ historiography of the discipline of IR. This is an area that has grown considerably in the last decade, prompting one scholar to ask rhetorically whether we are witnessing the 'dawn of a historiographical turn [in IR]?' (Bell 2001: 15). However, to some such a focus will hardly be welcome, leading one prominent IR scholar to confess that he 'shudders at the thought of the history of [the discipline] becoming a recognized research field' (Brown 2000: 118). And no less an authority, David Lake, complained that 'I have relatively little patience for the great debates in IR and IPE ... I often wish that [historiographical] scholars would stop contemplating *how* to do research and simply get on with the business of explaining, understanding and possibly improving the world' (Lake 2009: 48). But the immediate problem here is that the discipline *already* functions on the basis of one particular (heart-warming) Whiggish reading of its intellectual history. The 'noble identity myth' works in tandem with the 'foundationist myth'.[18] That is, it is deemed to be a self-evident truth that the discipline had been conceived on the blood-stained battlefields of Europe, with the infant child of IR having been delivered in 1919 after a gruelling 48-month gestation period. In this Whiggish self-imaginary it is assumed that the IR infant had been born with the noblest of moral purposes, for in order to overcome the traumatic experience of his birth he became determined to find ways of exorcizing the spectre of warfare from the world body-politic – notwithstanding the point that the cynic who had constructed this foundationist myth in the first place proclaimed such motives to be typical of the naivety associated with infants (Carr 1946/1981).

In this book I want to directly challenge this noble identity myth by revealing the dark side of the discipline. This will simultaneously enable me, albeit indirectly, to challenge the foundationist myth by showing how international theory has, at least ever since 1760, been underpinned by various Eurocentric metanarratives, all of which in one way or another work to defend or celebrate the West as the highest normative referent in world politics. In the process this reveals the strong continuities between pre-1914 international theory and its interwar successor. And in turn this argument contributes to the revisionist research

---

[18] These two myths are interlinked in Duncan Bell's (2009) idiom of the 'progressivist myth'.

programme that is associated primarily with the brilliant and pioneering works of Brian Schmidt and Robert Vitalis, as well as Torbjørn Knutsen (as I explain in Chapter 6).

Finally, it is worth returning to David Lake's anxiety over historiography's growing place within the discipline. For if my claim that international theory takes the form of a multivalent/polymorphous Eurocentric construct is at all persuasive, the upshot necessarily gives rise to the fundamental question as to how we can adequately research, theorize, or even teach IR (and IPE), let alone 'improve the world', before we have dealt with the prior, fundamental issue as to whether the discipline subconsciously embodies a particular metanarrative, Eurocentric or otherwise. Failure to uncover these hidden discourse(s) of power and prejudice means not only that we will fail to understand IR/IPE adequately but that we will continue, often unwittingly, to reproduce this discourse of power through our own writings. And in any case, to ignore this task is to assume that a neutral reading of disciplinary history is somehow possible. But to quote two prominent voices here: 'there can be no nonlegitimating or neutral stance from which a disciplinary history can be written. All such histories will be selective, and guided by some commitment (or opposition) to a particular identity' (Dryzek and Leonard 1988: 1248).

Above all, there are two inter-related reasons that underpin the necessity of engaging in a critical historiography of IR. First, international theory, past and present, has never been a passive reflector of Eurocentrism and scientific racism but has also played a role in *constituting* these discourses; that is, there is an elective affinity between international theory and Eurocentrism. Second, and above all, because international theory is inherently politically *performative* in that it is operationalized in the practice or performance of world politics, so the need to deconstruct it becomes all the more pressing.

2. The 'positivist myth' of international theory

That the discipline recounts in essence a 'West-side story' leads on to the claim, to adapt Robert Cox's well-known critical theory mantra, that 'IR theory is (almost) always for the West and for the Western interest' (1981/1986: 207); though that which defines the 'Western interest' necessarily varies over time according to which 'Eurocentric' metanarrative prevails at any particular point. I say 'almost' because not *all* of IR conforms to this Eurocentric mantra, with various postcolonial-inspired exceptions appearing mainly in the last decade.[19] And nor is this to elide a number of voices who have criticized Western racism in their own approaches to international relations in the past.[20] Exceptions aside, the immediate upshot of this assertion, as Cox originally argued, is to call into fundamental question not merely the noble image or identity of the discipline but also the common belief that IR theory is founded on a positivistic, value-free epistemological base. This then, is the second myth that this book seeks to critically expose; one that is necessarily attached to the 'noble identity/foundationist myths'.

Here I am reminded of a recent visit in 2008 to the Department of Politics at the University of Sheffield by one of the world's most influential IR scholars, Robert Keohane. In his first talk that opened the Politics Graduate School, he gave a bold and impassioned presentation that celebrated the virtues of positivism and dismissed critical theory outright, arguing that while political values are indeed important they should nevertheless always *follow* rather than precede positivistic analysis. And in a follow-up talk he gave an equally impassioned and impressive presentation that ranged across a variety of normative issues that included the importance of various forms of Western intervention in the 'South'. The immediate question that sprung to my mind (though I dared not ask it!) was: what if the values you and other IR theorists adhere to turn out to emanate not from an *a priori* positivistic value-free method but from an underlying Eurocentric metanarrative? If so, this would mean that claims to be scientifistic/rationalist and value-free could no longer hold. Indeed my rhetorical question seemed to be confirmed by Keohane's impassioned argument that Western humanitarian interventionism and structural adjustment programmes (to name just two examples) were necessary in order to retrack the

---

[19] Rather than cite the extensive and growing non-Eurocentric literature I point the reader to some key journal fora and edited volumes which exhibit a range of representatives: Persaud and Walker (2001); Nair (2007); Chowdhry and Nair (2002); Gruffydd-Jones (2006); Jahn (2006a); Hall and Jackson (2007); Tickner and Wæver (2009); Seth (2011a); Shilliam (2011); Millennium (2011) – special issue on 'Dialogue in IR' (see the articles by J. Ann Tickner, Amitav Acharya, Kimberly Hutchings, Robbie Shilliam, Gurminder Bhambra, Mustapha Kamal Pasha, Carvalho *et al.*, Meera Sabaratnam and Fabio Petito). Note that other key representatives are mentioned in Part 3 of the book.

[20] Most notably a group of African-American Marxists, the most famous of whom were: Ralph Bunche (1936), W. E. B. Du Bois (1905, 1915); cf. C. L. R. James (1938/1980) and Eric Williams (1944). For a much fuller discussion here see Krenn (1999); Vitalis (forthcoming). Note that these aforementioned scholars provided a different critique of racism to that which was made by various white Eurocentric institutional thinkers (including John Hobson, Norman Angell and Leonard Woolf).

non-Western world onto a more progressive Western path of liberal capitalism and democracy. And he added, answering a braver questioner than I, that if this smacked of neo-imperial interventionism, then better this than the alternative 'politics of malign neglect',[21] that would merely deny the backward East the privilege of developing into an advanced Western form!

Extrapolating out from this, the logical corollary of my claim that the discipline works to celebrate and defend Western civilization as the highest or ideal referent in world politics is that it fundamentally challenges the belief – one that is hegemonic in the United States in particular – that international theory is value-free and produces positivist, universalist explanations of world politics that apply to all states regardless of cultural or racial difference. For it turns out that when viewed through a non-Eurocentric lens the vast majority of international theory produces a parochial or provincial analysis of the West that masquerades as the universal.

3. The 'great debates myth' and reconceptualizing the idea of the clash of IR theories

It is a trope of the discipline that IR theory has been driven forward through a series of intense but 'healthy' intellectual clashes that are known as the 'great debates' and which take the form of Manichean battles between heroic combatants. These are thought to constitute the discipline's formative genealogy, such that the student can gain a picture of the discipline simply by understanding these great battles. It is conventionally assumed that there have been three great debates, or possibly four if we include the so-called 'inter-paradigm debate' of the 1970s. These have dealt with a series of controversies: between 'realism and idealism' in the interwar period;[22] between 'history versus scientifism' in the 1960s; between the three leading paradigms in the 1970s; and between 'positivists and postpositivists' in the 1990s. That these are important areas of debate is not the issue at stake here. Rather, my point is that when viewed through a non-Eurocentric lens these debates reappear as far less dramatic contests between surface-type issues. For the upshot of my argument is that beneath the sound and fury of these Manichean 'great debates' lies the hum-drum consensus of virtually all

---

[21] Though in fairness I am attributing this concept to him here.
[22] Notwithstanding the problem that a good deal of the assumptions that underpin the 'first debate' turn out to be highly problematic (see Chapters 6 and 7).

parties concerning the politics of defending and celebrating Western civilization in world politics. Moreover, while the student is introduced to the discipline via the clash between radically different theories – whether these be realist, liberal, Marxist, or constructivist – it turns out that when viewed through a non-Eurocentric lens they largely reappear as but minor variations on a consistent set of Eurocentric themes.

4. The 'sovereignty/anarchy myth'

It is, of course, a fundamental axiom of the discipline that IR theory is concerned to understand and theorize the relations between sovereign states in an anarchic world. It is also a fundamental axiom of the mainstream in particular that anarchy implies sovereignty. A key message of this book is that all the major theories of the international in the last quarter millennium begin their analyses not with the sovereign state but with a social analysis wherein inter-state relations are derived from the application of an *a priori* conception of the 'social standard of civilization'.[23] And, albeit in different ways, international theory has in effect focused not on the level-playing field of juridically-equal sovereign states but on the unequal field of global/civilizational hierarchy and gradated sovereignties.

More specifically, I argue that imperialist Eurocentric and racist international theory advances a conception of '*formal* hierarchy' which awards 'hyper-sovereignty' to Western states and either denies sovereignty to Eastern polities (as in post-1989 neo-imperialist international theory) or grants them 'conditional sovereignty' whereby sovereignty can be withdrawn if 'civilized' conditions are not met (as in post-1945, and especially post-1989, neo-imperialist international theory). By contrast anti-imperialist Eurocentric and racist international theory, while seemingly respecting the political self-determination of Eastern polities nevertheless denies them cultural self-determination, and requires them to abandon their civilizational identity and assimilate or culturally convert to Western civilizational norms. In this imaginary Western states are granted 'full sovereignty' while Eastern polities are granted either 'qualified sovereignty' or 'default sovereignty'. Here, then, we receive a conception of '*informal* hierarchy' and gradated sovereignties. I specify these variations here because they form an important part of the discussion undertaken in each chapter (an overall summary of which is

---

[23] See also Keene (2005); Long and Schmidt (2005b).

provided in Chapter 13). All in all, then, the notion that IR is concerned to understand and theorize the relations between sovereign states under anarchy turns out to be a fourth myth.

5. *The 'globalization myth'*

By the 'globalization myth' I am not claiming that globalization does not exist. My claim here is altogether different. It is naturally assumed within the discipline that globalization has only recently come to occupy the minds of its theorists in one way or another. But to my surprise I found that in many cases, including some though not all realists, international theorists since 1760 have placed considerable emphasis on globalization, even if they deploy different terms. Most significantly, I argue that globalization has been politically constructed in various ways. Thus one stream of international theory invents the construct of *globalization-as-barbaric threat*, as in parts of racist-realism and modern (post-1989) 'Western-realism', as well as in racist cultural realism (pre-1945) and Eurocentric cultural realism (post-1989). The other stream of international theory invents the construct of *globalization-as-Western opportunity* to remake the world along Western lines, as in the paternalist Eurocentrism of Marx, Hobson, Angell, Zimmern and Woolf, or in the liberal-imperialist offensive racism of Reinsch, Ireland, Sidgwick, Strong, Wilson and Kidd, as well as in some variants of socialist racism/Eurocentrism and in much of racist-realism. Significantly, this trope finds its modern equivalent in the manifest paternalist Eurocentrism of liberal international theory including Rawls, Téson, Fukuyama, Nussbaum and many others. Once again, then, when viewed through a non-Eurocentric lens the idea that IR theory has only recently turned to consider globalization constitutes a fifth myth of the discipline since it has been there, in one form or another, from 1760 onwards.

6. *The 'theoretical great traditions myth'*

Finally, one of the key upshots of this book is that it necessarily re-visions each of the major IR theories, producing alternative discontinuous visions precisely because it disturbs the standard linear idea of continuous theoretical 'great traditions' across time.[24] By this I am referring to the point that the key theories – liberalism, realism and Marxism – are

---

[24] See Schmidt (1998a: ch. 1); Keene (2005: ch. 1).

often presented in terms of ahistorical continuous 'great traditions' that stem back several centuries, if not millennia in the case of liberalism and realism. Such a reading has been aptly referred to as an 'epic rendering' of IR (Schmidt 1998a: ch. 1). Thus, for example, realism is traced back to Thucydides and then forward via Hobbes and Machiavelli to culminate in Waltz, Gilpin and Mearsheimer, via Carr and Morgenthau. In the process, all discontinuities become obscured and each theorist is (re)presented with isomorphic properties. The key move I make here is to reveal each major theory's *promiscuous/polymorphous* or protean properties, whereby each one crystallizes in radically different and discontinuous forms over time – either as pro- or anti-imperialist depending on which Eurocentric/racist metanarrative is deployed (and see Chapter 13 for a full overview of the three major theories of IR).

Cave: here be dragons!

And so in the light of all this I should warn my reader, if (s)he has not already realized, that the voyage into the dark side of international theory and of the discipline's past and present that this book plies is clearly neither for the faint-hearted nor for the impatient! For such a voyage of re-discovery will need to navigate an enormous literature that appears much as what the Arab sailors once referred to the Atlantic as – namely the 'green sea of darkness' – in which we will encounter all manner of conceptual dragons and strange creatures that inevitably confront the very identity of the discipline in ways that for some readers will undoubtedly be extremely uncomfortable and challenging. Indeed, such a journey is one that explores the dusky labyrinthine network of dank underground passage-ways and barely-lit chambers which exists deep beneath the surface of international/IR theory, within which are found all manner of trap-doors that drop the explorer into yet deeper hidden chambers, all of which ultimately reveal or reflect the dark side of that which exists back on the surface. There are even times when the exploration of these catacombs leads into the darkest chamber which houses the picture of Dorian Grey, whose distorted image is inversely proportional to the clean-cut figure that drifts smoothly on the surface in the bright light of day. And it is in this context that a discussion of the book's front-cover image is relevant.

Known as the 'Fool's Cap World Map', this highly enigmatic picture was painted around 1580 though the painter's name is unknown (given that he went by the name of Orontius Fineus – who had in fact died in 1555).

The image could be said to operate at various levels of meaning. As one expert points out, the Fool 'was a kind of scapegoat who drew upon himself the forces of evil, unreason or ill-fortune, and by confronting them, averted their power from the community. [As the Court Jester he] was licensed to break rules, speak painful truths, and mock at power' (Whitfield 1994: 78). Taking some hermeneutic licence here, my use of this map is intended to convey the point not that the world itself is a wholly irrational and threatening place (the meaning that Whitfield attributes to the picture), but that it is the various Eurocentric conceptions of the world found within international theory that largely create this distorted and sinister image in the first place.

In 1974 Arno Peters produced his radical world map projection, which sought to correct for the (Eurocentric) distortion that the famous Mercator maps suffered from (namely the exaggeration of the North and the under-estimation of the size of the Southern countries). Although no perfect map of the world exists, the Peters/Peters-Gall projection is certainly free of the Eurocentric distortion found in the Mercator. Either way, one of the most compelling reasons for exhibiting the Fool's Cap World Map on the front-cover is that the size of the Northern Continents, especially North America and Europe, is exaggerated even further relative to South America, Africa, India and China than they are on the Mercator. This is relevant because such a distortion constitutes the very essence of the vision of the world that Eurocentric and racist international theory constructs between 1760 and 2010.

To close this section I argue that the message of this book can either be accepted so that we can move forward into a genuinely brighter future or be resisted, no doubt implacably by some who might prefer to attack the author rather than intellectually engage with the *actual* arguments of the book. Either way, though, resisting the message of this book serves only to freeze us into the status quo of the Eurocentric theory and practice of IR, with its many attendant problems left unresolved. And as an addendum here it should be noted that while I shall use the terms 'East' and 'West' throughout the book, this will undoubtedly appear perplexing to some readers given the objection that Africa and Latin America do not reside geographically in the East but on the same lines of longitude as Europe and North America respectively. But I deploy these terms because they are fundamental to the lexicon of Eurocentrism/racism and that, as such, what matters is not the geographical dimension but the ideational. That is, within Eurocentrism and scientific racism, East and West are constructs that are differentiated not by geography but either by a rationality/civilizational divide or a rationality/racial divide.

Defining imperialism and anti-imperialism in international theory

And so I now turn to the final conceptual area that needs to be dealt with before we can begin our journey. For given that imperialism and anti-imperialism feature prominently in this book, it is necessary for me to lay out my own conceptualization or definitions, while simultaneously locating the key dividing line that separates imperialist from anti-imperialist theory. This is in any case important to determine because the vast literature on imperialism and anti-imperialism generally lacks conceptual precision, the effect of which is that scholars frequently talk at cross purposes on the topic, thereby producing all manner of confusion over what at first sight seems such an obvious and intuitive concept. And, of course, such confusion is exacerbated further by the point that 'imperialism' is a highly emotive term.

Here I confront two broad definitional approaches: the 'narrow Eurocentric' and the 'expansive postcolonial'. Most of modern Eurocentric international theory embraces a narrow definition, which allows for considerable wiggle room when confronted with the imperialist charge. By contrast, postcolonial theorists seek to completely shut down this wiggle room by assuming that Eurocentrism is inherently imperialist, using as it does an extremely broad or expansive definition of imperialism. My own position resides mid-way between these two polarities. Given the sensitive, if not explosive, nature of the issue at stake, it behoves me to provide a definition that might hopefully be accepted by my readership. For if my definitions are rejected at this point then the rest of the book will simply fall at the first hurdle. Figure 1.1 produces a conceptual continuum that sets out the extreme conception of imperialism and then shifts rightward through to the softest case.

Boxes 1–3 on the left-hand side of Figure 1.1 are uncontentious as far as the definition of imperialism is concerned so that a consensus of agreement can be readily secured. At first sight the common denominator appears to be the idea of formal territorial control over colonies. Such positions range from the coercive extreme (Box 1) through to the softer notion of the 'benign' paternalist civilizing mission, where the latter entails formal territorial control and the 'cultural conversion' of

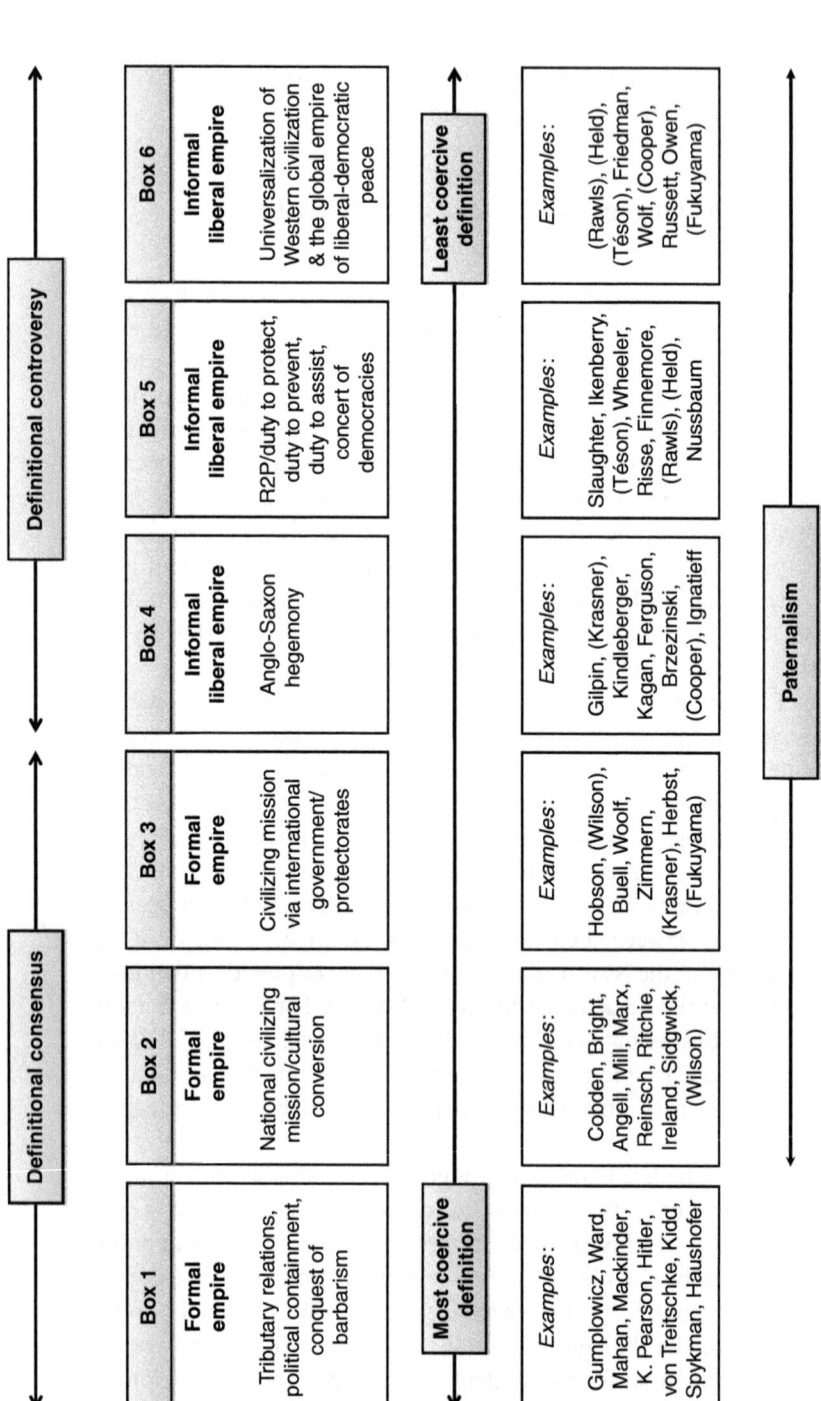

Figure 1.1 The definitional continuum of imperialism, past and present.
Note that some thinkers feature in more than one box and are therefore placed in brackets.

Eastern societies to Western civilizational norms and institutions (Boxes 2–3). Another way to express the definitions based in these three boxes is to say that imperialism entails the universalization of Western civilization through cultural conversion as well as through formal territorial control; though Box 1 achieves this via the application of coercion while for the most part Boxes 2 and 3 reject coercive modes of imperialism (with Marx and Mill constituting the exceptions).[25]

The controversial part, of course, rests with the three boxes on the right-hand side (Boxes 4–6), which have existed within significant parts of international theory in the post-1945 era and especially since the end of the Cold War. Many of the representatives of these categories would deny that they advocate imperialism or neo-imperialism. Hegemonic stability theorists such as Robert Gilpin, for example, counterpose 'liberal hegemony' to 'autocratic imperialism', much as liberal humanitarians and cosmopolitan liberals view humanitarian interventionism as embodying a benign and 'emancipatory/*non*-imperialist' purpose. Such claims, however, presume that 'imperialism' implies not merely formal territorial control/conquest but, above all, the *coercive economic* exploitation of colonial victims; hence liberal humanitarian interventionists' sincere bewilderment at the imperialist charge.

But imperialism – in theory *rather* than practice – need not rest on an exploitative definition, not least because most, though by no means all, liberal imperialists of the nineteenth and first half of the twentieth centuries explicitly rejected coercive and exploitative imperialism. Indeed this non-coercive/non-exploitative definition was a stock-in-trade position of the paternalist-Eurocentrics who included Hobson, Cobden, Angell, Murray, Woolf and Zimmern, as well as the racist-liberals such as Reinsch, Ireland, Sidgwick, Wilson and Buell. Moreover, a nascent or infant conception of humanitarianism underpinned these approaches to imperialism, all of which advocated a paternalist challenge to Eastern 'barbaric practices' – as in, for example, the outlawing of the Hindu practice of *Sati* (widow burning) or the Chinese practice of *foot binding*. Indeed, such a humanitarian sensibility can reasonably be extrapolated out to incorporate the very essence of the nineteenth-century conception of the benign civilizing mission, since

---

[25] John Stuart Mill and Karl Marx provided the exceptions that in fact prove this rule. For Mill believed that a despotic colonialism was necessary if the inferior peoples and races were to be pushed towards a liberal democratic state in the long run, while Marx, though clearly lamenting the violence of global primitive accumulation that imperialism entails, nevertheless viewed it as a political necessity.

replacing irrational savage and barbaric institutions – political, social, economic, humanitarian and religious – served an emancipatory purpose for the object of intervention. The essence of this 'benign' conception of imperialism was well captured by one of its advocates, Ramsay Muir, back in 1917:

> We may rightly and without hesitation continue to employ these terms [imperialism and empire], provided that we remember always that the justification of any dominion . . . is to be found, not in the extension of mere brute power, but in the enlargement and diffusion . . . of those vital elements in the life of Western civilisation which have been the secrets of its strength (Muir 1917/2010: 4).

Or, as one of his contemporaries put it in 1897 rather more pithily, by colonizing Africa so Europe would perform a noble task – 'namely, to elevate a race from a lower plane, and to draw it into the stream of the active development of mankind'.[26]

So how then does this relate to the more modern definition of imperialism that I outline in Box 4? Turning to the claim that Anglo-Saxon hegemony is a form of liberal-imperialism, it is interesting to note that while Gilpin would reject such a charge, other advocates explicitly equate hegemony with the noble project of liberal-imperialism. Michael Ignatieff labels US hegemony 'empire-lite',[27] and sees in it a vital and noble moral purpose to ensure global order and progress. Niall Ferguson is primarily concerned to bring the 'E-Word' (Empire) out of the closet and similarly imbibe US hegemony – as he does British hegemony in the nineteenth century – with a noble liberal-imperial purpose, holding it up as the last best hope for maintaining civilization and world order.[28] Others such as Robert Kagan, Charles Krauthammer and Zbigniew Brzezinski echo Gilpin by calling it a hegemon or a 'behemoth with a conscience', but in effect advocate the same liberal-imperial policies that Ferguson and Ignatieff call for. And yet the irony, as I explain in Chapter 8, is that Gilpin openly equates hegemony with a noble civilizing mission that underpins the praxis of the British Empire. This irony notwithstanding, we find that the same phenomenon is termed either 'liberal-empire' by one set of advocates or anti-imperialist 'hegemony' by others.

Overall, I argue that what defines US hegemony as 'neo-imperialist' or liberal-imperialist as it is deployed in theory rather than practice is that by intervening in other states it seeks not necessarily to enhance its own

---

[26] Carl Peters cited in Hawkins (1997: 204).   [27] Ignatieff (2003a, 2003b, 2005).
[28] Ferguson (2002, 2004); see also Mallaby (2002).

national interest at the expense of others but, above all, because it actively *imposes cultural conversion of non-Western states to a Western civilizational standard*. It is this *interventionist* assimilationist rationale – one that intentionally strips the identity of Eastern societies so as to reconfigure them along more 'progressive' Western lines – that can be defined as a key aspect of imperialism and neo-imperialism. But in turn, what above all underpins this assimilationism is perhaps *the* key property that links modern neo-imperialist theory with much of its traditional ancestors (represented in Boxes 2 and 3) – the idea of international paternalism.

Turning now to consider Boxes 5 and 6, I argue that these thinkers embrace international paternalism as a *discourse of benevolence* rather than of exploitation or oppression, where the intervening *subject* acts 'on behalf of' the weak/inferior *object* in ways that are allegedly closed to the latter. That the practice of such interventionism may have negative unintended consequences is beside the point. Much of modern neo-imperialist theory invokes precisely this kind of reasoning, harking back to the pre-1945 liberal paternalist thinkers who argued for the benign civilizing mission on the grounds that only the West could and should *uplift* the inferior peoples/societies (as in the White Man's Burden). The same logic underpins much of modern liberal international theory, as for example in John Rawls' *Law of Peoples* (1999), where he speaks of the paternalist 'duty to assist' Third World 'burdened societies' (or 'savage societies' in nineteenth-century speak). In all cases, the intended outcome is, in theory at least, the improvement of the welfare of the objects of intervention.

So to sum up this discussion of what constitutes imperialist theory it is worth noting that the assumption of formal territorial control is not required given that, as Niall Ferguson (2002, 2004) following Gallagher and Robinson (1953) rightly argues, empire can take informal as much as formal expressions. But as I explain below, much hinges on how informal imperialism is defined. For the moment, though, I want to conclude by noting that imperialist theory can stand for an exploitative and/or repressive mode of intervention exercised either through formal or informal control, though for the most part within international theory it rests on the notion of *interventionist paternalism*; a discourse which links the theories of Hobson, Reinsch and Wilson before 1945 to those of Rawls, Téson and Nussbaum after 1989. Thus if the reader can accept this definition, then the final two categories (Boxes 5 and 6) can be accepted as examples of imperialist/neo-imperialist theory.

This definition of imperialist theory flows logically into my definition of *anti-imperialist theory* where the latter rejects what it deems to be the arrogant paternalist politics of imperial intervention. This is as true of the pre-1945 anti-imperialist theories found in Spencer, Sumner, Jordan and Blair on the scientific racist side as it is of the anti-paternalist Eurocentric theories of Smith and Kant. Accordingly, the issue of 'paternalism versus anti-paternalism' constitutes one of the key dividing lines between imperialist and anti-imperialist theory, especially within liberalism (as I explain throughout the book). But while this definition might be accepted as reasonable by some, it will undoubtedly sit awkwardly with postcolonialists given their insistence that *all* Eurocentric theory is inherently imperialist. In essence, while Eurocentric scholars tend to embrace a fairly narrow definition of imperialism that is confined to the issues of coercive exploitation and a largely, though by no means exclusively, *formal territorial* conception, postcolonial-inspired thinkers by contrast adopt the broadest definition that places much emphasis on *informal* imperialism.

Although, I shall discuss this in some detail in Chapter 3, here it is useful to pre-empt that discussion in order to pinpoint my definition of anti-imperialism and locate the dividing line between imperialist and anti-imperialist theory. While some postcolonial scholars might agree with my claim that both Adam Smith and Immanuel Kant rejected formal imperialism, nevertheless they would indict them both in the discursive *informal* imperialist court on various charges, three of which are pertinent here. The first of these asserts that both thinkers believed that all non-European countries *should*, and in Kant's case *must*, adopt Western civilizational practices – specifically liberal-democratic capitalism. However, I argue that *wishing* or even prescribing non-European societies to become European ultimately betrays a Eurocentric- rather than imperialist-mindset, for they both believed that non-European societies will naturally develop into Western-type capitalist democracies *of their own accord* and that this would in any case be undermined should Western imperialist intervention be imposed. The second informal imperialist charge confronts the Kantian/Smithian support for the extension of trade, especially free trade, to the non-European countries on the grounds that this exploits Eastern economies. But both of them rejected any type of trade that would be based on unequal exchange and, in Kant's case, Europeans must not be allowed to trade with non-Europeans should the latter not grant formal consent in the first place.

And so we turn to a third informal imperialist charge that flows on ineluctably, which asserts that imperialism is inherent to capitalism in that it forces non-Western societies to adopt capitalist ways; an argument that dovetails with the Marxist critique, most especially that of Leon Trotsky's (1967) concept of 'uneven and combined development'. Here the claim is that anyone who supports capitalism is necessarily an imperialist, and that only radical critics of capitalism can be said to be properly anti-imperialist. The problems with this formulation are essentially three-fold: first, that it lowers the threshold of the definition of imperialist theory virtually to the ground since much of international theory supports capitalism in one guise or another; second, that some of the radical Marxists critics of capitalism advocate the civilizing mission (most notably Marx and Engels), and even the majority of Marxists who do not, turn out to be for the most part Eurocentric (including Trotsky). Third, and most importantly of all, such an approach is problematic because it imputes a rationale that was not intended by the author concerned; a key point that deserves further elaboration.

Rather than read international theory by what might be called 'interpretivist imputation' – that is by imputing a hidden imperialist politics into the text that the author did *not* intend – I have chosen to read the author in the spirit of that which I believe (s)he intended. Of course, I fully recognize that there could be a range of possible interpretations to any one text. But what I have not done is *impute* a certain rationale behind the back of the particular author. For example Kant would, I imagine, have found bewildering the claim that he was in fact an imperialist because he believed that liberal-capitalism and democracy are the highest forms of societal and political expression and that all societies should embrace them. And both Smith and Kant would have been surprised to learn that advocating capitalism is inherently imperialist because it is a structure of power that forces non-Western societies to adopt Western ways or risk military defeat (as in Trotskyism), precisely because such a conception of capitalism is not one they would have recognized. But had they insisted that capitalism must be actively imposed either by a colonial power or, had they been alive today, by the IMF/GATT/WTO, then this would meet my designated threshold of imperialism. That neither of them went this far is a product of their anti-imperialist posture.

To deal with the problem of interpretivist imputation, I have chosen to pitch my designated threshold of imperialism, so far as is possible, at a level that meets all of the authors on their own terms such that none of them would find reason to challenge such a definition. Put differently, had I deployed a much lower threshold, then most if not all of the authors I discuss in this book would I suspect, were they all alive today, reject it outright. Thus in this context it is worth noting my claim made in Chapter 8 that hegemonic stability theory entails an imperialist and neo-imperialist politics despite the fact that Gilpin explicitly rejects such a charge. But I deduce this not via interpretivist imputation, but according to the *logic* of the theory that is advanced *explicitly* by the author. That is, by explicitly advocating the need for the hegemon (as well as the British Empire in the nineteenth century) to pacify the world and to *proactively impose* cultural conversion upon Eastern societies to a Western standard of civilization, so it meets my designated imperialist threshold. This, I believe, runs truer to the spirit of the theorist's intention than that which might be imputed by the expansive postcolonial definition. Of course, whether this will satisfy my postcolonial reader remains to be seen. But either way, though, I have now laid out my store so that we are now in a position to begin the long journey into the Eurocentric heart of the dark underworld of international theory.

PART I

1760–1914
Manifest Eurocentrism and scientific racism in international theory

2

Eurocentric imperialism: liberalism and Marxism, c. 1830–1914

Introduction: paternalist-Eurocentric imperial conceptions of world politics

This chapter focuses on what I call 'paternalist Eurocentric institutionalism' and examines its embodiment in classical liberal/Marxist theory, focusing specifically on Cobden, Bright, Angell, Hobson and Marx. It is, of course, an axiom of IR that liberal internationalism and classical Marxism stand as the antitheses of imperialism. This received normative vision presupposes that imperialism and internationalism are situated within a binary relationship, in which imperialism is thought to stand for hierarchy, exploitation/inequality and the denial of sovereignty, while internationalism stands for anti-imperialism and sovereign equality/self-determination for all. But as I mentioned in Chapter 1, liberal internationalism and classical Marxism often constructed a *formal hierarchical* conception of gradated sovereignties.

As Figure 2.1 reveals, this normative formal hierarchical conception of gradated sovereignty rewards European states with *hyper-sovereignty* and the privilege of non-intervention on the grounds that they are deemed to be civilized. By contrast, because Eastern polities are deemed to be either 'barbaric' (the second world of Oriental despotisms), or 'savage' (the third world of anarchic societies residing within a domestic state of nature), so they are deemed to be unworthy of, and hence denied, sovereignty. Equally, the notion of a European imperial civilizing mission in the East rests on a shared conception of Eastern agency. While postcolonialists assume that such a discourse denies Eastern agency outright, it seems clear that Eastern societies are granted *conditional* agency within this variant. That is, they *are* capable of attaining rationality but that this can only be realized *on condition* that the 'rationality requirement' is satisfied – i.e., that the necessary rational institutions are delivered courtesy of the European civilizing mission. In this imaginary,

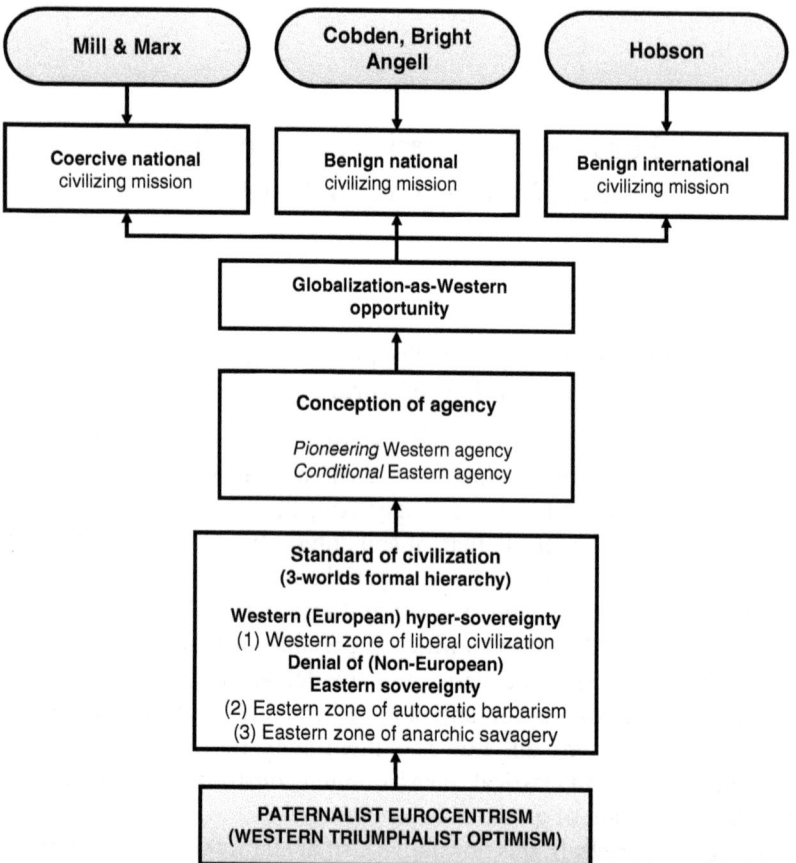

Figure 2.1 Paternalist Eurocentrism and the imperial civilizing mission, c. 1830–1913

the Western civilizing mission acts as a catalytic trigger, retracking non-European societies onto the progressive developmental path that had been laid down by the pioneering Europeans, with autonomous Eastern development proceeding thereafter into modern 'civilization'.

Naturally, though, this conception of agency falls short of the degree accorded to European countries, which are credited with making the pioneering breakthrough to modernity all by themselves in the absence of non-European help, given their exceptional institutional/cultural genius and hyper-agency. That is, development unfolds naturally and spontaneously within European societies as a result of their rational institutions via the Eurocentric process of the 'logic of immanence'. In addition, these thinkers emphasize the importance of global interdependence and perceive it as an *opportunity* for Europe to remake the world in its own rational-civilizational image. And in conjunction with the 'social efficiency' argument, it is claimed that the 'strenuous conditions of global interdependence' require that the West develops Eastern lands and resources 'on behalf of global humanity' in what amounts to the 'white man's burden'.

For all these similarities, however, there are some notable differences and variations within this category. It is not their rationale for imperialism that differentiates them so much as the *form* that imperialism should take. Thus Mill, and to an extent Marx, represent the harsher pole, advocating despotic colonial overlordship while at the other extreme lies Hobson, who insists that imperialism must be governed by a high degree of empathy and that it must be supervised, regulated or guaranteed by an independent international government. Nevertheless, it should be emphasized that Mill positively advocated despotic colonialism while Marx lamented the harshness of colonialism even though such coercion was functionally required as a means of imposing primitive accumulation.[29] Either side of these two extreme polarities lies the mid-ground position held by Cobden, Bright and Angell, all of whom argue against *coercive* imperialism but stop short of Hobson's more empathic approach, particularly via their calling for *national*-based civilizing missions rather than one in which impartial international governmental regulation ensures a non-coercive imperialism (as it does for Hobson). I shall deal with the middle-ground position first before considering the outer poles. I omit a discussion of Mill because his imperialist-Eurocentrism has been covered in detail by others,[30] and because the coverage of four liberals should be sufficient to illustrate the basic ingredients of liberal paternalist Eurocentrism.

Richard Cobden and John Bright: for 'peaceful universal interdependence' or 'English nationalism and national imperialism'?

While Richard Cobden (1804–65) and John Bright (1811–89) are often paired together in the popular historical imagination, within IR the figures of Cobden and Norman Angell (1872–1967) are generally paired

---

[29] Mill's despotic-imperialist claims can be found in various places: Mill (1859/1984: 119; 1861/1998: 453–4; 1859/1998: 14–15).
[30] E.g., Sullivan (1983); Parekh (1997); Mehta (1999); Hindess (2001); Jahn (2005); Pitts (2005: 133–62); Bowden (2009); McCarthy (2009: 171–7).

together as the outstanding representatives of classical liberal internationalism. In this chapter I concur with the assessment that these thinkers indeed overlap but I argue that they do so because they represent a liberal-paternalism that calls for the liberal-imperial civilizing mission in the East. The conventional assumption, of course, is that such a theory stands for self-determination, non-interventionism and anti-imperialism, all of which is founded on a cultural pluralist base. This conventional reading of Cobden is perhaps nowhere better summarized than in his own posited description of the British statesman's idiom:

> 'Men of war to conquer colonies, to yield to us a monopoly of their trade' must now be dismissed, like many other glittering but false adages of our forefathers, and in its place we must substitute the more homely but enduring maxim – *Cheapness*, which will command commerce; and whatever else is needful will follow in its train (1868a: 290, his emphasis).

Or, as he put it in a letter to Goldwin Smith in 1836: 'The colonies, army, navy, and church are with the Corn Laws, merely accessories to our aristocratic government. John Bull has his work cut out for the next 50 years to purge his house of these impurities' (Cobden cited in Bodelsen 1960: 33). Similarly in a letter to one of his constituents written in July 1850, John Bright asked rhetorically whether the foreign minister of Britain should:

> advise and warn, and meddle in matters which concern only the domestic and internal affairs of other countries? I say that such a policy necessarily leads to ... quarrels with other nations, and may even lead to war; and that it involves the necessity of maintaining greater armaments, and heavier expenditure and taxation ... It is a policy, therefore, which I cannot support under any pretence whatever (Bright 1895: 4).

But it turns out that this non-interventionist stance applies only to the case of relations between civilized European states.

Perhaps the best place to start is with Bright's and especially Cobden's views on the Crimean War, in which they were highly critical of Britain's decision to go to war with Russia on behalf of the Ottoman Empire. Indeed it is this argument for which Cobden gained an immediate notoriety, and sealed his reputation as the non-interventionist liberal-internationalist thinker *par excellence*. However, this posture was derived from a manifest paternalist Eurocentrism. For his key claim is that relatively civilized Russia should have been allowed to colonize Turkey precisely because this would deliver the blessings of civilization to this backward, barbaric Eastern country. Moreover, his Eurocentric analysis is not confined to various one-off statements but is sustained across no less than 443 pages out of a total 991 in Cobden's posthumously published two volume set, *Political Writings* (Cobden 1868a, 1868b).

For Cobden, Turkey was undermined by its barbaric institutions, especially its Oriental despotic state and its regressive Islamic religion. Thus while Turkey's lands had once been fertile, nevertheless 'despotic violence has triumphed over nature' such that this country 'has by the oppressive exactions of successive pachas, become little better than a deserted waste' (Cobden 1868a: 19). Or as he put it in his 1836 pamphlet, a once great country has been reduced to a 'desolate place of tombs' by a rapacious despotism given that it privileges war and militarism over peace and commerce (Cobden 1868a: 173-4). This point was echoed with equal force by Bright when, in an 1854 letter to Absalom Watkin, he asserted that

> We are building up our Eastern Policy on a false foundation – namely on the perpetual maintenance of the most immoral and filthy of all despotisms over one of the fairest portions of the earth which it has desolated, and over a population it has degraded but has not been able to destroy (Bright 1895: 14).

Cobden then engages in a thought experiment, asking what would happen if the population of the United States was substituted for the Turkish people and transplanted into Turkey. And he replies by painting an image of the ravaged hell of barbaric Turkey being transformed into an earthly civilized paradise, on the grounds that the Americans would create a vibrant commercial and prosperous economy (Cobden 1868a: 22-4).

In turn, having demarcated civilized Europe from barbaric Turkey, the bipolar or formal hierarchical imperialist conception of the international flows on immediately. For not only does Cobden dismiss the claim that a Russian acquisition of Turkey would harm British interests but, he insists:

> On the contrary, we have no hesitation in avowing it as our deliberate conviction that not merely Great Britain, but the entire civilized [i.e., Western] world, will have reason to congratulate itself, the moment when [Turkey] again falls beneath the sceptre of any other European power whatever. Ages must elapse before its favoured region will become ... the seat and centre of commerce, civilization, and true religion; but the first step towards this consummation must be to convert Constantinople again into that which every lover of humanity and peace longs to behold it – the capital of a Christian [civilized] people (1868a: 33).

Thus Cobden positively endorses a Russian colonial take-over of Turkey on the grounds that this Western civilizing mission would yield considerable benefits not just to Turkey but also to Europe in general and to Britain in particular (1868a: 33–7, 189–91). Speaking of this imperial mission of civilizing Turkey, he argues that it will

> put into a peoples' hands the bible in lieu of the Koran – let the religion of Mohamet give place to that of Jesus Christ; and human reason, aided by the printing press and the commerce of the world, will not fail to erase the errors which time, barbarism, or the cunning of its priesthood, may have engrafted upon it (1868a: 33–4).

This argument underpins his general claim that Turkish society was, in the typical paternalist Eurocentric institutionalist position, 'unchanging and stationary', whereas Russian society was 'progressing' (1868a: 187–8). And in Bright's case, as with Cobden's, standing for the doctrine of non-intervention by Britain logically entailed supporting a policy of Russian imperial intervention in Turkey, not least because 'the danger of the Russian power was a phantom . . . [and] the necessity of permanently upholding the Mahometan rule in Europe is an absurdity' (Bright 1895: 15).

At this point it might be suggested that perhaps Cobden and Bright condoned colonialism so long as it was not undertaken by Britain. But this is problematized most clearly by Cobden's calling for British imperialism in Ireland. And while Ireland is clearly a European country, it is the exception that proves the Eurocentric rule in the minds of many nineteenth-century thinkers, including Cobden. For in the grand civilizational league table that was invented by many British thinkers, the Irish were consigned to Division Three alongside the primitive Negroes on account of their laxity and 'savage' cultural behaviour. Reflecting this judgment, in the chapter on Ireland contained within his 1835 pamphlet, Cobden argues that the Irish are savages and that their Catholic form of persecution has 'enabled [Ireland] to resist, not only unscathed, but actually with augmented power, the shock of a free press, and the liberalizing influence of the freest constitutional government in Europe' (1868a: 63). And the rest of the chapter is given over to an argument that advocates an English colonial civilizing mission in Ireland that is wrapped up within a fervent English-nationalism. It is vital to 'raise Ireland up' through a civilizing mission, Cobden insists, for failure to do so 'will inevitably depress [England] to a level with [the Irish]' (1868a: 69). Precisely because savage habits are contaminating England through Irish immigration – a kind of 'Irish Peril' type-argument – so it is imperative that Irish savagery be eradicated (see esp. 1868a: 70). But in contrast to the racist anti-imperial position of Robert Knox, which insisted that the Irish must be ejected from English soil outright,[31] Cobden provided an alternative paternalist-Eurocentric solution.

To solve the Irish problem required an English civilizing mission in Ireland on the grounds that a '[p]arliament in Dublin [self-determination] would not remedy the ills of Ireland. That has been tried, and found unsuccessful; for all may learn in her history, that a more corrupt, base, and selfish public body than the domestic legislature of Ireland never existed' (1868a: 82). And so it was to the English parliament that Ireland must look for salvation. In particular, an English civilizing mission would entail building infrastructure (e.g., roads and railways) and the exporting of English capital and civilization. 'We confess we see no hope for the eventual prosperity [of Ireland] . . . except [through] . . . the instrumentality of English capital, in the pursuit of manufactures or commerce' (1868a: 90). Bright echoed this, reiterating in many letters the point that an Irish government would succeed only in creating disorder as well as the destruction of Irish industry (e.g., Bright 1895: 126, 138). Cobden concludes that where England has gone wrong vis-à-vis the 'problem of Ireland' is not in colonizing it but in neglecting to submit Ireland to a full colonial civilizing mission. Ultimately, however, it is the serving of the English national interest that underpins his calling for colonialism, given his belief that Ireland 'remains to this hour an appalling monument of our neglect and misgovernment. . . . The spectacle of Ireland operat[es] like a cancer in the side of England' (1868a: 95).

It is also instructive to note here that in a series of letters Bright provides strong support for maintaining British colonial rule of India. The solution to India's problems that emerged in the wake of the 1857 'Mutiny' was not the granting of independence but was, rather, a more empathic and benevolent British colonial government that could confer 'on the Indian people whatever good it is in our power to give them', and that good can 'only come from the most just government which we are able to confer upon [the] countless millions [of Indians]'. In turn, this led him to conclude that 'I hope every future Governor-General may merit the confidence of our Government at home and of the vast population whose interests may be committed to his charge' (Bright 1895: 182–3). All in all, then, both Bright and Cobden in effect constructed a paternalist Eurocentric conception of world politics, wherein European states gained imperial hyper-sovereignty while non-European polities were denied sovereignty.

[31] Knox (1850: 41, 89–90).

Finally it is worth responding to two possible objections to my argument. First, it might be objected that the Cobden/Bright stance towards Turkey and Ireland, as well as Poland in the case of the former,[32] contained no Eurocentric tendencies but was, rather, a function of an *ad hoc* illiberal argument that emanates rather from a Protestant prejudice towards Islam and Catholicism. But the criticism of these countries reflects a liberal-Eurocentric predisposition wherein those societies that were founded on irrational institutions did not qualify for self-determination and could only do so once the *full gamut* of rational institutions had been set up courtesy of an imperial civilizing mission (of which 'rational Protestantism' was only one such institution). And liberal prescriptions of non-intervention and tolerance can only apply once the 'irrational Other' has been remoulded along rational European lines.

Second, it might be argued that the 'Other' in Cobden's work does not simply refer to Eastern countries but includes various European states. But this serves not so much to disrupt Cobden's Eurocentric conception of an Eastern Other but reinforces the point that the level of civilization that a country occupies is measured according to the degree of rationality attained. For Cobden all of Europe, bar Ireland and Poland, qualified as rational and civilized even if the ultimate phase of civilization would not be reached until free trade and full parliamentary democracy had been installed throughout. Thus I argue that at worst Cobden and Bright's paternalist Eurocentric pro-imperialist posture supersedes entirely their non-interventionist doctrine since this holds only for intra-European relations (barring Poland and Ireland), or at best, that there are two Cobdenite theories – one pro- and the other anti-imperialist – which reside side-by-side in a contradictory fashion.

Norman Angell: for Western civilizational interdependence and the British civilizing mission in the East

The idea of 'interdependence' is conventionally thought to be a generic feature of the linear construction of the 'great liberal tradition' that IR historiography presents, comprising an imaginary line that begins with Adam Smith and then moves forwards through Immanuel Kant, David

---

[32] Cobden justified Russia's colonization of Poland on the grounds that the latter was a backward country that had been sacrificed at the altar of an all-powerful and selfish feudal aristocracy.

Ricardo, Richard Cobden, John Bright and Walter Bagehot,[33] before culminating in its classical guise with Norman Angell's seminal text, *The Great Illusion* (1913).[34] Angell's argument is reported to be a universal theory that applies equally to *all* countries, peoples and races. Indeed it is generally thought of as the last instance, or climax, of classical liberal internationalism, in which the realist assumption that economic gain can be secured through realpolitik and/or colonialism is denounced as but 'the great illusion' of the times. This is assumed on the grounds that Angell viewed the world on the eve of WWI as fully interdependent and that under such conditions economic gain could be maximized for *all* states through peaceful cooperation rather than through military conquest.

When viewed in this light Angell's anti-imperialist credentials appear to be impeccable. Indeed, as one IR scholar notes: Angell's 'acute comments on the role of colonies advanced the liberal critique of empire and was similar to the arguments of other radicals regarding the negative balance sheet of the empire-builders, such as J. A. Hobson ... and Leonard Woolf' (Miller 1995: 106). However, in this chapter I argue that Angell and Hobson can indeed be linked but for precisely the inverse reason to that supplied by Miller, given that they both shared in various imperialist visions of IR that emanated from their common paternalist Eurocentric-institutional base. I also make the same argument with respect to Woolf in Chapter 7.

As with Cobden, so I identify in Angell's text a formal hierarchical conception of the international that implies a conception of gradated sovereignties. The first clue to this alternative reading appears relatively early on in the book. Angell makes it clear that the discussion of interdependence, upon which his whole book is allegedly based, turns out to apply *only to the civilized states of Europe*. 'We are concerned with the case of fully civilized rival nations in fully occupied territory or with civilizations so firmly set that conquest could not sensibly modify their character' (Angell 1913: 52, 54–5, 197). Although this vital insight has been either unwittingly forgotten or consciously elided by modern IR historiography, it was revealed incisively in a 1911 review of *The Great Illusion*, the key part of which notes that '[i]t is important that the exact

---

[33] Walter Bagehot was editor of *The Economist* between 1860 and 1877.
[34] We could add to this list Jean de Bloch's *The Future of War*, which was published in English in 1899, nine years before the early version of Angell's book came out. This is also pertinent because Bloch's argument fully pre-empted the one that Angell became famous for (see Crook 1994: 99–101; Dawson 2002).

scope of the author's proposition be understood. He does not assert that all war is unprofitable to the average man, but only a war between civilized nations' (Snow 1911: 558). The immediate implications that flow from this point are two fold: first, that what has been read as a universal thesis turns out to constitute a parochialism or provincialism that applies only to civilized European states; and second, that while imperialism between civilized states is counter-productive, it can, however, be worthwhile when applied to uncivilized polities and societies.

Like Cobden and Bright, Angell argued that Britain had no place in militarily engaging Russia in the Crimean War not because of his inherent non-interventionist/pacifist credentials but more because of his belief that the realist-militarists had 'backed the wrong horse' – i.e., barbaric Turkey rather than civilized Russia (1913: 387). For his vehement objection to defending Turkey was based on a paternalist Eurocentric analysis that effectively depicted the Ottoman Empire as ripe for colonization. Echoing Cobden's analysis, the problem with Turkey is that its Oriental despotic state engages in militaristic imperialism abroad and coercion of its own people at home. In turn, the despotic backwardness of Turkey is in part a result of the fact that the country is not economically interdependent with Europe. For Europe's interdependence has, unlike in the case of Turkey, enabled her to progress out of 'primitive religious and racial hatreds' as well as despotism. The Turk 'has learned none of the social and moral lessons which interdependence and improved communications have taught the Western European, and it is because [of this] . . . that the Balkanese are fighting and that war is raging' (1913: 402).

The Eurocentric analysis of Turkey is helped along by an extensive quote from Sir Charles Elliott, the most notable part of which is the claim that the Turk's 'contributions to art, literature, science and religion, are practically nil. [His] desire has not been to instruct, to improve, hardly even to govern, but simply to conquer . . . The Turk makes nothing at all; he takes whatever he can get, as plunder or pillage' (Elliott cited in Angell 1913: 390–1). This is reinforced further by a series of impassioned claims including the points that: 'The Turk cannot build a road or make a bridge or administer a post office or found a court of law', and that the Turkish 'Government will take the form of the obscene torture of children, of a bestial ferocity which is not a matter of dispute or exaggeration, but a thing to which [many] . . . credible European witnesses have testified' (1913: 404, 393).

With his bipolar formal hierarchical construction of the international already in place, so his prescription of imperialism naturally follows.

Significantly, Angell's paternalist Eurocentric conception of imperialism is directly articulated against the racist-realist conception of imperialism. In explicit contrast to those scientific racists who deny the East any development agential capacity (though as I explain in Chapters 4–7 not all subscribed to this view), Angell proclaims that development is not the sole preserve of the West but can be achieved by *all* societies, though initially this can only be triggered by the catalytic impulse of a Western civilizing mission in the East. Such a conception implicitly awards the East a 'conditional agency'. And directly challenging some of the social Darwinian racists he presents a progressive evolutionary schema, arguing that '[i]f at any stage of human development war ever did make for the survival of the fit', today the imperial civilizing mission in the East provides 'added chances of life by introducing order' which enables the survival of the weakest rather than the fittest. The civilizing mission has enabled 'race conservation' (1913: 189). Moreover, later on he asserts that:

> Great Britain has conquered India. Does that mean that the inferior [Indian] race is replaced by the superior? Not the least in the world; the inferior race not only survives, but is given an extra lease of life by virtue of the conquest.... War, therefore, does not make for the elimination of the unfit and the survival of the fit. It would be truer to say that it makes for the survival of the unfit (1913: 236–7).

Such a statement signals the point that Angell embraced a paternalist-Eurocentric institutionalism in contrast to the offensive racism that underpinned the realist imperialists such as Alfred Mahan and Halford Mackinder.[35] Here Angell, though he does not use the terms, is effectively differentiating 'coercive colonialism' from the 'benign' formal paternalist civilizing mission. For as he goes on to say:

> [w]here the condition of a territory is such that the social and economic co-operation of other countries with it is impossible [i.e., where interdependence does not exist] we may expect the intervention of military force, not as the result of the [coercive] 'annexationist illusion', but as the outcome of real social forces pushing to the maintenance of order. That is the story of England in Egypt, or, India (1913: 146).

[35] Though a different reading is provided by Paul Crook who sees in Angell's book strong signs of the racist 'peace biology' of Jacques Novicow (Crook 1994: 117–18). Even so, as Crook concedes, Angell only read Novicow's (1911) book after the publication of the first 1908 edition of his own book; see Angell (1913: 184). And, in any case, I reject the claim that Angell's book was racist.

44   CHAPTER 2 : EUROCENTRIC IMPERIALISM: C. 1830–1914

Above all, Angell's notion of a benign and peaceful imperialism finds its ultimate normative expression in British imperialism. In offering up a critique of racist-coercive imperialism he asks: '[W]hat has caused the relative failure and decline of Spanish, Portuguese, and French expansion in Asia and the New World, and the relative success of English expansion therein?' (1913: 239–40). And he answers by claiming that:

> the methods and processes of Spain, Portugal, and France were military, while those of the Anglo-Saxon world were commercial and peaceful.... The difference ... was that one was a process of conquest, and the other of colonizing, or non-military administration for commercial purposes. The one embodied the ... Cobdenite idea ... the other the lofty [realist] military ideal. The one was parasitism; the other co-operation (1913: 240).

Added to this is the point that 'the work of policing backward or disorderly populations is ... often [wrongly] confused with the annexationist illusion .... England is doing a real and useful work for the world at large in policing India' (1913: 151). This is only possible because the Briton has reached the peak of rationality; something which was the result of Britain's superior institutions, to wit:

> Not that Fuzzy-Wuzzy is not a fine fellow. He is manly, sturdy, hardy, with a courage, and warlike qualities generally, which no European can equal. But the frail and spectacled English official is his master, and a few score of such will make themselves the masters of teeming thousands of Sudanese; the relatively unwarlike Englishman is doing the same thing all over Asia, and he is doing it simply by virtue of superior brain and character, more thought, more rationalism, more steady and controlled hard work.... Force is indeed the master, but it is the force of intelligence, character, and rationalism (1913: 280–1).

It is therefore the British Empire rather than the presence of an antiimperialist universal interdependence that will produce a future civilized world that enjoys the fruits of peace. For Britain has furnished the world with progressive ideas concerning political economy, human freedom and parliamentary government; ideas that need to be embraced by others courtesy of the British civilizing mission (e.g., 1913: 380).

When viewed in this light we can now appreciate the imperialist motives that informed Angell's belief in the folly of Britain going to war with Russia to defend the Ottoman Empire. For what particularly bothered Angell about the realist conception of statecraft that still lingered among European states on the eve of WWI, is not simply that this makes possible economically futile wars within Europe but that it must bear 'a large part of the responsibility for this failure of European civilization [insofar as it] has caused us to sustain the [barbaric] Turk in Europe, to fight a great and popular war with that aim' (1913: 390). To this end he closes the appendix to his book with the claim that

> It is because these false [realist] beliefs prevent the nations of Christendom acting loyally the one to the other, because each is playing for its own hand, that the Turk, with hint of some sordid bribe, has been able to play off each against the other. This is the crux of the matter, when Europe can honestly act in common on behalf of common interests some solution can be found. And the capacity of Europe to act in harmony will not be found as long as the accepted doctrines of European statecraft remain unchanged, as long as they are dominated by existing [realist] illusions (1913: 405–6).

Here it is apparent that Angell critiques racist-realism on the grounds that it prevents Western states from bandwagoning together so as to unify civilization. Or put differently, Angell rejects realism for its implicit politics of dividing and ruling Western civilization.[36]

In the light of all this, then, an alternative conclusion can be drawn regarding the essence of Angell's theory. For it turns out that for Angell, only *civilized* states (i.e., European states) should avoid going to war with each other and should instead bandwagon together in order to unify Western civilization. In short, the 'great (war) illusion' and the (colonial) 'annexationist illusion' turn out to apply only to *intra-European* state relations. For colonial annexation was deemed to be entirely appropriate when it came to Europe's relations with the East. And so in the end, Angell's politics were founded not upon a pristine liberal internationalist pacifism that advocates interdependence over imperialism, but upon an extension of imperialism that would deliver the non-Western societies to full rationality and interdependence with the West, thereby harmonizing the world according to the universal rhythmic beat of the provincial liberal empire of Western civilization in general and the British Empire in particular.

J. A. Hobson: paternalist Eurocentrism and the quest for a 'pure humane' Western civilizing mission

The inclusion of John Atkinson Hobson (1858–1940) in the category of paternalist-Eurocentric imperialism will undoubtedly appear to most of my readership as entirely counterintuitive given that he is, of course,

---

[36] Though the paradox here is that various racist-realists (such as Mahan and Mackinder) called precisely for the unity of Western civilization as I explain in Chapter 5.

famous for his radical critique of imperialism advanced in his well-known book, *Imperialism: A Study* (Hobson 1938/1968), first published in 1902.[37] Indeed, his theory is still discussed on undergraduate development courses, often treated alongside Vladimir Lenin's equally famous theory of imperialism in what is known as the 'Hobson/Lenin thesis'. But here and in Chapter 6 I argue that while both were Eurocentric, Lenin's anti-paternalist Eurocentrism made him a strong critic of imperialism whereas Hobson supported a certain kind of imperialism that his paternalist-Eurocentrism generated. In this respect, it is particularly striking that Hobson's thesis on imperialism is so poorly understood, for unbeknown to the majority of IR scholars, though an open secret among Hobson experts,[38] Hobson had several theories of imperialism. These he referred to as *sane* and *insane* imperialism, both of which are contained in his book *Imperialism*.[39]

Conventional received wisdom holds that Hobson produced an *economistic* critique of imperialism that revolved around a finance capitalist imperial conspiracy, which ensured that the distribution of resources at the domestic level was skewed in favour of the elites, and that this inequity problem under conditions of underconsumption constituted the 'tap-root' of imperialism.[40] But no less than 70 per cent of the book is given over to considering the political and discursive origins of imperialism, leading one expert to note that 'Hobson's emphasis of imperialism's non-economic aspects are as important as, perhaps more important than, his economic studies' (Mitchell 1965: 414). In my view and others', Hobson rejected economism and argued that politics and discourse must be accorded a certain ontological weighting.[41] Here I argue that Hobson's first theory of (insane) imperialism was the subject of an economic critique in part 1 of the book and a discursive and political critique in part 2. Most importantly, though, his political solution to imperialism was not simply to cut off its 'tap-root' by

---

[37] All references to this book are to its third edition. Note that his theory was first advanced in an 1898 article and possibly an 1897 one, entitled 'Ethics and Empire'; for a discussion of the latter see Porter (1968: 177); Särkkä (2009: 151, 152); for the former see Hobson (1898).

[38] E.g., Mitchell (1965); Porter (1968); Townshend (1990); Cain (2002); Long (2005); Sylvest (2009); Boucher (1997b); Särkkä (2009).

[39] Note that elsewhere I argue that Hobson had three theories of imperialism (J. M. Hobson 2011a).

[40] Of the countless examples available see Waltz (1979: ch. 2); Gabriel (1994: 59–65).

[41] J. M. Hobson (2011a); Magnusson (1994: 143–62); Long (1996: 86–90); Allett (1981: 157–64); Mitchell (1965: 397–416). Jules Townshend (1990: 110) is a notable exception.

overcoming the domestic economic problem of underconsumption. For no less importantly, Hobson sought to undermine insane imperialism by critiquing the scientific racist discourse of empire and replace it with an empathic 'sane' conception of an international imperial civilizing mission.

Turning therefore to part 2 of *Imperialism*, Hobson begins his critique of insane imperialism by revealing its scientific racist discursive roots. Critically, scientific racism was not dreamed up by capitalists to legitimise their imperial interests but came first, to which imperial interests instinctively attached themselves subsequently.[42] In particular, he singles out the racist 'social efficiency' argument that is found in the works of Benjamin Kidd, Karl Pearson and Franklin Giddings. As he put it: '[t]his genuine and confident conviction about "social efficiency" must be taken as the chief moral support of imperialism' (1938/1968: 155). Here he has in mind the extreme biological Darwinian notion that the weaker races must yield in the face of the stronger, superior races and that the survival of the fittest is a law that cannot be mitigated. It is this discourse, he argues, that furnishes the justification to conquer, exploit and even exterminate the weaker races (1938/1968: 154ff). He is no less critical of the paternalist discourse of the civilizing mission as it transpired in practice rather than theory. For while it proclaimed to help the Natives in theory, nevertheless the practice of imperialism served merely to provide a legitimating cover for the naked pursuit of economic gain by private capitalist interests. Moreover, the claim to install democracy, he argued, is denied by the despotic version that is actually implemented (1938/1968: 113-24). All of which is summarized by his claim that '[t]he Pax Britannica, always an impudent falsehood, has become a grotesque monster of hypocrisy' (1938/1968: 126).

The trick for Hobson was to bring the practice of the benign civilizing mission into line with the theory. His conception of sane imperialism began with two initial paternalist-Eurocentric claims:

> [f]irst, that all interference on the part of civilized white nations with 'lower races' is not prima facie illegitimate. Second, that such interference cannot safely be left to private enterprise of individual whites. If these principles be admitted, it follows that civilized Governments *may* undertake the political and economic control of lower races – in a word, that the characteristic form of modern Imperialism is not under all conditions illegitimate (1938/1968: 232).

[42] Hobson (1901a; 1938/1968: esp. 197, 206).

And from this starting point he outlines his approach to sane imperialism in the long chapter in Part II of *Imperialism* entitled 'Imperialism and the lower races'. Here he begins by asserting that 'there is nothing unworthy, quite the contrary, in the notion that nations' which have become more advanced should communicate their ways to the backward nations 'so as to aid them in developing alike the material resources of their land and the human resources of their people' (1938/1968: 228-9). Thus he takes issue with those who argue that the native peoples should be left alone in sovereign isolation to develop the resources of their lands because, he insists, they will *not* do so. Indeed, he reasons:

> [a]ssuming that the arts of 'progress', or some of them, are communicable, a fact which is hardly disputable, there can be no inherent natural right in a people to refuse that measure of compulsory education which shall raise it from childhood to manhood in the order of nationalities. The analogy furnished by the education of a child is prima facie a sound one (1938/1968: 229).

Such a metaphor was directly applied to the 'races of Africa [whom] it has been possible to regard as savages or children, "backward" in their progress along the same general road of civilization in which Anglo-Saxondom represents the vanguard, and requiring the help of the more forward races' (1938/1968: 285). And while the Asiatic races of India and China could not be likened to children owing to their higher levels of civilization, nevertheless in terms of civilizational attributes he states that '[i]f Western civilization is richer in these essentials, it seems reasonable to suppose that the West can benefit the East by imparting them, and that her governments may be justified as a means of doing so' (1938/1968: 286).

This social efficiency argument was complemented by his interpretation of emergent global interdependence. For under these conditions, he argues, it is now impossible for even 'the most remote lands to escape the intrusion of "civilized" nations ... The contact with white races cannot be avoided' (1938/1968: 230, also 231). Or as he put it later on in his life:

> For [backward] countries may contain material resources the development of which is of prime importance to world prosperity, and the claim that the people in occupation of a country are the absolute owners of those resources, and entitled to leave them undeveloped, is a quite inadmissible assertion of national sovereignty (1934: 141-2).

Moreover, he blends with this his critique of national or insane imperialism on the grounds that private Western interests seek to exploit the

Eastern lands and peoples in pursuit of profits. Accordingly, in the context of global interdependence the West must not 'abandon the backward races to [the] perils of private exploitation' as in insane imperialism, for this would constitute a 'barbarous dereliction of a public duty on behalf of humanity and the civilization of the world' (1938/1968: 231). But this is not merely a critique of the predatory interests that lie within Western civilization, for he was equally as concerned with the weak governing institutions of the Eastern countries. Thus failure to intervene to protect the backward countries

> opens grave dangers in the future, from the ambitions of native or imported rulers, who, playing upon the religious fanaticism or the combative instincts of great hordes of semi-savages may impose upon them so effective a military discipline as to give terrible significance to some black or yellow 'peril' (1938/1968: 231).

It deserves emphasizing that at first sight this social efficiency argument undoubtedly appears perplexing given that Hobson's key criticism of the scientific racists was precisely their resort to the 'social efficiency' justification for imperialism. But Hobson's rendition was, for the most part, shorn of its racist basis, and was used to justify what he believed would be a 'genuine' or 'sane' civilizing mission. Of what did this comprise? The most interesting aspect of his proposal for a sane imperialism is that it is ideologically schizophrenic: invoking many sympathetic, even postcolonial, ideas but ultimately deferring to a paternalist-Eurocentric institutionalism. Thus while the advanced nations must educate the backward races through transplanting various rational Western institutions and practices, albeit on a gradualist basis, this can only be achieved with a strong degree of empathy for the Natives. This requires understanding Native cultures, languages and environment. And he insists that the Eastern peoples should be approached carefully and should be legitimately persuaded of friendly motives while simultaneously discouraging any private imperial attempts to exploit their economies; an argument that is reminiscent of Kant's insistence that Western incursion into non-European lands must be undertaken in a non-exploitative and genuinely consensual manner. Indeed the Natives 'should be gainers, not losers' and that 'the direct gains of development should pass on equal terms to all the world and not to the capitalist exploiters of a single nation' (Hobson 1932: 78). Moreover, he objected to the *wholesale* transplantation and imposition of *all* Western institutions in the East, which underpinned his criticism of those American imperialists who in effect sought to 'carry "canned" civilization to the heathen' (Hobson 1938/1968: 245).[43]

In addition to various discursive building blocs, sane imperialism would be guaranteed by an independent international government, ensuring that the development of Native lands would be conducted in their own interests, as well as those of global humanity's, over and against the exploitative private interests of individual imperialist capitalists. Importantly, this fed into his theory of 'constructive internationalism' – or what David Long (1996) aptly dubs the 'new liberal internationalism' – which was mooted in the second part of *Imperialism* and developed much further in a number of key works including *Towards International Government* (1915a), *A League of Nations* (1915b), *The Morals of Economic Internationalism* (1920), *Problems of a New World* (1921) and *Democracy and a Changing Civilisation* (1934). Ultimately, as I explain elsewhere in detail, international government could only be secured by a prior epistemic shift entailing the construction of the progressive international mind (see J. M. Hobson 2011a). Moreover, there had to be a democratization of international government so that it could not be dominated by the great powers as, he argued, had occurred in the case of the League (Hobson 1921, 1934: esp. ch. 8). The key point as far as this chapter is concerned is that while Hobson converged with other liberal international theorists on the need for a civilizing mission, the central difference is that for Hobson all national-imperialisms were necessarily coercive and could only be 'socially sanitized' or 'truly civilized' by the intervention of an impartial and democratized international government through 'international imperialism'.

Significantly, Hobson's conception of sane imperialism and 'constructive internationalism' as a solution to the world's problems was, in effect, a conceptual blueprint both for the Mandate System as well as the ideas that informed the interwar 'international imperialists', including Woodrow Wilson, Alfred Zimmern, Leonard Woolf, Raymond Buell and Norman Angell (see Chapter 7).[44] It is also the case that while

---

[43] Interestingly, this particular sensibility was one that others had developed earlier, most notably Richard Congreve and Frederic Harrison, as well as William Knight and Mary Kingsley (Porter 1968: 181–3).

[44] It is noteworthy that Hobson was a member of the Union for Democratic Control and the Bryce Committee that in turn played a formative role in establishing the League of Nations.

Hobson was the most prominent New Liberal, others such as Leonard Hobhouse (1904/1972) and William Robertson (1900) shared in Hobson's paternalist-Eurocentrism. There was also considerable overlap here with the British idealists including John Muirhead (1900/1997) and David G. Ritchie (1900), notwithstanding the social Darwinian approach of the latter. Notable too is that a 'progressive' conception of imperialism served to link many members of the Rainbow Circle, who included representatives from a range of political perspectives such as Fabianism and Socialism, in addition to New Liberalism.[45] Indeed one expert notes that the majority of the membership of the Rainbow Circle subscribed to the belief that 'Britain should own as much of the earth's surface as possible, and that it was the duty of the British to see that what they had colonized was well governed' (Särkkä 2009: 73). Overall, these various political and intellectual movements exhibited a range of pro-imperial arguments that were couched either in social Darwinian, Eugenicist, or paternalist-Eurocentric terms; a theme that I extend further in Chapters 5 and 7.

But I shall conclude this section in the context of the twin-charge levied most recently by the prominent Marxist scholar, Alex Callinicos (2009: 46): that Hobson's theory of imperialism 'betrays a broader racialized ideology that denies the right of lower races to self-determination', and that it is this which differentiates Hobson from the Marxist theories of imperialism in which 'racial categories are wholly absent'. But, as we have seen, the first charge mistakenly conflates Hobson's paternalist Eurocentrism with a scientific racist ideology; one that he critiqued in an extensive way (though this is not to absolve Hobson entirely, since on various occasions during his life he adhered to certain Eugenicist ideas).[46] And with respect to the second charge, while Hobson was no Marxist, he nevertheless shared in common with Karl Marx a pro-imperialist paternalist-Eurocentrism that denied the concept of self-determination to non-Western societies, to a consideration of which I now turn.[47]

---

[45] For the former see especially George Bernard Shaw (1900) and Ramsay MacDonald (1907).

[46] See J. M. Hobson (2011a: 32); Etherington (1984: 71–6); Freeden (1979: 657–8); Särkkä (2009: 137–40); but see Long (2005: 83).

[47] While in no way wishing to smear Marx as a racist, nor even an anti-Semite given his Jewish origins, nevertheless Callinicos's charge innocently elides the many harsh, if not outright condemnatory, criticisms of the Jews that Marx meted out in his *A World Without Jews* (Marx 1843/1959).

Karl Marx: paternalist Eurocentrism and the 'political necessity' of the Western civilizing mission

Nineteenth-century Eurocentric institutionalism also found its voice in the writings of Karl Marx (1818–83) and Georg Hegel (1770–1831), as well as the liberal sociologist, Max Weber (1864–1920). Here, though, I shall focus on Hegel and especially Marx, having discussed Weber's Eurocentrism elsewhere (Hobson 2004: 14–19). While Marx might well have inverted Hegel's idealism to produce a dialectical-materialist theory of history, nevertheless the prospect of inverting Hegel's Eurocentric institutionalism to produce some kind of non-Eurocentric cultural pluralism is a move that was never effected by Marx. That Marx could be described as Eurocentric might come as a surprise to many, especially those of a Marxist persuasion who have not read Said's *Orientalism*, given the immediate retort that Marx was the critic of Western capitalism *par excellence*. But this defence rests on a common misperception of what Eurocentrism comprises, for as I shall argue in this section and in Chapters 6 and 10, Eurocentrism need not imply a *moral* celebration of the West, as Marx's approach bears ample testimony.

Interestingly, in his defence of Marx, Aijaz Ahmad rails in particular against the Eurocentric charge originally made by Said (1978/2003: 153–7), not least because *inter alia* he insists that Marx was no racist (Ahmad 2008: ch. 6). I agree with the latter point but disagree with the former: for while Marx was certainly no racist he did work within a paternalist Eurocentric-institutionalism, as did Hegel. And this, of course, returns us to one of the abiding themes of the present book: that Said's mistaken conflation of Eurocentric institutionalism and racism constitutes the source of Ahmad's misplaced consternation. However, as I explain below, I endorse Ahmad's criticism of Said's claim that Marx's 'Orientalism' implies on Marx's part a dissolution of 'human sympathy' for the non-Western peoples. But equally, where I differ with Ahmad is that it was precisely Marx's human sympathy for the oppressed Eastern peoples that underpinned his paternalist-Eurocentric theory of imperialism.

Marx's brand of imperialism

Although Marx had little to say directly about international relations, it is well-known that in various pamphlets and newspaper articles published in *The New York Daily Tribune*, his pro-imperialist stance comes to the fore. For there he insisted that the East, especially China and India, could only be emancipated from its backwardness in the first instance by the imperial mission of the British capitalists (e.g., Marx 1969: 93–5). This stance emanated directly from his paternalist Eurocentrism. Indeed, much as Hegel claimed that traditional customs of India 'are fixed and immutable, and subject to no one's will',[48] such that India lies 'outside of ... World's History',[49] so Marx famously asserted that:

> Indian society has no history at all, at least no known history. What we call its history, is but the history of the successive intruders who founded their empires on the passive basis of that unresisting and unchanging society. The question, therefore, is not whether the English had a right to conquer India, but whether we are to prefer India conquered by the [backward] Turk, by the [backward] Persian, by the Russian, to India conquered by the Briton (Marx 1969: 132).[50]

Equally as well known was Marx's claim that 'England has to fulfil a double mission in India: one destructive, the other regenerating – the annihilation of old Asiatic society, and the laying of the foundations of Western society in Asia' (Marx 1973a: 320). And '[w]hile China and India remain stationary, and perpetuate a natural vegetative existence' (Hegel 1837/2001: 191), so for Marx, China was but a 'rotting semicivilization. ... vegetating in the teeth of time', and existed merely as 'a fossil form of life',[51] such that its only hope for progressive emancipation or redemption lay with the 'emancipatory' Opium Wars and the incursion of British capitalists who would 'open up barbaric' China to the energizing impulse of capitalist world trade (1969: 442–4). Thus whatever moral crimes the British committed in the process, and he argues that they were considerable, could not detract from his abiding belief that without British intervention there would be no future emancipatory socialist revolution in India or China (1973a: 320) – or indeed anywhere else in the East. To be clear, Marx had no moral truck with the imperial process given that it enforced violent primitive accumulation on Eastern societies. But despite this he viewed imperialism as an instrumental political necessity since this constituted the initial stepping stone to the future rise of the East into communism via capitalism.

This analysis ties in directly with Marx's view of incipient globalization, which he conflates with the expansion of European capitalism.

---

[48] Hegel (1837/2001: 172). [49] Hegel (1837/2001: 133).
[50] For his discussion of Persia and Turkey see Marx (1969: 51–8, 184–90).
[51] Marx (1969: 184, 343, 444).

The 'terrible-twins' – Western globalization and imperialism – were charged with performing the vital functional requirement of 'global primitive accumulation', which entailed the violent propulsion of non-Western societies out of their backward static collective systems of rural production and onto the dynamic track of capitalism. This is also worth noting in the context of this chapter since it reveals Marx's imperialism as one that resides at the harsh/coercive end of the spectrum (as noted in Figure 2.1). Indeed, for Marx, global primitive accumulation is an inherently violent process, albeit one of global social necessity since only on pain of extinction can non-Western countries refuse the path of capitalist modernity, and thereby refuse undertaking the 'real civilizing process' that delivers them to a future communist society. As Marx and Engels put it in the well-known passage in *The Communist Manifesto*:

> The bourgeoisie, by the rapid improvement of all instruments of production, by the immensely facilitated means of communication, draws all, even the most barbarian, nations into civilization. The cheap prices of its commodities are the heavy artillery with which it batters down all Chinese walls, with which it forces the barbarians' intensely obstinate hatred of all foreigners to capitulate. It compels all nations, on pain of extinction, to adopt the bourgeois mode of production; it compels them to introduce what it calls civilization into their midst, i.e., to become bourgeois themselves. In one word, it creates a world after its own image (Marx and Engels 1848/1967: 84).

Although it is certainly possible to see in Marx and Engels' pronouncements in *The Communist Manifesto* a celebration of the Western bourgeoisie as it serves to civilize the East, this is heavily qualified by Marx's moral disgust for the process of violence that accompanies both globalization and imperialism (or what he called 'primitive capital accumulation'). This is clarified in the first volume of *Capital* where he asserted, not without a degree of sarcasm, that

> The discovery of gold and silver in America, the extirpation, enslavement and entombment in mines of the aboriginal population, the beginning of the conquest and looting of the East Indies, the turning of Africa into a warren for the commercial hunting of black-skins, signalised the rosy dawn of the era of capitalist production. These idyllic proceedings are the chief moments of primitive accumulation (1867/1954: 703).

Equally it is undeniable that his many articles on India in particular evince a moral condemnation of Britain's imperialist intervention.[52] One

---

[52] Marx (1973a: 301–25; 1969: 81–108, 115–39, 191–335).

notable authority got it right when he asserts that 'Marx was as ambivalent on colonialism as he was on capitalism – both were destructive and inhuman but at the same time regenerative in that they laid the foundations for a new form of society' (McLellan 1975: 83). At this point Ahmad (2008) seeks to defend Marx from the Eurocentric charge by claiming that Marx viewed primitive accumulation as an equally 'barbaric' process in Europe, thereby implying that it was a normal part of capitalist development. But this misses the key point that the process of primitive accumulation in the Asian context, in contrast to the European situation, had to be imposed from without by the European imperialists. And, as noted, emancipation was the flip-side of the violence of the civilizing mission.

Thus it was only through the imperialism of the globalizing Western bourgeoisie, which was in effect the backward East's 'conquering liberators' (i.e., the 'Western fifth column'), that the 'static Eastern peoples' could belatedly jump aboard the Western progressive developmental train – the Oriental Express – which would deliver them to capitalism. And from there the Western working class would come to the aid of the Eastern peoples in order to deliver them to the terminus of communism. Ultimately, it is precisely this emancipatory-socialist logic that makes Marx an 'admirer' of colonialism, or better still, a 'sympathetic-critic' given that he was highly critical of its brutalizing modus operandi. And it is this which reveals the defensive claim by Ahmad as missing the target: that 'any attempt to portray Marx as an enthusiast of colonialism would logically have to portray him as an admirer of capitalism as well' (Ahmad 2008: 226). In sum, as Jorge Larrain puts it: 'Marx and Engels at this time did not believe in the right of self-determination of backward [Eastern] nations and thought that the national struggles for liberation and independence had to be subordinated to the needs of the stronger and more progressive nations' (1991: 231). Indeed, Marx constructed a formal hierarchical conception of the international which granted hyper-sovereignty to the key Western states while simultaneously denying sovereignty to the Eastern polities.

Nevertheless, at this point many neo-Marxists respond by making two defensive claims: first, that these statements on imperialism were contained within various *ad hoc* newspaper articles,[53] which did not reflect the core substance of his writings on historical materialism; and second, that these articles were in any case moribund after about 1860 when in

---

[53] No less than 74 articles between 1848 and 1862.

56 CHAPTER 2 : EUROCENTRIC IMPERIALISM: C. 1830–1914

the second half of his career he turned to provide a critique of imperialism. Indeed the latter point, it is often argued, is evident in his critique of English imperialism in Ireland (Marx and Engels 1971).[54] Answering these responses is the task of the next subsection.

Marx's paternalist-Eurocentric theory of history

The main problem with both of these twin defensive responses is that Marx's paternalist-Eurocentrism awards Eastern societies with only *conditional-* rather than the pioneering-agency that he grants the West. And critically, this forms the lynchpin or foundation of his whole theory of history. Crucial here was his concept of the 'Asiatic mode of production' in which private property and hence class struggle – *the* developmental motor of historical progress – was notably absent in the East. As he explained in *Capital*, in Asia 'the direct producers ... [are] under direct subordination to a state which stands over them as their landlord. ... [Accordingly] no private ownership of land exists'.[55] Thus it was the failure to produce a surplus for reinvestment in the economy that 'supplies the key to the secret of the *unchangeableness* of Asiatic societies' (1867/1954: 338, my emphasis). Marx, as did Hegel, subscribed to the Eurocentric concept of Oriental despotism wherein the key dynamic features of private property and class struggle were choked off. Indeed social actors were quashed not least through massive 'taxes wrung from them – frequently by means of torture – by a ruthless despotic state'.[56] By contrast, the European situation was presented as the binary opposite case, wherein states cooperated with key social actors in order to nurture capitalist development. Thus the presence – as opposed to its absence in the East – of the dynamic motor of class struggle ensured that economic progress constituted the unique preserve or monopoly of the West. It was precisely this analysis that underpinned Marx's imperialist stance, given that the East had no prospects for progressive self-development and could only be rescued by the capitalist (and hopefully the British) imperialists in the first instance and the Western proletariat in the last.

---

[54] The strongest case is made by Davis (1967) and Mori (1978), with a more qualified version advanced by Larrain (1991).
[55] Marx (1867/1959: 791, 333–4; 1867/1954: 140, 316, 337–9).
[56] Marx (1867/1959: 726); cf. Hegel (1837/2001: 124). For a much lengthier elaboration of this point on Marx see O'Leary (1989) and Turner (1978). And for Hegel see Whelan (2009: ch. 5).

No less importantly, Marx's whole theory of history faithfully reproduces the teleological Orientalist story, which rests fundamentally on the Eurocentric concept of the 'logic of immanence'. In *The German Ideology* (1845/1965) Marx traces the origins of capitalist modernity back to Ancient Greece – the fount of civilization – thereby eliding the Egyptian origins of Ancient Greece (Bernal 1991: 296), while in the *Grundrisse* he explicitly dismissed the importance of Ancient Egypt (1973b: 110). No less an important omission is Ancient Sumer in present-day Iraq, which pioneered many ideas that would later be developed by the Greeks and others. Either way, though, Marx's theory of history recounts the rise of the West through, in effect, an immanent journey of the European developmental train which, having departed Ancient Greece, steams through the Roman Empire, then onto European feudalism, before passing through the European capitalist way-station on its way to the terminus of communism. No such spontaneous progressive developmental journey could occur in the East.

For Marx the *Western* proletariat is global humanity's 'chosen people' no less than the *Western* bourgeoisie is global capitalism's 'chosen people'. To paraphrase Marx's discussion of class consciousness, it is as if Marx saw the East as a 'being-in-itself' but could only become a 'being-for-itself' once it had been retracked onto the capitalist path by the Western capitalist civilizing mission. By contrast, the West was from the outset a 'being-for-itself'. Moreover, it seems no coincidence that the Hegelian influence in Marx's work should have produced this binary 'progressive West/regressive East' couplet, precisely because for Hegel the superior Spirit of the West is progressive freedom, whereas the inferior Spirit of the East is regressive, unchanging despotism (Hegel 1837/2001). Here it is salutary to note Jorge Larrain's conclusion, who himself questions the reading of imperialism I produce here: that 'on the whole, even when Marx and Engels advocated the independence and self-government of some colonies, their point of reference and their main objectives were the liberation of the British proletariat and the advance of socialism in the most developed countries of the world as a precondition for the liberation of the rest of humankind' (Larrain 1991: 240).

All in all then, the paternalist-Eurocentric foundations of Marx's theory of history rests on the familiar series of binaries which include: 'European pioneering agency versus Eastern conditional agency'; and 'rational capitalist states in Europe versus irrational Oriental despotisms'; 'capitalist modes of production in Europe versus the Asiatic modes of production'. In turn, these binaries reveal the highly charged debate on Marx's imperialism as missing the critical point: for the more fundamental prior issue concerns his Eurocentric theory of history that counterposes a 'dynamic West' and a 'static East'. Indeed, Marx's universalist claim that 'the history of all hitherto existing society is the history of class struggles' (Marx and Engels 1848/1967: 79), should accordingly be amended to reflect the provincial Eurocentrism that underpins his whole theory of history: 'that the history of all hitherto existing *European* societies is the history of class struggles'. In this respect it is curious that the key problem – that of the Asiatic mode of production – has been subjected to far less debate or revisionist reinterpretation within Marxist circles, having gained only a small handful of such interventions; notably Hirst and Hindess (1977) and Perry Anderson (1974). And equally, to return to the cue signalled earlier, while much emphasis is accorded by neo-Marxists to Marx's denunciation of colonialism in the Irish context, clearly Ireland was not characterized by the Asiatic mode of production.

I, therefore, concur with Jorge Larrain who concludes his article by asserting that 'this strand of Eurocentrism does not totally impair Marx and Engels' thought. . . . so long as they are reconstructed and reworked' (Larrain 1991: 240). But while I agree that there is certainly scope for reconstructing Marx's theory along non-Eurocentric lines, surprisingly this is a task that has been undertaken by only a small minority of Marxist IR scholars, as I signal in Chapters 10 and 13.

3

Eurocentric anti-imperialism: liberalism, c. 1760–1800

Introduction: constructing an idealized European conception of world politics

If the last chapter conformed to the postcolonial critique of both classical liberalism and Marxism by revealing their imperialist face, this chapter takes us into anti-imperialist territory that is unchartered by postcolonialism. Here I focus on the two key pioneers of classical liberal internationalism: Adam Smith (1723–90) and Immanuel Kant (1724–1804). As noted in the last chapter, the conventional IR reading views these original liberal internationalists as standing for an anti-imperialist politics that is wrapped up in liberal cosmopolitanism and a cultural pluralist tolerance of non-European societies. However, while in the last few decades a number of postcolonial-inspired writers have argued that classical liberalism is Eurocentric and inherently imperialist,[57] the traditional conventional reading has been rescued most recently by two political theorists – Sankar Muthu (2003) and Jennifer Pitts (2005). They argue that many Enlightenment thinkers – including Burke, Diderot, but especially Smith and Kant – were anti-imperialist cultural pluralists after all, exhibiting sympathy and tolerance for non-European societies.

In this chapter I shall draw from both sides of this interpretative great divide in order to carve out an interstitial space between them. Here I agree with the postcolonial-inspired position that both Smith and Kant were Eurocentric and exhibited various degrees of intolerance of non-European societies, though I also agree with Muthu and Pitts that both stood for anti-imperialism. Of course, as I clarified in the opening chapter, the claim that a Eurocentric stance need not imply an imperialist politics is one that is confounding for postcolonial scholars. But equally, my claim that Smith and Kant's anti-imperialism stemmed not

[57] See most notably: Tully (1995); Pagden (1995); Mehta (1999); Hindess (2001); Pateman and Mills (2007); Bowden (2009).

from a cultural pluralism but from an anti-paternalist Eurocentric monism will be equally as challenging to the conventional IR reading. Here I advance my critique of the conventional ahistorical 'great tradition' narrative of liberalism. Thus the pro-imperialist paternalist-Eurocentric liberals – Cobden, Bright, Angell and Hobson all of whom I examined in the last chapter – were pre-figured at the end of the eighteenth century by the late-Enlightenment anti-paternalist Eurocentric liberalism of Smith and Kant that rejected imperialism. Nevertheless this is not to elide the pro-imperialist politics of various Enlightenment thinkers,[58] and nor is it to ignore the point that various Enlightenment thinkers viewed Egypt and especially China as more civilized than Europe at least down to the 1770s;[59] the upshot of which is to reveal the Enlightenment as far more heterogeneous than is generally recognized by postcolonial critics.

Turning to Figure 3.1 I begin by noting that the anti-paternalists, as do the paternalist Eurocentrics, imagine a world in which Western civilization is demarcated off from the Eastern world of barbarism and savagery. But in strong contrast to the paternalist-Eurocentric formula, European states are denied the imperial-normative status of *hyper-sovereignty*. Significantly, while the liberal paternalist Eurocentrics who were examined in the last chapter emphasize the *social efficiency/terra nullius* trigger for imperialism, this is rejected explicitly by Kant and, for the most part, by Smith.[60] In essence, European states have *no* right to imperially intervene in non-European ones. Moreover, while the paternalists award non-European societies *conditional* agency insofar as they can auto-generate but *only on condition* that rational Western institutions are delivered through the civilizing mission – the liberal anti-paternalists award Eastern peoples a more robust degree of agency, even if this fails to reach the superior heights and qualities of European agency. In this imaginary the Eastern peoples are granted a *derivative* agency, wherein non-European societies will in the fullness of time auto-generate in the *absence* of a Western civilizing mission. I term it 'derivative' agency because the non-European societies are said to follow the 'natural' developmental path that was trailblazed by the Europeans.

---

[58] A useful place to start here is with Whelan (2009).
[59] See especially Voltaire, but also Malebranche, Leibniz and Quesnay. Many saw China as a 'model for Europe' (Hobson 2004: ch. 9), though equally, others such as Montesquieu and Fénelon were highly critical of China.
[60] Though Smith accepts the '*terra nullius*' argument in the initial context of the colonization of the Americas – an ambiguity that I explain later.

INTRODUCTION: AN IDEALIZED EUROPEAN CONCEPTION 61

Figure 3.1 Anti-paternalist Eurocentrism and the critique of imperialism, c. 1760–1800

It is this capacity for auto-development that principally differentiates Kant and Smith from their liberal paternalist 'brethren'.

Accordingly, given the capacity of the Eastern peoples to auto-generate so there is no need for the catalytic trigger of a Western civilizing mission. Importantly, Smith and Kant were clear that not only would development be undertaken by Eastern societies but that it *should* be. Thus, far from espousing a cultural pluralism, they embraced a Eurocentric cultural monism and saw as both irrational and intolerable the existence of pre-modern, barbaric and savage non-European societies under conditions of emergent global interdependence (though Kant's intolerance of non-European societies was far more visible than was Smith's). This led them to prescribe the 'developmental requirement' in the context of non-European societies, thereby leading them to construct an informal hierarchical conception of world politics and its associated idiom, or cascading scale, of gradated sovereignties. That is, European states should enjoy a *full* conception of sovereignty while non-European polities were, in effect, awarded 'qualified sovereignty' given that they must relinquish their cultural self-determination and become European. In this way they constructed an idealized European conception of world politics. And while most postcolonialists would see in this an imperialist stance I shall argue that both Kant and Smith's positions accord with an anti-paternalist rather than a paternalist outlook.

Immanuel Kant: anti-paternalist Eurocentric foundations of cosmopolitan anti-colonialism

To make my case, I shall enter into a part-sympathetic and part-critical dialogue with Sankar Muthu's analysis of Kant that is advanced in his pioneering book, *Enlightenment Against Empire* (Muthu 2003: chs. 4–5). I shall deal first with Kant's anti-imperialist stance before proceeding to consider his anti-paternalist Eurocentrism.

Kant's theory of cosmopolitan right as critique of empire

As indicated earlier and explained in the last chapter, many so-called liberal 'critics' of empire ended up by embracing imperialism often because they subscribed to the 'social efficiency/*terra nullius*' argument. Indeed, it is here where James Tully's postcolonial-inspired argument intervenes, claiming that this imperialist cue is endorsed by Kant in his third definitive article for a perpetual peace. Tully claims that for Kant (as with Locke in particular), the Aboriginals must be punished if they resist those Europeans who take their land, since the latter have a right to hospitality and settlement in the formers' lands (Tully 1995: 88–9). But in *The Metaphysics of Morals* Kant asserts unequivocally that the right to establish community with such natives 'does not, however, amount to the right to *settle* on another nation's territory ... for the latter would require a special contract' (1970c: 172, his emphasis). Moreover, he goes on to say that where Europeans seek to settle on non-European lands occupied by shepherds or hunters 'who rely upon large tracts of wasteland for their sustenance, settlements should not be established by violence, but only by treaty [i.e., indigenous consent]; and even then, there must be no attempt to exploit the ignorance of the natives in persuading them to give up their territories' (1970c: 173). In short, without genuine Native consent European settlement must not proceed.

In *Perpetual Peace* Kant condemns outright the European imperialists for offending this responsibility that goes hand-in-hand with cosmopolitan right. In the discussion of the third definitive article, which Tully sees as providing the imperialist cue, Kant takes precisely the opposite stance by taking European imperialists to task for their inhospitable conduct abroad, emphasizing the point that the 'injustice which they display in *visiting* foreign countries and peoples (which in their case is the same as *conquering* them) seems appallingly great' (1970b: 106, his emphases). Combining this with a critique of the social efficiency/*terra nullius* argument, Kant asserts on the same page that 'America, the negro countries, the Spice Islands, the Cape, etc. were looked upon at the time of their discovery as ownerless territories [*terra nullius*]; for the natives were counted as nothing'. But far from justifying the imperial mission, Kant then argues that under the pretext of spreading trade the natives were oppressed through widespread wars, famine 'and the whole litany of evils which can afflict the human race' (1970b: 106). For Kant, such intolerable cruelty is the trade-mark of European imperialism and, in a well-directed jibe aimed at the concept of the imperial civilizing mission, he concludes that all this is 'the work of powers who make endless ado about their piety, and who wish to be considered as chosen believers while they live on the fruits of their iniquity' (1970b: 107). He then immediately reiterates the point that such behaviour violates cosmopolitan right, so that as long as this continues no progress towards a perpetual peace is possible (1970b: 108). In sum, then, it seems fair to conclude that the 'social efficiency trap-door' which leads back into the pro-imperialist chamber – one that exists within the corridors of the theories espoused by Vitoria, Gentili, Grotius, Locke, Vattel and others – is locked tight in Kant's schema.[61]

Muthu, then, is surely correct to note that Kant's conception of 'cosmopolitan right' is formulated precisely so as to *critique* imperialism

---

[61] Vitoria (esp. 1539/1991: 278–85); for Gentili, see Tuck (1999: 47–50); for Grotius, see Grovogui (1996: 58–9); Locke (1689/2005: 309, 312, 339); for Vattel, see Pateman (2007: 53). More generally see Pagden (1995); Grovogui (1996); Inayatullah and Blaney (2004); Anghie (2005); Pateman and Mills (2007); Bowden (2009).

(Muthu 2003: 187–8). As Kant put it, '[y]et these [European imperial] visits to foreign shores and even more so, attempts to settle on them with a view to linking them with the motherland, can also occasion evil and violence in one part of the globe with ensuing repercussions which are felt everywhere else' (Kant 1970c: 172; also 1970b: 107–8). Significant too is that in *Perpetual Peace*, Kant approves of the Japanese and Chinese practice of placing heavy restrictions on the entry of European traders since the latter had failed to act peaceably and fairly in accordance with the strictures of cosmopolitan right (1970b: 106–7). Ironically, Jacques Derrida (2000) unwittingly reinforces my claim here when he critiques Kant for precisely the opposite reason to that of Tully: that Kant 'contradicts' his own commitment to cosmopolitanism precisely because of his insistence that visitors (specifically asylum-seekers in today's context) who seek to settle abroad can only do so once consent has been given through the signing of a contract by the receiving society. But equally, as one Kantian expert rightly notes, Derrida's critique of Kant's arguments misunderstands the historical context, wherein Kant's major concern was to protect non-European peoples from marauding European imperialists; hence the 'laws of hospitality' were framed very much with the critique of imperialism in mind (Brown 2008, 2009: 59–66).

However, postcolonial-inspired critics might well offer up the claim that Kant's theory endorsed an informal imperialism that is found specifically in his positive support for the extension of trading relations between Europe and the East. Against this, though, is the point that for Kant such commercial relations must *not* involve unequal or exploitative exchange; and, moreover, that such trading relations can only be extended once *consent* has been gained by the non-European peoples.[62] Here I concur with Muthu's claim, that Kant's 'category of cosmopolitan right attempts to articulate an ideal which can both condemn European imperialism *and* encourage nonexploitative and peaceful transnational relations' (Muthu 2003: 192). Nevertheless, postcolonialists might respond by arguing that even the extension of non-exploitative trading relations serves to informally promote Western norms across the world, on the grounds that trade, especially free trade, allegedly pacifies and socializes or *civilizes* non-European societies. Moreover, they might argue that such trading relations socialize/civilize non-European

---

[62] On this point see also: Doyle (1983a: 227; 1983b: 325, 331); Muthu (2003: 155–62); Jahn (2006b: 187–8).

societies into an economically interdependent relationship that in turn propels them into commercial society. And this in turn, they would point out, is viewed by Kant as a partial antidote to warfare given that 'the spirit of commerce sooner or later takes hold of every people, and it cannot exist side by side with war' (1970b: 114).

The claim that trade between European and non-European societies entails an implicit or informal imperialism is problematic not least because for the vast majority of the second millennium, it has been the Eastern peoples – especially the Chinese, the Indians and the Muslims – who led world trade and extended its currents into Europe, principally via Italy.[63] Critically, while such Eastern trade helped spur on European commerce, as I have argued elsewhere (Hobson 2004), no one argues that this process entailed an Eastern informal imperialism. And overall, as I explained in Chapter 1, my position is that for the conceptual threshold of imperialism to be reached, either formal or informal, there must be present a degree of compulsive interventionism. Had, therefore, Kant insisted that European states had a right to force non-European states into adopting free trading relations with themselves, then this would certainly meet my designated threshold. But Kant's arguments in this respect fall short. And as I explain in the next sub-section, while Kant was unapologetic that non-European societies *should* renounce their 'lawless savagery' and move towards a capitalist-republican state-form, but for a few ambivalent statements, he never advocates the need for pro-active European intervention to push non-European societies to proceed into civilization.

One particularly notable exception is worth exploring for several reasons, the first of which sees Kant drawing perilously close to my designated imperial threshold when he asserts that:

> It is usually assumed that one cannot take hostile action against anyone unless one has already been *injured* by them. This is perfectly correct if both parties are living in a *legal civil state*. For the fact that the one has entered such a state gives the required guarantee to the other, since both are subject to the same authority. But man (or an individual people) in a mere state of nature robs me of any such security and injures me by virtue of this very state in which he coexists with me. He may not have injured me actively ... but he does injure me by the very lawlessness of his state [or condition] ... for he is a permanent threat to me, and I can require him either to enter into a common lawful state along with me or to move away from my vicinity (1970b: 98).

---

[63] Hobson (2004); Frank (1998); cf. Abu-Lughod (1989).

This quote in particular suggests that for Kant, peace cannot be achieved so long as (non-European) pre-civil societies exist, given that they comprise a permanent threat to civilized states on the one hand and that they are incapable of entering into a lawful relationship with such states on the other. Indeed, with respect to the latter point Kant prefaces this by saying that 'unless one neighbour gives a guarantee to the other at his request (which can only happen in a lawful state), the latter may treat him as an enemy' (1970b: 98). Moreover, the quote also suggests that civil states might compel uncivilized societies to undertake a social contract (thereby meeting the imperialist threshold that I have set). And while Muthu might emphasize Kant's claim that savage societies can always move away from the vicinity of civil states and thereby avoid undertaking a social contract, against this is the very point that Muthu also highlights elsewhere with respect to Kant's argument about globalization: that because humans live in a 'sphere [so] they cannot dispense infinitely but must finally put up with being near one another' (Kant cited in Muthu 2003: 192). This effectively means, in terms of the quote above, that there is no longer any hiding place where savage societies can maintain their cultural self-determination, so that civil states might indeed compel savage societies to enter a social contract. It is precisely this claim that one postcolonial-inspired scholar has used to confirm his belief that Kant's politics were imperialist (Bowden 2009: 147–8). And there can be no doubt that Kant comes perilously close to jeopardizing his otherwise robust anti-imperialist posture.

Either way, though, by way of prefacing the next subsection, the second and principal point that I take from this discussion is that it registers Kant's explicit intolerance of non-European 'savage' and 'barbaric' societies in no uncertain terms. And as I argue shortly, it is precisely this that underpins his theory of perpetual peace and his notion of gradated sovereignties in world politics.

Kant's anti-paternalist Eurocentric theory of history

While I have supported Muthu's claim that Kant was anti-imperialist, here I turn to interrogate his claim that such a politics emanates from a cultural pluralism that evinced a tolerance for non-European societies. Muthu believes that Kant's ethnology that was developed in his political writings stood outside of the 'common scientific racist' markers of eighteenth century European thought. This is significant given that postcolonial-inspired critics sometimes denounce Kant precisely for his scientific racism.[64] But while Kant was certainly one of the first constructors of scientific racism, nevertheless his racism was confined to his geographical and anthropological writings,[65] and played no part in his *political writings* on international relations (see also Muthu 2003: 181–4). Kant's avoidance of scientific racism in his political writings leads Muthu to conclude that Kant advocated a 'cultural pluralism' that was premised on what Muthu calls 'cultural agency'. For Muthu, this presumes a respect for the equality of all peoples and, therefore, by implication, a tolerance of non-European societies.

Muthu also claims that Kant did not privilege civilized European- over uncivilized non-European societies with all of them held on an egalitarian, non-hierarchical normative footing; the upshot of which is that Kant rejected judging non-European societies against a universal Western norm. To this end Muthu emphasizes the consistent claim made by Kant that civilized European societies were far from perfect and were shot through with all manner of injustices and conflicts between individuals, which emerged as a function of the quest for gratification through power and prestige both at home and in relation to the non-European world abroad. The key argument that Muthu makes against the Eurocentric charge is that while Kant envisaged a moral duty on each individual to self-improve, nevertheless Muthu insists that Kant saw no corresponding duty for *whole peoples* to improve or perfect themselves and thereby move towards an idealized Western terminus. He claims that 'it is possible that Kant saw no inevitability in the transition from a non-settled [pre-civil] to settled society [i.e., civil states]', offering up Kant's claim in *The Anthropology*: that it is unusual for peoples to move from a non-settled/pre-civil to a settled/civil society (Muthu 2003: 204), thereby suggesting that Kant was tolerant of 'pre-modern' non-European societies.

Part of the problem here lies in Muthu's assumption that the alternative to scientific racism is cultural pluralistic tolerance. But this binary construction is problematic because there is a third alternative available here: that of Eurocentric institutionalism. Here I suggest that Muthu's position is problematized by two inter-related Eurocentric arguments that form the basis of Kant's theory of politics and history. First, Kant

---

[64] Notably Eze (1997); Bernasconi (2001); Bowden (2009: 146); Tully (2002: 342–3).
[65] See especially Kant (1997a, 1997b, 1997c, 2001a).

presents a progressive teleological theory of history that develops through a sequence of stages and culminates in an idealized Western civilizational terminus. Second, and inter-relatedly, Kant viewed it as a categorical imperative that savage societies enter into a domestic social contract in the first instance and then progress through the stage of barbarism into that of capitalist-republican civilization, precisely because this was the vital pre-requisite for the eventual creation of an international federation of civilized republican states, upon which perpetual peace could one day be realized.

Indeed the essential point of his famous essay, 'Idea for a Universal History with a Cosmopolitan Purpose', was precisely the positing of a progressive teleology to the unfolding of human societies. At the very outset Kant asserts that while recognizing that the laws of human history are very difficult to detect, nevertheless 'we may hope that what strikes us in the actions of individuals as confused and fortuitous may be recognized, in the history of the entire species, as a steadily advancing but slow development of man's original capacities' (1970a: 41). Nature intends, almost behind the backs of individuals, an advance in human societies. Interestingly, Kant effectively deploys an argument that is almost identical to the role played by Adam Smith's 'invisible hand'. Thus while society develops according to the invisible hand of selfish individual competition for Smith,[66] so in the discussion of his 'fourth proposition' Kant sees in the selfish and egoistic intentions of individuals and their resulting antagonisms (their 'unsocial sociability') a *necessary* but *progressive* 'evil' that propels all societies automatically forward towards the terminus of human history – the pacific federation of capitalist republican states.

Here Muthu conflates Kant's emphasis on evil and selfish antagonisms within civilized Europe with a critique of its societies. But these evils function in a progressive rather than regressive way in Kant's schema. Thus, he argues that facing up to these antagonisms comprises

> the first true steps taken from barbarism to culture [civilization], which in fact consists in the social worthiness of man. All man's talents are now gradually developed, his taste cultivated, and by a continued process of enlightenment, a beginning is made towards establishing a way of thinking which can ... transform the primitive natural capacity for moral discrimination into definite practical principles, and thus a pathologically enforced social union is transformed into a moral whole (1970a: 44–5).

[66] Smith (1776/1937: 14, 421, 423).

This culminates in the unequivocal claim that civilized societies are indeed superior to non-civil ones and that mankind has a duty to proceed out of barbarism and savagery into civilized society; the very inverse claim to that ascribed by Muthu. Thus, Kant asserts:

> Without these asocial qualities (far from admirable in themselves) which cause the resistance inevitably encountered by each individual as he furthers his self-seeking pretensions, man would live an Arcadian, pastoral existence of perfect concord, self-sufficiency and mutual love (1970a: 45).

For Kant, such qualities of 'perfect concord' and mutual love' are not symptomatic of a 'noble savage' discourse that is used by some to critique various aspects of Western society. In fact Kant claims just the opposite by saying that within pastoral societies

> [A]ll human talents would remain hidden forever in a dormant state, and men, as good-natured as the sheep they tended, would scarcely render their existence more valuable than that of their animals. The end for which they were created, their rational nature, would be an unfilled void (1970a: 45).

He then concludes that nature should be thanked for fostering this *unsocial sociability* since without it 'all man's excellent natural capacities would never be roused to develop. Man wishes concord [i.e., pre-civil social existence], but nature, knowing better what is good for his species wishes discord'. Thus, reminiscent of Smith, individual selfishness or even maliciousness is the motor that drives *progressive* historical development towards civilization (1970b: 108–14).

The anti-teleological stance that Muthu attributes to Kant in order to support the conclusion that Kant saw no duty of peoples to self-improve runs up against a second major inter-related problem, which concerns his calling for a pacific federation of republican states. In essence, if there is *no* mechanism for progress from pre-civil societies to civilized states – either one that is imposed from without via European imperialism (as indeed there is not in Kant's schema) or through some kind of endogenous motor operating within pre-civil societies including the role of human agency – then the very idea of movement towards a pacific federation becomes logically unattainable. This is so not least because such a federation cannot come about until all societies undertake a social contract and proceed on into civilization.

Kant's normative insistence that all peoples *must* leave the state of nature is a running theme of his most famous work, *Perpetual Peace*. In rejecting a cultural-pluralist vision of the world based on cultural heterogeneity in which civilized, barbaric and savage societies co-exist, he insists that a perpetual peace will be violated if just one party remains in a '*separate state of nature*', which would result in a risk of war (1970b: 99). Moreover, in discussing his second definitive article he asserts that 'each nation, for the sake of its own security, can and ought to demand of the others that they should enter along with it into a constitution, similar to the civil one, within which the rights of each could be secured. This would mean establishing a federation of peoples' (1970b: 102). This, of course, returns us to the discussion at the end of the last section concerning a possible imperialist cue in Kant's thought. Crucially, Kant morally dismisses savage/barbaric societies asserting that 'we look with profound contempt upon the way in which savages cling to their lawless freedom ... [and] prefer the freedom of folly to the freedom of reason. We regard this as barbarism, coarseness, and brutish debasement of humanity' (1970b: 102). Thus for Kant, those individual societies that live within a *domestic* state of nature 'must renounce their savage and lawless freedom, adapt themselves to public coercive laws, and thus form an international state [i.e., a pacific federation of republican states]' (1970b: 104). That is, they must move towards a capitalist-republican form as a pre-requisite for the creation of a future pacific international federation. This is reinforced by the eighth proposition outlined in his essay 'Idea for a Universal History' where he asserts that 'the history of the human race as a whole can be regarded as the realisation of a hidden plan of nature – one which begins with the internal construction of a political constitution and culminates in a pacific federation of republican states' (1970a: 50). Accordingly, Muthu's defensive claim that Kant believed that non-European savage societies should avoid the 'civilizing process' seems unsustainable.

However, one possible rebuttal here could be that when Kant talks of savage, anarchic, lawless freedom he is referring to the international state of nature. But while Kant certainly viewed the international realm in this way, he also applied this concept to particular or individual savage societies. Testimony to this point is found in *The Metaphysics*, where he asserts that 'there can only be a few in a state of nature, as in the wilds of America' (1970c: 166). And a second rebuttal might be made on the grounds that I have presented an overly teleological reading of Kant's historical schema. Defenders of Kant insist that his progressive theory of history is not teleological on the grounds that this reading obscures Kant's vision of the role of human agency and choice in the making of historical progress.[67] From here they might jump to the conclusion that this reading of Kant's theory of history as teleological is not only problematic in itself but that it simultaneously undermines the Eurocentric charge, not least because European societies had not reached the height of civilization (thereby negating my assumption that Kant conflated civilization with Europe at that time). But what such defenders really seem to be concerned with is less Kant's teleology and more the imputation of a *deterministic* historical schema. It would seem entirely fair to suggest that Kant ascribed a clear role for human agency. Indeed, men make their own destiny, but not simply from constraints laid down by the past (as Marx argued), but also from the future: 'men act freely, to whom, it is true, what they ought to do may be dictated in advance' (Kant 2001b: 141). The similarities here with Marx's conception of agency are striking and yet, of course, few would deny that Marx's theory of history was teleological. Adding in the role of human agency, then, does not immunize Kant from the teleological charge even if it certainly qualifies the determinist charge.

Indeed, Kant very much had a normative telos in mind – the federation of advanced capitalist republican states (as opposed to Marx's future federation of stateless societies) – and this was a projection of how he wished European history would progress given that it had clearly not yet arrived at this terminus, though he was also clear that this endpoint could only be realized through human agency girded with cosmopolitan intent. And yet his ultimate stage of human destiny was an extrapolation forward of the stages model that he had derived from reading Europe's past (see especially 1970a: 52). Note that almost all stagist theorists of the eighteenth and nineteenth centuries adopted teleological schemas on the basis that the final stage had not yet been reached, including Hegel, Marx, Smith and Spencer. Indeed the whole point of their theoretical interventions was precisely to advocate the political means that were necessary to reach the end of history. But that does not immunize them from the Eurocentric charge because their normative prescriptions were – in all cases – derived from their tendency to naturalize and idealize the European developmental experience.

Thus Kant's approach exemplifies a Eurocentric stadial model of development, while defending an idealized conception of European civilization to which all non-European states should and would

---

[67] E.g., Apel (1997); Wood (2006); Brown (2009: 37–44).

eventually conform (see also Tully 2002). But in the light of Muthu's argument, the irony is that the underlying rationale for Kant's anti-imperialist posture lies in his anti-paternalist Eurocentric 'cultural monism', which asserts that non-European societies did *not* require imperial intervention precisely because they would *auto-develop* through the various stages to arrive at the terminus of an idealized European civilization. And only once they had achieved this could a federation of republican states be established. In short, Kant's Eurocentrism means that the solution to the problem of war requires precisely the opposite condition to that suggested by Muthu: that far from being content with cultural heterogeneity, Kant stood for the construction of a single idealized 'Western-civilizational world of uniformity'. It was in this way that Kant's writings were designed to 'defend the idea of European civilization as the highest referent in world politics'. Accordingly, while he resisted the idea of European imperial hyper-sovereignty nevertheless Kant subscribed to an informal hierarchical conception of gradated sovereignties, reserving full sovereignty for European states and qualified sovereignty for Eastern polities.

Finally it is worth closing by turning to the acrimonious Kant–Herder debate, for the key difference that separated these thinkers in effect constitutes the litmus test for my argument as well as that of Muthu's. Here I am referring to Herder's cultural relativism and Kant's cultural monism. As James Tully notes, Herder entirely rejected Kant's Eurocentric assumption that 'all cultures can be ranked relative to a European norm and that they all develop ... toward the [idealized Western] apex' (Tully 2002: 344). This difference is clarified by Kant's rhetorical question, which echoes the claims made in his 'Idea for a Universal History' discussed above:

> Does [Herder] really mean that, if the happy inhabitants of Tahiti, never visited by more civilized nations, were destined to live in their peaceful indolence for thousands of centuries, it would be possible to give a satisfactory answer to the question of why they should exist at all, and of whether it would not have been just as good if the island had been occupied by happy sheep and cattle as by happy human beings who merely enjoy themselves? (Kant 1970d: 219–20).

This thrust of Kant's line of argumentation surely enables us to appreciate Tully's claim that 'Herder ... presents a cultural pluralism as an alternative to Kant's cosmopolitan universalism [or cultural monism] on the grounds that all cultures are of intrinsic worth' (Tully 2002: 344; also Parekh 1997: 186). And no less poignant is the conclusion reached by two critical scholars: that '[i]f ... Kant was the first to propose a rigorous scientific concept of race [outside of his political/IR writings], Johann Gottfried Herder was the first to deny it' (Bernasconi and Lott 2000: ix).

It is of particular note that the Kant–Herder controversy, which points up Kant's explicit cultural monism or cultural intolerance, is ignored by Muthu; a point that is surprising not least because almost 50 per cent of his book is given over to discussing Kant and Herder. Moreover, when Muthu does mention the debate, he seeks to downplay its significance on the grounds that it obscures the many similarities that exist between Kant and Herder (Muthu 2003: 257–8). Either way, though, it seems fair to conclude that whatever their similarities might have been, they diverged fundamentally on the key issue of cultural pluralism.

While I accept that Kant's racism is confined to his works *outside* of politics and IR, nevertheless it is striking not merely that Kant pioneered a racist approach to geography and anthropology at the very time that he was penning his cosmopolitan political writings, but also because these various bodies of writing came into fundamental contradiction. Indeed in Kant's various racist writings, the red and black races were deemed to be *incapable* of self-development; something which constituted the antithesis of his anti-paternalist Eurocentric political writings (cf. McCarthy 2009: 48–53). One of the most pertinent references here is found in his *Physical Geography*:

> [i]n the hot countries the human being matures in all aspects earlier, but does not, however, reach the perfection of those in the temperate zones. Humanity is at its greatest perfection in the race of the whites. The yellow Indians do have a meagre talent. The Negroes are far below them and at the lowest point are a part of the American peoples (Kant 1997c: 63).

And, moreover, his cosmopolitanism was problematized by his racist critique of miscegenation or race-mixing/blood mixing (Kant 1997a). A particular irony here is that it was the nationalist political economist, Friedrich List (1841/1909: 178–9), who produced a deeper cosmopolitanism in this particular respect since he argued that miscegenation is a positive good that would enhance economic development. Most curiously of all, it could not be claimed that Kant began as a racist and then moved beyond it into a cultural pluralist cosmopolitan phase later on in his life, for he developed and maintained both simultaneously in his final three decades.⁶⁸ And in any case the ultimate contradiction that underpins his cosmopolitan political/international theory lies in the point that Kant developed a cultural monism that cuts out the very principle that cosmopolitanism should logically stand for – specifically the possibility of a genuinely reciprocal process of inter-cultural or inter-civilizational learning (McCarthy 2009: 68; Adib-Moghaddam 2011: 178–9). The irony here is that only through a *non-Eurocentric dialogical* approach can we realize the grand aim that Kant's cosmopolitanism claims to stand for.

Adam Smith: anti-paternalist Eurocentric foundations of anti-imperial cosmopolitical-economy

A second key exemplar of anti-paternalist Eurocentrism is Adam Smith who, in so many respects, pre-empts Kant. Here I follow a similar path to that of the last section, for I shall make my case by entering into a part-sympathetic, part-critical dialogue with Jennifer Pitts' analysis of Smith that is advanced in her pioneering book, *A Turn to Empire* (Pitts 2005: ch. 2). In essence, in the first subsection I shall agree with her claim that Smith was an anti-imperialist but will present Smith in the second subsection not as a tolerant cultural pluralist, as Pitts contends, but as an anti-paternalist Eurocentric monist.

Smith's anti-paternalist critique of empire

Smith's anti-imperialist posture was motivated in part by his revulsion of the repressive imperial policies of the Europeans, and was typified by his claim that the colonial policy of Europe in the Americas

> has very little to boast of. . . . Folly and injustice seem to have been the principles which presided over and directed the first project of establishing those colonies; the folly of hunting after gold and silver mines, and the injustice of coveting the possession of a country whose harmless natives, far from having ever injured the people of Europe, had received the first adventurers with every mark of kindness and hospitality (1776/ 1937: 555, see also 590).

Nevertheless his critique of colonialism was for the most part a function of his liberal anti-mercantilist posture, given that imperialism was

---

[68] Thus the racist tract 'Of the Different Human Races' was first published in German in 1775; while the racist tract 'Of the Use of Teleological Principles in Philosophy' was published in 1785. Note that he died in 1804.

founded on state interventionism, monopoly commercial relations and predatory trading corporations (see also Muthu 2008). In essence his anti-imperialist argument has two core components: first, an emphasis on the economic costs of colonial monopoly trade; and second, the excessive fiscal costs of colonialism. Smith's key discussion of imperialism is contained in the long chapter 7 of Book IV of *The Wealth of Nations* (1776/1937: 523-607). And it is no coincidence that this discussion is contained there given that Book IV is concerned with the critique of all forms of political intervention in the economy.

Smith begins by arguing that colonialism in the most backward, savage societies such as the Americas can, at least initially, have a positive developmental impact.[69] Moreover, in this one context Smith, unlike Kant, draws close to invoking the imperialist concept of *terra nullius* to justify such intervention (1776/1937: 531-3; cf. 526). Nevertheless, he also criticizes exploitative and oppressive instances of colonialism and those tendencies to 'commit with impunity every sort of injustice in those remote countries' (1776/1937: 555, 535, 590). Either way, though, his initial pro-imperialist argument is then countered by the deployment of the liberal counterfactual argument concerning the economic opportunity costs of imperialism. Thus while colonialism has initially helped to augment industrialization within the European countries (1776/1937: 557-8), nevertheless colonization entails high economic opportunity costs that outweigh the aggregate benefits to the European countries.

The opportunity costs argument comprises the point that the monopoly colonial trade has the effect of keeping 'down below what they would otherwise rise to, both the enjoyments and industry of all those nations in general, and of the American colonies in particular' (1776/1937: 558). More specifically, England has suffered not just a relative but an *absolute* disadvantage from colonial trade. Here he discusses the act of navigation that resulted in the withdrawal or diversion of *foreign* (i.e., non-English) capital away from the English colonies, thereby prompting a diversion of domestic English capital into the empire to make good the deficit (1776/1937: 562-80). But this served only to reduce the aggregate production of English goods that would have otherwise been sold to the more competitive European countries. The colonial monopoly afforded

---

[69] See Smith (1776/1937: 531-7), and especially his positive discussion of British colonization of America (1776/1937: 538-53).

to English capital necessarily raised the rate of profit enjoyed by *individual* capitalists, which in turn served to divert yet more English capital into the colonies. And the resulting higher cost of colonial imports into Britain served only to make her own exports to her European competitors less competitive, thereby forcing an ever-greater dependence on the colonial trading system. The net effect of this was a situation in which the national economy became dangerously lop-sided, whereby one part of it becomes overgrown at the expense of the vast bulk of it which, in becoming increasingly undeveloped, serves only to weaken the whole economy. And though he does not use the term, he clearly has in mind the 'rent-seeking' activities of certain merchants and capitalists, to wit: 'the single advantage which the monopoly procures to a single order of men, is in many different ways hurtful to the general interests of the country' (1776/1937: 579, also 568).

The second critical argument that is mounted against empire derives from Smith's famous critique of the burden of excessive taxation. Defending the empire is a cost borne by all taxpayers on behalf of the monopolist, rent-seeking individual capitalist beneficiaries of empire (1776/1937: 580–1). Here, of course, he pre-empts the discussion of Book 5 ('Of the Revenue of the Sovereign or Commonwealth') by arguing that higher tax revenues crowd out the amount of savings available for investment in the productive part of the economy, thereby undermining overall economic growth. Moreover, defence expenditures that imperialism necessitates are inherently unproductive and are lost to the productive part of the economy. On this basis he advances a critique of realist-mercantilist theory, the essence of which boils down to the proposition that empire and imperial pride constitute a vain illusion because it serves only to undermine the imperial economy as well as that of the colonies.

All in all, then, combining these two critical arguments, Smith calls for a more balanced national economy which entails the weaning of Britain off the vain or *great illusion* of empire, wherein colonial monopoly and the costs of imperial defence sacrifice the interests of all Britons at the altar of a small minority of capitalist rent-seekers.

> If [ceding the monopoly trade] was adopted ... Great Britain would not only be immediately freed from the whole annual expence of the peace establishment of the colonies, but might settle with them such a treaty of commerce as would effectually secure to her a free trade, more advantageous to the great body of the people, though less so to the merchants, than the monopoly which she at present enjoys (1776/1937: 582).

One of the key upshots of this is the conclusion that Smith, in radical contrast to the likes of Cobden, Mill, Hobson and Angell but in common with Kant, utilized a consistent anti-state interventionist stance in the domestic and external arenas.

While some postcolonial critics might accept some of the interpretation so far, they would nevertheless argue that Smith embraced an informal imperialism. This is advanced in various ways. First and foremost, Smith's belief that extending European trade to the non-European world, particularly on a free trading basis, is thought to constitute an informal imperialist posture as it serves to contain or hold down their economies.[70] And, moreover, free trade, as it does for David Ricardo (1819), implies cultural conversion to European civilization on the basis that it dictates the need for a country to specialize in that which it has a natural or comparative advantage, thereby promoting a host of internal changes that would help spur on new capitalist social relations. But Smith believed that trade would have a positive rather than negative effect upon the Eastern economies. Moreover, the instructive comparison here would be between Smith on the one hand and the likes of John Rawls (1999) and Thomas Friedman (1999) as well as Robert Keohane (1984) on the other. For as I explain in Chapter 12, modern liberal internationalists insist that free trade *must be imposed* on non-Western societies. This, of course, is the allotted role of the post-1944 IFIs in general and the GATT/WTO in particular. Such a stance is an inherently informal imperialist one not because it *prescribes* free trade as the optimal form of exchange between countries, but because it *actively imposes* it on non-European societies. Although Smith, like Kant, believed unequivocally that all societies would be better off if they embraced free trade, neither of them argued for its active imposition on non-European countries. Moreover, there is no compunction for Eastern societies to specialize in that which they produce best and to introduce capitalist social relations and institutional practices; merely that should they choose to do so they would be better off in the long run.

Nevertheless, postcolonialists might still seek to indict Smith as well as Kant, in the discursive imperial court on two further grounds: first that their desire to see all non-European societies become capitalist betrays an imperialist mindset. But my point here is that this stance is one that betrays an anti-paternalist Eurocentric mindset rather than an

---

[70] As in the argument of Friedrich List (1841/1909); and Chang (2002).

imperialist one since wishing something does not make it so. And second, the informal imperialist charge is advanced further by Bhikhu Parekh who argues that Smith's critique of imperialism did not evince a sympathy for the colonial peoples but was more about helping metropolitan capitalism and reducing the European taxpayers' burden (Parekh 1997: 186). This is made on the basis that for Smith imperialism is bad because it provides a net drain on the metropolitan economy. But this is problematic because Smith is clear that in the long run imperialism hurts colonial societies as much as it does the metropolitan ones (e.g., 1776/1937: 576–7) and that trade with the non-European societies as conducted in a non-imperialist manner is infinitely superior. David Ricardo summarized Smith's position well, claiming that he

> has attempted to … show, that this freedom of commerce, which undoubtedly promotes the interests of the whole, promotes also that of each particular country; and that the narrow [imperialist] policy adopted in the countries of Europe respecting their colonies, is not less injurious to the mother countries themselves, than to the colonies whose interests are sacrificed (Ricardo 1819: 361).

But this debate with the postcolonialists on the one hand and Pitts on the other can be advanced further by considering the nature of Smith's ideological sensibilities and whether his anti-imperialist politics emanated from a cultural pluralist mindset.

The anti-paternalist Eurocentric foundations of Smith's cosmopolitical economy

Pitts accepts that Smith was a universalist who was committed to the stadial model of development, and that he also approved of commercial society over pre-modern ones. But, she argues, in his book *The Theory of Moral Sentiments* (1759/1982) Smith displayed considerable cross-cultural moral empathy or a 'tolerant impartiality' for the *cultural* practices of non-European peoples. And this, she argues, stands in marked contrast to the vitriolic Western triumphalism and dismissive contempt of non-European peoples that characterized mid-nineteenth-century (paternalist) liberalism, found most acutely in the writings of John Stuart Mill (Pitts 2005: 25, 26, 43–52). She also claims that Smith – as does Muthu with respect to Kant – viewed all societies as equally rational and equally able, leading to the conclusion that Smith evoked a cultural pluralist sensibility. While I concur that Smith's approach neither morally denigrated non-Western *peoples* nor celebrated the white race, and was certainly different to the triumphalist form of J. S. Mill's paternalist Eurocentrism – not to mention, I would add, the liberal-imperialist racism of the likes of Dilke (1868), Seeley (1883/1906), Strong (1885, 1889) and Fiske (1885) – nevertheless Smith's work displayed (anti-paternalist) Eurocentric properties that are elided by Pitts.

That said, though, there are occasions when Smith echoed the dismissive Eurocentric tone of Mill and other 'triumphalists'. Most notable is the extensive passage found in his *Lectures on Jurisprudence*, even though it stopped short of advocating imperialism.[71] This concerns his analysis of polygamous practices in the East where he concludes that *all* the institutions of certain societies, including the East Indies, Persia, Turkey and Egypt, were irrational and regressive (Smith 1762–3/1982: §6–§76, 143–71). There he reiterates all the familiar signs of the more triumphalist version of Eurocentric institutionalism, concluding that these countries suffered in large part as a function of their regressive Oriental despotic states. The key conclusion here is that such an analysis immediately qualifies Pitts's assertion that all societies are equally rational and able in Smith's eyes.

Moreover, while *The Wealth of Nations* is for the most part free of such triumphalism, it nevertheless exhibits occasional dismissive statements regarding the Other. Thus, for example, when discussing Columbus's discovery of a land that was void of the Chinese wealth that he had desperately hoped to discover, Smith describes it as comprising 'a country quite covered with wood, uncultivated, and inhabited only by some tribes of naked and miserable savages' (1776/1937: 526). Or in his discussion in Book V on religious practices Smith refers to 'the indolent, effeminate, and full-fed peoples of parts of . . . southern Asia' (1776/1937: 741). And last but not least, in Book I (chapter 1), he refers to the African king as 'the absolute master of the lives and liberties of ten thousand naked savages' (1776/1937: 12), while in a more extended discussion in chapter 3 he states that:

> [a]ll the inland parts of Africa, and all that part of Asia which lies any considerable way north of the Euxine and Caspian seas, the antient Scythia, the modern Tartary and Siberia, seem in all ages of the world to have been in the same barbarous and uncivilized state in which we find them at present (1776/1937: 20).

---

[71] I am particularly grateful to Martin Hall for bringing this to my attention.

Nevertheless, because the litmus test for Smith's Eurocentrism does not rest with such statements, I argue that Pitts is looking in the wrong place for signs of it. That is, she conflates Eurocentrism with a vitriolic Western triumphalism rather than an anti-paternalist Eurocentric discourse that, I argue, underpins Smith's whole cosmopolitical economic theory. The cue for this alternative reading lies in the point made originally by Ronald Meek: that stadial model theorists such as Smith 'interpret development in the pre-commercial stages in terms of the economic categories appropriate to contemporary [Western] capitalism' (Meek 1976: 222). Put differently, all societies are read or judged against an idealized European standard of civilization.

The backdrop to this Eurocentric stadial model is found in the analysis of the Americas. Meek and others points out that the stadial model theorists – from the crude versions found in Grotius, Pufendorf and Locke, through the intermediary versions found in the likes of Lafitau, Kames and Dalrymple, and finally to the fully developed version found in Smith – all emerged against the backdrop of American Indian society.[72] Indeed America was pronounced as the original state of nature and the first primitive age of subsistence. As Locke put it, 'in the beginning all the world was America', and that '*America* . . . is still a Pattern of the first Ages in *Asia* and *Europe*' (1689/2005: 301, 339). Critically, once America was deemed to be the first stage of development, so scholars and thinkers came gradually to draw a line between it and the stage reached by commercial Europe, thereby constructing a linear or near-linear developmental path. The task then became to understand the processes that led from one stage to the next. Two key relevant aspects emerge at this point.

First, there were two interpretive modes that could be utilized when constructing the stadial model. Those who were critical of certain aspects of contemporary Europe presented the American Indian as a *noble savage* 'holding [him] up as an ideal to be aimed at by Europe' (Meek 1976: 39). The main thinker in this category was Jean-Jacques Rousseau. Nevertheless, this often failed to offer up a non-Eurocentric sensibility because the idiom of the noble savage tended to be deployed so as to critique the aristocratic/feudal aspects of European society in favour of a bourgeois sensibility rather than as a means to critique Europe *per se* (e.g., Montesquieu). Conversely, those who saw Europe as advanced

---

[72] See especially: Meek (1976); Jahn (2000); Inayatullah and Blaney (2004: ch. 2); Whelan (2009: ch. 2); Blaney and Inayatullah (2010).

presented America as the backward land of the *ignoble savage*. Meek claims that '[i]t is no accident ... that the majority of our [stadial model] pioneers were in one sense or another "perfectibilists"', by which he means that for most stadial theorists the whole process terminates in the final stage of perfectibility – the age of liberal Western Commerce. Whether this accords with a Western triumphalism in the case of Smith I shall not infer, though for many such thinkers this discourse was a symptom of the age of bourgeois optimism (Meek 1976: 129). Still, Pitts is certainly correct to argue that Smith perceived various problems with modern Western capitalism (such as the alienation that the division of labour entails or the selfishness of capitalists who desire to create monopolies),[73] which qualifies this assertion somewhat, though equally Meek is aware of this point. Nevertheless, it is also clear that fully-developed laissez-faire commercial Western society represents for Smith the highest stage of civilization. And it is interesting to note at this juncture that J. S. Mill (1836/1977) also perceived various problems with modern Western civilization and yet this was not mentioned in Pitts' narrative of Mill's triumphalism.

Most importantly, while Smith's 1762–3 *Lectures* present a universalist account of development in which each stage corresponds to a certain demographic threshold this is, however, replaced by a Western provincialist approach in *The Wealth of Nations*. Thus, rather than levels of population density determining the shift from one stage to the next that would apply equally to any society, Smith emphasizes specifically European institutional properties, which are then extrapolated back in time to create a 'universalist' stagist developmental model. That is, wealth is explained by the extension of the division of labour, the level of commodity exchange and the accumulation of capital, rather than in terms of demographic shifts (Meek 1976: 220–2). Critically, for Smith, these three factors had reached their most concentrated form within European commercial society. And from there Smith reasons backwards, explaining the lower stages through the absence or limited presence of these three factors that are associated with contemporary Europe. In this way, the non-European world is read or judged through a European standard of civilization and is found variously wanting. Notable here is that the discourse of 'presences' within the West and their 'absence' in the East is one of the leitmotifs of Eurocentric development theory.

---

[73] On this see Watson (2012), who also considers the similarities and differences between Smith and Rousseau.

While it was a leitmotif of liberal Enlightenment Eurocentrism that all peoples and all races are capable of developing,[74] nevertheless where the anti-paternalists differed from the paternalists was in their belief that Eastern societies could *spontaneously* auto-generate. Important here was Smith's assumption that modern commercialism is congruent with human nature such that modern capitalism is immanent within the make-up of *all* societies. For he defined human nature as 'the propensity to truck, barter and exchange one thing for another' (1776/1937: 13). But where anti-paternalist and paternalist Eurocentrics converged was in their belief that Eastern societies will develop by following a naturalized Western developmental path that will eventually deliver them to an idealized Western civilizational terminus. In this respect they adhered to Marx's claim that the advanced European society 'only shows ... to the less developed, the image of its own future' (Marx 1867/1954: 19). All in all, the conclusion is that what at first sight appears to be a purely universal model of development turns out to be one that is based on a parochial European model writ large. And so when Meek suggests that '[m]en like Turgot and Smith were apt to ascribe the superiority of contemporary European society ... to the existence of certain important socio-economic institutions and phenomena',[75] he was in fact describing the essential properties of Eurocentric institutionalism.

Once again, this reading might be challenged by the claim not only that Smith, like Kant, was at times critical of European capitalism (e.g., his critique of alienation), but that Smith's conception of the final stage was based not on what Europe looked like at the time, given its explicit preference for mercantilism, but on what he desired it to be. In this way, then, it could be claimed that Smith did not hold Europe as it stood at the time as the model for all others. But the political purpose of Smith's work (as it was for Kant) was *aspirational*, such that Smith urged European governments to consolidate their position within commercial-industrial civilization by adopting laissez-faire. Either way, though, this does not detract from his assumption that European society was closest in this regard and that the ultimate properties of a successful society were founded on an idealized European conception of civilization.

All in all, like Kant, Smith believed that *all* societies and peoples would traverse the different stages of development *of their own accord*, thereby implicitly negating the need for a civilizing mission that is deemed to be so important for paternalist Eurocentric liberals. In this way Smith

---

[74] Notwithstanding the climatic determinism of Montesquieu.   [75] Meek (1976: 129).

awarded the East a *derivative* agency that was clearly more robust to the *conditional* agency awarded by the paternalist Eurocentrics. And so the generic approach represented by Smith and Kant establishes its credentials as an anti-imperialist perspective, though one founded not on a cultural pluralism but on an anti-paternalist Eurocentrism that elicited various degrees of intolerance of non-European societies – moderate in Smith's case and highly pronounced in Kant's. It is for this reason that Smith, like Kant, smuggles in to his conception of world politics an invisible informal hierarchical line, the Western side of which (barring the Americas) enjoys full state sovereignty while the Eastern side (and the very far west) is downgraded to the status of *qualified sovereignty* precisely because cultural self-determination had to be ceded in favour of adopting a European identity.

4

Racist anti-imperialism: classical liberalism and cultural-realism, c. 1850–1914

Introduction: racial apartheid conceptions of world politics

As noted in Chapter 1, in the conventional or popular imagination scientific racism is thought to constitute the pinnacle of imperialist thought, especially in its Darwinian and Eugenicist guises with the latter often associated with Adolf Hitler. A typical characterization here has it that with the application of Darwinian science to human affairs in the nineteenth century so

> [i]t became much harder to see international politics in terms of a benevolent process leading towards [an] end goal, and the international system – much like Darwin's view of the natural world – became an arena of competition with no *telos* whatsoever (Keene 2005: 181).

But while this is certainly a fair summary of some parts of social Darwinism, nevertheless Herbert Spencer – often imagined as the godfather of this approach – expresses not only an anti-imperialist politics but also an optimistic, progressive teleological conception of historical development that would end with the inauguration of a peaceful world.[76] In this particular respect, Spencer's laissez-faire social Darwinism shares far more in common with the anti-paternalist/anti-imperialist Eurocentrism of Smith and Kant than it does with the various racist-imperialist conceptions. Paul Crook puts his finger on the acute paradox that emerges at this juncture:

> Spencer and Andrew Carnegie – the fiercest of social Darwinists in popular mythology ... were notorious pacifists, while apostles of [domestic] social co-operation like Lester Ward [an outspoken left-liberal] and Karl Pearson (an outspoken socialist) endorsed racial and global violence as the outcome of cosmic laws. Paradox abounded. Much depended upon [racist-discursive] context (Crook 1994: 29).

---

[76] Indeed, '[u]nlike Malthus, who was the bleakest pessimist, Spencer, beneath the gritty hardheadedness was a sunny optimist ... Unlike Darwin's evolution, which had no purpose or direction, Spencer's evolution – until late in life, when he lost faith in it – meant things could only get better' (Sewell 2009: 35).

INTRODUCTION: RACIAL APARTHEID CONCEPTIONS 85

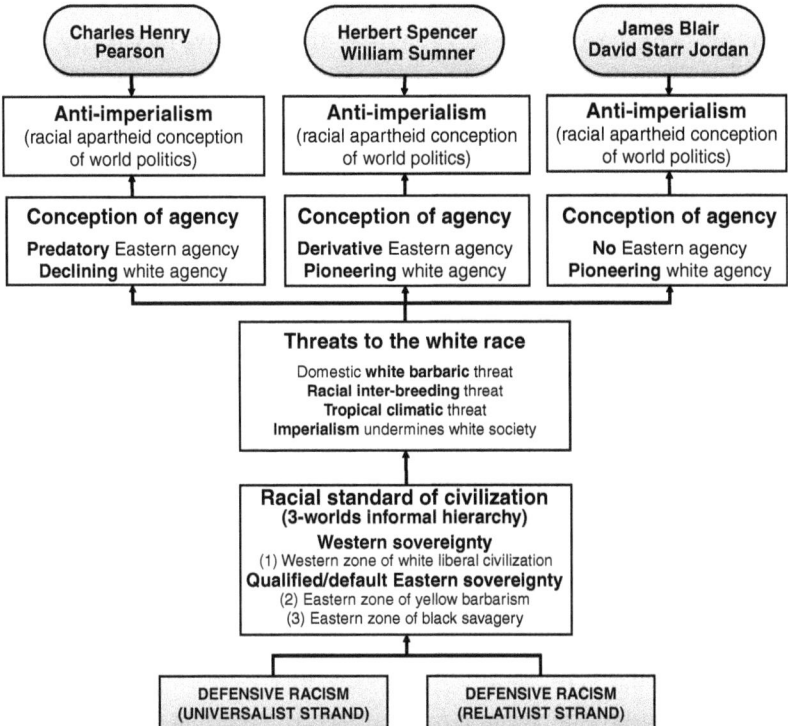

Figure 4.1 Defensive racism and the critique of empire, c. 1850–1914

And as he also notes, Spencer helped spawn a good deal of racist pacifist thought (Crook 1994: 36).

Indeed there was a significant group of scientific racists, albeit of various persuasions, who openly rejected imperialism and empire. Figure 4.1 summarizes the two wings of what I am calling the universalist and relativist streins of 'defensive racism'. And as should be apparent there are slightly different versions even within the universalist variant (which is why I distinguish C. H. Pearson from Spencer and Sumner). Even so, it should be noted that Sumner and Spencer did not produce identical forms of racism, with differences certainly apparent between them.[77] Rather I pair them together because of their shared anti-imperialist stance.

These variants, emerging in the second half of the nineteenth century, imagine the world in terms of an East–West division comprising a three-world *informal hierarchy* of white civilization, yellow barbarism and

---

[77] See Bannister (1979: ch. 5).

black savagery. Echoing the offensive (imperialist) racists to be discussed in the next chapter (see Figure 5.1, p. 109), the defensive racists envisage a similar string of threats to the white race – internal and external. For many of these thinkers the 'state socialism' of the emergent welfare states within the West constituted a key internal threat to white racial vitality since it props up socially inefficient poor white stock. Within this imaginary it was the white elites who constituted the custodian or guardian of white racial vitality. Although I return to this point in the next chapter, I shall discuss it here in the context of Spencer and Sumner.

Above all, though, the anti-imperialist racists examined here argue against imperialism because it brings the white race into racially-fatal contact with the contaminating influence of the non-white races. This occurs in various ways: first, because they believe that empire grants residence and citizenship to non-whites that emigrate into the imperial country which in turn undermine democracy as well as social order at home; second, because immigration and the consequent process of miscegenation leads to white racial degeneration at home; and third, because empire requires white residence within the colonies, where the spectre of miscegenation and the impact of the 'torrid' climate leads once more to white racial degeneration.[78] Accordingly, the defensive racists respond differently to the very same racial threats that concern the offensive-imperialist racists. And because most racists believed that miscegenation and the tropical climate promotes only white racial degeneration, it was the imperialist racists who had to find arguments to circumvent these problems (as I explain in the next chapter). To this can be added three further anti-imperialist arguments: first, the impossibility of Eastern progressive development renders the civilizing mission as all but futile (as in Blair and Jordan); second, imperialism blocks the auto-generation of Eastern as well as Western societies (as in Spencer, Sumner and to an extent, Charles Pearson); and third, warfare and empire serve only to diminish the pool of fit white stock, since the best or fittest elements are killed on the battlefield (as in a leading variant of so-called *pacifist Eugenics* that was typified by Jordan and Vernon Kellogg).

All in all, racist anti-imperialists in effect construct a racial apartheid conception of world politics. And while they reject Western hyper-sovereignty, equally Eastern state sovereignty is bequeathed *by default*, as a contemptuous residue of their racist politics. Clearly, this rejects an

---

[78] Cf. de Gobineau (1853–5/1970); Knox (1850); Ripley (1900: esp. ch. 21); Brinton (1901: ch. 10); Huntington (1915); Grant (1918).

equalitarian conception of sovereignty in favour of a gradated one that is based on an *informal* hierarchical conception of world politics, whereby Western states are awarded full sovereignty and non-European polities 'qualified' or 'default' sovereignty.

Universalist defensive racism and the critique of Western imperialism

Charles Henry Pearson: the decline of white supremacy and the rise of the yellow barbaric peril

Charles Henry Pearson (1830–94) achieved immediate fame with the dire prophecy that he issued to the white race in his book *National Life and Character: A Forecast* (1894), which was first published in 1893. There he argued that imperialism was no longer an option for the West and that white racial supremacy was being superseded by very high levels of predatory Eastern agency. Given the popular misconception that scientific racism stood for an unabashed sensibility of white supremacy and a harsh politics of imperialism, it might be thought that his approach was entirely anomalous. But, in fact, his book did much to inaugurate the new Western/white racial anxiety phase that emerged within scientific racism after 1889 – both within defensive and offensive racist thought.

Thus while the modern popular view perceives that scientific racism denies the East agency and revels in a sense of supreme white triumphalism, the analysis of Charles Pearson provided a near-inversion of this. Indeed, '[i]n attributing historical agency to the "black and yellow races", Pearson posed a radical challenge to conventional race thinking and to social Darwinists, such as Benjamin Kidd, whose *Social Evolution* was published the following year in 1894'.[79] Charles Pearson confronted those who claim that the higher races are destined to expand and triumph over the weaker races; a position held by many racist-liberals and racist-realists (as I explain in the next chapter). In many racist texts it was assumed that the whites are destined to expand while the lower races will remain within their stationary limits. But in Pearson's racist imagination it is the white West that is fated to remain within its stationary limits while the yellow races are destined to expand and triumph over the higher whites.

Pearson mixes and matches several of the key ideas of social Darwinism to produce a novel and radical picture. First of all, an important factor in

[79] Lake and Reynolds (2008: 88).

the rise of the Eastern races lies in the help that they have been given by the British imperial civilizing mission (1894: 40). For having delivered the accoutrements of Western civilization so the resulting prosperity triggered a non-white demographic explosion. Coupled with the point that the white races in the colonies seek to avoid work, so eventually they will be absorbed and displaced by the non-whites.[80] Important here is Pearson's argument that coloured and white races cannot exist side by side. This argument is complemented by his emphasis on the degenerative impact that the tropical climate imposes on the white race. Crucially, civilized white races cannot colonize India or China, Central Asia, Malaysia or Africa, owing to their hostile climates. This leaves only Eastern Afghanistan and Western Turkestan as possible outlets given that they could support the white race climatically. But, in turn, these were discounted as viable options on the grounds that they were destined to come under future Chinese control.

While Pearson awards the rising Eastern barbarian races extremely high, albeit regressive or barbaric, levels of agency – higher even than those enjoyed by the white race – it is the 'closing of the world' through rising global-interdependence that creates a significant problem insofar as it delivers a rampaging and predatory 'barbaric threat' right onto the doorstep of the West. In effect this gave rise to the construction of 'globalization-as-Eastern threat'. The Chinese are perceived to be one of the West's future primary racial threats. Not only is the Chinese population large, Pearson noted, but it is likely to mobilize against the West in the coming years as its burgeoning population inevitably spills out into the wider world. Moreover, this race's ability to flourish in the tropics and the Europeans' preference not to work alongside inferior races means that it is only a matter of time before the Chinese expand successfully at the expense of the whites.

> Thus a hundred years hence, when these races, which are now as two to one to the higher, shall be as three to one, when they have borrowed the science of Europe, and developed their still virgin worlds, the pressure of their competition upon the white man will be irresistible. He will be driven from every neutral market and forced to confine himself within his own. Ultimately he will have to conform to the Oriental standard of existence ... With civilization equally diffused, the most populous country must ultimately be the most powerful; and the preponderance of China over any rival – even over the United States of America – is likely to be overwhelming (1894: 137–8).

[80] The idea that the white races could not work in the open fields in the tropics as it would lead to racial degeneration was a trope of much racist thought more generally.

Accordingly, the most fertile parts of the earth will be taken over by the predatory and regressive barbaric races. And in general, he concludes that 'the black and yellow belt, which always encircles the globe between the Tropics, will extend its area and deepen its colour with time' (1894: 68). All of which leads him to argue that residing within the non-temperate zone offends natural laws, with the result being that the white race will be pushed back into the confines – or what he in effect envisaged as a ghetto – of the small temperate zone (1894: 17).

The net result of Pearson's dire prophecy is that Western civilization will be undermined from the barbaric threats both from within (as a result of the socialistic state's preference to prop up the unfit white working class), and from without via the yellow peril. The famous black intellectual and activist, W. E. B. Du Bois, opened his book, *The Souls of Black Folk*, with the prophecy that '[t]he problem of the twentieth century is the problem of the color line – the relation of the darker to the lighter races of men in Asia and Africa, in America and the islands of the seas' (Du Bois 1905: 13). Pearson did much the same but inverted the racial hierarchy that Du Bois had in mind: that the white races would be constrained and confined within a narrow belt of the temperate zone, while the black and yellow races would effectively hem them in and develop their own vitality while sapping that of the whites. And it is in this context that Pearson offers up his famous prophecy:

> The day will come, and perhaps is not far distant, when the European observer will look round to see the globe girdled with a continuous zone of the black and yellow races, no longer too weak for aggression or under tutelage, but independent, or practically so, in government, monopolizing the trade of their own region, and circumscribing the industry of the European. ... The citizens of these countries will then be able to take up into the social relations of the white race, will throng the English turf, or the salons of Paris, and will be admitted to intermarriage. It is idle to say that if all this should come to pass our pride of place will not be humiliated. ... We shall wake to find ourselves elbowed and hustled, and perhaps even thrust aside by peoples whom we looked down upon as servile, and thought of as bound always to minister to our needs (1894: 89).

Spencer and Sumner: the anti-paternalist critique of imperialism

Like Smith and Kant, Herbert Spencer (1820–1903) and his prominent protégé, William Graham Sumner (1840–1910), adhered to a consistent anti-paternalist, anti-interventionist posture in the domestic and international arenas. This approach can be unpacked by considering three key themes. First, I examine their anti-paternalist racist argument for the minimalist laissez-faire nightwatchman state; second I outline the nature of their racist conception of history; and third, I consider their anti-paternalist critique of imperialism. All in all, while Spencer is sometimes thought of as a liberal internationalist within conventional IR historiographies, or more frequently as the archetypal representative of social Darwinian imperialism, I argue that his anti-imperialism issues not from a tolerant liberal cultural pluralism but from a defensive racism, as is the case with Sumner.

Anti-paternalism and the laissez-faire state as the means to promote civilization

Spencer's extreme celebratory view of the 'laissez-faire state' is driven home in both *The Principles of Ethics*, II (1893/1966) and *The Man Versus the State* (1881). While Adam Smith presented a robust defence of the laissez-faire state, Spencer, like Sumner, takes the argument to vastly new rhetorical heights. Chapter 2 of the latter book, 'The Coming Slavery', reveals this clearly. Indeed, he opens the chapter with a characteristically unabashed critique of social reformist interventionism:

> Sympathy with one in suffering suppresses, for the time being, remembrance of his transgressions. The feeling which vents itself in 'poor fellow!' on seeing one in agony, excludes the thought of 'bad fellow', which might at another time arise. Naturally, then, if the wretched are unknown or but vaguely known, all the demerits they may have are ignored; and thus it happens that when, just as now, the miseries of the poor are depicted, they are thought of as the miseries of the deserving poor, instead of being thought of, as in large measure they should be, as the miseries of the undeserving poor. ... 'They have no work', you say. Say rather that they either refuse work or quickly turn themselves out of it. They are simply good-for-nothings, who in one way or other live on the good-for-somethings (Spencer 1881: 18).

The 'coming slavery' refers to the process whereby the protection of the poor white working class by an increasingly socially reformist interventionist state ends up by creating an overly regulated collectivist society that prevents the energizing impulse of individualism from realizing itself, thereby curbing freedom for all. This book echoes his earlier, *Social Statics*, which mounted an attack on Bentham's advocacy of social reform on the same lines (Spencer 1851/1864).

The key point to note is that Spencer's laissez-faire stance was a product of his belief in the process of natural evolution where conforming to the 'law of the survival of the fittest' (his term, not Darwin's) and *consciously* adapting to the social and physical environment, as in Lamarckianism, is essential for the maintenance of white racial vitality (as I explain later). Speaking of poor white stock as racially unfit, he announces that '[t]he whole effort of nature is to get rid of such, to clear the world of them, and make room for the better. ... If [individuals] are sufficiently complete to live, they *do* live, and it is well they should live. If they are not sufficiently complete to live, they die, and it is best they should die' (1851/1864: 414–15). While this has clear echoes of Eugenics, nevertheless it stops short insofar as Spencer rejects advocating the socially interventionist means by which the fit races should be encouraged to reproduce and the unfit ones actively discouraged. His solution to dealing with unfit white stock, by contrast, is to leave the market and the laws of nature to select out its irrational behaviour rather than directly punishing it through active state interventionism or 'negative Eugenics'.[81]

An equally uncompromising view on the dangers of the interventionist state is advanced in Sumner's books *What Social Classes Owe to Each Other* (1883/2007) and *The Forgotten Man and Other Essays* (1879/1969). The key thrust here lies in Sumner's antipathy towards social paternalism, which in turn underpinned his aversion to colonialism. Taking on the socialist paternalists he insists that, '[t]hey do not perceive ... that if we do not like the survival of the fittest, we have only one possible alternative, and that is the survival of the unfittest. The former is the law of civilization; the latter is the law of anti-civilization' (Sumner 1879/1969: 225). Thus progress rests only on the vitality of competition such that if unfit white individuals within society are to be selected out so that white society may survive and progress, then so be it. For the survival of the fittest white individuals is merely nature's way of ensuring the survival of white society at large.

The universalist defensive racist conception of history

For both Sumner and Spencer, the anti-paternalist approach to the state emanates from their particular racist discourse. As I noted earlier, while it is generally believed that Spencer was a pure social Darwinist, this ignores the point that while 'Darwin argued that organisms change through accidental variations which turn out to have survival value and thus perpetuate themselves, Spencer adopted the Lamarckian idea that acquired or use characteristics are inherited';[82] notwithstanding

---

[81] Nevertheless, Spencer did see a role for private philanthropy.
[82] Gossett (1997: 151–2).

the point that Darwin himself adopted certain Lamarckian principles. Arguably, Spencer was in fact one of the leading neo-Lamarckians.[83] Indeed, while David Boucher concludes that 'Spencer was far less convinced by the [Darwinian] explanatory force of Natural Selection than by Lamarck's theory of Use Inheritance, or inherited character',[84] Crook goes even further by claiming that 'Spencer, it appears, reluctantly squeezed Darwin's natural selection into his primarily Lamarckian theory'.[85] And while we shall see in the next chapter how the highly malleable discourse of Lamarckianism can yield a soft version of imperialism (e.g., Reinsch) as well as a harsh one (e.g., Ward), equally it can yield an anti-imperialist perspective (e.g., Spencer).

Spencer's neo-Lamarckianism is particularly evident in his *Principles of Sociology*, I, in which he defines the process of social evolution as governed by the complex interaction of extrinsic factors (climate, geographical surface and vegetation), intrinsic biological factors (biological male physicality, emotional and intellectual traits) and the reciprocal influence that society has on its constituent members (i.e., social factors) (Spencer 1896/2004: 9–11). This point has various ramifications, one of which is that progress can be directed through human agency and the concomitant process of *learning* to adapt. This stands in marked contrast to the radical contingency of Darwin's natural selection process with its conception of accidental mutation in which human agency is lost entirely. Thus while the conventional perception of Spencer's laissez-faire social Darwinism is that it was a highly deterministic theory where races had no choice but to follow the laws of the survival of the fittest, in fact Spencer's task was to reveal how races could improve themselves through conscious selection and education. As one astute observer put it, one of the reasons for Spencer's global popularity was his oft repeated insistence that 'despite all the "iron lawfulness" of evolution, its political control, instrumentalization, and indeed manipulation was possible – providing his readers with the hope of rationally controlling the evolution of their own race' (Geulen 2007: 79). Thus while many racist critics, and especially the Lamarckian-social Darwinist Lester Ward, attacked Spencer for allegedly ignoring the role of human agency this in turn ignores the neo-Lamarckian component that allocated a not inconsiderable degree of human agency within his stages theory of social evolution.

---

[83] Stocking (1982: 239–41); Campbell and Livingstone (1983: 269); Crook (1994: ch. 2); Jones (1980: 85–6). But see Hawkins (1997: 87–8).
[84] Boucher (1997b: xvi).   [85] Crook (1994: 41).

Reminiscent of the stages model of Kant and Smith, Spencer's theory of social evolution envisaged above all a universal developmental process, whereby *all* societies and *all* races naturally evolve over time from primitive savagery through barbarism and onto civilization. Overlaid upon this schema was his more famous conception whereby pre-modern 'militant' societies give way to modern pacific 'industrial' ones; the vision that has been extrapolated out of its defensive racist context by modern sociological interpreters of Spencer. And, like Smith and Kant, this places him in contrast with the paternalist Eurocentrics who subscribe to a *conditional* conception of Eastern agency, wherein non-Western societies can progress but *only on condition* that the West delivers rational institutions through the civilizing mission so as to 'jump-start' their developmental trajectory. For precisely like the anti-paternalist Eurocentrics such as Smith and Kant, Spencer awards the Eastern races *derivative* Eastern agency, wherein non-white races will auto-develop but *only in the absence* of Western imperialist interventionism. Moreover, they will do so only by following the 'naturalized' path that had already been pioneered by the white races. Interestingly too, this conception differentiates Spencer's approach from those offensive racists and relativist defensive racists who deny non-white races developmental agency (see Chapters 5 and 7 as well as the next section respectively).

As noted earlier, Spencer's racist universalism views the process of social evolution as being governed by the telos of human perfection (which awaits *all* societies and *all* races).

> The ultimate development of the ideal man is logically certain – as certain as any conclusion in which we place the most implicit faith; for instance that all men will die ... Progress, therefore, is not an accident, but a necessity. Instead of civilization being artificial, it is a part of nature [and is therefore open to all races] (1851/1864: 79–80).

Caspar Sylvest, while recognizing this point, nevertheless concludes that this renders Spencer a 'non-racist', given the assumption that 'references to lower races did not signify a *perpetual* stigma' (Sylvest 2009: 109, my emphasis). But I draw a different conclusion here: that Spencer's reliance on Lamarckianism within a social Darwinian approach rendered him a scientific racist. For the problem here is that racism is not a monolithic discourse that always invokes genetic characteristics that are conceived of as *permanent* features. Thus in contrast to the genetic-fundamentalists who saw racial characteristics as permanent,[86] Spencer's Lamarckian racism was

---

[86] E.g., de Gobineau (1853–5/1907); Knox (1850); Grant (1918); Hitler (1939).

far more malleable and allowed for race modification. For example, in *Social Statics* Spencer portrayed inferior races developing into superior ones gradually over time as the stronger racial elements fared best in battle and replaced the weaker ones through use-inheritance. And it was precisely his Lamarckian conception of anti-imperialism that frequently 'annoyed racists who favored imperialist domination of the primitive races' (Gossett 1997: 152). Crucially, Spencer was far from alone, since elements of neo-Lamarckianism were widely adopted, albeit to varying degrees, by many scientific racists especially after about 1890 (Stocking 1982), despite the revival of Mendelian genetic-determinism after 1900. Thus Spencer's work in effect cautions us to appreciate just how complex scientific racism was.

To reinforce this point it is worth returning to volume I of *The Principles of Sociology* where he develops a sustained Lamarckian/social Darwinian analysis of the differences between primitive, barbarian and civilized races. Chapter 5 reveals the physical differences between the races, arguing that the small size of many of the inferior races is partly original and partly acquired as a result of their environment, while the civilized race is physically larger and more powerful than the savages. Chapter 6 argues that the inferior races are given over to an irrational emotional predisposition in which passion and impulsiveness reign supreme such that the childhood of civilized man is essentially equivalent to the mind of the adult primitive (1896/2004: 59–60). The chapter also produces many of the familiar scientific racist tropes, with the Hottentots (the Khoikhoi of southwest Africa) described as lazy owing to their hot climate, and inferior races in general being described as highly conservative and averse to change. Last, but not least, in chapter 7 he argues that the intellect of the primitive mind is incapable of grasping abstract ideas that are arrived at through higher generalization and is therefore incapable of attaining truth and causality. He lacks, in clear contrast to civilized man, an inventive imagination and is governed by a manual dexterity and an inability to engage in critical thinking.

Drawing together the whole discussion thus far, it should by now be clear as to why Spencer's and Sumner's reified conception of the minimalist laissez-faire state rests on their particular brand of racism, as was signalled earlier. For the key point is that all races will auto-develop of their own accord so long as they are left free from all forms of *political intervention*. And it is precisely this particular racist conception of development that comprises one of the key factors in their rejection of imperialism.

The racist anti-paternalist critique of empire

The critique of imperialism rests on four inter-related arguments that I shall unpack in turn: first, imperialism entails an unacceptable, arrogant paternalist predisposition; second, imperialism undermines non-white and white development, as signalled above; third, imperialism leads to miscegenation and the degeneration of the white race; and fourth, colonialism entails residence in the tropical climate which also leads to white racial degeneration. Turning therefore to the first criticism, in his chapter 'Imperialism and Slavery' in *Facts and Comments*, Spencer takes to task the paternalist aspect of imperialism for its hypocrisy (1902: 157–71). He begins by summarizing this paternalist mentality accordingly:

> 'You shall submit. We are masters and we will make you acknowledge it'. These words express the sentiment which sways the British nation in its dealings with the Boer Republics; [a] sentiment [that] pervades indefinitely the political feeling now manifesting itself as Imperialism ... Actual or potential coercion of others ... is necessarily involved in [this] conception (1902: 157).

He then responds to this callous view by saying that 'there are others, unhappily but few, who think it ignoble to bring their fellow creatures into subjection, and who think the noble thing is not only to respect their freedom but also to defend it' (1902: 157–8). And in *The Man Versus the State* he revelled in pointing out the hypocrisy of those left-wing imperialist racists who criticized his own laissez-faire political economy as callous while in the next breath,

> you may hear them with utter disregard of bloodshed and death, contend that it is in the interests of humanity at large that the inferior races should be exterminated and their places occupied by the superior races ... Not worthy of much respect then, as it seems to me, is this generous consideration of the inferior at home which is accompanied by the unscrupulous sacrifice of the inferior abroad (1881: 71).

Equally his disgust of imperialism was driven home in the second volume of *The Principles of Ethics*, where simultaneously he indicts the hypocritical imperialist aggressive tendencies of Victorian Christian society:

> Throughout a Christendom full of churches and priests, full of pious books, full of observances directed to fostering the religion of love, encouraging mercy and insisting on forgiveness, we have an aggressiveness and a revengefulness such as savages have everywhere shown. And from people who daily read their Bibles, attend early services, and

appoint weeks of prayer, there are sent out messengers of peace to inferior races, who are forthwith ousted from their lands by filibustering expeditions authorized in Downing Street; while those who resist are treated as 'rebels', the deaths they inflict in retaliation are called 'murders', and the process of subduing them is named 'pacification' (1893/1966: 257).

And later on he asserts that '[t]he courage shown by one of those hired men who unite in conquering small semi-civilized nations and weak, uncivilized tribes, is to be admired as much as is the courage of a brute which runs down and masters its feeble prey' (1893/1966: 362).

Echoing this Spencerean theme, in Sumner's well-known 1898 essay, 'The Conquest of the United States by Spain', he launches into a critique of the imperial civilizing mission as but boastful paternalist hypocrisy that merely fans the national ego. Imperialism, as with social interventionism at home, begins 'by saying to somebody else, we know what is good for you better than you know yourself and we are going to make you do it'. But this, he insists, is false because it violates liberty (1911: 305). Moreover, in the case of the Americans, and pre-empting David Starr Jordan (1901: 47), he asserts that:

> We assume that what we like and practice, and what we think is better, must come as a welcome blessing to Spanish-Americans and Filipinos. This is grossly and obviously untrue. They hate our ways. They are hostile to our ideas. Our religion, language, institutions, and manners offend them. They like their own ways, and if we appear amongst them as rulers, there will be social discord (1911: 304–5).

Furthermore, he insists that 'expansionism and imperialism are nothing but the old [realist] philosophies of national prosperity [which] ... appeal to national vanity and national cupidity ... They are delusions, and they will lead us to ruin unless we are hard-headed enough to resist them' (1911: 297–8, also 313). But while such statements might be thought of as clear examples of liberal internationalism based on a cultural pluralist predisposition, it turns out that they emanate from their particular brand of defensive racism.

Turning to the second criticism of empire, Spencer argues that imperialist paternalism is unwise because it disturbs the natural evolutionary trajectory of non-white societies that is directed inevitably towards the telos of civilization in the long run. Worse still, imperialism leads to the 're-barbarization of civilization'. This is the international face of the argument he laid out concerning the 'coming slavery' within domestic white society, which is effected by the growth of collectivist institutions and the reformist interventionist state (see esp. Spencer 1881: 18–43). In *Facts and Comments* Spencer argues that the rebarbarization of civilization can be effected from outside through the negative blowback that imperialism imposes on the colonial power; an argument that is related in three key chapters in which he argues that imperialism necessitates the conversion of free individuals within the colonizer country into slaves (1902: 157–200). This is a function of the point that imperialism requires the coercion of the subject race, which in turn demands the development of a strong imperial army. And this in turn goes hand-in-hand with a remilitarization of civilized society and the introduction of a host of fiscal exactions and regulations, ultimately leading to a displacement of power away from the legislature into the executive. Civilization becomes re-barbarized as each individual is forced to perform compulsory service to the state in ways that are reminiscent of coercive feudalism or militant society. That is, civilized-pacific industrial society regresses back into the stage of pre-modern militant society; a point that also qualifies the conventional assumption concerning his determinist and linear conception of social evolution. Moreover, Spencer argues that imperialism is a harmful discourse, privileging physical superiority and military regimentation over mental superiority. Reminiscent of Hobson's critique of insane imperialism, Spencer argues that these discourses are propagated and diffused by all manner of domestic institutions within the colonial power, including the church, the Salvation army, public schools, as well as artists, journalists and novelists. And he concludes in characteristic fashion by asserting that '[s]urely a society thus characterized and thus governed is a fit habitat for Hooligans' (1902: 181).

The third argument against imperialism returns us to one of the common scientific racist themes, which concerns the degenerative impact of miscegenation upon the white race. Colonialism, by drawing the white and non-white races into close proximity necessarily leads to miscegenation. But, he insisted, inter-breeding between superior and inferior races was categorically wrong (though Spencer was extremely positive about mixing the allied varieties of the Aryan race). When asked in 1892 by a Japanese political leader, Kentaro Kaneko, concerning whether the inter-marriage of foreigners with Japanese people was a good idea, he replied by saying that:

> It should be positively forbidden ... There is abundant proof ... furnished by the inter-marriages of human races ... that when the varieties mingled diverge beyond a certain slight degree *the result is invariably a bad one* in the long run ... [I]f you mix the constitutions of two widely divergent varieties which have severally become adapted to widely

divergent modes of life, you get a constitution which is adapted to the mode of life of neither – a constitution which will not work properly, because it is not fitted for any set of conditions whatever . . . . [A]nd I end by saying as I began – *keep other races at arm's length as much as possible*.[87]

This argument against miscegenation is also deployed by Sumner, though it is used in tandem with the point concerning the inferior political and social capacities of the lower races. His ultimate rationale for why US imperialism should be avoided rests on the desire to preserve the uniqueness of American civilization, which in turn rests on the purity of white American racial stock. Poignantly, in his 1898 essay, following on from his previous criticism of colonizing the Philippines (as mentioned above) he asks immediately: 'But then, if it is not right for us to hold these islands as dependencies, you may ask me whether I think that we ought to take them into our Union, at least some of them, and let them help to govern us'. And he replies no less immediately, 'Certainly not. If *that* question is raised, then the question whether they are, in our judgment, fit for self-government or not is in order' (Sumner 1911: 310). In answering this question he then discusses the unique circumstances within which the American state was founded, going on to assert that

> It is the highest statesmanship in such a system . . . [above all] never to take in voluntarily any heterogeneous [racial] elements. The prosperity of such a state depends on closer and closer sympathy between the parts in order that differences which arise may be easily harmonized. What we need is more intension, not more extension (1911: 311).

And again,

> that it is unwisdom to take into a state like this any foreign [racial] element which is not congenial to it. Any such element will act as a solvent upon it. Consequently we are brought by our new conquests face to face with this dilemma: we must either hold them as inferior possessions, to be ruled and exploited by us or we must take them in on an equality with ourselves, where they will help to govern us and to corrupt a political system which they do not understand and in which they cannot participate (1911: 311).

Thus US imperialism is best avoided so as to prevent non-white immigration and the concomitant racial, social and political contamination that it necessarily brings in its wake. And this in turn leads him to the

---

[87] Spencer cited in Duncan (1911: 322, 323), emphasis in the original.

logical conclusion that '[f]rom that dilemma there is no escape except to give them independence and to let them work out their own salvation or go without it' (1911: 312). That is, the inferior races should be left to the laws of natural selection, which dictate the survival of the fittest; and should these races fail to adapt accordingly, then so be it. Thus rather than reflecting a tolerant cultural pluralism, it is clear that Sumner's calling for inferior racial self-determination issues from an intolerant racist predisposition. And as I explain shortly, this racist argument was a common mantra among the Progressive Liberal American anti-imperialists.[88]

Finally, the fourth argument against Western imperialism complements that of the third: the claim that tropical climatic trauma leads to the degeneration of the white race. But in contrast to the offensive racists, Sumner cited this as a key reason to reject imperialism outright. 'The Islands which we have taken from Spain never can be the residence of American families, removing and settling to make their homes there. The climatic conditions forbid it' (1911: 306).

Ultimately, the universalist approach of Sumner and Spencer represents that element of racism which demands white racial *isolation from* the non-white races, for imperialism would serve only to bring these antithetical forces together. Thus Sumner asserts in his essay, 'War', that '[n]o one has yet found any way in which two races, far apart in blood and culture, can be amalgamated into one society with satisfaction to both' (1911: 35). Better then to allow the non-white races to govern themselves rather than to allow them close contact with Aryan stock. It is in this racial sense that Sumner concludes his 1898 article by asserting that 'the United States has stood for something unique and grand in the history of mankind ... It is by virtue of these [unique] ideals that we have been "isolated", isolated in a position which the other nations of the earth have observed in silent envy' (1911: 193).

Relativist defensive racism and the critique of imperialism: Blair and Jordan

In the next chapter I note that the racist-realists, Franklin Giddings and Harry Powers, as well as Theodore Roosevelt and Henry Cabot Lodge, argued for US imperialism in the debate that emerged on that issue during and after the Spanish-American War of 1898. Here I focus on the other side of that debate by examining the liberal objections to US

---

[88] Leuchtenberg (1952); Lasch (1958); Gossett (1997: 336–7); Leonard (2005).

imperialism (even though I began this task with my discussion of Sumner in the last section, given that he was a significant voice in this debate). Two key points are noteworthy here. First, it would be problematic to assume that the American debate on empire was one that pitted pure realist militarists against liberal cultural pluralists. Rather, a good number of people on both sides of the fence based their arguments in part, at least, on racist logic: offensive racism on the part of the realist-imperialists and defensive racism on the liberal anti-imperialist side.[89] In particular, the defensive racist critique of empire took two main forms: the universalist approach advanced by Sumner and the relativist approach developed by the likes of David Starr Jordan (1851–1931) and James Blair (1854–1904). To reveal this latter strand I shall focus on Blair's *Imperialism, Our New National Policy* (1899) and David Starr Jordan's *Imperial Democracy* (1901).

The key dividing line within the defensive racist camp, which separates the 'universalists' from the 'relativists', hinges on the levels of agency awarded to the Eastern races. Spencer and Sumner awarded the Eastern races a moderately high level, insofar as they believed that such races could auto-develop in the fullness of time, while Charles Henry Pearson awarded the yellow races extremely high levels of, albeit regressive/barbaric, agency. By contrast, Blair and Jordan believed that the agency of the inferior races was neither *derivative*, in that they would not auto-develop, nor *conditional* precisely because the agency of the Eastern races was so low that they were incapable of being 'tutored' in the ways of Western civilization. Imperialism, therefore, was entirely futile; indeed it was worse than futile since it would cause only negative blowback on the West.

At first sight, these liberals passionately critiqued imperialism through what appeared to be a typical cultural pluralist sensibility. For example, William James (one time vice president of the Anti-Imperialist League) lambasted the idea of the expansionist civilizing mission in a letter to the *Boston Evening Transcript*:

> Could there be a more damning indictment of that whole bloated idolatered 'modern Civilization' than this amounts to? Civilization is, then, the big, hollow, resounding, corrupting, sophisticating, confusing torrent of mere brutal momentum and irrationality that brings forth fruits like this.[90]

---

[89] However on the anti-imperialist side George Hoar (1900) and Moorfield Storey (1901) constituted clear exceptions insofar as they avoided deploying racist arguments in their case against US empire.

[90] William James cited in Hofstadter (1992: 195).

Such liberal claims extended from upholding George Washington's insistence on resisting overseas imperial policies to celebrating Thomas Jefferson's principle of equality of all men, to ideas about the prohibitive costs of imperial militarism. Both Blair and Jordan insist that governing another race is to betray the American Constitution. Here they emphasize Washington's insistence on national isolation on the grounds that the nation has no rights to expand abroad and to oppress other nations. And they both provide a robust critique of the civilizing mission, the sum of which appears initially to constitute a robust defence of liberal cultural pluralist principles.

But behind these familiar liberal cultural pluralist arguments was a defensive social Darwinian racism, and in Jordan's case a 'pacifist Eugenics', all of which fundamentally denied the equality of all men. As one commentator points out, while

> [m]ost historians have in fact assumed that anti-imperialism was genuinely liberal in inspiration and that the anti-imperialists were voicing objections to colonialism now commonly accepted ... [But many of] the anti-imperialists, like the imperialists, saw the world from a pseudo-Darwinian point of view. They accepted the inequality of man – or to be more precise, of races – as an established fact of life. They did not question the idea that the Anglo-Saxons were superior to other people (Lasch 1958: 320, 321).

This relativist racist critique of empire comprised three key arguments. The first argument marshalled against imperialism was that the white race cannot survive in the tropics (much as we saw with respect to Sumner). For the heat of the tropics serves only to effect a degeneration of the physical and intellectual energy of the Europeans (Blair 1899: 13–14). Jordan goes into considerable detail on this point in several chapters. At one point he declares that '[c]ivilization is, as it were, suffocated in the tropics. It lives, as Benjamin Kidd suggests, as though under deficiency of oxygen. The only American who can live in the tropics without demoralization is the one who has duties at home and is not likely to go there' (Jordan 1901: 45). And in a long section later on in the book he asserts that the Philippines

> lie in the heart of the torrid zone, 'Nature's asylum for degenerates' .... [T]he conditions of life are such as to forbid Anglo-Saxon colonization ... Individual exceptions and special cases to the contrary, the Anglo-Saxon or any other civilized race degenerates in the tropics mentally, morally, physically.[91]

---

[91] Jordan (1901: 93–4 and 95–102).

Blair describes the temperament and behaviour of the inferior tropical races through the impact of climate. The Malay is a 'gambler, a profligate, indolent, untruthful, even in the confessional, disobedient, cruel to animals and enemies, superstitious', while the Moslems are 'warlike, fanatical and dangerous'. Above all, the Negroes are 'black savages, closely resembling apes in shape and tree climbing habits ... clothed only in girdles ... [T]hey have cannibalistic habits and are worshippers of the moon'. And he concludes this discussion by asserting that '[a] high authority is of the opinion that nothing short of actual imprisonment will ever subjugate either these blacks or the Malay population' (Blair 1899: 14–15).

The second anti-imperialist argument concerned the perils of immigration. At first sight such an argument is framed in the context of the racial egalitarian principle of the 14th and 15th Amendments. But these Amendments are invoked as a means to keep the inferior races *out* of the United States. This becomes a key argument in the rejection of imperialism. For colonizing the inferior tropical races will mean that they will inevitably gain access to the US through immigration. Echoing Sumner, they argued that the existence of these Amendments means that non-white racial immigrants will automatically gain the vote and will therefore be able to exercise some sort of political control on the American homeland. This would be intolerable because these races are incapable of living up to the duties and obligations of citizenship. Thus 'if we govern the Philippines, so in their degree must the Philippines govern us' (Jordan 1901: 48). Or as Camp Clark put it '[n]o matter whether they [the Filipinos] are fit to govern themselves or not, they are not fit to govern us' (Clark cited in Lasch 1958: 327).

In addition, the taking in of non-white racial elements will lead only to social chaos and breakdown. Thus Jordan insists that 'wherever degenerate, dependent or alien races are within our borders today they are no part of the United States. They constitute a social problem; a menace to peace and welfare' (Jordan 1901: 44). In the context of such immigration Blair asserts that the 'race question is perhaps the most serious of all problems arising in this connection' (1899: 23). Discussing the point that the US is receiving hundreds of thousands of Chinese Coolies, he asks rhetorically:

> Are we forgetful of the fact that the racial differences between the Oriental and western races are never to be eradicated? The Oriental is of the past; he has not progressed for centuries; he hates progress. The constitution of China it is said has not been changed for thousands of years. We are progressive, energetic and intolerant of the very thing which is his [the

Chinese race's] most marked characteristic – indolence. The two races could never amalgamate (Blair 1899: 23).

Accordingly, he poses a rhetorical question, asking why we are taking 'into our body politic millions of people – ignorant of and hostile to our laws, our language, our religion and the basic principles of our government?' (Blair 1899: 23). This was complemented by the likes of Edward A. Ross (1914) and John Commons (1907/1967), who argued against the importation of coolie labour on the grounds that this would displace the 'indigenous' white American working class from employment and would depress wages.

While the arguments thus far resonate clearly with those of Sumner, the one key difference between the universalists and the relativists is that for the latter the non-white races are incapable of auto-generating. As such this means that the civilizing mission is pointless given that these races are incapable of being uplifted. Indeed 'history shows no instance of a tropical people who have demonstrated a capacity for maintaining an enduring form of Republican government' (Blair 1899: 18). Or as Jordan put it, 'the race problems of the tropics are perennial and insoluble, for free institutions cannot exist where free men cannot live. The territorial expansion now contemplated would not extend our institutions, because the proposed colonies are incapable of self-government' (1901: 44). Jordan develops this anti-colonial argument in part through what appears to be a tolerant liberal critique of slavery. For in the tropics, he argues, the inferior races will remain slaves for centuries. 'These people in such a climate can never have self-government in the Anglo-Saxon sense. Whatever forms of control we adopt, we shall be in fact slave drivers' (1901: 32).

But the criticism of imposing slavery turns out to be motivated by the need to preserve white liberal-democratic civilization. For he immediately argues that imposing slavery will provide only negative blowback upon the United States insofar as it will undermine her republican constitution given that slavery is consistent only with oligarchic government (as found in Britain). Governing colonies necessitates the abandonment of democracy at home. Accordingly, he claims that '[t]he American merchant, missionary, and miner have taken up the white man's burden cheerfully; the American government cannot' (Jordan 1901: 106). For 'among hundreds of colonial experiments ... there is not to-day such a thing as a self-supporting European colony in the tropics' (Jordan 1901: 93–4).

Finally, a third argument against empire is found in Jordan's 'pacifist Eugenic' argument that warfare selects the best or fittest elements of the civilized white race to go out and fight but in so doing leads to a reduction in the numbers of the fittest element as they lose their lives in futile colonial wars; a problem that was exacerbated by his point that the weak, the infirm, the cowardly and feckless stay at home away from the battlefield. As he put it: '[i]ts call is ever in Kipling's words, "Send forth the best ye breed". And the best never return. With the selection of the best for exile and destruction the standard of the race at home inevitably declines' (Jordan 1901: 110). Importantly, this 'dysgenic racist' argument formed the key basis of the 'pacifist wing' of the Eugenics movement; a wing which in fact comprised a majority of the membership of the Eugenics movements in the United States and Britain – with Jordan comprising a key figure within the former. It also found its expression in the racist 'peace biology' of Jacques Novicow's *War and its Alleged Benefits* (1911: esp. ch. 4), Charles Richet's *Peace and War* (1906: 43–4), Vernon Kellogg's *Military Selection and Race Deterioration* (1916) and, not least, G.F. Nicolai's *The Biology of War* (1918). Crucially, biology and genetics were deployed to prove that warfare does not enhance white racial vitality but undermines it. It was this argument that comprised much of the discussion in Jordan's other books including *The Human Harvest* (1907), *War and Waste* (1914/ 2009) and *War and the Breed* (1915).

However, it would be remiss at this point to ignore the fact that the racist dimension of the school of 'pacifist Eugenics' led to a number of paradoxes and not infrequently to outright contradictions. For it turns out that many of these pacifists who advocated peace reserved such aspirations for relations between civilized European states, which in turn was a function of their desire to maintain white racial unity and supremacy. For when it came to specifying relations between the civilized and savage races warfare and colonialism were often advocated.[92] Hence we confront the paradox that someone like the social Darwinist, Ernst Haeckel, could set up the 'pacifist' German Monist League in 1906 while also being a founding member of the imperialist Pan-German League. No less paradoxical is the point that in both these organizations he was able to give vent to his brand of 'indirect' racial exterminism (a position which I discuss in the next chapter). The same position was held by G. F. Nicolai (1918), who had gone to prison for opposing World War I. And other well-known 'pacifists' such as Helene Stöcker and Christian von Ehrenfels were against war between white countries so

---

[92] Weikart (2003, 2004); Gasman (1971/2004).

that they could preserve white unity against blacks and especially the 'yellow peril' (Weikart 2003: 285).

But to return to the narrative by way of summary, it seems fair to conclude that the relativist defensive racists insisted that colonialism serves to undermine the vitality of the white race within the West, while doing nothing to promote non-white development abroad. In the light of all this there was only one thing to be done. For in addressing the point that the United States is already involved in the colonization of various tropical countries, Jordan concludes that 'the only sensible thing [for the US] to do would be to pull out some dark night and escape from the great problem of the Orient as suddenly and dramatically as we got into it' (Jordan 1901: 52, also 73). And to conclude the chapter more generally, while the critique of imperialism might at first sight imply some kind of anti-Eurocentric sensibility which suggests that Eastern polities should gain political and cultural self-determination, it should be apparent by now that this position invokes an informal hierarchical conception of world politics wherein 'existential equality' (the idea of cultural self-determination) – a *sine qua non* of sovereignty – turns out to be non-existent. Thus the defensive racists in general sought specifically to 'defend the West' by seeking to maximize the distance between the white and non-white races so as to maintain white racial vitality and the supremacy of Western civilization in what amounted to various 'racial apartheid' conceptions of world politics.

5

Racist imperialism: racist-realism, liberalism and socialism, 1860–1914

Introduction: racist-imperial conceptions of world politics

While conventional IR historiography assumes that realist international theory emerged initially in its classical form via the works of E. H. Carr and Hans Morgenthau round about the time of World War II, this obscures a range of thinkers writing in the post-1889 era who developed what I shall call racist-realism. In this chapter I shall explore some of the key exponents – notably the geopoliticians, Alfred Mahan and Halford Mackinder – and, albeit indirectly, the German racist-realists, Ludwig Gumplowicz and Gustav Ratzenhofer (via my discussion of Ward, given that his vision of imperialism drew directly from their work). Note that I shall reserve for Chapter 7 the discussion of the other racist-realists who wrote in the pre-1914 era, including Friedrich Ratzel, Rudolf Kjellén, Heinrich von Treitschke and Friedrich von Bernhardi. One of the main themes of my discussion of racist realism is that it was a multivalent approach that exhibited many different facets. In Chapter 7 I shall differentiate the German geopolitikers from Hitler and others according to their different brands of racism that in turn yield various conceptions of imperialism. Here it is noteworthy that Mahan and Mackinder differed not only to the likes of von Treitschke and von Bernhardi, Hitler and others, but also to the American racist-realists such as Theodore Roosevelt (1894/1897, 1905), Whitelaw Reid (1900) and Henry Cabot Lodge (1899). For these latter three thinkers embraced an optimistic white triumphalist sensibility, believing that the manifest destiny of the white race to expand and conquer the globe was at hand. Although Mahan and Mackinder did not express the extreme levels of anxiety associated with the likes of Stoddard, Charles Pearson and Hitler, nevertheless they were gripped by an imaginary discourse of the 'coming yellow barbarians'.

Of course, the popular imagination assumes that scientific racism was the preserve of right-wing thinkers. This, however, necessarily obscures the existence of a vibrant stream of liberal racism, not to mention a socialist strein as I explain below. If we zoom our focus out for a moment, it becomes apparent that taken as a whole, the racist-liberal imperialists evinced optimistic and, not infrequently, triumphalist visions of world politics, which contrasted with the more angst-ridden nature of much, though not all, of the racist-realist literature. Typifying such triumphalist liberals were the likes of Charles Dilke (1868), John Seeley (1883/1906), Josiah Strong (1885, 1889), John Fiske (1885), David Ritchie (1900) and Walter Bagehot (1974).[93] These thinkers constructed a vision of world politics that entailed the natural spread of the English or Anglo-Saxon race and which projected the piercing light of civilization into the dark places beyond Europe and the United States. Typical were Fiske's words: that it was the English race's 'manifest destiny' to conquer the barbarous regions so as to eventually create a world 'covered with cheerful homesteads, blessed with a Sabbath of perpetual peace' (Fiske 1885: 152). There were also various liberal-racists who very much echoed the conception of the 'benign' civilizing mission, which I shall mention later on in this introductory statement.

One of the most intriguing aspects of scientific racism in general and Eugenics in particular is that it was frequently embraced by left-liberals, radicals and socialists.[94] Jack London, at a meeting of the Socialist Party in San Francisco, when challenged by various members concerning his emphasis on the yellow peril, pounded his fist on the table and exclaimed: 'What the devil! I am first of all a white man and only then a Socialist!'[95] J. B. S. Haldane pointed out that Eugenics cuts right across the political spectrum, asserting for example that 'the English national Council of Labour Women had recently passed a resolution in favour of the sterilization of defectives, and this operation is legal in Denmark and other countries to the "left" of Britain in their politics' (Haldane 1938: 8). No less important is the point that Eugenics (and social Darwinism) embraced a pacifist, or more accurately a 'quasi-pacifist' strand, as I noted in the last chapter.[96] Indeed the pacifist German Monist

---

[93] While there are no imperialist cues in Bagehot's seminal social Darwinian treatise, *Physics and Politics* (1872/2010), nevertheless elsewhere he points towards the idea of the civilizing mission in the East – in Turkey and India in particular, not to mention his support for the English empire in Ireland (see Bagehot 1974: 77–135, 283–308, 335–43).
[94] For excellent discussions see: Freeden (1979); Paul (1984); Kevles (1985); Soloway (1995: 32–48); Crook (1994); Sewell (2009). And in the context of the US Progressive movement see the references in Chapter 4, fn. 88 (this volume).
[95] Jack London, cited in Gossett (1963/1997: 206).
[96] Cf. Jordan (1901, 1907, 1914/2009); Kellogg (1916); Nicolai (1918); Sanger (1932).

League and the Austrian Peace Society were set up by two 'pacifist-racists' – Ernst Haeckel and Bertha von Suttner respectively. But while they advocated peace between white nations, many of their socialist and left-wing members had no problem advocating the colonization of the inferior races by the superior whites. Also of note is that a good number of the left-wing Eugenicist membership of the Monist League believed that poverty was in significant part a function of defective working class stock (see Gasman 1971/2004: ch. 4).

One reason why Eugenics – especially its imperialist wing – found an almost natural home among socialists and left-leaning liberals was that it dovetailed with their preference for collectivism, state interventionism, social engineering and planning;[97] which is precisely why Spencer's 'conservative' anti-interventionist stance rejected Eugenics as I explained in the last chapter. Thus as the Fabian-Eugenicist, Sidney Webb, put it, '[n]o consistent Eugenist can be a "laisser faire" individualist unless he throws up the game in despair. He must interfere, interfere, interfere!' (Webb 1910–11: 237). No less poignant is the fact that the three key progressives who played a vital role in the development of the British welfare state – John Maynard Keynes, Richard Titmuss and William Beveridge – were all members of the Eugenics society.[98]

Figure 5.1 focuses on two particular variants of imperialist 'offensive racism'. On the left-hand side I note that both the racist-realists, Mahan and Mackinder, construct globalization – or what they call the 'closing of the world' – as delivering the yellow barbaric threat (the yellow peril) onto the doorstep of the West,[99] which in turn required an imperialist counter-offensive that should be conducted by an Anglo-Saxon racial alliance. A key aspect of their approach, as it was for Charles Pearson and later on, Lothrop Stoddard, comprises the awarding of high levels of, albeit regressive/barbaric, agency to the yellow race. By contrast, Benjamin Kidd, Karl

---

[97] See for example: Webb (1907, 1910–11); Shaw (1903/2009); Laski (1910); Money (1925); Huxley (1926); Carr-Saunders (1926); Haldane (1932, 1938); Wallace (1900); Wells (1902); K. Pearson (1905); Ellis (1911).

[98] Sewell (2009: 72–7).

[99] The term the 'yellow peril' was used first by Hungarian General Turr in relation to the rising Japanese threat in June 1895, as well as by Kaiser Wilhelm in September 1895 following Japan's victory over China. Wilhelm used this construct in order to support his militant imperialist posture, writing to Theodore Roosevelt in 1905: 'I foresee in the future a fight for life and death between the "White" and the "Yellow" for their sheer existence. The sooner therefore the Nations belonging to the "White race" understand this and join in common defense against the coming danger, the better' (cited in Weikart 2003: 287).

INTRODUCTION: RACIST-IMPERIAL CONCEPTIONS   109

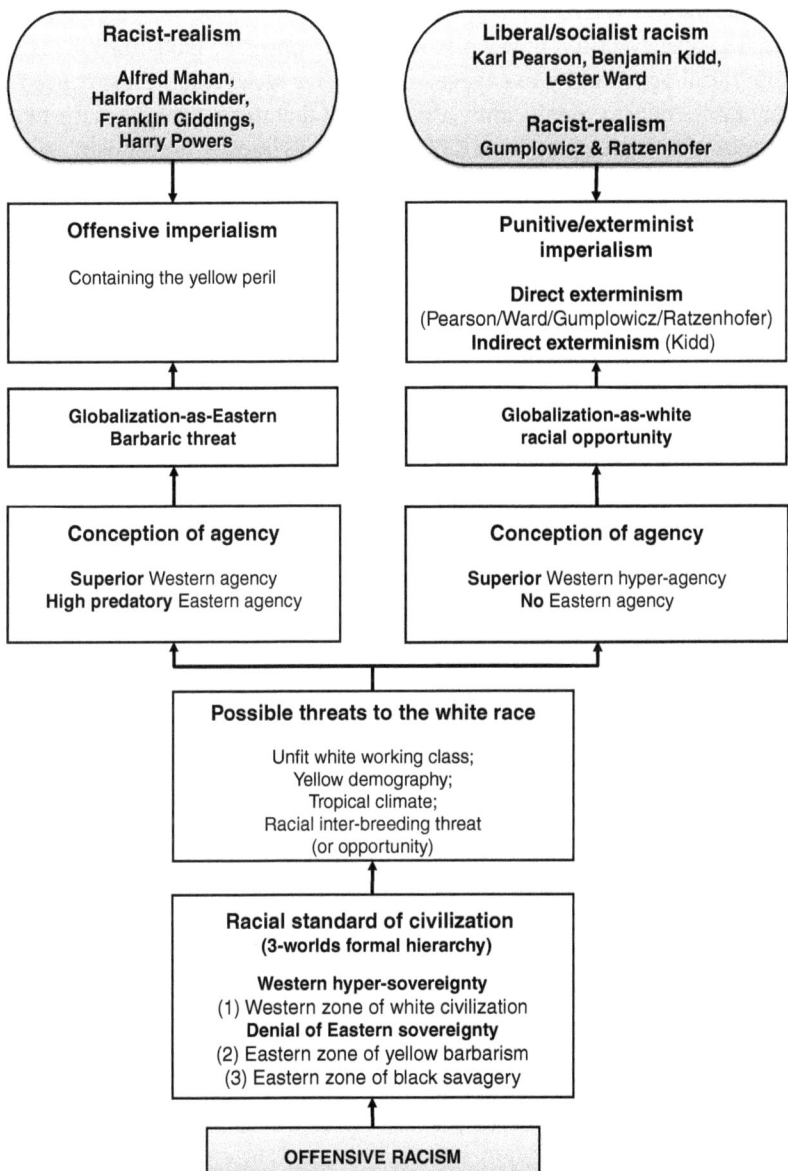

Figure 5.1   Offensive racist conceptions of imperialism, 1889–1914

Pearson, Lester Ward, Ludwig Gumplowicz and Gustav Ratzenhofer all deny the agency of the non-white races and construct 'globalization' as a white racial opportunity to engage in a punitive racial exterminist conception of imperialism. Significantly, this body of literature exemplifies the two wings of what Richard Weikart (2003, 2004) calls 'racial exterminism', with Pearson, Ward, Gumplowicz and Ratzenhofer representing what I shall call *direct* genocidal exterminist thought, and Kidd representing what I shall call *indirect* racial exterminist thought. Pearson and Kidd both constructed the tropics as posing various challenges to the white race, either as a result of the degenerative impact of climatic trauma (Kidd) or through miscegenation as the white colonists inter-bred with the non-whites (Pearson). While this was used by defensive racists as a rationale for avoiding imperialism as I explained in the last chapter, nevertheless it was the offensive racist imperialists that were forced to quietly rework the argument.

My reader might well anticipate from this that Kidd, Pearson and Ward represented an extreme version of right-wing racist-realism. But in fact Kidd's politics shared much in common with New Liberalism,[100] Pearson was a 'socialist' Eugenicist, and Ward was a left-liberal progressive who was extremely critical of Spencer's right-wing laissez-faire politics. No less surprising is that for Pearson, as was the case for many Eugenicists, a key danger to white racial vitality was the threat posed not simply by the non-white barbaric races but also by the 'enemy within' – the white working class.[101] Indeed for many Eugenicists and Darwinists, white racial vitality was a euphemism for white elite vitality. Thus the survival of the white race lay in the hands of the superior white elite which comprised the white 'neo-aristocrat' as opposed to the white working class 'under-man',[102] 'sub-man',[103] or as the socialist, Leo

---

[100] For an excellent discussion of this see Hawkins (1997: 171–7).

[101] But Pearson's socialism is one that we would not recognize today. In particular, he argued that the problem which Britain faces at the turn of the twentieth century is precisely that bad white stock has multiplied faster than the good white stock in large part as a result of the welfare state (1905: 58ff). This in turn points to a contradiction in his logic; for on the one hand he argued that limiting the competition within the white race would enhance rather than diminish white social efficiency, while on the other hand he called for breeding the working class out of existence (Crook 1994: 87–9). As Michael Freeden concludes of Pearson's thought '[i]f this was socialism at all, it was a regimented socialism ... devoid of humanity' (Freeden 1979: 668); see also Kevles (1985: 34).

[102] Stoddard (1922b).

[103] Freeman (1921). Significantly, Freeman sees in the British sub-man a lowlier figure than the Negro (1921: 249–52).

George Chiozza Money (1925) put it, the 'white peril'. As Alistair Bonnett explains, the white 'unter-mensch', to borrow a phrase that was later embraced by Nazism, constituted 'the enemy of whiteness, an enemy who is both a racial throwback and a harbinger of an anarchic future' (Bonnett 2004: 19). However, while I shall discuss this aspect briefly in relation to Karl Pearson in this chapter, nevertheless my gaze will be fixed firmly on the international vision that these thinkers constructed.

Finally, to counter the possible impression that liberal-racism was an inherently violent approach it is worth noting that a number of liberal-racist imperialists constructed, at least in their eyes, a more 'empathic' conception. These included Alleyne Ireland (1905) and Henry Sidgwick (1897). But probably the clearest example of this genre is found in Paul Reinsch's work, which stood at the opposite extreme to Ward and Kidd. Interestingly, Reinsch's approach shares many important overlaps with liberal paternalist Eurocentrism and its conception of the civilizing mission. To reveal this I shall discuss briefly Reinsch's 'benign' liberal racist conception of the civilizing mission at the end of the first section. Note, however, that most liberal racist-imperialists stood mid-way between the 'benign' and 'direct exterminist' conceptions – including Dilke, Seeley, Ritchie and Bagehot.

The indirect and direct exterminist imperial antidotes to Charles Pearson's dire prophecy: Benjamin Kidd, Karl Pearson and Lester Ward

The extreme response to Charles Pearson's prophecy that I discussed in the last chapter is found in the exterminist brand of racism, exemplified here by the liberals Benjamin Kidd (1858–1916) and Lester Ward (1841–1913) – alongside the racist-realists Ludwig Gumplowicz (1838–1909) and Gustav Ratzenhofer (1842–1904) – as well as the perverted 'socialism' of Karl Pearson (1857–1936). Nevertheless I should mention at the outset that while I pair Kidd and Pearson together in terms of their racist-imperial conceptions of world politics, it is noteworthy that Kidd 'detested Pearson's authoritarian Eugenics, and spent many years fighting it' (Crook 1994: 92), notwithstanding the irony that his own brand of social Darwinism drew in part on August Weismann's germ-plasm theory.[104]

---

[104] Here it is noteworthy that the link between Weismann's germ-plasm theory and Galton's Eugenic thinking is nicely captured in the statement that '[i]f Galton's

Most significant, though, is that while Kidd and Pearson both fit into the category of 'racial exterminist' theory, each represented one of its different wings as I mentioned earlier. More specifically, Kidd's *indirect* racial exterminism assumed that the policy of genocide was *not* required given that the inferior races would naturally die out of their own accord upon mere contact with the superior white races in the context of the survival of the fittest. This was a trope of much of social Darwinism and could be found in the 'pacifist Darwinism' of the likes of Ernst Haeckel and Bertha von Suttner, as well as in the 'pacifist Eugenicism' of G. F. Nicolai (1918) and many others, as I noted at the end of Chapter 4.[105] The other wing advocated a policy of *direct* racial exterminism or genocide which was represented, albeit in different manifestations, by Karl Pearson on the one hand and Lester Ward as well as Gumplowicz and Ratzenhofer on the other. It also found its expression in much of German race science (*Rassenwissenschaft*), including the likes of Erwin Baur, Eugen Fischer, Fritz Lenz, Friedrich Hellenwald, Otto Ammon, Ludwig Woltmann, Oscar Peschel[106] and, of course, Adolf Hitler (1939), as I explain in Chapter 7.

But while there *is* a distinction here that should not be dismissed so as to paint all imperialist social Darwinians as exterminists – as does Lindqvist (2002) – nevertheless it is not infrequently the case that the dividing line between these positions was very thin, and at times permeable. For many indirect exterminists were openly content for the law of the survival of the fittest to operate on behalf of the white races. That is, upon contact with the white races Nature saw to it that the inferior races would be 'selected out of existence' (e.g., Ernst Krause, Ernst Haeckel, G. F. Nicolai, Ludwig Woltmann and Otto Ammon). A typical example of this is provided by Nicolai:

> [W]ar as waged at present can be considered only a justifiable form of struggle for existence if the nations against whom we are waging war are not looked upon as human beings ... that is, if it is desired to carry on a war of extermination against barbarians so as to enable true humanity [i.e., the white race] to find room to spread over the earth. No European

statistical studies of heredity strongly suggested the constancy of populations for a given character, Weismann had seemingly provided a mechanical underpinning for the result in his germ-plasm theory that the force of heredity resided in a substance impermeable to environmental influence' (Kevles 1985: 70).

[105] See esp. Weikart (2004: chs. 9–10); Gasman (1971/2004: ch. 4); Hawkins (1997: 140–1). Note that other 'pacifist Eugenicists' who fitted into this imperialist approach included Wilhelm Schallmayer and Alfred Ploetz.

[106] See Weinstein and Stehr (1999); Weikart (2003, 2004: chs. 9–10).

will feel that he is justified in considering another European as a barbarian. . . . What will undoubtedly occur is that these people will gradually be exterminated by the white race, though it has long been clear that it would be foolish to make war upon them. They die out of themselves wherever they come in contact with whites, bloodless warfare being always more effectual than bloody (Nicolai 1918: 85).

In another version of this approach some argue that having colonized Eastern lands so the white races had to impose a harsh work routine on the inferior racial inhabitants in order to 'civilize them', even if this led to the paradoxical outcome that they might die out and become extinct in the process. Winwood Reade made this exact argument in the context of the African savages who are scarred by the racial trait of indolence.

> Africa shall be redeemed. Her children shall perform this mighty work. Her morasses shall be drained; her deserts shall be watered by canals; her forests reduced to firewood. Her children shall do all this. They shall pour an *elixir vitae* into the veins of her mother, now withered and diseased. . . . In this amiable task they may possibly become exterminated (Reade 1864: 452).

But did he advocate a compassionate policy that could prevent such a fateful outcome? At least he thought he was being compassionate when he asserted that '[w]e must learn to look on this result with composure. It illustrates the beneficent law of nature, that the weak must be devoured by the strong' (Reade 1864: 452).

More generally, many racists believed that while war was an absurdity between civilized white nations, it was deemed to be entirely natural between whites and non-whites (e.g., Fiske 1885: 146; Roosevelt 1905: 31); a position which many 'pacifist Eugenicists' also adhered to. In general, then, it is clear that in this genre the spread of the white races and the concomitant extinction of the inferior races – whether effected by man or nature – was a progressive good in that it was 'the price' of the spread of civilization, and therefore a price well worth paying; to wit the statement by Theodore Roosevelt (1905: 31):

> The growth of peacefulness between nations, however, has been confined strictly to those that are civilized . . . .. With a barbarous nation peace is the exceptional condition. On the border between civilization and barbarism war is generally normal . . . . [For] in the long run civilized man finds he can keep the peace only by subduing his barbarian neighbour. . . . Every expansion of civilization makes for peace. In other words, every expansion of a great civilized power means a victory for law, order, and righteousness.

Benjamin Kidd – white races wake up: the tropics are beckoning!

One response to Charles Pearson's 'dire prophecy' was found in Benjamin Kidd's book *The Control of the Tropics* (1898), which followed on from his seminal book *Social Evolution* in 1894. In the former book Kidd upbraids Charles Pearson in an extended footnote, suggesting that he erred by focusing too much on the non-temperate zone and ignored the 'racial fact' that only the white races are capable of inculcating progress in the world (1898: 79). More significantly, Kidd provides a clear alternative scenario for the future that plays directly on the phraseology of Pearson's famous prediction (as cited above on p. 89):

> The day is probably not far distant when, with the advance science is making, we shall recognize that it is in the tropics, and not in the temperate zones, that we have the greatest food-producing and material-producing regions of the earth; that the natural highways of commerce in the world should be those which run north and south; and that we have the highest possible interest in the proper development and efficient administration of the tropical regions, and in an exchange of products therewith on a far larger scale than has been attempted or imagined (Kidd 1898: 84).

Like Charles Pearson's text, Kidd's book is in effect a prediction of the future while at the same time issuing a wake up call to the white races. However, he sought to issue this warning not in terms of a looming Eastern *threat* but in the context of a vital Western *opportunity* to exploit the resources of the non-white lands so as to enhance white racial vitality and Western development. Moreover, Kidd inverts Charles Pearson's conception by denying the non-white races agency.

Importantly, although Kidd sought to challenge Pearson's dire prophecy, he was equally concerned to absolve the West of its home-grown 'liberal imperial guilt syndrome'; or what he referred to as the liberal 'altruistic doctrine'. 'It is this doctrine which has raised the negro on the southern states of North America to the rank of citizen ... [I]t is before this doctrine ... and not before the coloured races, that the European peoples have retreated in [the] tropical lands' (1898: 81). This mentality presumes that the rationale for colonialism is merely to prepare the inferior races to eventually take up the mantle of independent government and that the white races should accordingly govern only on a *temporary* basis (1898: 35–45); an idea that emerged at the end of the eighteenth century with the challenge to the slave trade and the French and American revolutions (1898: 67–72, 81).

The problem is that this liberal sensibility has crippled imperialist sensibilities and thereby prevented the West from going out to develop the tropics; a task which is crucial given that these lands are potentially so productive. And, above all, it has prevented the Western mind from appreciating the superior white race's monopoly of 'social efficiency', despite Charles Pearson's negative prognostications on this point. For he wants to impress upon his readership the point that the Native populations of the tropics are *socially inefficient* and are unable to develop their lands productively; the imperialist mantra that Kidd reiterates throughout the book. As he states at the beginning, all this results in the problem that what is missing in our collective white racial psyche is a justification for an incursion into, and the development of, the tropics. His book, then, is set up to furnish just such a justification.

The argument about the superior social efficiency of the white race is derived from his social Darwinian emphasis on the problems of the tropical environment, which prevents the coloured races from developing either an efficient government or the resources of their lands (1898: esp. 51–3). The liberal altruistic doctrine ignores the fundamental principle that the equality of all races fundamentally denies the logic of social evolution: 'The evolution which man is undergoing is, over and above everything else, a social evolution. There is, therefore, but one absolute test of [racial] superiority. It is only the race possessing in the highest degree the qualities contributing to social efficiency that can be recognized as having any claim to superiority' (1898: 98). And, of course, the social efficiency argument is a vital tool in legitimizing the cause of Western imperialism (as I explained in Chapter 2 with respect to the paternalist Eurocentrics).

Kidd's key concern about colonizing the tropics was the degenerative impact that the climate would have on the white imperialists. Speaking of the white man he asserts that

> In climatic conditions which are a burden to him; in the midst of races in a different and lower stage of development; divorced from the influences which have produced him, from the moral and political environment from which he sprang, the white man does not in the end ... tend so much to raise the level of the races amongst whom he has made his unnatural home, as he tends himself to sink slowly to the level around him (1898: 50–1).

This leads him to assert that '[t]he attempt to acclimatize the white man in the tropics must be recognized to be a blunder of the first magnitude' (1898: 48). For

> in the tropics the white man lives and works only as a diver lives and works under water. Alike in a moral, in an ethical, and in a political sense, the atmosphere he breathes must be that of another region ... Neither physically, morally, nor politically, can he be acclimatized in the tropics. The people among whom he lives and works are often separated from him by thousands of years of development (1898: 54).

This, then, has negative ramifications for his desired imperialist enterprise. At this point Kidd finds himself on the horns of a dilemma: between a pro-imperialist posture on the one hand and a rejection of white residence in the tropics on the other. But rather than reject imperialism, Kidd offers the solution wherein colonial government needs to be conducted mainly 'from a distance' – namely in the metropole, even though a small cadre of white administrators will be required to reside in the colonial tropics.

To conclude this discussion it is worth noting in the context of Kidd's analysis that he in fact describes colonialism in terms of a benign 'trust for civilization' (1898: 53, also 54). But it seems clear that this turns out to be merely a rhetorical device aimed to furnish imperialism with a noble liberal moral purpose so as to overcome the liberal 'imperial guilt doctrine' that Kidd so abhors. Moreover, it is highly likely that such rhetoric is also deployed to absolve the Anglo-Saxons of all responsibility for the fact that imperialism leads inevitably to the extinction of the inferior races. Voicing his indirect exterminist approach he asserts simply that 'the weaker races disappear before the stronger through the effects of mere contact' (1894: 268). And in any case, it is hard to square his rhetoric of imperialism as a *trusteeship* for the benefit of global humanity given his central argument that the West must colonize the tropics in order to exploit its mineral resources upon which the success of Western industrialization and white racial vitality depends. Accordingly it is clear that trusteeship applies to the diffusion and triumph of (Western) civilization. Indeed, he had no problem with 'the fact' that the weaker races die out upon mere contact with the white race. For had he been against this and been true to his professed noble moral purpose, would this not have urged him to rail against imperialism in the first place?

Karl Pearson: revitalizing white racial supremacy through imperialist genocide

Ironically, Karl Pearson, who was Francis Galton's brilliant protégé, not only shared a surname and the Germanic version of his first name with

Charles Henry Pearson, but the title of his 1905 book was also uncannily similar. Thus Charles's *National Life and Character: A Forecast* was followed by Karl's *National Life from the Standpoint of Science* (1905). But this is where any similarities ended, for while Charles prophesied the defeat of Western civilization at the hands of the yellow barbarian marauders and lamented the obsolescence of Western imperialism, Karl inverted this analysis in every respect. Indeed, Karl's use of Eugenics provided an antidote to Charles' somewhat unorthodox social Darwinism. Rather than produce a vision of an ascendant East and a retreating West, he insists that under the opportunity of rising global interdependence the West can and should colonize the East, while also directly exterminating the Eastern peoples in the process.

Given the conventional or popular perception that social Darwinism and Eugenics both presume the ineluctable or so-called 'iron laws' of natural selection, one might assume that Pearson would advocate letting nature and evolution take their course. But the Eugenicists were critical of this approach and were keen for humans to intervene in nature and the world. This was one of the original motivations that spurred on Francis Galton who, as the cousin of Charles Darwin, founded the school of Eugenic science and wrote the first book in this genre (Galton 1869). The term 'Eugenics' that Galton coined derives from 'Eu' (meaning good) and 'genics', which refers to the quality of human stock (see Galton 1883). Above all, the central thrust of Eugenics constituted the possibility of improving the quality of the human species through pro-active state intervention. This was to be achieved through 'positive Eugenics', which promotes good white stock, as well as through 'negative intervention' that actively discourages the reproduction of bad stock – white or non-white. Embracing this approach Pearson argued that while the laws of inheritance are inevitable, nevertheless 'this does not mean a fatal resignation to the presence of bad stock, but [that] a conscious attempt [should be made] to modify the percentage of it in our own community and in the world at large' (Pearson 1905: 20). That is, bad stock cannot be modified but its proportion to good stock can and must be reduced. For '[h]istory shows ... one way, and only one way, in which a high state of civilization has been produced namely, the struggle of race with race, and the survival of the physically and mentally fitter race' (1905: 21).

In particular, Pearson placed considerable emphasis upon the evils of miscegenation, claiming that mixing racial characteristics will only spoil 'good stock'; a key belief of the Eugenicist thinkers such as Madison Grant, Lothrop Stoddard and Adolf Hitler. Pearson argued that a 'physically and mentally well-ordered individual will arise as a variation in bad stock [through cross-breeding with good stock] ... but the old evils will in all probability reappear in a definite percentage of the offspring' (1905: 19). And while the non-white races represented bad stock, so too did the working class elements within the white race, such that bad white and non-white stock needed to be actively reduced in size relative to the white elites (1905: 57, 61).

The ultimate paradox of scientific racist thought is that in some key respects it logically implied an *anti*-imperialist posture, given the various degenerative challenges that imperialism entailed for the white race. As noted earlier as well as in the last chapter, the tropics were fraught with danger because on the one hand they would deliver the white race into a degenerative climate, while on the other colonialism would bring the white race into close proximity with the racially contaminating inferior races. Ironically, then, the onus to legitimize colonialism was placed squarely on the shoulders of the pro-imperialist rather than the anti-imperialist racists. Not surprisingly, therefore, both Kidd and Karl Pearson sought to re-work the argument so as to circumvent these problems in order to justify imperialism (even though they came up with two alternative but complementary formulations).

Thus Pearson begins this argument by proclaiming that: '[l]et us suppose we could prevent the white man, if we liked, from going to lands of which the agricultural and mineral resources are not worked to the full; then I should say a thousand times better for him that he should not go than that he should settle down and live alongside the inferior race' (1905: 23). Like Kidd, then, Pearson now found himself on the horns of a dilemma. But unlike the defensive racists such as Spencer and Sumner who rejected imperialism, Pearson invoked an alternative final solution as a means to rationalize his desire for Western colonialism. For '[t]he only healthy alternative' to abandoning imperialism because of the degenerative impact that miscegenation produces on the white man 'is that he should go and completely drive out the inferior race'. This happened in the United States, which saw the majority of an unproductive (Red Indian) race exterminated and replaced by a superior productive white race (1905: 25). Happily too the same beneficial result applied in the Australian case (1905: 27). Here the social efficiency argument becomes paramount given that the white conquering race was justified in displacing the native savages since, unlike the latter, it had succeeded in putting the acquired lands to productive use. Thus in direct contrast to Charles Pearson, and speaking of South Africa as an example, Karl asserts that the white man replace[s] the dark in the fields and in the mines, and the Kaffir is pushed back towards the equator. The nation organized for the struggle must be a *homogeneous* whole, not a mixture of superior and inferior races. For this reason every new land we colonize with white men is a source of strength (1905: 50).

Lester Ward: progressive 'social interventionist liberalism' and direct racial exterminism

Here it is helpful to note that I include a brief discussion of Lester Ward for five key reasons. First, he reveals that even 'progressive social liberalism' could support a direct exterminist conception of imperialism; second because he doubles up as a summary of the pre-1914 racist-realists, Gumplowicz and Ratzenhofer; third, because his conception of exterminist imperialism differed in various respects to those just described; fourth, because his theory reveals that Lamarckian Darwinism can yield an exterminist racial conception of imperialism which contrasts to the 'benign' neo-Lamarckian conception of colonialism offered by Paul Reinsch, as well as to that of the anti-imperialism of Spencer's Lamarckian Darwinism. Fifth and finally, Ward is particularly interesting because he represents the *interventionist* brand of social Darwinism that sought to critique the laissez-faire approach of Spencer and Sumner. Above all, he saw in their theory an elitist defence of the rich classes within white society and deployed his working class sensibilities to debunk their defence of the minimalist, laissez-faire 'nightwatchman' state (see esp. Ward 1884). To challenge this he developed a left-liberal theory of the socially-interventionist state, which was charged with the task of defending the interests of the working classes. In turn, one might very well infer from this political stance that Ward would develop a more progressive theory of international relations to that espoused by Spencer and Sumner. But the irony is that while Ward's domestic reformist politics indeed provided a socially progressive alternative to that of Spencer and Sumner, nevertheless he advocated a direct exterminist conception of imperialism abroad that contrasted starkly with the anti-imperialism of Spencer and Sumner.

In particular, it is important to emphasize that Ward departs from the likes of Karl Pearson, Hitler, Grant and most other racists by *positively* embracing miscegenation (blood/race-mixing). Nevertheless, this should not be read as some kind of commitment to multiculturalism given that race war and miscegenation are vehicles for enhancing white supremacy. Inverting the standard racist trope he asserts that 'the mixture of blood conduces to race vigor',[107] and to this end Ward insisted that the socially efficient races must expand and colonize the socially inefficient races. This argument begins with his discussion of the race theory of the state that was formulated by Gumplowicz and Ratzenhofer.[108] This process begins with the conquering of an inferior race by a superior one, with the latter setting up a new state in the conquered territory. This new state, which begins with race-struggle, is completed with the creation of a new racial amalgam.

Nevertheless, it would be wrong to infer from this that racial antagonisms in world politics are capable of reconciliation. For this brand of racism leads to the mantra that 'races, states, peoples, nations are always forming, always aggressing, always clashing and clinching, and struggling for the mastery, and the long, painful, wasteful, but always fruitful gestation must be renewed and repeated again and again' (1903/2002: 213). Thus racial-resolution is rejected in favour of *permanent* race struggle (1903/2002: esp. 231–41). It is vital that races keep moving across the face of the earth, for fixity within one specific environment leads to mental deterioration and racial degeneration. For such stationary peoples '[t]heir whole lives, physical, mental, and moral, become fixed and monotonous, and the partners chosen for continuing the race have nothing new to add to each other's stock' (1903/2002: 235). Thus once a new race has been consolidated, nevertheless over time it would stagnate given that racial progress results only from 'the fusion of unlike elements' (1903/2002: 237). This leads to the conclusion that race 'war has been the leading condition of human progress. ... When races stop struggling progress ceases ... [T]he condition of peace is a condition of social stagnation' (1903/2002: 238). Ironically, Ward's progressive liberalism contrasted radically with those liberals who believed in a future perpetual peace.

It is significant to note at this point that Ward, as did Benjamin Kidd (1898), Franklin Giddings (1898) and Harry Powers (1898), was openly critical of the so-called liberal 'altruistic doctrine', arguing that '[c]ertain tender-hearted persons have almost always uttered a faint protest against [war and race struggle], but it has been utterly powerless to stem the current' (1903/2002: 239). And echoing Gumplowicz's dictum that '[t]he perpetual struggle of the races is the law of history, while perpetual peace is nothing but the dream of the idealists',[109] so this culminates in Ward's theory of permanent race struggle:

---

[107] Ward (1903/2002: 210, also 214).   [108] See Ward (1903/2002: 203–16).
[109] Ludwig Gumplowicz (*Der Rassenkampf*), cited in Novicow (1911: 116).

THE INDIRECT AND DIRECT EXTERMINIST ANTIDOTES 121

> Under the operation of such a [doctrine] it seems a waste of breath to urge peace, justice, humanity, and yet there can be no doubt that these moral forces are gaining strength and slowly mitigating the severity of the law of nature. But mitigation is all that can be hoped for. The movement must go on, and there seems no place for it to stop. ... If the peace missionaries could have made their counsels prevail there might have been universal peace, nay, general contentment, but there would have been no progress (1903/2002: 239–40).

Finally, in chapter 11 of his book Ward ties these claims directly into his triumphalist white racist conception of world politics. For there he argues that the civilized European white races

> have led the civilization of the world ... They are and have been ... the repository of the highest culture, they have the largest amount of social efficiency, they have achieved the most ... The several nations into which this race is now divided are the products of compound assimilation of a higher order than other nations. As a consequence of all this this race has become the dominant race of the globe. As such it has undertaken the work of extending its dominion over other parts of the earth (1903/2002: 238–9).

And he then proceeds to support the argument for social efficiency/*terra nullius*, wherein the Western colonial take-over of socially inefficient native peoples is deemed to be entirely legitimate. Ultimately he advocates the need for the white race to effectively exterminate the inferior colonized races by breeding them out of existence.

Appendix: the 'empathic' brand of liberal-racist imperialism – Paul Reinsch and the 'benign' civilizing mission

At first sight it will appear counter-intuitive to find that racism could yield a 'benign' vision of imperialism as a civilizing mission, given the common misconception that racist imperialism implied the virtual destruction of the native races. But this misses many points, not the least of which is that the injection of neo-Lamarckianism produced a range of different postures vis-à-vis imperialism as I noted earlier and in the last chapter. For its emphasis on genetic characteristics *and* social behaviour makes it equally at home with imperialism as it is with anti-imperialism. Thus if changes in social behaviour of a 'progressive' kind are to be effected so this could promote movement towards civilization in the absence of external imperial intervention (as in Spencer), or equally to development into civilization as a result of the progressive impact of a 'benign' civilizing mission (as in Reinsch 1905a, 1905b; Sidgwick 1897; Ireland 1905), or equally to the cause of punitive, exterminist imperialism (as in Ward). Having covered Ward as well as Spencer in the last chapter, I shall discuss Reinsch as the clearest exemplar of the liberal-racist conception of the 'benign' civilizing mission.

In two key publications that place special emphasis on Europe's relations with Africa, *Colonial Administration* (1905b) and 'The Negro Race and European Civilization' (1905a), Reinsch produces an argument that contains many of the same 'empathic' sensibilities to those developed by J. A. Hobson in part 2 of his 1902 book *Imperialism*, as I explained in Chapter 2.[110] Echoing Hobson, Reinsch insists that the chief extant problem in Western imperial thought lies with the belief that the native populations are expected to adopt Western rational institutions and norms of behaviour *in toto*. For such a programme of complete cultural conversion/assimilation has 'in practice proved unsuccessful and at times even disastrous' (Reinsch 1905a: 15). Indeed, 'Natives are [required] to abandon the entire complex of customs and beliefs which have thus far guided them through life, and by an act of selective reason, to adopt institutions foreign to their social experience' (1905a: 21). Throughout, he argues, not always consistently it should be noted, the first requirement of Western colonial administrators should be to study the ethical character of the natives, as did Hobson and Alleyne Ireland (1905), if they are to deploy an *effective* imperial mission.

But it would be wrong to infer from this that Reinsch adopted a liberal cultural pluralist disposition, for this seemingly empathic sensibility was significantly informed by his Lamarckian racism. Rational institutions cannot simply be imposed on the Natives for they will be unable to work with them given their inferior physiologically or mentally maladaptive condition. Thus he argues that '[n]ew ideas may be poured into the consciousness, may even be understood by the rational faculties, but they will leave no trace upon the mental constitution and upon the real spring of action' (1905a: 21). In this context he discusses how similar psychological traits of the same conquered race are reproduced through heredity over many generations. Thus parts of the Malay race, the Filipinos and Javanese, under the control of different powers 'all display identical characteristics and have the same intellectual constitution which the earliest explorers noted in their day' (1905a: 21). This led Reinsch to invoke Lamarckian logic arguing that 'psychological

---

[110] Interestingly, Reinsch was well aware of Hobson's work, having reviewed *Imperialism* in *Political Science Quarterly* (1903).

characteristics are perhaps subject to modification, but only very gradually, in the course of centuries' (1905a: 32). Accordingly the policy of total assimilation 'runs counter to the scientific laws of psychic [hereditary] development' (1905a: 22). Simultaneously, and reminiscent of Hobson and Ireland once more, he notes that the different races have different civilizational achievements leading to the conclusion that 'the very idea that one set of [Western] institutions ... could be applicable to all these multiform societies, would seem to be the result of pure ignorance'.[111] In short, the backward hereditary condition of the African peoples meant that assimilation to Western civilization could only be achieved very slowly, probably over a matter of centuries, and that in the short-to-medium term it was necessary to retain traditional 'irrational' African institutions which were congruent with the backward state of the Native mind-set.[112]

It was precisely this racist belief, then, that led Reinsch to call for a *selective* 'uplift'; one that would entail introducing settled agriculture and industrial pursuits, infrastructures and Western capital, as well as guaranteeing peace. The Natives would also require technical training to educate them in the ways of such productive pursuits. In general, he argues that the 'substitution of intensive methods for the exhaustive barbarous exploitation [undertaken by Western imperialists] which is now the rule throughout Africa as well as in other undeveloped regions of the world is an essential purpose of a civilizing policy' (1905a: 31). Beyond this selective remit the Western colonialists should not tread – at least not in the medium term – and should allow the maintenance of Native cultures and religions in their irrational forms.

The racist-realist offensive imperialist antidote to Charles Pearson's dire prophecy: Alfred Mahan and Halford Mackinder

As I explain in Chapter 13, modern conventional IR historiography effectively *whitewashes* geopolitical theory of its racist base, assuming instead that it was based on the universalist logic of national realpolitik. But in this section and in Chapter 7 I argue that the generic school of

---

[111] Reinsch (1905a: 22); cf. Hobson (1901b: 275, 276; 1938/1968: 245).
[112] However, this logic led Ireland to argue that a future Filipino self-determination is impossible because the native character had 'not been changed by a large admixture of European blood' and that accordingly, it would always remain incapable of maintaining order and secure government (Ireland 1905: 276).

geopolitics was founded on various provincial discourses of *racist realpolitik* that gave rise to a variety of imperialist conceptions of world politics.[113] Here I shall focus on Alfred Mahan (1840–1914) and Halford Mackinder (1861–1947), not least because they have at least some resonance within the conventional IR historiographical imagination, reserving my discussion of the wider school for Chapter 7. I also supplement this discussion with a few quotes from Franklin Giddings (1898) and Harry Powers (1898), both of whom echoed a great deal of that which was advanced by Mahan and Mackinder.

'White Races wake up: the barbarians are coming!': or, 'the coming anarchy and the barbaric threat'

Although Mahan and Mackinder were far less sanguine about the white race's future than were the likes of Theodore Roosevelt, Henry Cabot Lodge and Whitelaw Reid, nevertheless they did not subscribe to the highly pessimistic vision that had been constructed by Charles Pearson in 1893 (as was explained in the last chapter). Thus Mahan and Mackinder believed that the Barbaric Peril had not yet reached a critical mass and, above all, that it could be defeated in the coming decades so long as the West – especially the Anglo-Saxon races that were situated either side of the Atlantic – unifies against it through an offensive imperialism.

Crucial to the geopolitical discourse is the perception of global interdependence, or what Mahan and Mackinder called 'the closing of the world'. This was perceived or constructed as dangerous because it brought the Eastern barbaric races right onto the doorstep of the West. It is the rapidity of movement and the minimization of distances that is crucial.

> Events which under former [isolated] conditions would have been distant and of smaller concern, now happen at our doors and closely affects us. Proximity ... is a fruitful source of political friction, but proximity is the characteristic of the age. The world has grown smaller .... [All states are] touching each other throughout the world (Mahan 1897: 60, 66).

Likewise Franklin Giddings asserted that an emerging threat via global interdependence 'has awakened a dormant sense of geography that will never again permit the American voter to look at his domestic problems

[113] Cf. Vitalis (2005: 167); Knutsen (1997: 192–201); Tuathail (1994, 1996); Ashworth (2011, 2012).

with the time-old satisfaction in our secure isolation' (Giddings 1898: 596).[114] For Mahan, the breaking down of distance is important in terms of the great Eastern challenge to the West insofar as it delivered a strengthening Japan onto the West's doorstep; something which constituted 'a striking illustration of the somewhat sudden nearness' of the Eastern Other through the 'closing' of the world (1897: 66). Or as he also expressed this anxiety: 'civilizations on different planes of material prosperity and progress, with different spiritual ideals, and with very different political capacities, are fast closing together' (1897: 109).

Similarly, Mackinder's essay is written with a clear sense of Western anxiety that finds its initial expression in the 'closing of the world'. Thus, he asserts, in the post-Columbian age

> we shall again have to deal with a closed political system [that is] worldwide [in] scope. Every explosion of social forces, instead of being dissipated in a surrounding space and barbaric chaos, will be sharply re-echoed from the far side of the globe, and weak elements ... will be shattered in consequence (Mackinder 1904: 422).

By 'weak elements' he is referring to those European societies that were vulnerable economically or politically. The solution in part to this closing of the world would be to enhance the internal-domestic relative efficiency of those vulnerable Western societies.

In addition, Mackinder's angst-ridden perception of globalization refers to the point that all spaces within the world have now been filled up as a result of Western imperialism. This vision is eloquently summarized by Gearóid Tuathail:

> Underpinning this argument is an unquestioned geographical ethnocentrism, an ethnocentrism that initially sustained the belief that certain regions of the world political map were blank, undiscovered, and unoccupied and is now proclaiming the world political map a closed system of space, settled, occupied, and named (Tuathail 1996: 27–8).

In this context Mackinder designates the period running up to 1900 as the *Columbian epoch*, which was characterized by the unchallenged imperial expansion of the West after 1492. The problem was, he believed,

---

[114] Note too that in the American context, this anxiety was fuelled further by the official closing of the internal frontier in 1890. For if white racial vitality could no longer be maintained through war on the American Indians, then it was imperative to open up a new global frontier so that white racial vitality could be maintained through a war on the non-white races abroad; see especially Keene (2002: 182–3); Hunt (1987: 55); and more generally Slotkin (1973); Drinnon (1980).

that by 1900 the Columbian epoch had run its course owing to the fact that most of the world had been colonized by the West and that now 'there is scarcely a region left for the pegging out of a claim of ownership, unless as a result of a war between civilized or half-civilized powers' (1904: 421). For Mackinder, the perceived ending of the Columbian epoch constituted an ominous portent for Western civilization, since it threatens to return Europe back to the anarchic pre-Columbian era in which world history witnessed a 'medieval Christendom [that] was pent into a narrow region and threatened by external barbarism' (1904: 422).

However, before I elaborate on Mackinder's vision of the pre-1492 era which is used as a direct analogy for the perils that confront the West after 1900, I need to preface that discussion with a focus on the conception of Eastern agency that both he and Mahan subscribed to. What is striking here are the high levels of agency that they award the Eastern races, particularly with respect to the oriental races (though they stop short of the extreme level ascribed by C. H. Pearson). Nevertheless, reminiscent of Pearson, Mahan asserts that at the very time that the United States slumbers in its isolation we witness the

> stirring of the East, its entrance into the field of Western interests, not merely as a passive something to be impinged upon, but with a vitality of its own, formless yet, but significant[;]. ... the astonishing development of Japan. ... [In India] there are signs enough of the awakening of political intelligence, restlessness under foreign subjection. ... And of China we know less, but many observers testify to the immense latent force of the Chinese character (Mahan 1897: 97).

Similarly, this strong conception of Eastern agency is a clear theme of Mackinder's, who implores his reader 'to look upon Europe and European history as subordinate to Asia and Asiatic history, for European civilization is, in a very real sense, the outcome of the secular struggle against Asiatic invasion' (Mackinder 1904: 423). Critically, neither Mackinder, nor Mahan and Pearson, granted Eastern agency a progressive role in the making either of the West or of world politics. Eastern peoples were cast with the negative stereotype or trope of barbaric atavism – i.e., *predatory* Eastern agency – contributing nothing positive either to progressive civilization or to world order and constituting merely the harbingers of an anarchic new world disorder. Moreover, Mahan describes the Chinese as 'unprogressive' and 'conservative' but as having 'unusual staying power, persistence of purpose, endurance' and 'vitality' (Mahan 1897: 97). Its ominous portent issues from the fact that it is a racially homogeneous people and is multiplying rapidly, all of which 'may be counted upon in the future to insure a substantial unity of impulse which, combined with its mass [or large demographic size], will give tremendous import to any movement common to the whole' (1897: 97).

Thus with this conception of Eastern agency out of the way I can now turn to Mackinder's historical analysis of the pre-1492 era, which forms the backdrop to his analysis of the post-1900 era. Here he argues that to the extent that the Eastern peoples contributed anything at all to the development of civilization, it was only as the unintended result of the West's defensive unification against the invading barbarian hordes. He traces this back into the thousand year period that marked the pre-Columbian epoch which began after the fall of the Roman Empire, asserting that as a result of defending against the successive waves of Asiatic barbaric invasions (the Huns, Magyars, Avars, Mongols etc.)

> a large part of European history might be written as a commentary upon the changes directly or indirectly ensuing from these raids. The Angles and Saxons ... were ... driven to cross to England. The Franks, the Goths and Roman Provincials were compelled, for the first time, to stand shoulder to shoulder on the battlefield of Châlons, making common cause against the Asiatics who were unconsciously welding together modern France. ... Venice was founded from the destruction of Aquileia and Padua; and even the Papacy owed a decisive prestige to the successful mediation of Pope Leo with Attila at Milan (Mackinder 1904: 426-7).

Critically, this leads Mackinder to conclude that:

> Such was the harvest of results produced by a cloud of ruthless and idealess horsemen sweeping over the unimpeded plain – a blow, as it were, from the great Asiatic hammer striking freely through the vacant space. ... For a thousand years a series of horse-riding peoples emerged from Asia through the broad interval between the Ural mountains and the Caspian sea, rode through the open spaces of southern Russia, and struck home into Hungary in the very heart of the European peninsula, shaping by the necessity of opposing them the history of the great [European] peoples ... (1904: 427).

Gradually Europe's constituent states were marked out and forged in the heat of 'racial battle' as they sought to defend themselves against the successive pre-1492 waves of incoming Eastern barbarians, in the process creating a sense of nascent 'European' unity. Tracing forwards he then argues that although the Europeans ultimately lost the Crusades, the battles nevertheless served to unite Europe and 'we may count them as the beginning of modern history – another striking instance of European advance stimulated by the necessity of reacting against pressure from the heart of Asia' (Mackinder 1904: 429).

Echoing Mahan's argument that the Columbian epoch rested heavily on a preponderance of sea-power, nevertheless Mackinder emphasizes the centrality of land power in the post-Columbian era. In this respect he focuses on the importance of the land-locked corridor that existed mainly within Russia, the 'geographical pivot',[115] which constitutes the central strategic position of the world through which the Asiatic peoples had successively entered and invaded Europe during the pre-Columbian epoch. Moreover, while steam power and the Suez canal had enhanced sea power relative to land power, the balance of advantage was by the turn of the twentieth century shifting back to land-power as a result of the recently laid trans-continental railways (with the near-completion of the Trans-Siberian railway significantly influencing Mackinder in this respect). And he closes his article by warning that the closing of the Columbian epoch seems to be returning us to the familiar dangers of the pre-Columbian epochal situation which saw successive waves of Asiatic peoples invade Europe – to wit his assertion that 'were the Chinese, for instance, organized by the Japanese, to overthrow the Russian Empire and conquer its territory, they might constitute the yellow peril to the world's freedom' (1904: 437).

Echoing, or rather pre-empting Mackinder's argument, Mahan's 1890 essay 'The United States Looking Outward' claims that the United States needs to move out of isolation by developing a strong naval power base in order to confront the advancing Japanese and Chinese (1897: 9); an idea that was taken much further in his subsequent *Forum* essay in 1893. In this piece, 'Hawaii and Our Future Sea Power', China is singled out as a key threat to the West. This discussion focuses on the key strategic location of the Hawaii islands as the potential meeting point of a defensive West and an outward-bound aggressive East.

> It is a question for the whole civilized world [i.e., the West] and not for the United States only, whether the Sandwich Islands, with their geographical and military importance, unrivalled by that of any other position in the North Pacific, shall in the future be an outpost of European civilization, or of the comparative barbarism of China ... [Indeed] many military men abroad, familiar with Eastern conditions and character, look with apprehension toward the day when the vast mass of China – now inert – may yield to

---

[115] Or what he called 'the heartland' in his 1919 book.

one of those impulses which have in past ages buried [Western] civilization under a wave of barbaric invasion (1897: 12).

Mahan's racist siege mentality led to his assertion that the West now constituted 'an oasis in the midst of a desert of barbarism' (Mahan 1897: 49). The Europeans need to turn away from any pacifist tendencies, insists Mahan, because Europe constitutes a crucial land barrier to a potential Asian land movement westward, as much as the Americans need to mobilize their sea-power so as to block a coming eastward invasion by the Chinese from across the Pacific.

> China ... may burst her barriers eastward as well as westward, toward the Pacific, as well as toward the European continent ... By its nearness to the scene, and by the determined animosity to the Chinese movement which close contact seems to inspire, [the United States], with its Pacific coast, is naturally indicted as the proper guardian for this most important position (Mahan 1897: 12–13; also 51).

This led Mahan to warn his Western readers that insufficient attention 'is paid to the possible dangers from those [barbarians] outside, who are wholly alien to the spirit of our civilization; nor do men realize how essential to the conservation of [Western] civilization is the attitude of armed watchfulness between nations, which is maintained now by the great states of Europe' (1897: 49). Accordingly, in his famous 1897 essay, 'A Twentieth Century Outlook', Mahan chastises the United States for its 'ideal of isolation' and its refusal 'to recognize the solidarity of interest with ... European civilization' which surely awaits it in the coming years (1897: 97). For as he warned: '[w]e stand at the opening of a period when the question is to be settled decisively, though the issue may be long delayed, whether Eastern [barbarism] or Western civilization is to dominate throughout the earth and to control its future' (1897: 100).

Thus echoing the likes of Giddings and Powers and many others,[116] an Anglo-Saxon racial alliance could unify the West and contain the incoming waves of yellow barbarians (1897: 51–2, 105–7). Such an idea might be termed a kind of Anglo-Saxon 'racial ultra-imperialism' (to paraphrase Lenin's concept). Thus '[w]hen we begin really to look abroad, and to busy ourselves with our duties to the world at large in our generation ... we shall stretch out our hands to Britain, realizing that

---

[116] Other imperialists who called for an Anglo-Saxon racial alliance between the English and the Americans included John Fiske (1885); Josiah Strong (1885, 1889); John Burgess (1890); Henry Cabot Lodge (1899); Whitelaw Reid (1900); James Hosmer (1903).

in unity of heart among the English-speaking races lies the best hope of humanity in the doubtful days ahead' (1897: 107). Only in this way could the white citadel of civilization be protected. And, moreover, Western leaders needed to colonize the remaining lands of the world as a result of the imperative of social efficiency (1897: 68–9).

All in all, then, behind the universalist veneer of 'geopolitics among nations' lurked the sound and fury of race struggle. And, as we shall see in Chapter 11, their racist-realist idiom, 'The barbarians are coming! The barbarians are coming!' or equally 'the coming anarchy and the barbaric threat', would find its direct corollary in 'Western-realism' after 1989 with its signature tune of the 'new barbarism and the coming anarchy'.

PART II

1914–1945
The high tide of manifest Eurocentrism and the climax of scientific racism

6

Anti-imperialism and the myths of 1919: Marxist Eurocentrism and racist cultural-realism, 1914–1945

Introduction: critiquing imperialism, defending the West

In certain respects this and the next chapter that cover the 1914–45 era take on a special significance given that this period is conventionally held by IR scholars to be that of the discipline's 'infant stage'. For it is a now conventional axiom that the discipline was born in 1919, and that it was furnished with the noble moral purpose of finding ways to solve the universal problem of war for all. Such a purpose derives from the belief that the 'infant child' was conceived on the blood-stained battlefields of Europe and whose mother had gone through an extremely traumatic 48-month gestation period. This now conventional view was originally constructed by E. H. Carr in his classic text *The Twenty Years' Crisis* (1946/1981), even if it has only been internalized within the historiographical self-imagination of the discipline more recently.[117] In this and the next chapter I want to contribute to the now vibrant revisionist literature, which produces an alternative account and understanding of what might better be called the thirty years' crisis (i.e., 1914–45).[118] I do so by making five specific revisionist arguments, which hinge on the pivot of my core claim that our conventional image of the birth of IR and of its 'interwar infancy' is to an important, though not complete, extent an exercise in myth-making that serves to make IR scholars feel good about themselves and their discipline.

---

[117] Indeed according to Jack Donnelly even as late as the early 1980s the standard overview of the discipline is that it only started with the classical realists of the post-war generation; see the discussion in Carvalho, Leira and Hobson (2011).

[118] Ashworth (2002, 2006, 2011, 2012); Schmidt (1998a, 1998b, 2002, 2008); Wilson (1998); Quirk and Vigneswaran (2005); Long and Wilson (1995); Long and Schmidt (2005b); Osiander (1998); Vitalis (2005); Thies (2002); Knutsen (1997, 2008); Guilhot (2008). For an overview of this literature as well as my own take on this see Carvalho, Leira and Hobson (2011).

My first revisionist argument problematizes the 'foundationist/progressivist myth' by pointing up the deep continuities that the 1914–45 period of international theory exhibits with the pre-1914 era. More specifically, I argue that while the interwar period comprises a not unimportant *moment in the development* of the discipline, it is problematic to treat it as an autonomous temporal domain because the Eurocentric and racist metanarratives that underpinned it had been forged in the previous century.[119] That is, IR theory did not suddenly spring up from the ground in one particular year unannounced as some kind of miraculous virgin birth following a gruelling 48-month gestation period. To be clear, though: this is not to deny the point that international theory starts to take on its more familiar modern form where concepts such as 'anarchy' appear in a more sustained way.[120] But arguably this marks a surface shift in focus rather than a deep rupture given the strong continuity with the pre-1914 Eurocentric and racist metanarratives. Moreover, it is noteworthy that the 1914–45 period marked the final climax of scientific racism and the high tide of manifest Eurocentrism. But unlike scientific racism, manifest Eurocentrism receded between 1945–89 on an ebbing tide only to wash back in on the crest of a returning high tide after 1989.

Second, while 1919 was by no means an unimportant moment it was so in part because that very year witnessed an explosion of anti-colonial resistance, with Western colonialism placed in the dock of the social court of global justice. Indeed, that year saw the tectonic plates of East and West collide, the effect of which was to convulse Europe in an identity-crisis of near earth-shattering proportions. It was this, at least as much as solving the problem of war, that exercised the concerns of many international theorists – especially liberals and 'cultural-realists'. And, moreover, solving the problem of war was often couched in terms of preventing a future race war between the colonized and the colonizers. Important too was the emergent European perception that hitherto 'civilized Europe' had devolved into barbarism through the suicidal intra-Western civil war between 1914 and 1918. And it was this perception in particular that galvanized the anti-colonial nationalist

---

[119] Such a claim complements the brilliant and pioneering revisionists interventions which revised the birth-date of the discipline – either to 1880 (Schmidt), the 1890s (Knutsen) or to the 1910s (Vitalis); see Schmidt (1998a); Vitalis (2000, 2005); Knutsen (2008).

[120] Ironically, the term 'international anarchy' was invented by the liberal thinker, G. Lowes Dickinson (1918) but found its place in much of liberal and left-liberal writings including Woolf (1916, 1933a, 1933b); Hobson (1915a, 1915b, 1921, 1932, 1932–1938/2011); Brailsford (1915); Buell (1925); Zimmern (1936); Angell (1933); and Laski (1933, 1940).

movements in their campaign of 'the Empire strikes back'.[121] The resulting crisis of Western self-doubt and deep anxiety was reflected in a host of books which included Oswald Spengler's Eurocentric-institutionalist text, *The Decline of the West* (1919/1932), Madison Grant's *The Passing of the White Race* (1918), Lothrop Stoddard's *The Rising Tide of Color against White-World Supremacy* (1920), and Sigmund Freud's later book *Civilization and its Discontents* (1930/1989), to name but a few. Indeed '[n]ever before had the possibility of the downfall of Western culture and civilization been as intensively discussed and imagined as in the years after 1918' (Geulen 2007: 87). But most importantly, it was within this fiery crucible that much of post-1914 international theory – liberal, racist-realist and racist cultural realist – was forged.

Third, not only is liberal institutional theory assumed to have dominated interwar IR, but equally our conventional historiographical imagination views it as a harmonious and optimistic discourse that stands for peace and cooperation between self-determining states. But rather than evincing a strong degree of optimism, many liberals were wracked with anxiety concerning the future of Western hegemony and sought ways to restore its imperial mandate. Moreover, some of the best-known interwar liberal international theorists even went so far as to argue that the League would be rendered impotent without the supporting role that the British Empire could provide – most notably Alfred Zimmern, Gilbert Murray and Norman Angell. It is, however, ironic that this imperialist aspect of interwar 'idealist' theory has not been widely noticed by modern IR scholars,[122] given that Carr had, in fact, made it one of the key defining features of what he called idealism's 'utopian' politics (as I explain in the next chapter).

Fourth, the thirty years' crisis is conventionally thought of as one that was dominated by liberal international theory. But in this chapter I argue that this necessarily elides or obscures the development of racist cultural-realism, as much as it does racist-realism (which I discuss in the next chapter). These approaches developed throughout the 1889–1945 era, which provides further testimony to my 'continuity' claim.

Fifth, to characterize the interwar period as one which hosted the 'first great debate' between 'realists and idealists' is problematic for a whole host of reasons (the details of which are found in the sources referenced in footnote 118 above). But in the context of this book's perspective I argue

---

[121] See more generally Mazrui (1984); Lauren (1996).
[122] Notable exceptions are: Rich (2002); Morefield (2005); Long (2005); Vitalis (2005, 2010).

that realists and the so-called 'idealists' were united by the concern to restore the mandate of Western civilizational hegemony in one guise or another. The conclusion to this claim is that beneath the sound and fury of an imaginary 'great debate' lay the humdrum consensus on the need to defend and celebrate Western civilization as the highest normative referent in world politics. But while this rationale could issue an imperialist politics (as I explain in the next chapter), equally it could take the form of a critique of Western imperialism, as I explain in this chapter. Even so, for the defensive racists such as Stoddard and Grant such a critique was issued in the context of maintaining white racial supremacy. Moreover, behind the Marxist critiques of imperialism lay a defence of the West such that it constitutes the highest progressive referent of world politics. And though clearly anti-imperialist, nevertheless the Marxists joined hands with the liberal imperialists insofar as they all believed that the progressive re-making of the world could only be achieved by the actions and initiative of the progressive West.

With these five revisionist claims in place it is worth noting that a key purpose of this and the next chapter is to reveal how all four of the key Eurocentric/racist metanarratives underpinned much of Western international theory between 1914 and 1945. I shall focus on the Eurocentric and racist *anti*-imperialist theories in this chapter before turning to the imperialist theories in the next. More specifically, I focus in this chapter principally on the subliminal Eurocentric anti-imperialism of Lenin and the qualified anti-imperialism of the defensive Eugenicist racists, Lothrop Stoddard and Madison Grant.

Inter-war anti-imperialism: critical subliminal Eurocentrism

While there are a good number of anti-imperialist thinkers in the 1914–45 period, I shall argue that they not infrequently conformed to what I call 'subliminal Eurocentrism'. These comprised a motley crew of individuals who ranged from the left-liberal/socialism of Harold Laski (1933, 1940) and H.N. Brailsford (1915), through to the classical Marxism of Vladimir Lenin (1916/1973), Rosa Luxemburg (1915/1951) and Nikolai Bukharin (1929/2003). While the Marxists also drew from Rudolf Hilferding's pre-war book, *Finance Capital* (1910/1985), nevertheless the key thinker who underpinned these aforementioned thinkers in one way or another was John A. Hobson and his critique of *insane* imperialism. Also of note is the work of Leon Trotsky (1932–33/1967) and his theory of uneven and combined development, even though

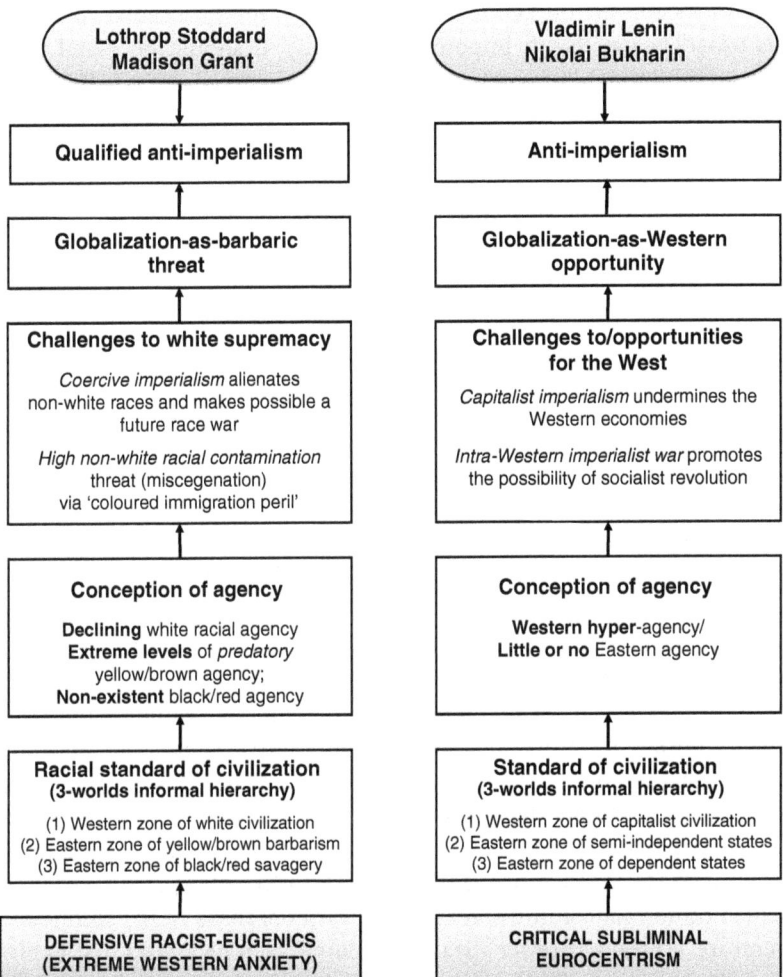

Figure 6.1 Defensive racism and critical subliminal Eurocentrism in the critique of imperialism, 1914–45

Trotsky had far less to say about imperialism than the others just mentioned.[123] Rather than focus on all of these writers in detail I shall

---

[123] The Eurocentric cue in Trotsky's theory of uneven and combined development is that it treats the original transition to capitalism in Western Europe in general and British industrialization in particular as something that was self-generated or *sui generis*, thereby reproducing the standard Eurocentric logic of immanence. Conversely the

hone in specifically on Lenin so as to establish the Eurocentric basis of this broad genre of anti-imperialism. Finally, it should be noted that because subliminal Eurocentrism is explained in detail in Part III of this book, and in Chapter 10 with respect to neo-Marxist IR theory, so I shall not detain the reader with a full discussion here. Suffice it to say, though, that in essence this brand is much more hidden and yet more subterranean than is manifest Eurocentrism, with the explicit language of 'civilization versus barbarism' missing.

Lenin: the Western behemoth and international relations as Westernization

Here my focus will be on Lenin's 1916 pamphlet, *Imperialism as the Highest Stage of Capitalism*.[124] It helps to begin by recapping the point that the key to Marx's Eurocentric theory of imperialism lay with his paternalist claim that the East is inherently incapable of auto-development and that accordingly, it is incumbent upon Western capitalists to deliver capitalism in the first instance through imperialist primitive accumulation. This was imperative since without capitalism, Eastern conditional agency meant that the East would not be able to progress into socialism and later communism and would, therefore, remain mired or imprisoned within the stultifying Asiatic mode of production. Lenin's version here echoes some of this but by no means replicates it. Certainly the all-important concept of the Asiatic mode of production is absent. But there is, however, a vagueness and ambivalence in Lenin concerning the propensity of the East to develop, which in turn has led on to much confusion and no clear consensus in the secondary literature. Anthony Brewer speaks for many when he argues that Lenin saw imperialism as effecting an acceleration of capitalist development in

---

Eastern states contributed nothing positive to world development in general or to European development in particular, and were condemned to copy, insofar as they could do so effectively, the achievements of the pioneering Western European societies (see also the discussion of neo-Trotskyism in Bhambra 2011; Hobson 2011b). The acute irony here is that one possible antidote to Trotsky's Eurocentrism lies with the application of his theory of uneven and combined development to the Western European societies in their transition to capitalism (see Hobson 2011b; Matin 2007, 2012; Shilliam 2009; cf. Rosenberg 2008).

[124] Note that Lenin was dependent upon Hobson's *Imperialism* as well as Bukharin's unpublished book manuscript, *Imperialism and the World Economy*. This book manuscript was completed in 1915 and Lenin had read it before he wrote his own treatise on imperialism.

the East (Brewer 1980: esp. 126–7), thereby implying a convergence with Marx. There are two references to this proposition. First, Lenin asserts that '[i]n these backward countries profits are unusually high, for capital is scarce, the price of land is relatively low, wages are low, raw materials are cheap' (1916/1973: 73). And second, he asserts that:

> The export of capital affects and greatly accelerates the development of capitalism in those countries to which it is exported. While, therefore, the export of capital may tend to a certain extent to arrest development in the capital exporting countries, it can only do so by expanding and deepening the further development of capitalism throughout the world (1916/1973: 76).

Nevertheless these two references aside,[125] thereafter Lenin develops a clear critique of imperialism.

As is symptomatic of subliminal Eurocentrism, references to racial difference or explicit 'civilizational' difference are all but absent. Instead, in critical subliminal Eurocentrism the East is portrayed as a helpless victim that is entirely defenceless and is stripped of both agency and dignity by a reified Leviathanesque West that struts the world stage like a Behemoth. Or, to use another analogy, the West is portrayed in effect as the engine room or cockpit of global politics and global capitalist development. Although neither Lenin nor Bukharin used the term 'globalization' it seems clear that their theories double up as a critique of incipient capitalist globalization not least because imperialism, like globalization, imposes capitalist exploitation on the East. Critically, imperialist globalization is recounted within what I call the Eurocentric big-bang theory of world politics (BBT). This comprises a two-step narrative where in the first step the West is understood to have endogenously self-generated through the Eurocentric logic of immanence, such that having risen to the top in economic and military terms the West then expands outwards across the world in the second step in order to remake the East in its own civilizational image and/or to exploit it for its own advantage. Put simply, the big bang of modernity explodes within Europe before European civilization expands or diffuses outwards to remake the earthly universe according to its own civilizational rhythm. In Lenin's version, this promotes a kind of Western 'Panopticon' or 'Big Brother' discourse, for having expanded outwards the West then entraps its Eastern victim in a kind of iron cage or steel net in order to control and surveil its each and every move. Indeed for Lenin, as for the vast

---

[125] Though he does make this argument elsewhere; see Lenin (1917/1975: 741).

majority of neo-Marxists,[126] the West is akin to a predatory vampire that sucks the life-blood out of its inert and dependent Eastern victim thereby leaving it exhausted and under-developed. I shall take the two steps of Lenin's Eurocentric BBT briefly in turn.

The first step concerning the Eurocentric logic of immanence is contained within the first three sections of his pamphlet, where Lenin focuses on endogenous developments within the West as a result of Europe's own exceptional properties. As is well-known, he discusses how the period of free competition within Europe was succeeded after 1873 with the rise of cartels which, in turn, intensified much further after 1903 into the full-fledged development of monopoly capitalism and 'finance capitalist combines' (the fusion of monopoly financial capital with monopoly industrial capital). Equally important is the emergence of capitalist crisis within the West, which exhibits a crisis of profitability within the context of rising levels of class struggle. Whether this is due to a 'crisis of underconsumption' (as in Hobson) or to the 'rising organic composition of capital' (as in Marx),[127] matters less than the point that both of these arguments presuppose that the causes of the crisis lie squarely *within* the West in accordance with the Eurocentric logic of immanence. Once capital becomes concentrated into a small number of gigantic combines, which is in full swing by the early twentieth century, so capital is exported to the backward countries in order to counteract the declining rate of profit at home; a process that constitutes the 'tap-root' of capitalist imperialism (to coin Hobson's phrase).

The second step of this imperialist-globalization theory, therefore, flows on automatically. This refers to the way in which Lenin portrays imperialism as that of the total domination of the East by the West. It is here where we encounter the 'Panopticon' or 'predatory vampire' discourse, wherein a dominant West sucks the lifeblood out of the East. Thus, citing Hilferding and echoing Bukharin, Lenin proclaims that 'finance capital does not want liberty, it wants domination' (1916/1973: 100–1). Moreover, in the 1920 Preface to the French and German editions, Lenin (as does Bukharin) takes issue with the notion that the export of capitalism and imperialism is a natural and 'civilizing enterprise', and views such a discourse as merely a form of bourgeois apologia

---

[126] One well-known exception which harks back directly to Marx's pro-imperialism is found in Warren (1980).

[127] See the ambivalent statement in Lenin (1916/1973: 73). See also the discussion in Brewer (1980: 111–12).

for both capitalism and imperialism. Clearly the irony that this so-called 'bourgeois criticism' would apply equally to Marx's conception of imperialism was lost on Lenin. Moreover, the irony that Lenin replaced this so-called 'bourgeois apologia' with an anti-paternalist subliminal Eurocentrism was also lost on him. For his Eurocentrism emerges in the point that he effectively awards the West a hyper-imperial agency while simultaneously relegating the East to all but its passive victim. Thus, he argues, using the building of railways in the colonies as a representative example:

> [A]s a matter of fact the capitalist threads, which in thousands of different intercrossings bind these enterprises with private property in [the] means of production in general, have converted this railway construction into an instrument for oppressing a thousand million people (in the colonies and semicolonies) ... Capitalism has grown into a world system of colonial oppression and of financial strangulation of the overwhelming majority of the population of the world by a handful of 'advanced' Western countries. And this 'booty' is shared between two or three powerful world marauders armed to the teeth ... who involve the whole world in *their* war over the sharing of *their* booty (1916/1973: 5–6, his emphases).

Or as he puts it later, 'finance capital, literally, one might say, spreads its net over all countries of the world' (1916/1973: 78), and that 'a financial oligarchy ... throws a close network of dependence relationships over [the whole world]' (1916/1973: 149).

Indeed, it is precisely here, in the context of the total subjection of Eastern countries, wherein his discussion of dependence resides. Thus

> [Western] finance capital is such a great, it may be said, such a decisive force in all economic and in all international relations, that it is capable of subjecting, and actually does subject to itself even states enjoying the fullest political independence. ... [F]inance capital and its corresponding foreign policy, which reduces it to the struggle of the [Western] Great Powers, for the economic and political division of the world, give rise to a number of transitional forms of state dependence. Typical of this epoch is not only the two main groups of countries: those owning colonies, and colonies, but also the diverse forms of dependent countries which, officially, are politically independent, but in fact, are enmeshed in the [Western] net of financial and political dependence (1916/1973: 97, 101).

In this characterization, then, the non-Western world is effectively presented as a large carcass that is tossed onto the Western table and whose belly is carved down the middle and divided up between the greedy Western capitalist predators. Both finance capital and its political representative (the Western nation-state) gain total control over an agency-less East in what amounts to a fetishized, anthropomorphic West.

The problem with this approach, indeed what ultimately makes it Eurocentric, is its inability to factor in even a semblance of Eastern agency within the narrative, either of a developmental or a resistance capacity. For it was the West that dictated the East's destiny. As one Marxist critic of Lenin not unreasonably concludes

> [i]t is perhaps remarkable ... that there is no mention in the section on colonialism in Lenin's pamphlet on possible resistance in the colonies, past or future. The world would remain divided, or would be re-divided, and all that the colonial people could do was wait for new 'owners' to appear (Hirson 1991: 4).

For Lenin, the 'new' owners were not so much the Western bourgeoisie but more the revolutionary vanguard of the Western working classes.[128] Tellingly, even when the debates on the question of colonial struggle took off in the early 1920s within Marxist circles, Lenin rigidly maintained his pre-1918 views. And moreover, the same conclusion applies to Bukharin (1929/2003: 176–7), though his overall analysis is focused even more on conditions within the West. Thus while Lenin and others are highly critical of globalization and imperialism, nevertheless in the last instance they serve a positive political function because in leading to war between the colonial powers an opportunity emerges for the making of socialist revolution in the West before it is exported to the Eastern societies. All in all, it is this very privileging of Western agency that leads me to conclude that the classical Marxists sought, perhaps unwittingly, to defend Western civilization as the higher normative referent in *progressive* world politics – even if this argument took a very different form to that which was advanced by defensive racist cultural-realism, to a discussion of which I now turn.

Qualified anti-imperialism and racist cultural-realism ('pacifist Eugenics'): Stoddard and Grant

As noted earlier, the 1914–45 period represented the climax – or the nadir – of Eugenicist international thought, and was articulated famously by Lothrop Stoddard and Madison Grant. The paradox, however, is that the

---

[128] See also Lenin (1915/1975: 631–2; 1917/1975: 741–2).

climax of Eugenics reflected not the moment of supreme white confidence but the most acute sense of anxiety regarding the future place and hegemony of the white race. And this paradox deepens when we recognize that the white supremacy literature was the logical expression of this underlying Western identity crisis (Bonnett 2004: chs. 1–2). Put simply, then, the label of triumphalist 'white supremacy' as it applied to much of the Eugenicist literature was an oxymoron. This racist anxiety could be expressed in either a pro-imperialist stance – as we shall see in the next chapter in the context of Adolf Hitler's imperialist Eugenics – or in an anti-imperialist stance, as I explain here. More specifically, I shall examine this racial anxiety in the ambivalent anti-imperialist work of Stoddard, found in various books the most notable of which is *The Rising Tide of Color Against White World Supremacy* (1920), while supplementing this with a brief discussion of Grant's seminal book *The Passing of the Great Race Or the Racial Basis of European History* (1918).

Although neither Stoddard nor Grant, of course, are considered as part of the IR canon, they are particularly interesting not just because they can be linked up with other 'pacifist Eugenicists' such as David Starr Jordan (pre-1919) but also because they link up with other defensive racists such as Spencer (1902), Sumner (1911) and Ross (1914). Of particular note here is that both Stoddard and Grant fit into what can be called 'cultural realism', which reaches back to the defensive racism of Charles Pearson (1894) and B. L. Putnam-Weale (1910), and forwards to the defensive Eurocentrism of Samuel Huntington (1996) and William Lind (1991).

Stoddard's book updates the dire prophecy that was issued by Charles Henry Pearson back in 1893 and upgrades that issued by B. L. Putnam Weale in his *Conflict of Colour* (1910). Moreover, as with Pearson – but also reminiscent of the offensive imperialist racists such as Mahan and Mackinder, Giddings and Powers – Stoddard's message is an alarmist one that in effect proclaims: 'White races unite – the Barbarians are coming!' And he upgrades their construction of 'globalization-as-barbaric threat', asserting that

> [t]oday the earth has grown small and men are everywhere in close touch. If white civilization goes down, the white race is irretrievably ruined. It will be swamped by the triumphant colored races, who will obliterate the white man by elimination or absorption ... Unless we set our house in order, the doom [of the white race] will sooner or later overtake us all (1920: 303).

Like all defensive racists, Stoddard's approach insists that the greatest threat to white racial existence, not to mention white racial supremacy, lies with the 'colored immigration peril'. For Stoddard in particular, the rising economic power of the East coupled with a demographic explosion of coloured races lies at the base of this threat. This is dangerous because should the coloureds be allowed access to the all-important white homelands (what he calls the 'inner dikes'), then the inevitable process of miscegenation will lead to white racial degeneration. Echoing Grant he advocates a 'world-Eugenicist solution', or what might be termed a 'world-apartheid solution', citing from Prescott Hall to the effect that 'immigration restriction is a species of segregation on a large-scale, by which inferior stocks can be prevented from both diluting and supplanting good stocks' (1920: 259). The eloquent terminology with which Stoddard paints his alarmist vision is poignant. Highly reminiscent of Pearson, he paints an image of the white races under siege and disunited within their inner sanctum, exacerbated by the Trojan horse of Western liberalism and democratic sentimentalism which, in betraying the cause of white unity and white supremacy, opens in insidious fashion the floodgates of the citadel to a tsunami-like wave of coloured peoples. He prescribes, in effect, a 'penultimate solution', prescribing that the whites must batten down the hatches, raise the drawbridge, huddle together in a revitalized sense of white unity and block coloured immigration. How then does Stoddard arrive at this conclusion?

In four separate chapters he constructs a hierarchical five-worlds picture with whites at the top, followed closely by browns (in Asia and North Africa) and yellows (in East Asia), with the largely degenerate reds (in Central America and the northern zone of South America) and the savage blacks (primarily in Africa) placed at the bottom given that their inherent stasis meant that they posed no threat to the white race (1920: chs. 4–5). Indeed the blacks are especially savage and primitive and have no 'constructive powers'; a fact which is confirmed by the point that they have contributed nothing to world-civilization. To the extent that Black progress has been effected at all, it has been merely as a result of the 'quickening powers' that brown-Islamic and white imperialism has bequeathed. Ominously, however, Blacks have a 'superabundant animal vitality. ... [based] on an intense emotionalism' (1920: 90), which accordingly makes them extremely susceptible to external influence (on which more later). The Reds were one notch up on the racial scale from the Blacks but their static and conservative nature meant that their achievements even at the beginning of the twentieth century ranked 'well

DEFENSIVE RACIST CULTURAL-REALISM   145

below [those] of European and Asiatic races in medieval and even in classic times' (1920: 126). And, in any case, Red racial unity had been lost to degenerate half-breeds through centuries of inter-racial breeding.

The key problem is the threat that the browns and yellows pose to the white race. Here he takes the notion of predatory Eastern agency to vastly new rhetorical heights, at least on a par with Charles Pearson and certainly above that which was awarded by Mahan and Mackinder (see pp. 87–89 and pp. 123–30, respectively, in this volume). A key reason for the issuing of his dire warning lies in his desire to upbraid the hubris of the white race, which rested on its laurels secure in the belief of white supremacy and brown/yellow racial inferiority.

> Too many of us still think of the Moslem East as hopelessly petrified. But those Westerners best acquainted with the Islamic world assert that nothing could be farther from the truth; emphasizing on the contrary, Islam's present plasticity and rapid assimilation of Western ideas and methods (1920: 60).

The various references to Henry Hyndman's *The Awakening of Asia* (1919/2010) are particularly interesting given that this text ascribes high levels of constructive agency to the Asians, thereby reminding us that Eurocentrism and racism do not always deny the non-white races and societies agency and can, at times, award them very high levels. Indeed, as Stoddard notes in his book *The New World of Islam*, Islam has not passively imitated the West but is attempting 'a new synthesis – an assimilation of Western methods to Eastern ends' (1922a: 50, also 1920: 229). Ultimately, though, for all its vibrancy and indeed creativity, Islamic agency is constructed as predatory, given his claim that 'Islam is militant by nature, and the Arab is a restless and war-like breed' (1920: 102). Likewise he views the yellows – the Chinese and especially the Japanese – as equally plastic and capable of significant material development, as well as being capable of inflicting imperial conquest upon much of the world.

Lying behind this racial analysis lies Stoddard's deep anxiety, if not sheer panic, which had emerged initially on the back of the Japanese victory over the white Russians in 1905. Indeed references to this 'seismic' event are peppered throughout the book, the most dramatic of which asserts that

> [m]ost far-seeing white men recognized [the Japanese victory] as an omen of evil import for their race-future . . . [The Japanese victory was] momentous. . . . for what it revealed. The legend of white invincibility was shattered, the veil of prestige that draped white civilization was torn

aside, and the white world's manifold ills were laid bare for candid examination (1920: 171, 154, also 12, 21).

The general direction of Stoddard's thinking lay in the perception that after 400 years of white racial pre-eminence during the Columbian Epoch, the Japanese defeat of Russia marked the very high tide of white supremacy, with only its subsequent ebbing away in prospect. For this event signalled in no uncertain terms the rapid and virulent rise of the yellow and brown tide.

As noted above, despite the fact that many 'far-seeing' white men perceived this Japanese victory as an omen, what concerned Stoddard most was the continuity of the belief that most Westerners held concerning the inviolability of white supremacy. Indeed Stoddard laments the point that 'prophets' such as Meredith Townshend and Charles Pearson have been largely ignored (e.g., Stoddard 1920: 151).[129] Seeking to puncture this bubble of white hubris he proclaimed that the white race must wake up and acknowledge both its relative and absolute decline. Regarding its 'absolute decline' Stoddard emphasizes its internal decay that he relates in terms of the Eugenicist emphasis on a demographically expanding white under-class and a shrinking white elite, coupled with the dysfunctionalism of 'socialist' state interventionism; something which is developed in detail in his book *The Revolt Against Civilization* (1922b). This was coupled by the decline of whites relative to the coloured races, with the latter not only expanding demographically at terrifying rates but, to compound the problem, the browns and yellows were also advancing rapidly in material power which served to fuel their imperialist desire to conquer new lands – especially in Latin America and Africa. Moreover, the demographic expansion of the browns and yellows fuelled the export of 'surplus coloured people' that washed up against the high walls of the white citadel.

While the pre-1914 situation witnessed a series of omens it was the First World War that issued a major blow to the cause of white racial supremacy. Stoddard's largely anti-war/anti-imperialist Eugenics, which echoed others such as Jordan and Kellogg, led him to emphasize the *dysgenic* effect of WWI as the best of the white stock was lost on the battlefields of continental Europe thereby resulting in 'a headlong plunge into white race suicide' (1920: 179).[130] Equally as problematic was that in general the war served merely to self-divide and conquer the unity and solidarity of the

---

[129] Townshend (1911/2010); Pearson (1894).
[130] Note that the term 'race suicide' was invented by Edward A. Ross in 1899.

white race. Here Stoddard describes WWI as the 'modern Peloponnesian War'; an argument which fed directly into the arguments of a string of 'pacifist Eugenicists' such as G. F. Nicolai (1918), Helene Stöcker and Alfred Ploetz, all of whom lamented the war on the grounds that it weakened and divided white civilized Europe. And this in turn feeds directly into his critique of the cause of national-imperialism; for it was the 'Prussian plotters of Weltmacht' whom he indicts for the conflagration that unintentionally undermined white racial unity while simultaneously enabling the coloured racial cause (1920: 175). Here he singles out for particular criticism the famous racist, Houston Stewart Chamberlain (one of the precursors to Hitler) and his Pan-Germanic propaganda. And, at this point, he also singles out Russian Pan-Slavism and the rise of Communism on the grounds that this dealt a similarly cruel blow to the noble cause of white racial unity (also 1922b: chs. 5–6). Ultimately he is highly critical of the cause of national-imperialism not for the destruction that it caused in the East but for the fact that it has shown a 'callous indifference to larger [white] race-interests' (1920: 204), effectively sacrificing white racial unity on the altar of arrogant and short-sighted national-imperial politics. What then is to be done?

Stoddard constructs a world in which the whites occupy the 'outer dikes', which comprise those areas where they have imperial control over coloureds, while the 'inner dikes' constitute the white racial homelands (Europe, North America and parts of South America, Australia/New Zealand and South Africa). His political prescription is to take on the majority of Western imperialists and to insist on the need for the whites to retreat from their imperial bases in Asia thereby leaving the land to yellow and brown rule. For as he explains elsewhere, while Western imperialism had been previously beneficial nevertheless by the twentieth century its repressive *modus operandi* served only to thoroughly alienate the rising brown and yellow races (1922a: ch. 3). And, in particular, because the yellow races had always sought to develop in isolation of others so he deemed it an egregious mistake that the white race had ventured there in the first place. Given the strength of these rising races and their desire for emancipation in the face of declining white vitality, the whites would be far better off relinquishing their imperial control of Asia. For this might also help placate these coloured races in the hope that this could act as an implicit quid pro quo for maintaining the security and purity of the inner white dikes.

However, despite Stoddard's general anti-imperialist thrust, his position in this respect is certainly qualified by the fact that he was not calling for a complete end to white imperialism. For, he insisted, the present white imperial strongholds in Black Africa and Red South America must be retained as strategic outposts that can act as giant barricades or breakwaters to any potential advancing brown/Islamic and yellow imperialist wave. And this in turn issued from his belief that 'Pan-Islamism once possessed of the Dark Continent and fired by militant zealots, might forge black Africa into a sword of wrath, the executor of sinister adventures' (1920: 102). For as noted earlier, the blacks are susceptible to this kind of external influence given their passivity coupled with their intensely emotional predisposition. Moreover, in Latin America too, which is populated by a similarly static, albeit highly degenerate, coloured race, 'the whites must stand fast – and stand together', in the face of an impending yellow imperialist invasion.

But to conclude it is useful to draw together the strong parallels between Stoddard's and Madison Grant's 'pacifist Eugenics'. Three areas are of particular note. First, Grant echoes Stoddard's ambivalent critique of white imperialism. Drawing on the familiar racist tropes of the perils associated with tropical climate and miscegenation, Grant argues that colonialism in Africa, Asia and Latin America has served only to weaken the white race (1918: ch. 7). He even goes so far as to argue that the Nordic race is unable to survive south of the line of latitude on which Virginia is placed owing to the detrimental impact of the hot climate. But like Stoddard, Grant produces an ambivalent and at times contradictory critique of white imperialism. In particular, he argues that the whites have successfully exterminated the natives of Australia and New Zealand and will accordingly play a significant role in the future history of the Pacific (1918: 70). And, although the climate of India undermines white genetic vitality, nevertheless he suggests at one point that colonizing India *is* possible so long as it is done by a very small group of Nordics who must keep away both from the native population for fear of racial contamination and from the degenerative effect of the sun's actinic rays.

A second parallel that exists between Stoddard and Grant concerns their peculiar brand of 'pacifist Eugenics'. As Henry Fairfield Osborn explains in the preface, for Grant '[w]ar is in the highest sense dysgenic rather than Eugenic. It is destructive of the best strains, spiritually, morally and physically' (Osborn 1918: xi). Grant also echoed Stoddard and the German 'racial hygienists' that culminated with Hitler's geneticdeterminism by believing that it is race that underpins everything in society and world politics. Indeed both Grant and Stoddard embraced the Mendelian laws of inheritance. Moreover, both shared a propensity for the politics of negative Eugenics. Thus the latter closed his 1920 book by prophesying that:

> We ... or the next generation will take in hand the problem of race depreciation, and segregation of defectives and abolition of handicaps penalizing the better stock, will put an end to our present racial decline ... Those splendid tasks are probably not ours. They are for our successors in a happier age (Stoddard 1920: 308).

And elsewhere he devotes a whole chapter to outlining a noble Eugenicist programme that the state needed to adopt (1922b: ch. 8). Likewise Grant insisted that

> A rigid system of selection through the elimination of those who are weak or unfit – in other words, social failures – would solve the whole question in a century, as well as enable us to get rid of the undesirables who crowd our jails, hospitals, and insane asylums. ... [T]he state through sterilization must see to it that his line stops with him or else future generations will be cursed with an ever increasing load of victims of misguided [socialist and liberal] sentimentalism. This is a practical, merciful and inevitable solution ... beginning always with the criminal, the diseased and the insane and extending gradually to other types which may be called weaklings rather than defectives and perhaps ultimately to worthless race types (Grant 1918: 51).

It was not surprising, then, that Hitler drew inspiration from Grant's book, which he described in a letter to the author as his 'bible'. And thus the irony emerges in the point that while Stoddard's 'qualified' anti-imperialist Eugenics led him to criticize the racial-suicidal actions of the 'Prussian plotters of Weltmacht', his ideas – and especially those of his mentor Madison Grant – helped provide part of the intellectual base that drove on the future 'Nazi plotters of Weltpolitik'.

Third and finally, both were major figures who railed against non-white immigration in the United States. For Grant like Stoddard insisted that miscegenation would always lead to the decline of the whites. But while this brand of cultural realism died with the Nuremburg Trials in 1945 it would re-emerge after the end of the Cold War, albeit in Eurocentric clothing, in the works of Samuel Huntington and William Lind (as I explain at the end of Chapter 11).

7

Racist and Eurocentric imperialism: racist-realism, racist-liberalism and 'progressive' Eurocentric liberalism/Fabianism, 1919–1945

Introduction: racist and Eurocentric imperial conceptions of world politics

In the introduction to the last chapter I laid out five key revisionist arguments that challenge the conventional 'mythical' historiography of 1919 and the interwar period. In this chapter I shall elaborate on several of those key claims, the first of which proposes that IR theory did not appear all of a sudden after World War I in some kind of miraculous virgin birth, but continued on from its pre-1914 roots in paternalist-Eurocentrism and offensive racism. And this in turn links up to my second revisionist claim: that interwar international theory was not monopolized by 'idealism' or liberalism because it also exhibited a vibrant racist-realist stream that had emerged after 1889 (as I discussed in Chapter 5). Notwithstanding the references to the usual suspects – Carr, Morgenthau, Niebuhr and Spykman – nevertheless, as Lucian Ashworth perceptively notes, what demands attention is the *silence* in the IR historiographical imagination concerning the place of realism in the pre-1945 era; an omission that is made all the more curious in the light of the conventional belief that the interwar period is supposed to have witnessed the so-called 'realist-idealist debate' (Ashworth 2011: 3).[131] Thus this discussion will provide further justification for the need to reduce the ontological status of 1919.

A third myth that I will challenge concerns the conventional image of interwar 'idealism' (or liberalism and left-liberalism). Rather than viewing it as entailing an optimistic vision of a world based on the inherent harmony of interests between cooperating self-determining states – a vision that is most closely associated with Woodrow Wilson – I seek here

---

[131] And for an excellent discussion of the realist political geographers see Ashworth (2011, 2012).

to reveal its dark imperialist side, which rests on the idea of Western hyper-sovereignty and the continuing denial of sovereignty to many of the Eastern polities. Paradoxically, my argument here dovetails to an important extent with Carr's critique of 'idealist' imperial politics. For his critique of the 'idealist' conception of the 'harmony of interests' is related directly to an imperialist political sensibility (Carr 1946/1981: 75–80). As he put it, the so-called utopian

> argues that what is best for the world is best for his country, and then reverses the argument to read that what is best for his country is best for the world, the two propositions being, from the utopian standpoint, identical. . . . British writers of the past half-century have been particularly eloquent supporters of the theory that the maintenance of British supremacy is the performance of a duty to mankind (Carr 1946/1981: 76).

Moreover, he closes this discussion by asserting that 'the English-speaking peoples have formed the dominant group in the world; and current theories of international morality have been designed to perpetuate their supremacy and expressed in the idiom peculiar to them' (Carr 1946/1981: 80). It is this part of Carr's vision of interwar liberal/left liberal IR theory that I draw out in the second and third sections of this chapter.

And finally, this in turn leads me to provide support for Carr's claim that interwar 'idealism' sought to maintain the status quo of world politics. For just as the defensive racists who I examined in the last chapter were wracked with high degrees of white racial anxiety, so the liberal-racist imperialists and many of the liberal paternalist Eurocentrics were no less profoundly anxious about the future of Western imperial hegemony in general and/or British imperial hegemony in particular.

Racist-realist imperialism: neo-Lamarckian Darwinism versus Eugenicist genocidal racism, c. 1889–1945

Here the majority of my focus will be on the generic school of geopolitics which includes Mahan and Mackinder – both of whom I discussed in Chapter 5 – as well as Ellen Churchill Semple, Nicholas Spykman, Karl Haushofer, Friedrich Ratzel, Rudolf Kjellén, Richard Hennig and 'ostensibly' Adolf Hitler. I shall also supplement this with the pre-1914 writings of Heinrich von Treitschke and Friedrich von Bernhardi. While it would be impossible to do full justice to all the twists and turns of this highly complex and heterogeneous body of literature in the half-century prior

CHAPTER 7: RACIST AND EUROCENTRIC IMPERIALISM

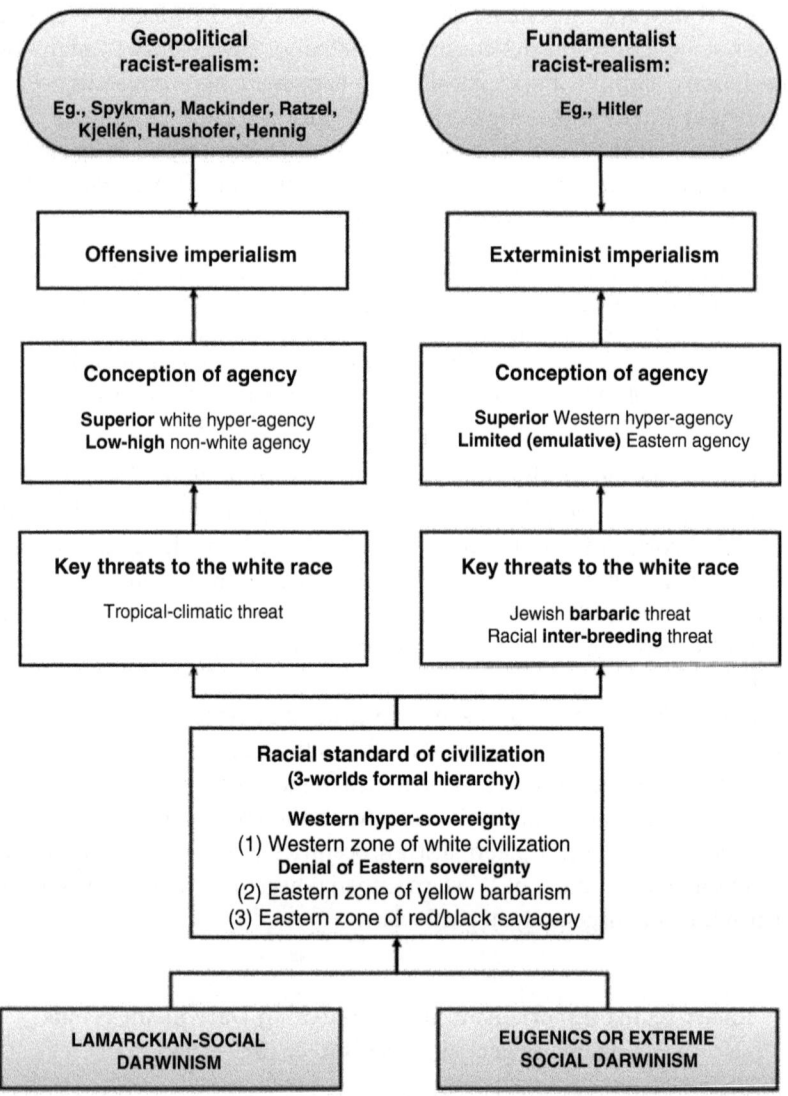

Figure 7.1 Racist-realist conceptions of imperialist world politics, 1889–1945

to 1945 in just one short section, I shall advance my analysis in three subsections. These focus in turn on the key propositions that: realism in its near-modern recognizable form existed in the half-century prior to 1945; that it gave rise to a *variety* of imperialist conceptions of world politics; and that the origins of these different conceptions derived in

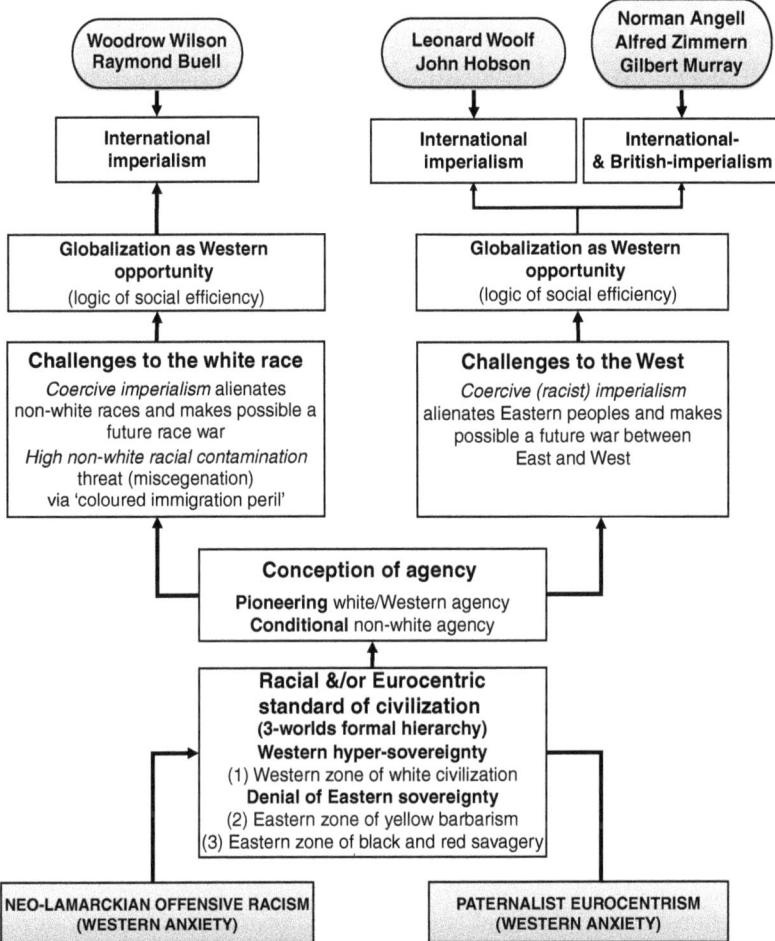

Figure 7.2 Offensive racist and paternalist Eurocentrism in liberal and Fabian interwar 'international imperialism', c. 1900–45

part from the competing strands of racism that underpinned these approaches. None of this is intended to smear realism *per se* as a racist enterprise, given that the classical realism of Carr and Morgenthau as well as neorealism in general exhibited subliminal Eurocentric, rather than racist, metanarratives. The wider significance of my analysis is that it counters the popular or conventional assumption that pre-1919 scientific racism in general, and the German school of *Geopolitik* in particular, followed a teleological path which steamed towards the terminus of

154 CHAPTER 7: RACIST AND EUROCENTRIC IMPERIALISM

Auschwitz. For scientific racist-realism was far more multivalent than this misconception recognizes. Although I have provided a summary diagram of this literature (Figure 7.1), I have simplified this so as to signal the point that racist-realism is essentially divided by two distinct racist metanarratives.

The political realist dimension of 'racist-realism'

Possibly the clearest statement of realist principles that would be most recognizable to a modern IR audience is found in Nicholas Spykman's racist-geopolitical book *America's Strategy in World Politics* (1942). Indeed his assertions in chapter 1 are virtually indistinguishable from the 'offensive realism' of John Mearsheimer (2001). Thus, for example, he asserts that

> The struggle for power is identical with the struggle for survival, and the improvement of the relative power position becomes the primary objective of the internal and external policy of states. All else is secondary, because in the last instance only power can achieve the objectives of foreign policy (Spykman 1942: 18).

And he goes on to assert the standard realist maxim that

> War is unpleasant, but it is an inherent part of state systems composed of sovereign independent units. To forget that reality because wars are unwelcome is to court disaster.... In a world of international anarchy, foreign policy must aim above all else at the improvement or at least the preservation of the relative power position of the state (Spykman 1942: 25, 41).

This 'offensive realist' strand is endogenized throughout the literature, albeit in a variety of ways. Von Treitschke asserts, for example, that '[t]he grandeur of history lies in the perpetual conflict of nations, and it is simply foolish to desire the suppression of their rivalry. Mankind has ever found it to be so' (Treitschke 1898/1916: 20–1). And in any case, should the state recoil from engaging in international conflict it would become 'an anomaly' and fall prey either to domestic anarchy or a foreign enemy (Treitschke 1898/1916: 15–16). Moreover, he insists that war and justice are chief tasks of the state, though these tasks 'are only conceivable where a plurality of States are found existing side by side. Thus the idea of one universal empire is odious' (Treitschke 1898/1916: 18–19). Such realist statements can be supplemented by Halford Mackinder who in his book *Democratic Ideals and Reality* pre-empts the thesis on the rise and fall of the great powers found in Kennedy (1988) and Gilpin (1981), to wit:

> The great wars of history – we have had a world-war about every hundred years for the last four centuries – are the outcome, direct or indirect, of the unequal growth of nations, and that unequal growth is [due to] the uneven distribution of fertility and strategical [sic] opportunity upon the face of our globe. In other words, there is in nature no such thing as equality of opportunity for the nations (Mackinder 1919: 4).

And last but by no means least is the racist-realist, Isaiah Bowman, who asserts that 'this is a *competitive* world, and to the costs of ordinary competition must be added the cost of the supreme competition of war. National and racial ambitions, hatreds, and rivalries will continue to the end of time, though they may be reduced in scope and intensity' (Bowman 1922: 11).

Some of the geopolitical thinkers portray the state as an *organism* (e.g., Ratzel 1898; Kjellén 1917; Haushofer 1938/2002), which requires living space (*Lebensraum*) that is commensurate with the vitality of the race existing within its borders. Thus successful races would require more *Lebensraum*, though as we shall see later, for many geopoliticians this rested on an environmentalist-racism rather than the genetic-biological conception that Hitler and other German 'race scientists' adhered to. Even so, there was certainly a number of important parallels, not the least of which is Hitler's claim that '[t]he State is only a means to an end. Its end and its purpose is to preserve and promote ... the race. ... Those States which do not preserve this purpose have no justification for their existence. They are monstrosities' (Hitler 1939: 330). And moreover, he describes a state as bad if it 'dooms to destruction ... the bearers of that culture by breaking up their racial uniformity' (Hitler 1939: 331). For the geopolitikers more generally, although international anarchy is important nevertheless it is the social Darwinian side of their theories which ultimately drives the conflict of states, conceived of as races and nations. Notable here is von Bernhardi's social Darwinian argument concerning the biological necessity of war:

> War is a biological necessity of the first importance, a regulative element in the life of mankind which cannot be dispensed with, since without it an unhealthy development will follow which excludes every advancement of the race, and therefore all real civilization. 'War is the father of all things'. The sages of antiquity long before Darwin recognized this. The struggle for existence is, in the life of Nature, the basis of all healthy development (Bernhardi 1911/1914: 18).

Accordingly, when seen in the round, these racist-realist theories overlap with but also depart from modern neorealism wherein international political conflict emerges as a *pure* function of anarchy and where 'race' finds *no* place (e.g., Mearsheimer 2001; Waltz 1979; Gilpin 1981).

Racist-realist imperial conceptions of world politics

One of the pervading themes of racist realism is the belief that large states are better than small ones. And greater size is to be achieved, of course, through colonization. Indeed von Treitschke spoke for many when he stated that the 'colonizing impulse has become a vital question for a great nation' (Treitschke 1898/1916: 115, also 221; also Bernhardi 1911/1914: 83). Colonization would not only benefit the colonizing state but it would also impart rapid economic development 'once the trained resources of labour and capital of a civilized nation are poured forth upon the virgin soil of a savage country' (Treitschke 1898/1916: 113). Nevertheless there is an indirect exterminist conception that von Treitschke adheres to, typified by his claim that Native populations are faced with a choice: 'extirpation or absorption into the conquering race'. And, he insists, '[c]ruel as these processes of transformation may be, they are a blessing for humanity. It makes for health that the nobler race should absorb the inferior stock' (Treitschke 1898/1916: 121). This is rationalized further by his claims that '[b]rave peoples alone have an existence, an evolution or a future; the weak and cowardly perish, and perish justly' (Treitschke 1898/1916: 121, 21). Overall, his imperialist dictum asserts that '[t]he rational task of a legally constituted people, conscious of its destiny, is to assert its rank in the world's hierarchy and in its measure to participate in the great civilizing mission of mankind' (Treitschke 1898/1916: 22).

The imperialist mandate was a staple of the school of geopolitics. The Germanic thinker, Friedrich Ratzel, expressed it thus:

> A great territory invites to bold expansion; a small one engenders a faint-hearted huddling of the population. . . . Just as the struggle for existence in the plant and animal world always centers about a matter of space, so the conflicts of nations are in great part only struggles for territory; and in all wars of modern history acquisition of land has been the prize to be gained by victory (Ratzel 1898: 449, 458).

One unifying factor that underpinned geopolitical thinking is that behind the politics of *Lebensraum* lies the old imperialist 'social efficiency' construct (which I examined in Chapters 2 and 5). One critic summarized the standard geopolitical formula thus: 'space and resources ... are wasted on those who cannot or will not exploit them. And should be given to those who will' (Paterson 1987: 112).[132] Moreover, Paterson reinforces this by reproducing a 1944 quote from Karl Haushofer: 'What is the ultimate goal of geopolitics? It is a fairer and better distribution of the world's living space, and of control over that space; a fairer distribution made in accordance with the numbers of each group and *their capacity for achievement*'.[133]

Nevertheless, while there are indeed various ideas that link up the different geopolitical and racist-realist thinkers, this should not elide the point that imperialism took on a wide range of forms. One reason for this is that different writers adhered to different forms of racism (as I explain later), while a second reason, of course, derives from the fact that they wrote from different nationalist perspectives. Thus the German racist-realists advocated German colonialism; the English such as Mackinder supported the British Empire; and the Americans supported US imperialism. A good illustration of this can be found by juxtaposing the vision constructed by the American geopolitical scholar, Nicholas Spykman, with that of the Germanic thinker, Karl Haushofer.

Writing in the middle of WWII Spykman constructs a potential imperialist conception of world politics that would emerge should Germany and Japan win the war. Here he constructs a coming 'yellow peril' argument wherein the Japanese are looking to threaten US security through their creation of an Asian imperial bloc. But he no less constructs a 'white peril' argument in which the potential of a Nazi empire that colonizes Europe and passive Africa looms large. The upshot of this is the possible geopolitical encirclement, and hence strangulation, of the United States. Thus to the west, he argues, might be the Japanese Empire in Asia and Australasia, while to the east might be the German Empire in Europe and Africa. Worse still, the Japanese would likely steal from the Americans their colonies – the Philippines, Guam and probably Samoa – while America's Open Door into China would be slammed shut such that the United States would unavoidably become dependent on Japanese goodwill for the strategic raw materials of the 'Asiatic Mediterranean' (1942: chs. 5–6).

Particularly important within this vision is the struggle for South America between the United States and the Nazi Empire (1942: ch. 7).

---

[132] A similar conclusion is reached by Jacobsen cited in Heske (1987: 136).
[133] Karl Haushofer cited in Paterson (1987: 112, my emphasis). And see the discussion in Heske (1987: esp. 136).

The thrust of the first half of the book asserts that the United States has developed and prospered owing to the stalemated balance of power between the great powers in Europe. But if the Nazis consolidate Europe into a single colonial bloc this breathing space that has hitherto nurtured the United States will necessarily be lost. And finally, a Nazi-Japanese pact would prevent the United States from playing off its encirclers who would be able to plot as one against the Americans. For Spykman it is imperative that the United States colonizes South America so as to provide a stronger economic pool that can promote American military self-sufficiency. Indeed, 'only the conquest of the [Western] hemisphere by the United States and the ruthless destruction of existing regional economies could bring the necessary integration' (1942: 451–2). Equally, should this possible future scenario of world politics not transpire, he advocates instead an informal US neo-imperialism in the world (Spykman 1942: 446–72).

A near mirror-image conception of imperialism is constructed by Haushofer, though it is also important to note that its details and racist origins differed considerably to that of Hitler's (as I explain in the next subsection). This is significant not least because Haushofer and Hitler are so often linked in the popular imagination. Thus Haushofer was adamant that an expanding imperialist Germany must form an alliance with Russia (which explains equally his joy at the formation of the Nazi-Soviet Pact in 1939 as much as his despair when Hitler broke that agreement in 1941). Moreover, he prescribed the formation of a German alliance with Japan, China and India in order to conquer space so as to defeat France and, above all, the Anglo-Saxon imperial powers, Britain and the United States. And finally, he prescribed that Japan should conquer Southeast Asia, the Philippines, the Dutch East Indies, Australia and New Zealand. Accordingly, his vision very much forms the counterpart to the vision that Spykman had constructed. Noteworthy here is that many of the German racist-realists, though preferring not to go to war with England, nevertheless came to realize that an Anglo-German alliance would not be accepted by the English. Accordingly, a key theme revolved around the need to defeat England so as to expand German colonial power and German *Lebensraum*.[134]

For Adolf Hitler colonization is, of course, a paramount objective of the German state. The precise details of his vision concern me less than its underlying racist aspects. Thus I shall leave aside the contradictions

---

[134] This was the central theme of von Bernhardi's book, *Britain as Germany's Vassal* (1912/1914).

within the Nazi vision of imperialism – particularly that concerning the conflict between the competing economic dimensions associated with the conceptions of *Lebensraum* and *Weltpolitik* that Woodruff Smith (1986) has ably drawn our attention to. And the point that he desired to create a Greater Germany that would link up all the German people, many of whom lived in Europe beyond Germany's borders at that time is in any case well known. Turning therefore to consider the racist origins of his vision it is notable that in *Mein Kampf* Hitler speaks frequently of the need to 'Germanize' other lands. Crucially, though hardly surprising, this 'culturalization process' did not imply any notion of a *civilizing mission* as it did for some racists such as Wilson and Buell, not to mention Reinsch (1905a, 1905b), Ireland (1905) and Sidgwick (1897) as I noted in Chapter 5. Socializing inferior races into Germanic Kultur was simply impossible. 'Germanization can be carried out only as regards territory but not as regards human beings' (Hitler 1939: 326). By this he meant that 'it is almost inconceivable how such a mistake could be made as to think that a Nigger or a Chinaman will become German because he has learned the German language' (Hitler 1939: 326). Such a process would serve only to bastardize Germanic culture; and in any case, a successful socialization/assimilation process could work only if 'that process could change the blood of the people who would be subjected to it, which is obviously impossible' (Hitler 1939: 326, 261). It would be impossible, Hitler reasoned, because miscegenation would lead only to the debasement or degeneration of the superior race: for 'hybrids ... are always in a state of cultural retrogression' (Hitler 1939: 327). This is important to note because it is this very racist idea which obviously played such a crucial role in determining his exterminist conception of imperialism.

The multivalent foundations of racist-realism

Hitler's uncompromising Eugenicist racial-biological fundamentalism has quite different implications for imperialist politics to that found in the school of geopolitics. The latter's emphasis on climate/environment coupled with its emphasis on social habits reflected a standard neo-Lamarckian-infused social Darwinism. Moreover, in clear contrast to Hitler's Eugenics, but in agreement with Gumplowicz and Ratzenhofer, Ratzel viewed race-mixing as producing fruitful outcomes while maintaining that races are not immutable as they evolve under environmental influence. And this in turn led in his case to reject the excesses of Hitler's vision (Bassin 1987: 119).

Various geopoliticians argued that exterminating inferior races could lead only to negative blowback for the white colonial races in the tropics. Thus Spykman argues that in

> the humid tropical zones only Blacks can do sustained manual labor, and on the high plateaus of the Andes physical work can be done only by native Indians whose barrel-shaped chests and enormous lung capacity are an indication of their adjustment to high altitude (Spykman 1942: 222).

The white colonizers must preserve such races if only to supply the labour-power that the whites are unable to provide, to wit: 'Except for central and southern Chile, all of South America's west coast lies in the tropics. Only high up in the mountains is the climate suited for permanent settlement by white men, and then only as employers of native labor' (Spykman 1942: 52). Haushofer made the exact same argument, and argued that even the indirect exterminism of the 'entombed races' upon contact with the whites constitutes a major problem for the latter. The task, he argues, is that

> Pacific problems are nothing else but a *regeneration question of the colored races*. Because in the long run only human beings with dark pigmented skin are competitive under the sun of the richest island region on Earth. Only they can work out in the open ... [For many areas] can simply not be developed fully without dark workers. This work force, however, is provided by the primitive substrata which can be sure of their resurrection in the new race mixture for this very reason (Haushofer 1938/2002: 61, my emphases).

The radical divergence concerning their chosen brands of racism was a key factor in why Hitler came to distance himself from Haushofer. A further difference lies in the point that one cannot find in Haushofer's writings a critique of the Jews; something which reflected the point that he had chosen to marry a Jewish woman.[135]

Most importantly this neo-Lamarckian based social Darwinism was widely deployed across the school of geopolitics in general, comprising the likes of Semple (1911), Spykman (1942), Kjellén (1917), Ratzel (1898), Hennig (1931), Bowman (1922), Mahan (1897) and Mackinder (1904,

---

[135] Added to this was that Hitler had Haushofer's son, Albrecht, executed for having had connections with the people who were involved in the failed plot to kill the Führer; see Heske (1987: 138–9).

1919).¹³⁶ Thus, for example, the American disciple of Ratzel, Ellen Semple, offered up a typical neo-Lamarckian statement on race-formation: 'In every problem of history there are two main factors, variously stated as heredity and environment, man and his geographic conditions, the internal forces of race and the external forces of habitat' (1911: 2).¹³⁷ This approach was also embraced by the man who was often referred to as the 'American Haushofer', Isaiah Bowman (1922), even though he renounced this term in a hostile critique of German Geopolitik (Bowman 1942),¹³⁸ and notwithstanding the point that Nicholas Spykman was much the better candidate for such a title. Some, though not all, of the geopoliticians openly criticized the genetic fundamentalism of Eugenics – Hennig and Ratzel being two notable examples. Moreover, they placed racial genetics in the distant background while very much foregrounding the effect of environment on race behaviour, all of which promoted a view of racial mutability (see Bassin 1987: 118–21). Interestingly, their racist approach overlapped with the neo-Lamarckian racist-environmentalists who worked within Political Geography, including William Morris Davis (1898), Albert Brigham (1903), Robert DeCourcy Ward (1908) and, most famously of all, Ellsworth Huntington (1915, 1919).¹³⁹ Note, however, that in this wider geographical literature the heavy emphasis on climate could also on occasion be turned into a critique of colonialism on the grounds that white residence in the tropics leads only to racial degeneration (e.g., DeCourcy Ward 1908: esp. chs. 7–8); a position that returns us to the anti-imperialists who I discussed in Chapter 4.¹⁴⁰

---

¹³⁶ See Campbell and Livingstone (1983); Livingstone (1992: ch. 7); Heske (1987); cf. Bassin (1987). For a more complex analysis of Mackinder's racism see Kearns (2004).
¹³⁷ See also the discussion in Peet (1985).
¹³⁸ On this see the discussion in Tuathail (1994: 320–5).
¹³⁹ Significantly, with respect to the critique of environmental-determinism Huntington stated in the preface to *World-Power and Evolution*: 'training, heredity, and physical environment are like food, drink, and air. One or another of these may be placed *first* according to the individual preferences, and one or another may demand more attention according to circumstances. It is idle, however, to say that one is any more important than the others. All are essential ... [T]raining, heredity, and environment receive exactly equal emphasis (Huntington 1919: 8, his emphases; see also Huntington 1915: v). A much clearer statement of neo-Lamarckianism would be hard to find! That said, later on Huntington turned to Eugenics, serving as President of the American Eugenics Society between 1934 and 1938, while also writing the book *Tomorrow's Children: The Goal of Eugenics* (Huntington 1935).
¹⁴⁰ E.g., Sumner (1911); Brinton (1901: ch. 10), de Gobineau (1853–5/1970); Knox (1850); Ripley (1900: esp. ch. 21); Jordan (1901), Blair (1899).

Hitler's Eugenicist approach did not dismiss the role of climate outright, but at most it comprised an 'intervening variable'. For he insisted that the unique Aryan capacity for civilization has always lain in that race's blood. And to those who argue that the pre-Christian Germans were barbarians he replies by saying that

> the severity of the climate that prevailed in the northern regions which they inhabited ... [initially] hampered a free development of their creative faculties. If they had come to the fairer climate of the South ... and if they had acquired the necessary human material – that is to say, men of an inferior race – to serve them as working implements, the cultural faculty dormant in them would have splendidly blossomed forth. But this [unique capacity] was not solely due to their northern climate. For the Laplanders or the Eskimos would not have become creators of a culture if they were transplanted to the South. No, this wonderful creative faculty is a special gift bestowed on the Aryan (Hitler 1939: 330).

Important to this particular racist argument is Hitler's claim that modern German national being is blighted by the lack of a uniform racial Aryan base given that Germany had admitted into its racial body politik various alien races, the most insidious and virulent strein of which is the Jew. Hitler's paranoid obsession with the Jews led him to construct a multidimensional conception of the Jewish Peril that was internally inconsistent and contradictory, one notable example of which was that the 'Jewish Peril' could take the form of the 'Jewish Bolshevik' one minute and that of the 'Jewish finance-capitalist threat' the very next. Indeed in Hitler's mind Jewish threats seemed to spring up anywhere and everywhere. But alongside the political aspect of the 'Jewish threat' was a strong racial component, the substance of which had in fact already been constructed by earlier anti-Semitic tracts.

Unlike some of the geopolitical theorists already discussed – for example, Mahan (1897) and Mackinder (1904) – Hitler was worried not so much by the 'coming yellow barbarians' but by the 'white Jewish barbarians already here in our midst' (see esp. Hitler 1939: 258–76). He writes of the insidiousness by which the Jewish race arrived in Germany many centuries ago, at first openly marking itself out as Jewish but then at some point hiding this in order to masquerade as German or, worse still, as Teutonic. Critically, the Jewish *racial* peril is manifested by the 'fact' that while the Jewish male reproduces only with his own race, nevertheless the Jew

> poisons the blood of others ... The Jew scarcely ever marries a Christian girl [in order to preserve Jewish racial purity], but the Christian takes a Jewess to wife. The mongrels that are a result of this latter union always declare

themselves on the Jewish side. Thus a part of the higher [Aryan] nobility in particular become completely degenerate (Hitler 1939: 264–5).[141]

Given Hitler's fundamental belief that the results of miscegenation always leads to a degeneration of the superior race, so he viewed this act as constituting 'a sin against the will of the Creator. And as a sin this act will be avenged' (Hitler 1939: 240). Critically, it is this racial contamination threat that made possible the Final Solution. Still, he believed sincerely that such an act would serve as a progressive good for the world in general and the Aryan in particular – given that the Aryan is the universal race. For he argued that should the Aryan 'be forced to disappear, a profound darkness will descend on the earth; within a few thousand years human culture will vanish and the world will become a desert' (Hitler 1939: 243). And this was premised on his belief that only the Aryan has a creative capacity to achieve civilization, with all others – the Jews in particular – having only an inferior imitative capacity. There is, therefore, much sense in a recent claim that Hitler adhered to an 'evolutionary ethical conception' of world politics, albeit the most tragic one yet conceived (Weikart 2011). For this in turn means that Hitler's *Mein Kampf* was not a set of random musings penned by a madman but was a text that stood firmly within the tradition of racist-realism.

Moreover, while Hitler's concern with the Jews was especially pronounced, it is worth noting that his anti-Semitic arguments were not original and so could not have been simply conjured up in a fit of madness, his extreme paranoia of the Jews notwithstanding. Daniel Gasman has argued strongly that much of Hitler's general ideological vision, including his racist approach, was derived from the founder of the 'pacifist' German Monist League, Ernst Haeckel (Gasman 1971/2004: esp. chs. 4 and 6).[142] One critical difference, though one that Gasman concedes,[143] concerns their differing stances regarding the solution to the 'Jewish problem'. For Haeckel was adamant that the Jews had to be *assimilated into* German society (Gasman 1971/2004: 158). But as I explained earlier, Hitler's brand of genetic racism led him to believe that 'Germanizing' the Jews was simply impossible, and was in any case to be avoided because the concomitant inter-breeding that followed would ensure only the degeneration of the Aryans. And this critical

---

[141] An argument that had been developed in detail much earlier by Houston Stewart Chamberlain (1910/1977: ch. 5).
[142] Though for an equally forceful renunciation of this link see Kelly (1971: esp. ch. 6).
[143] Gasman (1971/2004: 165).

difference points to the wider divergence between Hitler and Haeckel, where the former's direct exterminist racism contrasted with Haeckel's indirect exterminist brand.

Hitler's links to Houston Stewart Chamberlain, who devotes much discussion to the conflict between the Aryan and Semitic races in his two-volume set, *The Foundations of the Nineteenth Century* (1910/1977, 1912), are obvious. But less often commented upon is the link with Heinrich von Treitschke, who pre-empted many of the arguments that Hitler would deploy much later on. For example, in his book *Politics* (1898/1916: 278–301) von Treitschke argued that Jews never amalgamate with an alien people and 'wear their foreign nationality like a garment'; that they have a 'strong imitative faculty and no inward originating power'; that it had become apparent 'what a dangerous disintegrating force lurked in this people who were able to assume the mask of any other nationality'; and, last but not least, was his venomous claim that '[w]henever he finds his life sullied by the filth of Judaism the German must turn from it, and learn to speak the truth loudly about it'.

Here it is noteworthy that Hitler's extreme anxiety over the 'Jewish Peril' and the racial threat it posed for the Aryan emerged, of course, from his particular brand of anti-Semitic Eugenics. As I noted in Chapters 5 and 6, Eugenics was especially prone to constructing paranoid conceptions of a threatening Other. Proof of Hitler's hysterical paranoia concerning the dysgenic impact of the Jew upon the Aryan race lies in the simple point that the Jews comprised a mere 0.76 per cent of the total German population (Mann 2004: 141). Clearly Hitler's anxiety was inversely related to the demographic size of the 'contaminating threat' that the Jewish population allegedly constituted. But more confounding still is that if the Jews were a despicable race in part because they *mostly* insisted on maintaining their racial purity – something which had it been achieved by the Aryans would have been celebrated by Hitler – then this surely begs the question as to how such tiny numbers (which would have stood at most at 0.25 per cent of the total German population) could have been the source of the degeneration of the Aryans in the first place.

The key point for our purposes, though, is that in the light of this discussion it should be apparent by now as to why Hitler had such difficulty with the Lamarckian brand of social Darwinist racism that underpinned geopolitical theory. Indeed, the nub of the difference boils down to the point that

If traits could be acquired as the result of changes in the geographical environment or through socialization, and subsequently genetically passed on to future generations [as in Lamarckianism], then selective breeding would be an ineffective and otherwise doubtful technical application. Such a position ... was effectively excluded from German race science during the early 1920s ... By 1933 even the most remote suggestion that racial characteristics could be significantly altered through environment or education was considered to be, *ipso facto*, unscientific (Weinstein and Stehr 1999: 22).

Or as another expert notes more succinctly: '[u]nreformed geopolitics was regarded by the Nazi fraternity as placing an overdue emphasis on space and environment at the expense of inherent racial constitution' (Livingstone 1992: 247). In short, a *Judenfreie* world is only possible once it is accepted that races are the way they are 'because of deep, natural and unalterable genetic forces' (Weinstein and Stehr 1999: 34).

In this respect Hitler's brand of biological racism had far less in common with the German imperialist-geopolitikers and far more in common with the racial-determinist writings of Comte de Gobineau (1953–5/1970), the Germanic anti-Semitic imperialist, Heinrich von Treitschke (1898/1916), the pan-German anti-Semitic propagandist, Houston Stewart Chamberlain (1910/1977, 1912), as well as the qualified anti-imperialist Eugenicists, Madison Grant (1918) and Lothrop Stoddard (1920). And naturally, Hitler's Eugenics stood close to the German school of racial-hygiene – which included the likes of Fritz Lenz, Eugen Fischer and Erwin Baur –[144] which explains why something like 250,000 'physically defective' 'Aryan' *Germans* were 'mercifully culled' in the various Nazi Euthanasia Programmes (that went originally by the codename of T4).[145]

Liberal-racist and paternalist-Eurocentric imperialism, c. 1900–1945

As I explained in Chapter 5 the assumption that racist conceptions of imperialism are confined to right-wing realist thinkers elides the point that many liberals and left-wing thinkers embraced either various racist or paternalist-Eurocentric conceptions of imperialism. There I revealed how some liberals and socialists even embraced various 'exterminist'

---

[144] For a discussion of the connections between Hitler and the German racial hygienists see Weinstein and Stehr (1999); Weikart (2004: ch. 11).

[145] Taken from the street address of the Euthanasia programme's coordinating office in Berlin – Tiergartenstrasse 4.

brands of racist imperialism (i.e., Benjamin Kidd, Karl Pearson and Lester Ward). But while racist conceptions of imperialism were constructed by liberals and Fabians in the post-1914 period, these converged upon the less coercive conception of the *imperial civilizing mission*, in which the task of the West was to deliver the necessary rational institutions to the backward Eastern societies. This reflected the more progressive aspect of Lamarckianism, which differentiated them from the less progressive Lamarckian geopolitical realists. Here I remind my reader of the discussion in Chapter 1, which explained how Lamarckianism could yield a wide variety of conceptions of world politics. And this more 'progressive' application of Lamarckianisn, found in Wilson and Buell, converged with the interwar paternalist Eurocentric thinkers I examine below, while also being highly reminiscent of the pre-1914 works of Cobden, Bright, Angell and Hobson (see Chapter 2), as well as the racist-liberals such as Ireland, Sidgwick and, most especially, Reinsch (see Chapter 5).

However, the key difference here is that the interwar conceptions were based for the most part on the 'international imperialism' of the League of Nations Mandate System, notwithstanding the point that this idea was first mooted by Hobson in his 1902 book, *Imperialism* (Hobson 1938/ 1968). This formula, in principle that is, envisages that imperialism would be regulated and 'civilized' by the Mandate System so as 'to meet the interests of the Natives' (though, of course, such 'interests' were defined according to the Western standard of civilization). This argument might immediately be objected to on the grounds that these thinkers were not imperialist insofar as they believed that the formula which underpinned the League of Nations Mandate System constituted a genuinely *progressive alternative* to the old conception of national imperialism. David Mitrany was typical here when he argued that the Mandate System constituted a victory of international law over great power interests, such that the great powers 'have accepted of their own free will a restriction of rights acquired by conquest and placed their new acquisitions under the control of the League'. To this end Mitrany likened the Mandate System to an international commonwealth (1933: 79). But this system explicitly reconvened the very racist or Eurocentric assumptions that underpinned the old nineteenth-century conception of the civilizing mission. Indeed the Mandate System harked back directly to the 'trusteeship' conception of imperialism that was enunciated at the 1884 Berlin Conference and which was responsible for the imperial carve-up of Africa. Moreover, this conception also underpinned the idea of the British Empire. More specifically, the 'trusteeship' conception of the Mandate System rested on the paternalist Eurocentric and racist assumption that the uncivilized races were not yet ready to rule themselves and must therefore be held, as one postcolonial authority put it, in the colonial 'waiting room of history' (Chakrabarty 2000: 8-11). Accordingly, I believe it reasonable to conclude that the political project of the Mandate System was 'essentially colonialism in all but name' (Ambrosius 2002: 131; see also Tinker 1977: 33), even if its advocates believed sincerely that it would be far more humane than was its national imperialist predecessor.[146]

This 'international imperialist' vision provides a common denominator for many of these writers, linking up the liberal racist thinkers, Raymond Buell (1925) and David Starr Jordan (1919) with the likes of the paternalist Eurocentric Fabian thinker, Leonard Woolf. But there are two qualifications of note here. First, although Woodrow Wilson was an important figure in securing the Mandate System, he nevertheless constructed a racist conception of the 'national' civilizing mission in a series of writings that preceded 1919. And second, while various liberals such as Alfred Zimmern, Norman Angell, Ramsay Muir and Gilbert Murray embraced the idea of the League of Nations, they also argued for the continuity of the British Empire as a means of spreading peace and civilization across the world. This section is divided into two parts. Because of his iconic status as the most important interwar liberal, I shall begin by focusing on Wilson's imperial vision as the prime example of interwar offensive liberal-racism, before turning to consider Woolf and Zimmern as key exemplars of Fabian and liberal paternalist-Eurocentrism respectively.

The myth of Woodrow Wilson: the racist mission to 'Make the World Safe through Imperialism'

The received view of Wilson in standard IR historiography can be summarized by the claim that having sought to 'make the world safe for democracy' by sending the United States into World War I in 1917, his follow-up 'Fourteen Points Speech' to the US Congress in January 1918 placed the issue of national self-determination/anti-colonialism

---

[146] Though it is also notable that the failure of the League to realize these 'noble' ambitions prompted various liberal critiques; see Hobson (1921, 1932); Woolf (1933); Angell (1933).

and democracy at the centre of world politics. But this progressive and optimistic reading necessarily obscures the racist side of his politics that issued in no uncertain terms the need for a Western imperial civilizing mission in the primitive East.

The conventional benign vision of Wilson is problematized in the first instance by the complex goings on that culminated in his rejection of Japan's proposed racial equality clause in the final vote at the Paris Peace Conference. The obvious conundrum here emerges from the point that had Wilson been genuinely committed to the anti-imperialist idea of national self-determination then he would logically have had no problem in accepting the proposition. The question, then, is could this rejection provide a cue to an underlying racism in Wilson's politics? Circumstantial evidence for this is provided by a long list of racist policies and actions that Wilson had previously undertaken. Thus he had long been hostile to the 14th and 15th Amendments to the US Constitution, the sum of which gave the Negroes in the South the vote and various social and political protections. He also institutionalized the segregation of Negroes within his own Administration immediately upon taking office, informing various Black protesters that '[s]egregation is not humiliating but a benefit, and ought to be so regarded by you gentlemen' (cited in Lauren 1996: 89). This was in any case consistent with his banning of Black students from Princeton University when he served as its president, not to mention his decision to block the issuing of passports to many delegates who wished to attend W. E. B. Du Bois's Pan-African Congress in Paris, 1919, while simultaneously refusing to meet Du Bois as well as Ho Chi Minh. In this light, then, the rejection of the racial equality clause appears merely as another item in a long list of racist policies and actions. Actions and policies aside, though, this section hones in on Wilson's academic writings and argues that their racism helps explain why in the end Wilson played such a key role in denying the Japanese their wish. And it is within this wider racist context that we can make sense of his imperialistic vision of world politics that was institutionalized at the Paris Peace Conference.

While some historians would offer up non-racist reasons for the actions described above, such a response would necessarily ignore the fact that in his academic writings Wilson consistently deployed a neo-Lamarckian racism (Stocking 1982: 252–3). Reminiscent of Reinsch's neo-Lamarckianism, Wilson's racism was found in his belief that non-white races could be uplifted and prepared for future self-determination but only once they had been properly educated by the white colonial governors; a position which awards a *conditional* agency to the Eastern races. While this also resonates with the paternalist-Eurocentrism of Hobson and others, one key difference was that Wilson vehemently rejected non-white immigration into the West. All in all, Wilson's racist vision was based on a rejection of non-white immigration into the United States (and other 'white strongholds'); a containment of the Negroes in the southern states; and a paternalist civilizing mission abroad that would be secured through the independent oversight of the Mandate System.

Of course, this alternative picture of Wilson clashes with the conventional reading, which has been maintained in significant part by an overwhelming reliance on his Fourteen Points Speech; one that was highly ambivalent in any case since it did not stipulate self-determination for the non-white races. For when we examine Wilson's writings in the round, a clear offensive racist imperialist vision emerges; though this should perhaps not be all that surprising given that Wilson's politics typified the paternalist-imperialism of the American Progressive movement at the time (Leuchtenburg 1952). In particular, his political ideals were very much embedded within what one expert calls 'Wilson's historicism', and it is from this academic context whence Wilson's imperialism emanated (Ambrosius 2002: ch. 9). To be specific, Wilson's conception of self-determination and his views on imperialism can only be appreciated by understanding the racist 'historicism' of his theory of the state, found most clearly in *The State* (1898/1918) and *A History of the American People*, Vol. 5 (1902a).

In *The State* Wilson subscribed to the Teutonic race theory of the state that was developed by John Burgess and a host of other racist writers,[147] arguing that the development of constitutional states evolved over a period of millennia and that 'the lines of advance are seen to be singularly straight' (1898/1918: 534). His racist analysis asserts in particular that:

> In order to trace the lineage of the European and American governments which have constituted the order of social life for those stronger and nobler races which have made the most notable progress in civilization, it is essential to know the political history of the [ancient] Greeks, the Latins, the Teutons ... if not only, and the original political habits and ideas of the Aryans and Semitic races alone (1898/1918: 2).

Even so, he immediately discounts the role of the Semitic races on the grounds that their political development was secondary, for 'the main

---

[147] See Burgess (1890); Stubbs (1874), Freeman (1879), Strong (1889); Hosmer (1890); Fiske (1885).

stocks of modern European forms of government are Aryan' (1898/1918: 2). In essence, democratic genius is monopolized by the Teutons and Aryans, such that 'the Teuton brought into force, particularly in England, the principle of representation'. Indeed this fact is self-evidently

> familiar everywhere now that the world has gone to school to the English in politics ... [Representative institutions] were the peculiar fruit of Teutonic political organization. ... The Teuton seems to have known almost from the first: representation is one of the most matter-of-course devices of his mature polity, and from his the modern world has received it (1898/1918: 539–40).

And the parallel here with Burgess is striking when he announced that 'the race-proud Teutons ... preserved the Aryan genius for political civilization' (Burgess 1895: 406).

The thrust of the argument takes the 'fact' of Teutonic/Aryan constitutional achievement by the late-nineteenth century and then extrapolates it backwards all the way to Ancient Greece. He then traces the story of constitutional development forwards through the Romans, on to the Teutonic tribes that created feudalism and then on to British constitutional development from Magna Carta (1215) to the 1688/9 revolution, before culminating in the specific federal developments in Germany, Switzerland and the United States. In this way, a racist *logic of immanence* is constructed wherein democratic state-formation is seen to be an endogenous and wholly exceptional affair that unfolds only within the Aryan/Teutonic spaces of the West. The narrative can be likened to an Aryan/Teutonic relay race where the baton of political achievement and genius is passed from one member of 'team Teuton' to the next, with each subsequent runner taking forward the gains of the former. Complementing this story of political genius is the denial of Eastern political auto-development, with political stagnation being the lot of the non-white races. The Chinese and Indian races were 'stagnated nationalities', and their countries became backwaters, isolated from the mainstream of white success. 'China's wall had shut her in to a safe stagnation of monotonous uniformity', mainly because the 'Chins' had been conquered by backward races (1898/1918: 20).

His racist historical conception of political development is then taken forward in volume 5 of *A History of the American People* (1902a), as well as in his article in the *Atlantic Monthly* entitled 'The Reconstruction of the Southern States' (1901a). Both of these writings focus on the era of 'Reconstruction' following the American Civil War (1867–77). The overall argument dovetails with others that also appeared at this time, wherein '[t]he studies of Reconstruction which began to appear ... after the beginning of the twentieth century reflect among the historians mainly a criticism of the North for having allowed the Negroes in the South to vote and a sympathy for the South in having disenfranchised them' (Gossett 1997: 284). Indeed this is the abiding theme of Wilson's 300-page volume. Thus he viewed the result of the 14th and 15th Amendments as but the 'ruin' of the South, much as Burgess (1902) viewed them as a 'monstrous' action on the part of the Northern federal government. When the Southern states fought back and disenfranchised the Negroes so the former came into direct political conflict with the Northern federal government. Until they accepted these Amendments they would not be allowed to re-enter the Union and the white senators were effectively disenfranchised. Wilson's gloss on these developments was expressed thus: '[t]he first result of the Reconstruction under the Acts of 1867 was the disenfranchisement ... of the better whites and the consequent giving over of the Southern governments into the hands of the negroes' (1901a). And he insisted that once the legal means for the Southern states to exercise political control had been stripped away in the face of Federal government protection of the Negroes, so the whites had 'no choice' but to pursue extra-legal means, which included the formation of the Ku Klux Klan in 1867 (1902a: 59ff). This was rationalized accordingly: 'The white men of the South were aroused by the mere instinct of self-preservation to rid themselves, by fair means or foul, of the intolerable burdens of governments sustained by the votes of ignorant negroes and conducted in the interests of [Negro] adventurers' (1902a: 58). Later on, he sums up the period of Reconstruction in similar terms: 'It was plain to see that the troubles in the Southern States arose out of the exclusion of the better whites from the electoral suffrage no less than from the admission of the most ignorant blacks' (1902a: 82).

In his aforementioned cited 1901 article Wilson's racism was expressed in acerbic terms. Thus he asserted that:

> An extraordinary and very perilous state of affairs had been created in the South by the sudden and absolute emancipation of the negroes, and it was not strange that the southern legislatures should deem it necessary to take extraordinary [i.e., extra-legal] steps to guard against the manifest and pressing dangers which it entailed. Here was a vast 'laboring, landless homeless class', once slaves, now free; unpractised in liberty, unschooled in self-control; never sobered by the discipline of self-support, never established in any habit of prudence; excited by a freedom they did not understand, excited by false hopes; bewildered and without leaders, and

yet insolent and aggressive; sick of work, covetous of pleasure – a host of dusky children untimely put out of school (1901a).

Given that the era of Reconstruction came to an official close in 1877, it might be anticipated that Wilson's commitment to democracy would prompt him to celebrate the extension of the franchise to all groups. And indeed he celebrated the end of Reconstruction when the Southern states were readmitted into the Union, but he did so for the very inverse reason: that this era was happily resolved by the end of the century as the Southern states adjusted their electoral suffrage so as to 'exclude the illiterate negroes and so in part undo the mischief of Reconstruction [while] the rest of the country withheld its hand from interference' (1902a: 300).

Apart from Wilson's explicit racism, the highly qualified notion of democracy that he subscribed to is worth considering a little further. His desire to exclude the Negro race was based in part on a racist predisposition of course, but it also emanated from his elitist and conservative conception of democracy. As Ido Oren observes, Wilson's notion of democracy did not extend to universal suffrage and he was untroubled by the disenfranchisement of the Blacks in the South. He believed squarely in the top-down educative role of a political elite that exercised leadership on the basis of efficiency and 'character' (Oren 2003: 33–46). Wilson's vision of international politics in one key respect drew on the analogy of his domestic political vision, wherein his notion of 'character' was crucial to his theory of imperialism. For Wilson, character was synonymous with 'self-control and self-discipline'; and he saw these as *the* vital pre-requisites for democracy. Echoing the imperialist theory of John Burgess, Wilson believed that while the Aryan/Teutonic races had demonstrated the highest levels of character, nevertheless with the proper tutelage the non-European races could, albeit over a long period of time, be imbued with this quality. It was this very idea that formed the neo-Lamarckian foundation of his approach to imperialism.

While conventional IR historiography assumes that Wilson's conception of self-determination was anti-imperialist, the logic of his writings clearly suggest otherwise. In a 1902 article in the *Atlantic Monthly*, 'The Ideals of America', Wilson insisted that the colonization of the Philippines constituted a critical means by which the Filipinos could be uplifted towards civilization. There he concludes that the Filipinos 'must first take the discipline of law, must first love order and instinctively yield to it. We [the Americans] are old in this learning and must be their tutors' (1902b). Specifically, he argues that if the Americans can teach the Filipinos the noble ways of discipline and self-government – including justice and fairness in administration – so this 'will infinitely shorten their painful tutelage ... We must govern as those who are in tutelage. They are children and we are men'. In essence he argues that the Americans cannot 'give the Philippines independence/self-government now. To do so would be to leave them like a rudderless boat adrift'. Above all, self-government cannot be simply 'given' but must be earned, graduated into from the hard school of life.

The key idea – that of 'graduating' into self-government through imperial tutelage – means that self-determination for the colonized peoples would have to be postponed. This reflects his argument that constitutional political development is something that occurs over a very long period of time, as he argued in the case of Teutonic/Aryan constitutional state-formation in *The State*, as much as it reflected his neo-Lamarckianism in which race progress can be achieved but only very gradually. And it was precisely this gradualist idea that underpinned his understanding of the League of Nations Mandate System. For Wilson's paternalist racism was stamped all over Article 22, which spoke of 'peoples not yet able to stand by themselves'; 'that well-being and development of such peoples form a sacred trust of civilization'; and that 'tutelage should be exercised by [the colonial powers] as Mandatories on behalf of the League'.

While the Mandate System was thought to provide a much more empathic internationalized form of imperialism it was, as I noted earlier, premised on the same principle of the old national form of civilizing mission – specifically paternalism and the 'sacred trust of civilization'. And significantly, at the Paris Peace Conference Wilson was prepared to countenance self-determination only for the East and East-Central European peoples, whereas with respect to the non-European peoples, as 'in the Philippines earlier, he applied the principle of national self-determination with great caution. He did not undermine British rule in Ireland, Egypt and India, or French rule in Indochina' (Ambrosius 2002: 130). Moreover, the German colonial spoils were simply carved up and thrown to various Western powers (as well as Japan). In short, Wilson expected the great Western powers 'to fulfil the same [civilizing] mission in their League Mandates that the United States had assigned itself in the Philippines' (Ambrosius 2002: 130–1). Indeed Wilson viewed the Mandate System as an altruistic contribution to the Eastern societies on the part of the Western colonial powers: 'It is practical ... and yet it is intended to purify, to rectify, to elevate' (Wilson cited in Ambrosius 1987: 78).

Wilson's position is aptly summarized by Gordon Levin, who notes that unlike Lenin, 'Wilson was not prepared in the immediate post-war period to challenge the entire imperial system with a call for the instantaneous and universal establishment of self-determination for all colonial peoples'; and that 'Wilson was more opposed to the form than to the substance of the existing economic and political hegemony of the West in the international arena' (Levin 1973: 248, 249). Notable here is Wilson's response to Jan Smuts' desire for South West Africa to be 'annexed' by the Union of South Africa, stating that he 'could not return to America with the world parcelled out by the great powers' and instead advanced the more politically acceptable proposition that 'the fundamental idea would be that the world was acting as trustee through a mandatory' (Wilson cited in Alexandrowicz 1971: 157). In conclusion, then, it seems clear that Wilson's core objective was to keep the world safe for (Western) imperialism.

Having reached this point I now return to where I opened this discussion by considering the reasons for Wilson's rejection of the Japanese-proposed racial equality clause. Space does not permit an extended discussion of the various detailed goings on that surround this issue.[148] But the essence of the story is that Wilson, in collusion with his key adviser Colonel Edward House, having strung the Japanese along during the negotiations declared the defeat of the motion on the grounds that it was not unanimously approved. This shocked the delegates and it was pointed out by a French lawyer that on two previous occasions, when a vote was taken on an issue that was close to Wilson's political heart, the motions were passed according to a majoritarian rather than unanimous vote. Some historians might respond by arguing that Wilson's hand was forced by the implacable resistance to the clause made by Australia's Prime Minister, Billy Hughes and, though less vociferously, by Lord Robert Cecil and General Jan Smuts. And they might also point out that the racist policies and actions that Wilson had taken throughout his career were one way or another forced upon him by political pressures at home. But it should be obvious by now that even if all this did indeed press upon his mind, nevertheless Wilson's rejection of the clause was entirely in keeping with his racist worldview.

---

[148] For a full discussion see Lauren (1996: ch. 3); Allerfeldt (2004); Lake and Reynolds (2008: ch. 12).

The main objection to the passing of the racial equality clause was that it would not only threaten imperialism but that it would trigger unmitigated non-white immigration into the United States, Britain, Australia and South Africa. Such a fear, however, was one that was also felt deeply by Wilson. Indeed, in the aftermath of the Californian Alien Land Bill (1913), which denied Japanese and Chinese the right to naturalize and to own land, Wilson stated that:

> In the matter of Chinese and Japanese coolie immigration I stand for the national policy of exclusion. The whole question is one of assimilation of diverse races. We cannot make a homogeneous population out of a people who do not blend with the Caucasian race ... Oriental Cooleism will give us another race problem to solve and surely we have had our lesson (Wilson cited in Lake and Reynolds 2008: 271).[149]

In short, Wilson was as opposed to a potential wave of non-white immigration into the United States as was the political constituency that supposedly *forced him* to 'compromise his ideals'. But this in turn begs the question as to whether the rejection of the racial equality clause compromised his proclaimed objective of self-determination for all peoples. The problem with this question, though, is that Wilson did not have to effect a compromise given his belief that non-Western countries should be denied self-determination as they undergo the necessary corrective 'surgery' through international imperialism. In short, Wilson's conception of imperialism logically demanded that he reject the Japanese racial equality proposal not least because the demise of racism would inevitably trigger the unacceptable termination of Western imperialism in the world.

Leonard Woolf: Fabian paternalist Eurocentrism, international imperialism and the sane civilizing mission

Although the Fabian thinker, Leonard Woolf (1880–1969), is usually thought of as an anti-imperialist, nevertheless a clear argument for international imperialism emanates from his paternalist-Eurocentrism. In Woolf we find both prongs of Hobson's thought on imperialism: a critique of insane economic national-imperialism that is found in

---

[149] Once again, the parallel with Burgess is striking when he stipulates that the United States must not allow foreign non-Aryan races to 'pollute' the American nation; something which he describes as not only 'wicked' but 'sins of the highest order' (Burgess 1895: 407).

Empire and Commerce in Africa (1920),[150] and a commitment to a sane international imperialism that would be regulated by the League of Nations in his *Imperialism and Civilization* (1928/1933).

Interestingly, Woolf's sane imperialism is developed in the context of a strong critique of scientific racism. Thus he asserts that

> Nine-tenths of what is said and written about race and racial conflicts, about the inferiority and superiority of races, and about their inherent antipathies, is unmitigated nonsense, and any publicist who pretends to explain large conflicts between States or within States by racial differences which are physical differences should be viewed with the greatest suspicion (1928/1933: 19).

Rather, he insists that 'racial conflict is only a symptom on the surface, and that the real cause is the clash of civilizations under the impetus of [economic] imperialism and the reactions of the Far East against the imperialist West' (1928/1933: 20–1). The clash of civilizations is not the result of racial difference but is a product of Western coercive imperialist domination, leading him to conclude that Eastern resistance is entirely understandable since it constitutes a natural 'reaction against domination and exploitation of one civilization and one people over another. There is nothing racial in it except upon the surface' (1928/1933: 22).

But while Peter Wilson is surely correct to argue that Woolf refused 'to put the parlous condition of the African down to race or colour' (Wilson 2005: 139), this should not imply that he subscribed to some sort of cultural pluralist tolerance. Woolf's paternalist Eurocentrism yields the conceptions of Western hyper-agency and African conditional agency:

> One peculiar thing ... is that the political good and evil fortune of [Africa] and of its millions of inhabitants has been determined, during the last three hundred years, mainly from outside, by the social and economic ideals and philosophy of alien white men ... [Nevertheless] if they had had the psychology of European civilization instead of African savages, they would never have fallen under the dominion of Europeans. But the psychology of the African has been only the passive agent in the making of his life and history; the active agent has been the beliefs and desires of Europeans (1920: 352).

And, he insists, those who argue that Africa was better off before the Western imperialists arrived, enjoying a kind of historical Golden Age

---

[150] And for an excellent summary see Peter Wilson (2005: 120–32).

are wrong. There have been no Golden Ages of uncivilized peace and innocence... in the continent which was scourged by the slave trade. The African was a savage with all the vices of savagery. Not satisfied with the perpetual and unavoidable sufferings which Providence inflicts upon their species [the Africans] contrived to make their own and their neighbours' lives as miserable as possible (1920: 354).

Not surprisingly, in echoing Hobson's critique of insane imperialism, he insists that withdrawing from Africa should be avoided because this would enable the unregulated exploitation of Africa by Western capitalists to the detriment of the Africans. Here his Eurocentric denunciation of African societies is important.

There is no doubt that non-adult races like the Africans suffer worse things when they are left under 'independent' rulers to deal with white traders and financiers, than when the white man's State intervenes and conquers the African's country. Such intervention has, in fact, always proved to be inevitable (1920: 354).

In the face of this, Woolf's paternalism leads him to prescribe an 'ideational revolution' in the mentality of Westerners regarding Africa, the sum of which calls for an end to the mentality of treating Africa as a site for exploitation – or, to borrow Brailsford's (1915) term, as a site of 'human cattle farms' – as well as the political solution of governing Africa as a trusteeship. And like Buell, Reinsch and Hobson, so Woolf insists that trusteeship must entail *selective* rather than total assimilation of Africa to Western ways. For example, the African should be allowed to return to the communal system of land tenure given that Africans are too primitive to set up a system of private property or develop their lands autonomously. All in all, Woolf's arguments culminate in the support for the League of Nations Mandate System (1920: 364–8). And while it is the case that for Woolf international imperialism would be a temporary phenomenon, nevertheless even as late as 1943 he maintained that independence for Africa would still be highly premature (see Wilson 2005: 140).

Alfred Zimmern (Gilbert Murray and Norman Angell): restoring the British Empire in the face of racial revolt

It is important to correct the common misconception that interwar liberals placed all their political chips on the roulette wheel of the League of Nations as the means to create a more peaceful and prosperous world. For some of the most significant figures argued that the League was a necessary but insufficient factor, given that peace, prosperity and civilization could only be secured if the British Empire worked alongside the League. Norman Angell was one such figure, laying out his case in article-form (Angell 1931) as well as in his book, *The Defence of the Empire* (1937). However, because this updated the case he made for the British Empire in his 1913 book, *The Great Illusion*, the details of which I discussed in Chapter 2, I shall instead concentrate on Alfred Zimmern's defence that was advanced in his book *The Third British Empire* (Zimmern 1934). And I shall supplement this with some of the relevant arguments that Gilbert Murray made.

Far from espousing an optimistic and rosy scenario for the future, the immediate context of Zimmern's argument lay in the massive dent to Western self-confidence that the First World War and the Eastern revolt against the West imparted (as it did for many other interwar writers). Jeanne Morefield's eloquent summary here is noteworthy:

> Murray's and Zimmern's writing in the wake of the Great War suggest that they experienced [a] loss of racial identity acutely. Their prose were redolent with anxiety, heavy with the sense that Western culture was under attack. The hum of fear – of the encroaching 'Oriental mind', that the 'immense number of different breeds of men' were becoming less differentiated, that the war had shifted world power away from Europe and toward the 'politically immature peoples' of the world – played like a constant low drone throughout their work (Morefield 2005: 108).[151]

Zimmern himself testifies to the early birth of his anxiety vis-à-vis the 'Eastern threat':

> [T]he white man's prestige, in the old sense of the word, has become greatly weakened. That prestige, which was based on science/invention is weakened because the East has unlocked the secrets of the Western laboratory. This was demonstrated for all the world to see a generation ago, in the Russo-Japanese War. Well do I remember, as though it were yesterday, the impression made upon my mind when, as a young lecturer in Ancient History at Oxford, I read of the first great victory of the Japanese over the Russians. I went into my class and told them that I was going to lay aside Greek history for that morning, 'because', I said, 'I feel I must speak to you about the most important historical event which has happened, or is likely to happen, in our lifetime, the victory of a non-white people over a white people' (1934: 109).

---

[151] For Gilbert Murray, the racial threat was akin to a kind of 'Satanism', where '[s]atanic forces included all phenomena that threatened the imperial order, the movement of free trade and the idea of Western civilization' (Morefield 2005: 113).

It was this anxiety that led Zimmern to argue for the need to restore the British Empire. In essence he argues that the second phase of the Empire, which ran from 1776 through to 1919, was successful insofar as it promoted progressive world politics and governed the colonies as a form of trusteeship. Its success was partly reflected by the loyalty it commanded from the grateful colonial subjects, as well as constituting a harbinger of the idea of the Mandate System (1934: 11-12, 103-4, 106). One of the key factors that enabled this colonial loyalty was the prestige of the English gentleman, for it was this that constituted the legitimizing glue which sealed the Second Empire together. No doubt reflecting his Oxford identity, he asserts that

> The English gentleman represents a specific and clearly marked type of civilized humanity ... For courage, for honour and loyalty, for tolerance, for wisdom and calm judgment, for self-control in emergencies, I doubt whether the world has ever seen his equal ... The English gentleman has been, in fact, an unrivalled primary teacher of peoples (1934: 102-3).

Zimmern rejects the defensive racism of the likes of Blair, Spencer, Sumner, Stoddard, Grant and Ross, all of whom demand the separation of races from each other, arguing instead that what makes the British Empire the most special of all empires is that it allows for an amalgamation of races (1934: 167-74); to wit: 'the British Empire is ... the greatest political community the world has ever seen [because] it is also the most diversified' (1934: 6). But in addition to the problem of the declining prestige of the white English gentleman, the arrival of the League has led to the lamentable appropriation of many of the functions of the Second British Empire, prompting his rhetorical question: '[r]obbed of its special tasks of yesterday, our British genius needs new worlds to conquer. Our energy, our experience, our public spirit, our immense goodwill – how are we to employ them? (1934: 107). And he replies that 'the great task that lies before us in this generation [is that] of ensuring the peace of the world' (1934: 108).

Zimmern's principal concern is that of a potential coming race war. Indeed '[t]he race question, stirring as it does some of the most elemental of human passions, is the most urgent problem of our time ... It cannot be evaded ... It must be faced in all its unpleasantness – or the consequences of neglecting it will be a thousand times more unpleasant' (1934: 109). Interestingly, he argues that the causes of war are based on three prime factors: the racial conflict between whites and non-whites; the economic relations between the haves and have-nots; and the differences between the civilized and uncivilized peoples. How then is the race question to be solved? Notable here is that Zimmern critiques the racist claim that the Eastern peoples are incapable of being uplifted – articulated by the likes of the Eugenicist thinkers Karl Pearson (1905) and David Starr Jordan (1901) – on the grounds that were it to be true it would be a 'terrible tragedy'. For it would imply that the non-white peoples were 'stricken by an incurable infirmity', which in turn would 'throw an intolerable strain upon the superior race' precisely because '"[t]he white man's burden" would become almost too heavy to be borne. Happily the truth is otherwise' (1934: 112–13). For the fortunate fact is that the 'inferior' races are deemed capable of learning under the tutelage of the British – the very essence of the idea of 'conditional Eastern agency' that finds its clearest expression in paternalist Eurocentric institutionalism.

While the League was important for securing world order, nevertheless it was a necessary but insufficient component not least because it would require civilized nations to share power with non-white peoples (Morefield 2005: 137, 142). Only by restoring the legitimacy of the British Empire, through its evolution into a third phase, could world order and civilization be properly secured. This third phase comprised the form of a Commonwealth of Nations in which its members enjoy considerable autonomy. Nevertheless, this idea was to apply only to the white dominions, such that non-white colonies were to be retained in a formal dependent relationship (see also Morefield 2005: 146). Either way, though, the restoration of the legitimacy of the British Empire was vital for world order because the League could not act as *the* guarantor of world peace, though equally the Empire required the League. The British Empire, he argued, 'must survive as a league within the larger League ... Only in and through the League can the [Empire] solve its problems of to-day and take up the tasks reserved for it to-morrow' (1934: 75). Because the Empire is founded on law and liberty this enables it 'to set an effective standard for mankind' (1934: 87). Above all, he asserts:

> The work that the British Empire is called upon to do is to preserve the peace of the world. [It] is the surest bulwark against war in the present-day world – for this generation, at any rate, a surer bulwark than the League of Nations itself. If this Association were destroyed, if the communities that compose the British [imperial] Commonwealth separated in anger or broke up into two or more opposing camps, the outbreak of a new and more terrible world-war would only be a question of years. No League could prevent it ... If the League can keep the peace to-day, it is

because the British Empire provides the chief of its guardians and executants (1934: 94–5).

Importantly, while the League lacks international loyalty, by contrast the British Empire enjoys strong loyalties and affections among the dependent colonies. Accordingly, only this Third British Empire is able to unite the different races and thereby secure world order. Thus we can now appreciate Morefield's conclusion that 'the sense of chaos that Zimmern [as well as Murray and Angell] continually argued was so characteristic of the post-war world was largely a reaction to Britain's lost economic and military power. Without such an anchor the world appeared loosed from its moorings' (Morefield 2005: 105).

PART III

1945–1989
Subliminal Eurocentrism in international theory

8

Orthodox subliminal Eurocentrism: from classical realism to neorealism, 1945–1989

Introduction: realism in the postwar shift to subliminal Eurocentrism

If international theory had been divided between pro-imperialism and anti-imperialism as a function of varying scientific racist and 'manifest' Eurocentric metanarratives up to WWII, the post-1945 era exhibited, at least until 1989, a significant epistemic shift. Conventional IR historiographers might assume that if there was any racism or Eurocentrism within international theory in the past then this would have been exorcized, if not after 1919 then certainly after 1945. And because Eurocentric institutionalism and racism are usually conflated then the post-1945 era of international theory is thought to be free of subjective Western bias.

In the United States in particular, IR theory was allegedly founded on positivist principles, one of which is the assumption of value-neutrality. This, of course, is most closely associated with the rise of 'scientific' political realism in its 'classical' form (though equally it found its voice in the behavioural revolution in the 1950s and 1960s). As one of realism's key theorists argued, theory 'must be judged not by some preconceived abstract principle or concept unrelated to reality, but by its [scientific] purpose: to bring order and meaning to a mass of phenomena which without it would remain disconnected and unintelligible' (Morgenthau 1948/1967: 3). And it was upon this basis that the classical realists launched their sustained attack on 'un-scientific' interwar 'idealism'. However, this chapter argues that while IR theory did indeed take on a new guise after 1945 by discarding scientific racism, it nevertheless failed to escape the generic political bias of Western-centrism that had underpinned pre-1945 international theory. This 'Westphilian' or West-centric thinking took the form of what I call *subliminal* Eurocentric institutionalism. How then does realist subliminal Eurocentrism differ to that of its explicit or conscious Eurocentric predecessor?

CHAPTER 8: ORTHODOX SUBLIMINAL EUROCENTRISM

At first sight subliminal Eurocentrism appears to have escaped all the signs of pre-1945 manifest Eurocentrism. Thus all explicit talk of 'civilization versus barbarism' or 'whites versus non-whites' recedes from view. Moreover, normative politics is back-grounded while 'objective/positivist' analysis is fore-grounded insofar as the prime objective is simply to *explain* the operations of the international system free from any imputed value-bias. Above all, while normative prescriptions are allowed they must, however, flow directly on from a prior objective, scientific value-free analysis of international politics. In addition, realism deploys universalist analytical principles that supposedly apply to *all* states regardless of their culture or rank within a civilizational league table. But as I argue in this chapter, manifest Eurocentrism is not so much exorcized as turned inside out such that it takes on a 'subliminal' manifestation. This move allows its representatives to speak a language that has appeared to be more socially acceptable in the post-Nazi/postcolonial era. Thus while a surface reading of realism focuses on its universalist and ideologically un-biased principles of 'state-centrism under anarchy', my deeper reading reveals the Western provincial principles of its subliminal Eurocentrism.

Turning to Figure 8.1, which charts the subliminal Eurocentric properties of modern realism, I begin by noting that the world is once again divided between East and West. Critically, for all the talk of juridically equal sovereign states under international anarchy, the subliminal Eurocentrism of modern realism leads it to deploy the conceptions of formal- or informal-hierarchy and gradated sovereignty. For the most part the West is held to be the pioneering agent or subject of world politics while the East is portrayed as a passive object of the diktat of the Western great powers (though hegemonic stability theory provides a partial exception here insofar as it invokes a conception of 'predatory' Eastern agency that is reminiscent of the racist-realism of the post-1889 era that I discussed principally in Chapter 5). The vision of the international system takes slightly different forms across the realist spectrum. Both classical realism and hegemonic stability theory, which are interested in international change in the last four centuries, invoke what I call the two-step *Eurocentric big-bang theory of world politics* (BBT). In the first step the Europeans single-handedly create a European capitalist international states-system through their pioneering and exceptional institutional genius, while in the second step they export their civilization so as to remake the world, as far as possible, in their own image, either through imperialism or hegemony or both. Such a perspective is developed explicitly in hegemonic stability theory (HST) and parts of classical realism.

CLASSICAL REALISM: MORGENTHAU AND CARR

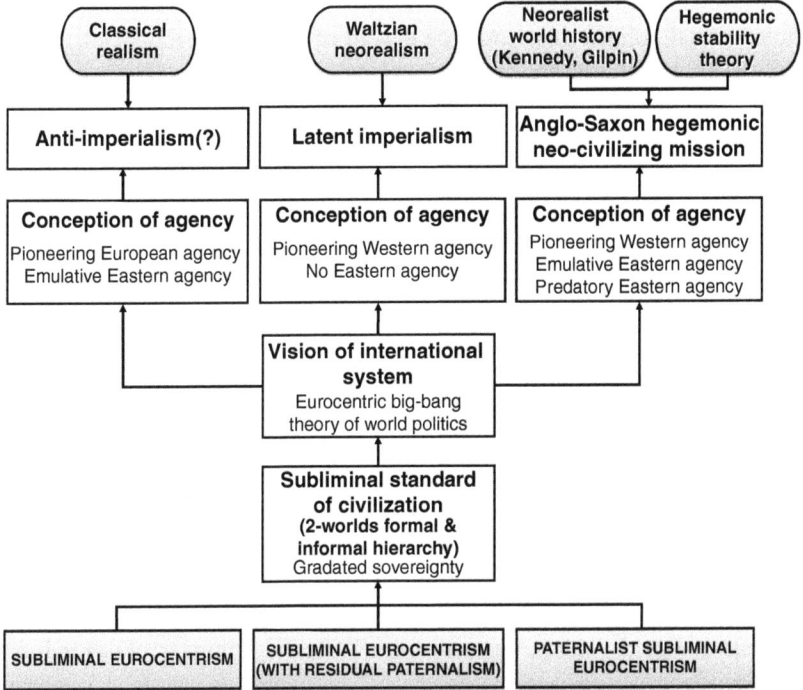

Figure 8.1 Subliminal Eurocentrism in classical realism and neorealism, c. 1945–89

Finally, like so much of post-1945 IR theory, much of modern realism does not explicitly uphold a commitment to imperialism (unlike its racist-realist predecessors). But once again the clear exception here lies with hegemonic stability theory, which explicitly justifies Western imperialism in the past, as well as in effect advocating a neocivilizing mission in the present. Accordingly HST provides a clear example of paternalist subliminal Eurocentrism. And to the extent that Waltz endorses US hegemony at the very end of his key 1979 book, so we find a residual paternalism in his approach. By contrast, although Morgenthau does not call for imperialism in the present, nevertheless he effectively naturalizes the earlier phase of European colonization through a series of subliminal Eurocentric moves.

Classical realism: Hans Morgenthau and E. H. Carr

Many readers would be immediately surprised by my claim that the classical realists such as Hans Morgenthau and E. H. Carr were Eurocentric. After all, their principal claim to fame within IR lies with their calling for a *science* of international politics that would be devoid of subjective tendencies, especially given their criticism of interwar idealism as 'utopian'. Nevertheless, it would be problematic to assume that classical realists (or neorealists for that matter) sought to eschew *all* normative claims. Morgenthau asserted that '[p]olitical realism contains ... a normative element.... [It] considers a rational foreign policy to be good foreign policy' (1948/1967: 7). Carr went even further in *The Twenty Years' Crisis*, insisting that a pure objective realism would be 'sterile' since it could not offer up policy prescriptions of any use (1946/1981: esp. chs. 2, 6). And in *What is History?* he went much further by taking on the many positivist historians who claim to be value-free and purely objective (Carr 1964). Nevertheless, as noted already, it remained a key claim that political realism was superior to interwar liberalism on the grounds that it derived its normative politics from a value-free universalist analysis of world politics, rather than deriving an analysis of world politics from an *a priori* value-biased framework. But, I argue, a subliminal Eurocentric bias underpins classical realism and that in the place of a universalist analysis the classical realists developed a normative/explanatory framework that was grounded within a Western parochial analysis of world politics, wherein intra-Western politics is presented *as* world politics.

Naturalizing imperialism and eliding the East–West hierarchical divide

Morgenthau's treatment of imperialism illustrates one of the key aspects of orthodox subliminal Eurocentrism. In his vision imperialism becomes defined in opposition to a 'status quo policy', where the latter refers to a state that seeks to preserve the existing distribution of power in the interstate system. Imperialism, by contrast, constitutes a foreign policy that aims at 'acquiring more power than [a great power] actually has, through a reversal of existing power relations' (1948/1967: 36–7). This definition is superior to all previous ones, he argues, because they all lacked ethical neutrality and objectivity given that the term tends to be deployed as a pejorative and is 'indiscriminately applied to any foreign policy, regardless of its actual character, to which the user happens to be opposed' (1948/1967: 41). The paradox here is that Morgenthau produces a definition which can be applied to any foreign policy that seeks to challenge the status quo, even if this has no relevance to colonies, thereby rendering the term far less precise than he would have us believe. Indeed, as one prominent critic put it,

Morgenthau 'dilutes the term beyond utility. Imperialism becomes the default action of any powerful state that is not pursuing a status quo policy' (Salter 2002: 117). The difficulty of this move emerges from the point that when a great power maintains its empire but does not seek to expand it, so it is following a policy of the status quo rather than an imperialist one. Thus with the exception of various key moments between 1800 and 1960/1980 – mainly between 1880 and 1910 – when the imperial powers did not significantly expand their colonial territory *ipso facto* the majority of the formal-imperial era logically drops out from view. Moreover, this no less 'precludes analysis of [neo-imperialism's] impact as a specific political practice on the contemporary states system' within the postcolonial era (Salter 2002: 117).

By effectively inverting the pre-1945 Eurocentric formulations of imperialism the paradox is that Morgenthau's universalized definition sanitizes or empties the concept of its European/Western particularities (1948/1967: chs. 4–5). This has the effect not only of letting the West off the moral hook but of relegating one of the crucial dynamics of world politics after 1800 to a stagnant backwater in the vibrant mainstream Western story. This is a striking move given that the pre-1945 Eurocentric tendency was to explicitly treat Western imperialism as *the* story of international politics. In this way, then, the East–West dynamic of world politics becomes obscured by an overwhelming focus on intra-Western relations (as I explain shortly). Thus in strong contrast to the 1889–1945 era of racist-realist international theory, between 1945 and 1989 realism's emphasis on empire and neo-imperialism was, with the exception of hegemonic stability theory, conspicuous mainly for its absence. But in the process, such a lacuna performs an important task in naturalizing the East–West imperial and neo-imperial division.

Significantly, the first four editions of Morgenthau's key text were published at a time when the politics of empire and of decolonization were reaching their climax. It is true that Morgenthau discusses the 'colonial revolution' but it is accorded a mere one per cent of the total text (1948/1967: 340–5); and, moreover, it is described in typically Eurocentric terms. Instead of awarding the East a substantial degree of agency in the overthrow of empire, he presents the story as a pure moment of Western triumphalism. Decolonization becomes reimagined as a result of the 'triumph of the moral ideas of the West', specifically the principles of national self-determination and social justice. And it was these ideas that were passively endogenized by an *emulative* East. Thus

> [i]n the wake of its conquests, the West brought to Asia not only its technology and political institutions, but also its principles of political morality. The nations of the West taught the peoples of Asia by their own example that the full development of the individual's faculties depends upon the ability of the nation to which he belongs to determine of its own free will its political and cultural destinies, and that this national freedom is worth fighting for; and the peoples of Asia learned that lesson (1948/1967: 344–5).

This story of Eastern emulation and learning in the face of the 'Western teacher' is a fundamental of much Eurocentric thinking (as we have seen in earlier chapters).

The subliminal Eurocentric politics of international change

But for all this, the key aspect of Morgenthau's subliminal Eurocentrism lies at the very heart of his theory of international politics. Key here is that his theory of world politics is conflated with the politics of intra-Western relations (as signalled earlier); so much so that reference to the non-Western world as an actor in its own right is all but absent. Moreover, the key to Morgenthau's subliminal Eurocentrism lies in the 'Eurocentric big-bang theory of world politics'. This assumes that the international system exploded into existence in the 'Westphalian big bang of 1648', whence it gradually expanded or diffused outwards to graciously deliver or bequeath modern international relations to the rest of the world. How then are intra-European relations conflated with the universal?

Conventional understandings of Morgenthau assume that he emphasizes the importance of state-centrism under international anarchy; and that through his 'six principles' he produces an ahistorical, materialist structural approach that consciously ignores historical discontinuity.[152] But, in fact, the core of the whole book rests on a simple historical sociological analysis of international change that contradicts this received view.[153] While Morgenthau, in classic realist terms, places much emphasis on the importance of the balance of power between states, nevertheless he argues that this has taken *different forms* across time. Indeed unlike Waltz he argues that there have been two key eras in the modern European system – the 'aristocratic international' (c. 1648–nineteenth century) and 'nationalistic universalism' (twentieth century).

---

[152] E.g., Smith (1986).
[153] Griffiths (1992); Hobson (2000: 45–55). Note, however, that his third principle points towards this alternative reading; see Hobson (2000: 47).

He argues that during the period of the 'aristocratic international' the balance of power worked to produce a relative peace and cooperation between states, while by contrast the age of 'nationalistic universalism' witnessed the effective breakdown of the balance of power and the ushering in of the era of total war. Unlike Waltz, for Morgenthau the balance of power is not self-regulating and self-equilibrating because its success depends upon certain social, normative and political prerequisites.

What, then, were these that made for the success of the balance of power during the aristocratic international and its failure under 'nationalistic universalism'? There are two basic factors that underpin the functioning of the balance of power. First, in the aristocratic international rulers enjoyed a significant amount of institutional state autonomy; and second, rulers were bound by shared European-based aristocratic norms that served to restrain the lust for power. As he put it:

> The fuel that keeps the motor of the balance of power moving is the intellectual and moral foundation of Western civilization, the intellectual and moral climate within which the protagonists of eighteenth-century society moved and which permeated all their thoughts and actions. These men knew Europe as 'one great republic' with common standards of 'politeness and cultivation' and a 'common system of arts, and laws and manners'. The common awareness of these common standards restrained their ambitions 'by the mutual influence of fear and shame', imposed 'moderation' upon their actions and instilled in all of them 'some sense of honour and justice' (1948/1967: 212-13).

These aristocratic norms ensured that the moral boundary expanded to the edges of European civilization, which in turn ensured the success of the balance of power and hence relative peace within Europe (see 1948/1967: chs. 16, 20).

However, a major shift in the European international system occurred in the nineteenth century following the democratic revolutions of the late-eighteenth century – particularly the French Revolution and the rise of nationalism that followed in its wake. 'When in the course of the nineteenth century democratic selection and responsibility of government officials replaced government by the aristocracy, the structure of international society and, with it, of international morality underwent a fundamental change' (1948/1967: 239). There were two key developments here. First, aristocratic rulers lost their institutional autonomy and were replaced by officials who were responsible to the wishes of the masses under the logic of democratic selection. Second, and inter-relatedly, the restraints associated with aristocratic norms were lost and replaced by nationalistic norms that were highly conducive to warfare. This is because nationalism entails not simply defending one's own country but is, above all, about exporting its norms to other states in an international Hobbesian war of all against all. Indeed international aristocratic morality was replaced by a nationalistic ethic of 'Right or wrong – my country' (1948/1967: 240). In essence, changes in norms coupled with the extension of citizenship rights underpinned the transformation of the international system into a harsh anarchy as the moral boundary shrank back to the level of the individual European nation-state.

This historical sociological analysis forms the centre-piece of Morgenthau's analysis of word politics in the last four centuries. For it is this framework which leads him to claim, for example, that there is no such thing as world public opinion in the twentieth century because people are socialized by the particularism of their own nationalistic universalism (ch. 17); that international law is now marginal as a force for restraint given the virulence of nationalistic states (ch. 18); and that in strong contrast to the balance of power under the aristocratic international, the modern balance of power is unable to constrain the lust for power, thereby leading to the era of total warfare (ch. 22).

Within this theoretical explanation lie two core inter-related Eurocentric properties. First, Morgenthau reads the international system through the specific lens of European political history. International developments and transformations within Europe are conflated with the operation of the international system at the global level. Second, he subscribes to the Eurocentric big-bang theory where the sovereign international states system was single-handedly created in Europe, exploding into existence in 1648 before it diffused outwards to remake the world in the West's own image. This becomes apparent in his, albeit brief, discussion of the 'colonial revolution' (i.e., decolonization), where, as was noted above, non-Western states emulated the West to achieve the status of sovereignty. Finally, returning to the first point, Morgenthau's analysis of the post-1947 Cold War era rests on the conflation of intra-Western relations with the universal, given his analysis of this era as determined almost solely by the Western superpowers, the United States and the Soviet Union.

By way of brief conclusion it is worth noting that Morgenthau's analysis of international change is also contained within two of E. H. Carr's books, *The New Society* (1951) and *Nationalism and After* (1945), where the latter was published three years before Morgenthau's text. Because the analysis is almost identical, I shall merely draw out the relevant connections rather than elaborate upon the whole argument.[154] In essence, Carr singled out three key eras that existed between 1648 and 1945. The first era of the 'monarchical international' (1648–c. 1815) is entirely congruent with Morgenthau's analysis of the 'aristocratic international'. This gave way to the second era of the 'bourgeois international' that was largely overseen by the Pax Britannica (1815–1919), and which was also peaceful due to the high autonomy of the state on the one hand and the presence of certain peaceful moral norms on the other. But the rise after 1870 of the 'socialized nation' (congruent with Morgenthau's 'nationalistic universalism') and its crystallization by 1919 was responsible for the period of total warfare between 1914 and 1945. The theory is almost exactly identical, with progressive extensions of citizenship rights coupled with the decline of international norms and their replacement by nationalistic ones lying at the heart of his theory of international change. Not surprisingly, therefore, the conclusion remains the same: that the story of world politics recounted by both Carr and Morgenthau is treated as the story of intra-Western relations, with the non-Western world all but banished from view. And the ultimate irony here is that while Carr's key critique in *The Twenty Years' Crisis* of interwar idealism is that it conflated the national interests of the leading great powers with the universal interest, so he echoes this by conflating intra-European politics with the universal.

Neorealist hegemonic stability theory: subliminal paternalist-Eurocentric imperialism

While there are a number of theorists who are closely associated with hegemonic stability theory including Charles Kindleberger (1973), here I shall focus on the most developed and extensive formulation that was constructed by Robert Gilpin (1975, 1981, 1987). In standard historiographies the rise of HST in the mid-1970s is generally explained either through an *internalist* methodological approach, where HST constitutes the neorealist response to the challenge of liberal interdependence theory, or via an *externalist-events* account, which views it as offering an explanation and solution to the unfolding global economic crisis. Not surprisingly, the elision of a discursive-contextualist historiographical interpretation means that in the secondary literature any potential Eurocentric context goes

---

[154] But for fuller discussions see Linklater (1998: 159–68); Hobson (2000: 55–61).

largely ignored.[155] Interestingly, Gilpin seems, at least superficially, to be aware of this possible context. Thus he argues at the beginning of his book *War and Change in World Politics* that one of the reasons why the study of international change has been neglected – to which his book would offer a remedy – is due to 'the Western bias in the study of international relations. For a profession whose intellectual commitment is the understanding of the interaction of societies, international relations as a discipline is remarkably parochial and ethnocentric' (Gilpin 1981: 5). And more recently, he dismissed the charge that HST defends the American interest by claiming that '[n]o proponent of hegemonic stability theory, at least to my knowledge, has been motivated to justify American behavior; to the contrary, most were very critical of the self-centered and irresponsible American behavior that began in the 1960s, if not earlier' (2001: 93–4).[156] Or as Stephen Krasner put it, 'realist prescriptions for the United States have hardly been imperialist and expansionary; in fact they have been just the opposite ... [M]ost prominent realist analysts have argued that the United States has engaged in [self-damaging] imperial overreach. It has tried to do too much' (Krasner 1992: 44).[157]

In this section, however, I argue that the substance of this theory contradicts these anti-imperialist sentiments, given that HST rests on the twin-biases of American ethnocentrism and paternalist subliminal Eurocentrism. For behind the universalist actions of the hegemons lies the provincial Anglo-Saxon civilizational interest masquerading as the universal. Here it is important to appreciate the point that external-events and discursive-contexts are rarely separable, given that events are interpreted within the particular discursive contexts that exist at the time of their occurrence. With this in mind I argue that the principal external-event challenge that HST was concerned with was not so much world recession and an imminent war of all against all but rather the *perceived* threat of the decline of American hegemonic supremacy in the world. For arguably the core rationale of the theory is to legitimize such

---

[155] Two clear exceptions are found in Nossal (2001: 172–5); Grunberg (1990).
[156] Such a defence, however, turns out to be a criticism of the few private gains actions that the United States undertook that did not conform to the altruistic provision of global public goods, and which in turn enabled an avoidance of undertaking the necessary domestic reforms to maintain US global competitiveness (especially the introduction of an industrial policy).
[157] But as I explain shortly, such a response reflects the paternalist-imperial basis of HST, wherein 'imperial overreach' is the product of the hegemon's self-sacrificial role as world policeman.

supremacy by revealing that what is good for America is good for the world and that what is bad for America is bad for the world (Nossal 2001: 174). In this vision, then, *all* countries have a stake in seeing a strong hegemonic America.

This American ethnocentrism is revealed further by the point that the student can learn all she needs to know about world politics and IPE simply by studying the actions and policies of the US hegemon, as well as the British hegemon should she be 'interested in history'. Significantly, one of the theory's prominent advocates replied to a question posed by an audience member (presumably a Luxembourg national) at the 1990 APSA conference: 'Sure people in Luxembourg have good ideas. But who gives a damn? Luxembourg ain't hegemonic' (Stephen Krasner cited in Higgott 1991: 99). Such a narrow focus necessarily precludes the actions of small Western states (i.e., American ethnocentrism) and Third World states (paternalist Eurocentrism). Analogous to 'World Series Baseball' that involves only North American teams, so for HST America *is* the world. This exclusive focus is predicated on the fact that the hegemon graciously provides the key services to ensure the development of the world economy under conditions of relative peace and stability. For the absence of hegemony leads to certain disaster in the shape of a reversion to the dark age of the interwar period. Accordingly, the theory encapsulates perfectly the well-known words of Madeleine Albright, uttered in 1998: 'We [the United States] are the indispensable nation. We stand tall. We see further into the future'. And this in turn propels us back to the point originally made in Stanley Hoffmann's famous essay 'An American social science: International Relations', where he pointed out that American students were drawn to the study of IR because '[t]o study United States foreign policy was to study the international system. To study the international system could not fail to bring one back to the role of the United States' (Hoffmann 1977/2001: 35; see also Smith 1995). Indeed, no other modern theory of IR conforms so closely to this American ethnocentric and Eurocentric idiom than does HST.

But the core of my argument will focus on the internal contradictions of HST. It is interesting to note that while Robert Keohane claimed that his theory of neoliberal institutionalism deployed realist premises in order to derive a liberal theory of inter-state cooperation (Keohane 1984: 29, 66–7), so I would suggest that Gilpin's HST drew on liberal (and realist) premises to derive a neorealist theory of inter-state co-operation. This is important to note because the most striking aspect of HST is that many of its components can only be maintained by suspending core neorealist principles. And as I shall argue throughout this section, it is the very lacunae and logical inconsistencies in the theory that require the import of subconscious exogenous ideas that in turn are derived from both an American ethnocentrism and a subliminal paternalist Eurocentrism. But equally, this could be rephrased by saying that it is the Eurocentric celebration of Anglo-Saxon hegemony in the first place that leads Gilpin to contradict some of the cardinal axioms of neorealism. Either way, though, focusing on the lacunae and logical inconsistencies of HST reveals the presence of these discourses. In doing so I divide this section into two subdivisions, the first of which examines the rise and exercise of hegemony while the second considers its decline.

Paternalist-Eurocentric foundations of the rise and exercise of hegemony

The rise and exercise of hegemony is captured within the two-step narrative of the Eurocentric big-bang theory of world politics (BBT). In the first phase, the hegemon rises to the top of the global material power hierarchy as a result of its own innate efforts that can be related through the endogenous process of the Eurocentric *logic of immanence.* Thus American development in the twentieth century, much as British development in the nineteenth, is recounted as an entirely endogenous process thereby revealing subliminally the point that their institutions are exceptional (Gilpin 1975; 1981: ch. 3). And having risen to the top in terms of material power it is deemed natural that such leading states would automatically convert their fungible economic power into global political hegemony.[158] That is, once the first step has been accomplished so the second step flows on naturally.

---

[158] This is complemented by an account of the rise of the European capitalist international system which, once again, reflects all the Eurocentric markers connected with the BBT (Gilpin 1981: 116–44; Kennedy 1988: ch. 1). That is, having been single-handedly created by the Europeans, the capitalist international states system was then exported so as to remake the world according to Western civilizational precepts (see especially Gilpin 1981: 133, 143). It is no less interesting to note that Kennedy (1988), Gilpin (1981) and Kindleberger (1996) recount the rise and fall of great powers through a Eurocentric narrative of a Western relay race, wherein the baton of global power is passed from one Western runner to the next. But this is problematized by the point that in the period up to 1800 none of the key powers in the world was Western. Indeed the Spanish, Portuguese, Dutch and British might all have been important powers *within* Europe up to 1800, but they were marginalized on the world stage by the Chinese

But at this point of proceedings the theory's explanation of the emergence of a hegemonic foreign policy is both under-specified and inconsistent with neorealist logic. This point emerges through the posing of two rhetorical questions. First, why would a great power want to become a hegemon whose charge it is to single-handedly pay to stabilize the world for the benefit of all other states who don't pay, and where the hegemon's ultimate reward is merely its decline relative to those it helps? Here I am referring to the point that hegemons are the exclusive providers and payers of 'global public goods' that benefit all states equally, and that all other states enjoy a free-ride because they fail to contribute to their payment.[159] Second, given that a key property of hegemony is the necessary *far-sightedness* to 'recognize' that all states would be better off if they followed long-term collective/ cooperative gains policies (as in neoliberal institutionalism), the question then becomes: why is the hegemon, therefore, unable to prophesy or foresee its own future demise and therefore do something to pre-empt it? (Grunberg 1990: 440). In both cases, the immediate problem here is that within standard neorealist logic all states seek to ensure their survival by maintaining or maximizing their position relative to others.[160] But here we have the leading great power choosing to sacrifice itself 'for the good or benefit' of other states. Indeed, even the most altruistic version of liberal IR theory would not subscribe to such a notion of self-sacrifice.

Moreover, the idea that a great power seeks to impose liberal-economic cooperation upon states through free trade (which comprises a key global public good) departs from all other variants of realism, which emphasize either the role of mercantilism and beggar-thy-neighbour as the appropriate national policy,[161] or that free trade cosmopolitanism represents the particular interests of the powerful *at the expense* of the weaker states.[162] And this is all the more perplexing given that Gilpin, alongside Mearsheimer, adheres to what is known as *offensive* realism, which asserts that states seek to maximize their relative

---

(1100–1800), the Safavid Persians (c. 1500–1700), the Ottomans (c. 1300–1800) and the Indians until about 1800 (see Frank 1998; Hobson 2004; O'Brien 2009).

[159] These 'hegemonic services' comprise the roles of: world policeman, promoter of free trade across the world, lender of last resort, and principal investor in countries around the world.

[160] Cf. Waltz (1979: 105–6): Grieco (1993); Mearsheimer (2001).

[161] E.g., Viner (1948); Waltz (1979).

[162] E.g., Carr (1946/1981: 81–2). This argument was developed most fully by the nationalist thinker, Friedrich List (1841/1909).

gains over others.[163] But it turns out that for Gilpin this principle applies to all states *bar the hegemon*. That the hegemon is exceptional is clear; why it is so is not explained other than through a circularity – that the hegemon self-sacrifices because that is what hegemons do. In essence there is no recourse within neorealist logic to explain the anomalous altruistic status that HST ascribes to the United States in the 1945–73 period or to Britain between 1845–73.

Explaining this gap in the theory requires focusing on the presence of a subconscious American ethnocentrism and subliminal paternalist Eurocentrism. That is, US hegemony reflects the nineteenth-century discourse of 'American exceptionalism' and its accompanying neo-imperialist idiom of America's 'manifest destiny'. For the notion of helping all other states, especially those in the Third World, conjures up the idiom of the civilizing mission and the 'white man's burden'. Indeed it is precisely this idiom that could be used to explain why the leading Anglo-Saxon great powers sacrifice themselves for the good of others. And this in turn forms an important imperialist trope that underpins Gilpin's analysis of the exercise of hegemony. Here it is important to note that Gilpin begins by differentiating hegemons from imperial powers. Thus in the modern world both British and American liberal-hegemons differ to the authoritarian imperial power of the Soviet Union (1981: 139). Moreover, he argues that (with the exception of the Soviet Union) the modern world is governed by the progressive non-imperialist politics of liberal hegemons whereas the pre-modern world was based on the cyclical and stultifying/regressive politics of despotic Eastern empires (1981: 106–15; also Kennedy 1988: ch. 1). Indeed the Eurocentric trope of Oriental despotism is effectively employed to account for this. But the presence of European and American imperialism in the 1800–1945 period undermines the apparently seamless differentiation of the pre-modern period of empires with the modern era of anti-imperial hegemons. And, of course, this is exacerbated by the obvious point that Britain was the greatest imperial power prior to 1945, as much as the United States has been the greatest neo-imperial power in the post-1945 era.

Gilpin attempts to circumvent this obvious inconsistency by resorting, paradoxically, to the nineteenth-century imperialist trope of the liberal civilizing mission. To this end he invokes Karl Marx's paternalist civilizing

---

[163] Gilpin (1975: 23, 34–6, 85–92); Mearsheimer (1995: 11–12); though Gilpin qualifies this assertion more recently (Gilpin 2001: 79).

mission conception (which I discussed in Chapter 2) wherein modern European imperial powers transferred capital and technologies to the colonies not so as to exploit, but in order to *uplift*, them (1981: 142–3). But in defending his 'non-imperialist' reading of hegemony it seems clear that Gilpin is addressing the wrong target. For his assumption is that imperialism is defined by the *exploitation* of the weak by the strong. What this misses, however, is that in Marx's vision – as well as that of the paternalist Eurocentric liberals such as Cobden, Angell and Hobson – imperialism is conceptualized as a *civilizing mission* precisely because it requires the West to engage in the paternalist uplift, rather than the coercive exploitation, of the East (as I also explained in Chapter 2). Significantly, Niall Ferguson makes almost exactly the same argument as Gilpin but refers explicitly to the benign *liberal imperialism* of Britain and America (Ferguson 2002, 2004).

When seen from this angle, the exercise of hegemony too can be explained in terms of the civilizing, or neocivilizing, mission. Indeed the whole purpose of British and American hegemony has been to uplift all states, but especially the backward (Eastern ones). Thus the principal institutions of US hegemony – the Word Bank, IMF and GATT – were established to enhance economic development across the world. Most importantly, the IMF and World Bank have offered the vast majority of their loans to the Third World through *conditionality* and the process known as *structural adjustment*. Key here is that indebted Third World states have been 'helped' by the IFIs on condition that they undergo *cultural conversion* according to Western neo-liberal civilizing principles. The reply might well be that this has been undertaken precisely so as to *help or uplift* rather than exploit Third World states, whose irrational short-termism prevents them from perceiving the gracious hand of these Western institutions. But such a reply merely confirms the point I am making, for the policies of diffusing free trade and neoliberal civilizational practices find their historical analogy in the actions of the British Empire in the nineteenth century, which sought above all to culturally convert Eastern societies to Western liberal-civilizational principles precisely so as to help and uplift them. Indeed it is this paternalist property that defines the liberal-imperial civilizing mission in the first place (as I explain in Chapter 1, pp. 23–30).

The paternalist-Eurocentric discourse of the decline of hegemony

If HST's conception of the exercise of hegemony can be explained through an underlying subliminal paternalist Eurocentrism, likewise a series of

Eurocentric monikers are evident in the theory's explanation of hegemonic decline. In this vision the hegemon is ungraciously dethroned by two processes that are connected to the 'free-rider problem' that was mentioned earlier.[164] Indeed, at the outset it is important to note that the 'free-rider' explanation of hegemonic decline conveniently scapegoats or blames all other states – especially Eastern ones – for the hegemon's problems.[165] But above all, the free-rider problem returns us to various nineteenth-century Eurocentric imperialist tropes, the first of which is the conception of 'ungrateful free riders' (see also Nossal 2001: 172–5). As Gilpin put it, '[t]he American Revolution began with the effort of the British crown to get "ungrateful" colonists to pay their "fair" share in the defense against the Indians and the French. And in the contemporary world, both Americans and Russians complain about defending "ungrateful", free-riding allies' (1981: 169). By definition, though, free-riders are ungrateful because they refuse to pay for the global public goods that they benefit from, despite repeated requests issued by the hegemon. Such an idiom returns us to Rudyard Kipling's conception of the white man's burden. For in his famous poem that was issued to an American audience in 1899 he warned that should the United States engage in a civilizing mission it should be prepared to court only unpopularity with those it would seek to help; that the imperial 'civilizer' should expect to incur only the 'blame of those ye better, the hate of those ye guard'.

Of course, it might be replied that free-riders include Western states as much as Eastern ones. Though true, nevertheless it turns out that non-Western free-riders are treated as egregious offenders, with Japan and the East Asian NICs in the 1980s being singled out consistently throughout Gilpin's 1987 book. Interestingly, the 1980s 'yellow peril' of Japan is now being superseded in the minds of contemporary neorealists by the coming 'Chinese peril' (e.g., Mearsheimer 2001). Ostensibly they are singled out because while they have been direct beneficiaries of US hegemonic largesse, their 'resulting' prosperity led to negative blowback in the guise of massive US trade deficits, particularly vis-à-vis Japan in the 1980s (and more recently vis-à-vis China in the 2000s). Interestingly, a clear sign of the 'ungrateful' Japanese could be found in the arguments

---

[164] And for the original position see Olson and Zeckhauser (1966); Kindleberger (1973); Gilpin (1975, 1981, 1987).

[165] Though Gilpin, as well as Krasner (1978), accepts that hegemonic decline is in part a function of the internal maladaptiveness of the hegemonic state as I explain elsewhere; see Hobson (2000: 31–5).

of Shintaro Ishihara's book *The Japan That Can Say No* (1991), which emerged at the peak of the Japanese Yellow Scare in America. The second aspect of the free-rider problem lies with the diffusion of advanced technologies from the hegemon which, when coupled with its exclusive provision of public goods and metropolitan investment abroad, enables the development of all other states and the relative decline of the hegemon. Worse still is that this all results in the rise of new great powers, one of which challenges and overthrows the hegemon, thereby reinforcing the altruistic notion of hegemonic self-sacrifice that underpins HST. Gilpin (1981: 178) invokes an argument that was deployed by Alexander Gerschenkron (1962) – the 'advantages of backwardness',[166] or what might equally be called the 'curse of forwardness'. This refers to the process by which the hegemon pays the substantial start-up costs of cutting-edge technologies – economic and military – before they diffuse outwards to free riding states.

Here we encounter the key imperial civilizing mission trope, where the hegemon takes on the guise of a benevolent father who teaches his children – both directly and by way of example – to embrace and develop that which it had already pioneered so that they too can grow up to prosper. And indeed it is precisely at this point that Gilpin explicitly invokes Marx's paternalist imperial argument to the effect that the imperial power stimulates the 'colonized peoples to learn its ways and frequently has taught them advanced military, political, and economic techniques' (Gilpin 1981: 176). Poignantly, Gilpin invokes Arnold Toynbee's two-fold argument about civilizational decline, to wit:

> The expansion of the center against the periphery arouses the peripheral peoples; they become aware of the superiority of the 'advanced' civilization and seek to adopt its ways. The diffusion of ideas and techniques from the center to the periphery narrows the gap in military and other capabilities between the advanced civilization and the barbarians. ... As a consequence, the difficulty and costs of dominating the periphery increase (Gilpin 1981: 184).

This in effect invokes the idea of *conditional* Eastern agency, which is the logical corollary of a paternalist Eurocentric discourse.

But this in turn flows directly into perhaps the deepest contradiction that underpins the analysis of hegemonic decline. This comprises the idea that the weak states can bring down the mighty hegemon, which is

---

[166] Although this was first discussed by Leon Trotsky, who spoke of the 'privileges of historic backwardness' (Trotsky 1932–3/1967: 22).

clearly anomalous within realist/neorealist logic. Indeed it offends the pivotal realist maxim first articulated by Thucydides, that 'great powers do what they can and the weak suffer what they must'. Instead this maxim becomes inverted within HST: 'weak (free-riding) powers do what they can and hegemons suffer what they must'. Mancur Olson originally summarized this as the 'tendency for the "exploitation" of the great by the small' (1965: 35). Once again, this contradiction within HST can be squared only by the importation of Eurocentric ideas; or equally that this contradiction emerges as a result of Eurocentrism and American ethnocentrism in the first place.

In singling out Asian states as particularly egregious free-riders Gilpin likens the decline of British and American hegemony to the fall of the Roman Empire, invoking the trope of the 'barbarian hordes' bringing down an internally weakened hegemon (e.g., 1981: 162, 189, 198). Here he asserts that 'the diffusion of military techniques from advanced societies to more primitive societies [constitutes] a principal factor in the rise of new powers .... Thus the diffusion of Roman military skills to the barbarian Germanic tribes was a major factor in the collapse of ancient Mediterranean civilization (1981: 177). However, at this point it might be responded that this argument in effect invokes a kind of Eastern *hyper-agency* – one that even trumps American agency – and thereby implies a break with Eurocentrism. But here Gilpin returns us directly to one of the principal arguments deployed by some of the scientific racist-realists who emerged after 1889. To recall from my discussion in Chapter 5, the likes of Mahan (1897) and Mackinder (1904) argued that Western civilization was under siege at the hands of the yellow barbarians. In this construction the Eastern barbarians were cast with the negative stereotype or trope of barbaric atavism and were endowed with high levels of predatory agency, serving to bring only chaos to world politics while simultaneously threatening Western civilization. By analogy, in his theory of hegemonic decline Gilpin inscribes a predatory agency to the Eastern barbarian free-riders, for they serve only to bring down Western hegemony while being unable to restore world order by offering a positive alternative. Thus on the one hand Japanese and East Asian free-riding has helped promote the decline of US hegemony, while on the other hand 'the *Japanese* have been ... poor candidates to assume economic leadership'. Their domestic protectionism and free-riding more generally have 'made it difficult if not impossible for them to carry out hegemonic responsibilities' (1987: 376). And it is precisely this vacuum that leads to a world of chaos and a return to the dark ages.

Nevertheless, though clearly reminiscent of Mahan and Mackinder, there is also an overlap with the defensive racist cultural realism of Charles Pearson (1894) and Lothrop Stoddard (1920), given their extreme claim that yellow barbarism might succeed in undermining Western civilization. Once again, the analogy of the fall of the Roman Empire is deployed in the case of modern hegemonic wars: 'the combatants may exhaust themselves, and the "victorious" power may be unable to reorder the international system. The destruction of Rome by barbarian hordes led to the chaos of the Dark Ages' (1981: 198). Moreover, it is possible to discern an underlying Christian metanarrative wherein the American saviour of the world, king of the chosen people, sacrifices itself for the good of all others; and where the ungrateful beneficiaries turn round later only to kill their saviour.[167] Either way, though, the Eurocentric/American ethnocentric message of HST is clear: US hegemonic civilization must be restored (or resurrected) and all free-riding terminated if the *whole* world is to be spared the chaos of a new dark age. For it is precisely here where the provincial interests of the United States masquerade as the universal.

All in all, it seems fair to conclude that HST does *not* provide a universalist conception of hegemonic power that ignores East–West divisions because it is based on a paternalist Eurocentric metanarrative. Nor could it be viewed as exemplifying solely an American ethnocentrism given the equally pivotal role that British hegemony is accorded in the creation of the liberal capitalist world order in the nineteenth century. Rather, what could be said is that HST simultaneously invokes a defence of Anglo-Saxon civilization in particular and of Western civilization in general. Accordingly, the irony is that Gilpin's proposed antidote to the problem of parochial Western bias that he correctly accuses other IR scholars of turns out to be guilty of the very same charge. Thus HST might be relabelled *Western Stability Theory* or even *Western Instability Theory*, where the most striking parallel between parts of racist-realism and HST lies in the point that both are ultimately derived from an angst-ridden perception of the decline of Anglo-Saxon civilizational supremacy.

Waltzian neorealism: the highest phase of postwar subliminal Eurocentrism?

Although the theories advanced by Carr, Morgenthau and Waltz are in certain respects quite different in that the classical realists produce a

---
[167] For a deeper exploration of this theme see Grunberg (1990).

theory of international change whereas Waltz denies that structural international change is possible, nevertheless they all converge upon a shared subliminal Eurocentric base. Again, as with Carr and Morgenthau, at first sight the possibility of value-bias, Eurocentric or otherwise, seems to be ruled out by Waltz's rigid insistence on the need for a scientific theory of international politics (1979: ch. 1). Though not a purely positivistic theory, given that the structure of the international system cannot be observed directly, nevertheless he ascribes to the positivist definition of theory as based on universal laws and the fact/value distinction. Indeed this universalist analysis is, of course, supposed to apply to *all* states, regardless of their cultural foundations or identity, whether they be Eastern or Western. But here I shall argue that these objectives are contradicted by the point that his theory rests predominantly on a subliminal Eurocentric base, with a dash of paternalism and American ethnocentrism thrown in for good measure at the very end of the book.

Waltz's theory provides an excellent example of *subliminal* Eurocentrism; arguably one of the clearest examples of subliminal Eurocentrism but for its more overt manifestation which comes in the guise of a cameo performance of US hegemony at the very end of the book. For while pre-1945 manifest Eurocentric international theory made East–West relations a key focus of its enquiry framed within the discourse of the standard of civilization, this becomes sublimated in Waltz's approach such that East–West relations all but disappear from view. Equally, but for his discussion of US hegemony, Waltz's denial of Eastern agency and his reification of Western agency is hidden within the apparently universalist framework of the theory. And, with the exception of his discussion of US hegemony, the appearance of Western imperialism all but disappears.

Eurocentric ahistorical structuralism: the elision of modern imperial hierarchy

Central to Waltz's theory is his view that international anarchy – the notion that there is no higher authority or world government that stands above states – is the prime feature of world politics, past, present and future. This operates in tandem with his insistence that in the modern post-1648 era of international politics, the sovereign state has been the key political unit under anarchy. In constructing this vision of a pure anarchy he discards the possibility that hierarchy of any sort can exist in the international system. Indeed hierarchy and anarchy, he insists, are mutually exclusive (1979: 114–16). The subliminal Eurocentric cue rests with the point that this emphasis necessarily occludes the possibility of revealing various hierarchical international political formations, especially of an inter-civilizational nature, which have existed not just in the pre-1648 era,[168] but above all within the post-1648 'anarchic' era.[169] The immediate problem here is that the post-1648 era witnessed the *proliferation* of international *imperial*-hierarchies, which comprised a series of single sovereign colonial powers, each of which stood atop of a conglomerate of dependent non-sovereign polities (Hobson and Sharman 2005).

Pointedly, the world was almost completely carved up by these various imperial hierarchies between 1800 and 1980, such that it was only during the period between the 1960s and about 2000 that the world came to be uniformly characterized by a sovereign multi-state system (notwithstanding the existence of various imperial legacies). As one prominent historical sociologist of IR put it: 'if we are to speak of a Westphalian political imaginary, we should recognize that it has reached its zenith rather than its nadir in the post-Cold War era, a period in which state sovereignty ... has become much more available than in previous epochs' (Lawson 2008: 890).[170] That is, hierarchies under anarchy have been the norm in the practice of world politics in the last 400 years, the sovereign state the bare exception. The key point, though, is that Waltz's proclivity to obscure the politics of hierarchy means that the role played by Western imperialism/neo-imperialism in international politics in the modern era (1648–2010) is necessarily obscured or sublimated. And given that this phenomenon was in place in one way or another for over 90 per cent of this period if we include European colonialism in the Americas after 1492, such an elision becomes all the more poignant.

Another example of this elision of Western imperialism and neo-imperialism is found within Waltz's well-known claim that bipolarity

---

[168] These would necessarily include a range of Eastern formations that were the leading 'powers' in the world such as the Ottoman Empire and the Chinese tribute system, as well as the lesser regional power of medieval Christendom. For an excellent exploration of the pre-modern era of hierarchy see: Buzan *et al.* (1993); Kaufman *et al.* (2007).

[169] For the references concerning subsystems hierarchy see footnotes 285 and 286 in Chapter 13.

[170] Nevertheless, as I explain in Chapters 11–13, the paradox is that at the very time when the sovereign state has become for the first time universalized in world politics, so we witness a return to one of the aspects of the nineteenth-century discourse – namely the notion of the *hyper-sovereign* Western state and the *conditional sovereignty* of the Eastern state.

during the Cold War created the most peaceful and stable era that the world has ever known (1979: chs. 8–9). But this holds true only if we conflate world politics with *intra-Western* relations. For intra-Western relations were peaceful only because conflict between the United States and the Soviet Union had been displaced away from Europe and on to the terrain of the East. In other words, many countries in Afro-Asia and Latin America suffered from Western great power military invasions, various forms of political destabilization and infringements on their sovereignty throughout the Cold War era.[171] Here Odd Arne Westad's conclusion is particularly apt:

> In a historical sense – and especially when seen from the South – the Cold War was a continuation of colonialism through slightly different means ... For the Third World, the continuum of which the Cold War forms a part did not start in 1945, or even 1917, but in 1878 – with the Conference of Berlin that divided Africa between European imperialist powers (Westad 2007: 396).

Heonik Kwon expressed this point thus: 'it appears that cold war history has a concentric conceptual organization, consisting of a "formal" history of relative peace in the center and "informal" violence in the periphery' (Kwon 2010: 154–5). In short, American and Soviet military interventions in the Third World have been the price of the West's peace. Thus for those non-Western peoples caught up in all of this, the claim that 1947–90 was the most peaceful era in history would strike them as curious to say the least. And much the same conclusion could be drawn vis-à-vis the commensurate story of the nineteenth-century 'long peace' that neorealists talk of, given that intra-European violence was similarly displaced onto the terrain of the colonial East. More generally, though, Waltz's vision is one that glosses over what one scholar calls the 'silent war' between East and West throughout the period of the Cold War (Füredi 1998a).

A more general Waltzian move that serves to elide Western imperialism is one that returns us directly to Morgenthau (see pp. 188–90). And this is tied in with the specific nature of Waltz's ahistoricism – what I call 'tempocentrism' (Hobson 2002: 9–13). Tempocentrism in effect takes a snapshot of the present system and then extrapolates this picture back in time so as to (re)present all previous periods in the same image. In the process of effecting a rigid form of retrospective path-dependency,

---

[171] See Cumings (1992); Acharya (1997); Barkawi (2001).

all actors and structures situated throughout time and space are imbued with isomorphic, transhistorical properties. It is precisely this move that enables Waltz to posit a series of transhistorical equivalences: British and Athenian imperialism; British and American hegemony; or the bipolar contests between the US/USSR and Athens/Sparta. Most generally, the international system is (re)presented throughout its history by a uniform and parsimonious conception of anarchy. The key point is that in echoing Morgenthau, Waltz tempocentrically universalizes imperialism back through time and space while simultaneously removing *European* imperialism from its specific place in modern world politics. This move is effected in chapter 2 where he critiques the theories of European imperialism advocated by Hobson and Lenin. There he removes a key aspect that links modern imperialism with Europe, namely capitalism, and then replaces it with a universalized definition of the 'imperialism of great power', as did Morgenthau (Waltz 1979: 26–7). Thus because great powers have existed throughout history then, *ipso facto*, so too has imperialism. In standard tempocentric fashion, then, Waltz takes the *particular* imperialist tendency of leading Western powers in the last two centuries as the norm and then extrapolates this conception back in time, thereby universalizing it as a generic and isomorphic property of *all* great powers throughout world historical time.

It is certainly true that imperialism is not unique to the post-1800 era, and nor has it been the monopoly of the West (think of early Islam as well as the Mongols). But it is also the case that imperialism (like the institution of slavery) has taken quite different forms over time and operated according to differing moral principles, identities and normative visions that are specific to the relevant actors.[172] Indeed the same might be said of Waltz's master-variable – anarchy (Wendt 1999). However, such critical differences are elided by Waltz's tempocentrism on the one hand, and his bracketing of cultural-identity factors in the making of great power politics on the other. Of course, Waltz celebrates his ahistorical-materialist parsimony and defends hard against the sort of historical sociological insight that I am eliciting here (see Waltz 1979: ch. 3). And while he is, of course, entitled to this approach, nevertheless the conclusion to my discussion is that in universalizing imperialism as a generic and isomorphic policy of all great powers at any point in time

---

[172] Thus Chinese great power politics took on a very different form to that of European imperialism largely owing to their different identities; see Hobson (2004: ch. 13); cf. Zhang (2001); Kang (2007).

and space, so he necessarily exorcizes the particular or specific place of European imperialism in world politics in the modern period. Indeed, it is curious that such a momentous phenomenon as European imperialism finds no place in his structural theory of international politics.

The elision of Eastern agency in Western great power politics and world politics

While this elision of Western imperial hierarchy in world politics forms one prong of Waltz's subliminal Eurocentrism, equally his effective refusal to entertain the prospect of Eastern agency within his general theory forms a complementary one. In the first instance he echoes Carr and Morgenthau. This elision emerges from the fact that his theory places exclusive focus on the Western great powers. As he put it, his

> theory, like the story of international politics, is written in terms of the great power of an era. ... In international politics, as in any self-help system, the units of greatest capability set the scene of action for others as well as for themselves. In systems theory, structure is a generative notion, and the structure of a system is generated by the interaction of its principal parts (1979: 72).

But this elision of Eastern agency is problematic for a number of reasons, which in effect disturb the foundations of his theory, both directly and indirectly.

First, it is often asserted that the end of the Cold War caught Waltz's theory off guard, revealing its inability to explain international change on the one hand, while simultaneously problematizing Waltz's belief that Cold War bipolarity was a particularly stable system on the other. But what has not usually been noticed at this juncture is the point that some appreciation of Eastern agency is necessary if we are to begin to construct an adequate explanation of the end of Cold War bipolarity. Such a point is, however, explicitly denied by Waltz. Thus writing on the eve of the Second Cold War he announced that

> the waning of hegemonic competition in an era of détente and the increased prominence of north-south relations led many to believe that the world could no longer be defined in bipolar terms. But the waning of American-Russian competition and the *increased importance of third-world problems* do not imply the end of bipolarity (1979: 204, my emphasis).

However, while the Second Cold War was initiated by the Soviet invasion of Afghanistan in December 1979, nevertheless it was in Afghanistan that the Soviets experienced their own 'Vietnam', with an exhaustive decade-long war ending in defeat at the hands of the Mujahideen fighters. While defeat at the hands of 'small-scale' Eastern agents could not wholly account for the end of the Soviet Union – and notwithstanding the point that the Mujahideen resistance which was aided by Osama Bin Laden, was supplied by the United States with Stinger missiles – nevertheless the defeat itself would have to be explained in significant degree by the role of Eastern resistance agency (cf. Sebestyen 2009). Thus the end of bipolarity which, of course, entails a fundamental change in the distribution of power in the international system, was at least in part brought about by Eastern agency, none of which registers on Waltz's theoretical radar screen. Equally, the defeat of the United States in Vietnam in the face of intransigent Vietnamese resistance agency gave rise to the 'Vietnam Syndrome', which in turn significantly affected American military thinking in the aftermath of 1975 and placed certain limits on potential future US military actions – notwithstanding President George H. W. Bush's hubristic words uttered in the euphoric afterglow of the 1991 victory in Iraq: 'By God we've kicked the Vietnam Syndrome once and for all!' Critically, that such Eastern resistance agency has had a profound impact on the American superpower refutes Waltz's claim that '[t]he United States need worry little about wayward movements and unwanted events in weak states ... The principal pains of a great power, if they are not self-inflicted, arise from the effects of policies pursued by other great powers' (1979: 202).

From these two examples alone, and many others could be offered, it would seem clear that Third World/Eastern agency needs to be factored in for understanding both the restrictive milieu within which the superpowers operate, as well as shaping some of the crucial contours that guide the reproduction and development of international politics.[173] And so to return to the Waltz quote posted at the beginning of this discussion of Eastern agency, his words could be rephrased to the effect that 'Eastern agents (in part) set the scene of action for the Western superpowers', and that 'the structure of the system is partly generated by the interactions of East and West'. Equally, to counter Waltz's claim that '[i]t would be ... ridiculous to construct a theory of international politics

---

[173] For the best discussions of this point see Barkawi (2005); Barkawi and Laffey (2006); Laffey and Weldes (2008).

based on Malaysia and Costa Rica ... To focus on great powers is not to lose sight of lesser ones. Concern with the latter's fate requires paying more attention to the former' (1979: 72–3), a more preferable statement would be that 'it would be ridiculous to construct a theory of international politics based exclusively on the United States and the USSR. To focus on small Eastern powers and actors is not to lose sight of the bigger ones. Concern with the latter's fate requires paying at least some attention to the former'.

However, at this juncture Waltz might well invoke one of his defensive delimiting arguments – in this case the defence that 'interaction relations' should be ignored when constructing a proper structural theory of international politics. Such interactions are dismissed as but irrelevant 'unit-level' attributes, the inclusion of which would only blur the strict parsimonious definition of international structure that he polices with vigilance. As he put it:

> Abstracting relations means leaving aside questions about the cultural, economic, political, and military interactions of states ... To define a structure requires ignoring how units relate with one another (how they interact) and concentrating on how they stand in relation to one another (how they are arranged or positioned). Interactions ... take place at the level of the units (1979: 80).

While such a move might well enable him to conveniently restrict the parameters of his theory in order to shield him from criticism, this does not enable an escape from the Eurocentric charge. For it is precisely *this* move that elides or dismisses the many East–West interactions that shape the actions and indeed the inner constitution of the Western great powers that in turn informs their outward trajectories. Ignoring this dimension leads in short to a reified conception of Western great powers as self-constituting, autonomous entities, whose societies and economies develop entirely independently of non-Western economic, military, political and cultural interactions; the very leitmotif of Eurocentric theory.

The Eurocentric basis of Waltz's key variables

Waltz's master-variables in world politics – anarchy, sovereignty, self-help, balance of power, and great power politics – are all derived from his reading of the modern European inter-state system. Thus in viewing these specifically European norms and practices as natural, he both tempocentrically extrapolates them back in time, as well as universalizes these provincial features through space so as to present a uniform and even canvas of world politics upon which these practices naturally occur. Had he examined non-European international politics, however, he might well have come up either with different variables, or he might have recognized the limits to how far universal generalizations can be generated from the experience of one small continent.

One pertinent example will suffice to illustrate my point. Given that China was arguably the leading power in the world from c. 1100–1800 and was certainly the leading power in the East Asian region, one would anticipate that the smaller powers in that region would have balanced against it. But this in fact did not happen. The reply might be in turn that this was because China was the kingpin within the international tribute system, and was therefore an imperialist power. But arguably this system was neither imperialist nor could it be explained through the 'conventional' practices associated with Western great power politics.[174] Moreover, the example of the Chinese system is also relevant because it constitutes a long-lasting example of hierarchy under anarchy, which in turn undermines Waltz's assumption that anarchy precludes international hierarchy of any description given the role that the balance of power plays in maintaining anarchy. In addition, one could also point to the fact that within the Chinese Warring States period (c. 475 to 221 BCE) the balance of power failed to cut in. One state, Qin, was able to defeat the other six, one by one. From these few examples alone, and there are many more that I could have selected,[175] we can see that Waltz universalizes through all time and space the provincial characteristics of one small 'continent', Western Europe, in one particular time period. Not surprisingly, then, this generates a distorted picture of the international system throughout world historical time.

US hegemony/neo-imperialism and the contradictions of Waltz's Theory

Finally, I turn to consider a number of fundamental contradictions that lie in Waltz's *Theory*, which in turn reveal a residual paternalist Eurocentric dimension to his approach. All of this emerges in the context of his discussion of US hegemony and his denial of the presence of American neo-imperialism in the post-1945 era. Much as Waltz elides the politics of

---

[174] See Hobson (2004: chs. 3 and 13); Kang (2007); Zhang (2001).
[175] See especially Kaufman *et al.* (2007).

Western imperialism between c. 1800 and c. 1960, so he seeks explicitly to sanitize or whitewash the postcolonial era of its American neo-imperialist properties. Like Morgenthau, Waltz dismisses neo-imperialism on the grounds that it is a fuzzy concept that is utilized by radical theorists in an inconsistent way. In particular he objects to the point that the 'concept' is often deployed by Marxist scholars as a means to 'salvage' the theory of imperialism, given that capitalism continued on *after* colonialism (1979: ch. 2). But Waltz contradicts this by celebrating and defending US hegemony at the very end of the book (1979: 199–210).[176]

Of course, Waltz would no doubt reply, as would Gilpin, by insisting that US hegemony has been anti-imperialist such that it has provided beneficial services to much of the world, thereby negating the 'contradiction charge'. Indeed he argues that the US serves as the global policeman and has borne the overwhelming burden of keeping the peace (1979: 206, 208), and that in the absence of US hegemony there would be no one to take the lead in solving the problems of poverty, population growth, pollution and proliferation (1979: 210). But once again, the problem here is that even formal imperialism, never mind informal neo-imperialism, need not imply an exploitative politics but can be said to exist when a great power seeks through paternalist intervention to 'civilize' and culturally convert others to its own core civilizational values. And as I explained in the section on HST earlier, this is precisely the definition of US hegemony that Waltz and Gilpin deploy.

What then of the contradictions that Waltz's celebration of US hegemony implies for his own neorealist theory? Because I have dealt with this in detail viz. HST in the last section, I shall move quickly through this discussion. The first contradiction, as with Gilpin, concerns the point that for Waltz great powers and states more generally seek at a minimum to maintain their own interests and power relative to those of others rather than sacrifice for the good of others. As he put it:

> In a self-help system each of the units spends a portion of its efforts . . . in providing the means of protecting itself against others. . . . When faced with the possibility of cooperating for mutual gain, states . . . must ask how the gain will be divided . . . Even the prospect of large absolute gains for both parties does not elicit their cooperation so long as each fears how the other will use its increased capabilities (1979: 105).

---

[176] It is curious, to say the least, that Waltz's defence of US hegemony has not been picked up in the vast secondary literature on his 1979 book.

Thus the presentation of American hegemonic self-sacrifice contradicts this fundamental neorealist maxim. This in turn leads directly into the second contradiction, wherein Waltz's discussion of the decline of hegemony leads him, as we saw with Gilpin in the previous section, to contradict his fundamental claim that weak powers are irrelevant to international politics (as I explained earlier). For it is at this point that he explicitly invokes Mancur Olson's argument that the free-riding weak states effectively undermine (or at least weaken) the American hegemon (Waltz 1979: 208).

Overall, I close by noting that Waltz is prepared to jeopardize some of the most fundamental and cherished tenets of his structural third image theory in order to celebrate American hegemony. In the process, then, he jeopardizes the strictures of his parsimonious theory. Moreover, as I explained vis-à-vis Gilpin, US hegemony is not merely exceptional to the logic of Waltz's neorealist theory but can itself only be explained through the old nineteenth-century imperial trope of *American exceptionalism* and its duty to civilize the rest of the world in order to heroically rescue it from chaos.[177] Of course, Waltz might reply by arguing that if his theory is Eurocentric it is nevertheless superior to any non-Eurocentric one. But if so, then it is clear that Waltz's stated claim for a value-free objective universalist theory of international politics (IP) is thereby undermined. And to respond to Waltz's claim that the success of a theory of IP must be measured in terms of its ability to 'explain the small number of big and important things',[178] there are surely few larger and more important things in international politics than Western imperialism/neo-imperialism in particular and East–West interactions in the last few centuries more generally. Accordingly, the conclusion might be that the aperture of his theoretical lens is fixed so narrowly that his theory is simply too limited to be able to pick up, let alone explain, some of the crucial dynamics of the international system – past, present and future – even though several of these are directly relevant even to the abnormally narrow remit of Waltz's theory.

---

[177] It is, however, the case that in a later article Waltz is far less sanguine about the continuing role of US hegemony, arguing that the trappings of unipolarity are likely to lead to the abuse of that power by the United States with negative consequences for world politics (Waltz 1993a, 1993b). That said, though, in a later article Waltz reverts back, albeit briefly, to his support for US hegemony (Waltz 1999).

[178] Waltz (1979: 71–2, 121–3; 1986: 329, 344, 345).

9

Orthodox subliminal Eurocentrism: neoliberal institutionalism and the English School, c. 1966–1989

Introduction: imperialist and anti-imperialist conceptions of world politics

This chapter carries the story of subliminal Eurocentrism a notch further by examining post-1945 liberal international theory, focusing specifically on the classical English School (ES) and neoliberal institutionalism (NLI).

Turning to Figure 9.1 we see once again how post-1945 liberal IR theory overlaps with, but also differs from, its manifest Eurocentric predecessors. Thus although there is no explicit discussion of 'civilizations versus barbarians', or of 'whites versus non-whites', nevertheless the traditional civilization/barbarism discourse is sublimated rather than exorcized. For the ES and the NLI the West is viewed in effect as the civilized realm of inter-state cooperation. And significantly, Western states are in effect imbued with levels of super-rationality, as I explain later. Moving up one level in Figure 9.1 I focus on the different degrees of agency that are awarded to the East and West. In Keohane's theory the West is awarded the highest degree of agency, in terms of its ability to pioneer development (political and economic) as well as its progressive capacity to remake world politics along Western lines. In his discussion, moreover, the Third World is implicitly allocated 'conditional agency' and is depicted as a largely passive recipient of the largesse that is delivered courtesy of the key benign international institutions. The ES awards the East various degrees of agency though these are always inferior to the pioneering agency that is awarded to the West. Specifically, it implicitly delineates two conceptions of Eastern agency. In the first incarnation the East is awarded emulative 'conditional agency' whereby it assimilates the institutions and practices that were pioneered by the Europeans as they were delivered courtesy of the Western civilizing mission, ultimately so that the East could join, and therefore enjoy the benefits of, Western international society. And second,

214

INTRODUCTION: IMPERIALISM AND ANTI-IMPERIALISM 215

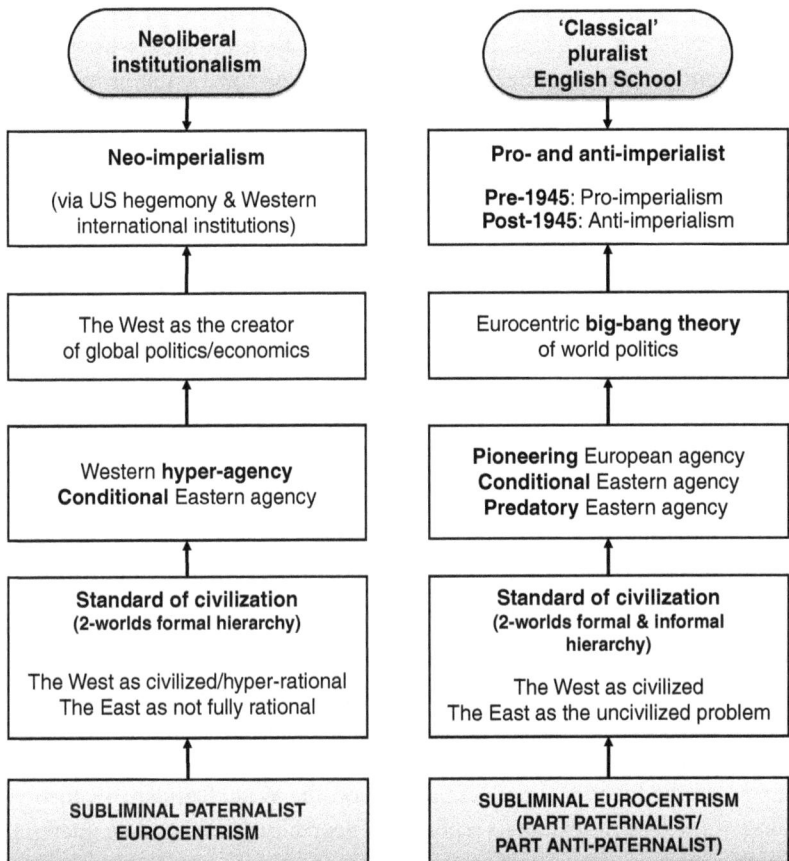

Figure 9.1 Subliminal Eurocentrism in liberal international theory, post-1945

the East is awarded a degree of 'predatory agency', which emerges in Bull's fifth 'revolt against the West', in which the refusal to fully Westernize gives rise to the contemporary 'Eastern problem' that in turn destabilizes both global international society/world order and Western civilization.

Moving up another level in Figure 9.1, classical ES theory visualizes IR through the Eurocentric 'big-bang theory' of world politics. Thus Europe pioneered development and self-generated through the Eurocentric *logic of immanence* before exporting its institutions (via imperialism) to the East in order to remake the world as far as possible in its own image. The approach undertaken by NLI is different. Here there is unsurprisingly no discussion of the rise of the West and the rise of the Western state, given the theory's lack of interest in historical international systems. Rather, it treats Western states as fully formed and then considers how they subsequently come together to create and reproduce the major international institutions through iterated cooperation.

What are the political prescriptions that these theories advance? In classical pluralist ES theory there are in fact two self-contradictory approaches. The first naturalizes European imperialism before 1945 viewing it as a functional-requirement for the creation of a progressive and orderly global international society, while the second thrust is of an anti-imperialist nature that cuts in for the post-1945 era. While NLI does not openly advocate imperialism and ostensibly rejects it, nevertheless a paternalist conception of neo-imperialism creeps in through the subliminal Eurocentric back door. For the key international institutions are portrayed as paternalist Western vehicles for the cultural conversion of Third World states to Western liberal-civilizational precepts.

Western interdependence theory and neoliberal institutionalism: subliminal Eurocentrism and latent neo-imperialism

Robert Keohane's seminal 1984 book, *After Hegemony*, is typical of postwar subliminal Eurocentric texts in which all talk of 'civilizations and barbarism' and explicit pro-imperialist references are conspicuous for their absence. Moreover, as with the classical realists and neorealists I examined in the last chapter, so the focus is almost exclusively on the West. Standard IR theory courses as well as IR textbooks report how neorealism endows state interests with the universal property of pursuing short-term, zero-sum 'relative gains', while NLI posits that of long-term collective-sum 'absolute gains' (e.g., Baldwin 1993; Hasenclever 1997). This description assumes the positing of *universal* characteristics to states: that *all* states, regardless of their culture or position in the international system, will adopt one or other of these postures depending on which theory we are dealing with. But in what follows I want to argue that this so-called value-free posture elides the point that the theory advances a provincial Westernism masquerading as the universal.

It is an axiom of constructivism that NLI is *a-sociological* since it purportedly treats state interests as fully formed prior to social interaction. Accordingly, constructivists insist that NLI is problematic because it fails to recognize the role of the identity of the agent in shaping its interests.[179] But here I want to suggest an alternative interpretation

---

[179] E.g., Finnemore (1996a); Wendt (1999); Reus-Smit (1999); Ling (2002).

that shall inform the rest of my discussion. In the first instance it could be claimed that Keohane in fact recognizes that the ethical relationship or identities of the actors within a Prisoner's Dilemma situation *can* impact on the outcomes (1984: 74–5), with him concluding this discussion by noting that 'we can just as well assume that the actors are imbued with values transmitted by society ... as that they are pure possessive individualists' (1984: 75). Much more significant, though, is that throughout the book Keohane explicitly reiterates that his analysis is generated by observing the advanced capitalist states of the West – with Japan included as an honorary member of the Western club – and that it is their *common ideological outlook* which ultimately serves to promote inter-state cooperation (1984: 5–7, 43, 182). As he put it:

> [b]ecause I begin with acknowledged common interests, my study focuses on relations among the advanced market-economy countries, where such interests are manifold. These countries hold views about the proper operation of their economies that are relatively similar – at least in comparison with the differences that exist between them and less developed countries, or the nonmarket planned economies (1984: 6).

Thus Keohane not only looks specifically at Western states but he argues that Western states already have shared cultural values *before* they interact in PD games. And he is explicit that such states take specifically Western cultural values to the table, which then directly inform how they interact in the subsequent iterated PD games. These common values, which comprise the core belief in liberal free market capitalism and liberal democracy are, of course, signifiers of contemporary Western civilization. As he put it towards the end of the book, '[g]iven the desire of European and Japanese governments to achieve rapid economic growth with democratic political institutions and capitalist economies, they had good reasons to join the Americanocentric system [of international institutions]' (1984: 182). Nor were these one-off assertions since he repeats them elsewhere.[180] This implicit civilizational definition dovetails with his Eurocentric assumption that the process of cooperation requires 'super-rationality' given that (Western) states must forego their short-term interests in favour of long-term ones.[181]

---

[180] E.g., Keohane (1989: 2–3; 1993: 274–5, 277–8).
[181] Interestingly, Ling (2002: ch. 1) also argues that NLI is Eurocentric but does so on the basis that it posits a universalist theory of state interests and behaviour, which in turn are fully formed prior to social interaction.

218 CHAPTER 9: ORTHODOX SUBLIMINAL EUROCENTRISM

Interestingly, Keohane tacks on to this framework the claim that his theory is supposed to have *some* relevance for 'North–South' relations. Thus, he claims, his prescriptions

> surely apply to some relationships between the advanced countries [the West] and the less developed countries [the East]. . . . The focus of this book on cooperation among the advanced industrialized countries by no means implies that cooperation is impossible, or unnecessary, between North and South (1984: 6–7).

So where interests are shared then East–West relations are assumed to be potentially cooperative, though presumably such a positive outcome would not prevail where such interests diverge. Indeed as he put it elsewhere, '[f]or situations with little mutual interest . . . states will be reluctant to cooperate with each other' (Keohane 1989: 18, n. 20). Even so, analysing this aspect is explicitly closed off and, in its absence, he posts an invitation to other scholars to develop this angle in the future (1984: 7). But the problem here is that North–South relations inevitably enter his discussion of international institutions because the key IFIs that he examines predominantly interface with Third World societies. And it is here, I argue, where we can detect a latent liberal-paternalist neo-imperial posture. Moreover, by appearing to flatten out the international system and obscuring the hierarchical relationship between East and West so he naturalizes this neo-imperial relationship.

To advance my claims it is instructive to note the parallels between Keohane and Angell (1913) given that both developed theories of cooperation under conditions of interdependence (see pp. 40–5, this volume). As with Keohane's theory, the conventional wisdom assumes that Angell's theory has universalist prescriptions in that *all* states are better off when cooperating under conditions of strong global interdependence rather than from going it alone. But as we saw in Chapter 2, Angell argued that interdependence only existed between European states and he *explicitly* advocated a hierarchical-imperialist relationship between East and West. Keohane mirrors Angell insofar as both construct *relativist* theories of cooperation that apply most robustly to intra-Western state relations; or put differently, their theories of interstate cooperation are derived from their reading of intra-Western state relations. The key question, then, revolves around Keohane's conception of East–West relations and whether, like Angell's, this entails any imperialist cues.

Early on in the book Keohane announces his disapproval of *ultraimperialism*, which entails the wealthy Northern states cooperating to exploit poor, weaker countries in the South (1984: 10–11). Here it is clear that he equates imperialism or neo-imperialism with economic exploitation. Moreover, by definition, his liberal political economy envisages the spread of liberal capitalism as an inherent public good that is non-exploitative. Thus while he concedes that '[t]he principles underlying the rules and practices of the IMF, GATT . . . reflect the interests and ideologies of the most powerful states in the international system' (1984: 256), nevertheless, he insists, such regimes are deemed to be *beneficial* for third world states. Indeed it is axiomatic, for example, that the spread of free trade can only benefit the Southern economies within his liberal Eurocentric approach. But there are two possible neo-imperialist cues in Keohane's argument, the first of which is contestable while the second is, I believe, incontrovertible.

First, using a standard neo-Listian framework it could be argued that the proactive spread of free trade by the Western hegemon and hegemonic international institutions (IFIs) serves to benefit the richer countries at the expense of the poorer ones, given that it enables the former to export their superior goods unimpeded into the latters' domestic economies thereby flooding their markets and undermining their infant industries. Moreover, speaking of the adoption of free trade by the richest nations Friedrich List originally claimed that

> [i]t is a very common clever device that when [someone] has attained the summit of greatness, he kicks away the ladder by which he has climbed up, in order to deprive others of the means of climbing up after him. In this lies the secret of the cosmopolitical doctrine of Adam Smith (List 1841/1909: 295).

This refers to the fact that both the United States and Britain industrialized on the back of extremely protectionist regimes and only turned to free trade once they had arrived at the top of the global economic hierarchy.[182] Thus the imposition of free trade on developing countries by Britain after 1846 and the United States after 1945 prevents Third World states from using tariffs to protect their infant industries, thereby denying them the developmental privilege that propelled the advanced Western economies to the top of the global hierarchy in the first place. On this reading, therefore,

---

[182] List (1841/1909); Weiss and Hobson (1995: chs. 4 and 7); Hobson (1997: 150–8; 2004: ch. 11); Chang (2002).

the projection of free trade by the American-led IFIs constitutes an 'economic containment' strategy to keep the Third World down; that is, *free* trade turns out to be *unfair* trade. However, this argument would be ruled out by Keohane's liberal political economy perspective, which holds that free trade benefits *all* states (e.g., 1984: 148-9).

A second neo-imperialist cue in Keohane's work emerges from the point that the key IFIs have acted as paternalist neo-imperial vehicles for the assimilation or *cultural conversion* of non-Western states along liberal capitalist lines (as noted in the last chapter). Clearly the GATT and WTO have discharged the duty of spreading free trade, while before 1973 the IMF was responsible for preventing a return to protectionism via its prohibition of currency devaluation. But after 1982 the IMF, as well as the World Bank, lent money to non-Western states with *conditionality* attached – specifically in the form of structural adjustment programmes – such that the social price of accepting financial aid has been the cultural conversion of Third World states to Western neoliberal policy architectures. And much like the nineteenth-century system of 'capitulations', the parallel is found in the point that modern Eastern states need to harmonize their domestic legal systems according to Western principles (Fidler 2000). Moreover, one notable scholar argues that the paternalist role of the IFIs finds its historical parallel with the League of Nations Mandate System (Anghie 2005: ch. 5).

However, describing these as 'neo-imperialist' arguments would be ruled out by Keohane on the grounds that assimilation to Western norms can be only a progressive good. But, as I explained in the last chapter and in Chapter 1 (pp. 23-30), this elides the simple point that such a paternalist rationale echoes that which nineteenth-century imperialism embodied. By analogy, the contemporary key IFIs act as 'paternalist civilizers' of the East, serving to 'uplift' the Eastern societies by remaking them in the Western image for their own betterment. Keohane might reply by saying that *if* this is imperialism of sorts, then it would dovetail with the popular *benign* notion of 'liberal imperialism' or 'empire-lite' that is advocated by neo-Conservatives and liberals such as Michael Ignatieff. But this would only reinforce my point that his argument constitutes a form of liberal *paternalist* neo-imperialism.

This implicit neo-imperialist framework is reinforced by Keohane's analysis of US hegemony. A significant part of his argument is that US hegemony was vital in establishing the key international institutions after 1944 (1984: ch. 8). He also provides a highly consensual vision in that the United States could not simply 'proclaim' its legitimate hegemonic power but was forced to negotiate with its partners in all manner of ways (1984: 138). But the key Eurocentric moniker emerges here in the guise of a *consensual* approach; one which can be maintained only by focusing on intra-Western relations given that US hegemony and the IFIs have often driven through their demands against the opposition of many Third World states. Thus when Keohane asserts that international institutions work because they do not trammel the sovereignty of states, so he elides the many infringements on the economic and fiscal sovereignty of Southern states that were imposed through structural adjustment programmes. Instead Third World 'recipients' are imagined as but passive beneficiaries of paternalist Western largesse. In this way, Western hegemony is naturalized while inter-civilizational resistance and dialogical interactions are ignored (thereby returning to my discussion of Waltz – see pages 203–10, 211–13).

To conclude, then, I would suggest that the Eurocentric parallels between Keohane and Angell are striking. Angell privileged Europe as the zone of civilized cooperation but demoted the non-European world to a zone of uncivilized conflict, such that only a Western civilizing mission could remedy the 'Eastern problem'. Likewise, Keohane views the West as the zone of civilized cooperation while much of the East is, albeit implicitly, denigrated as uncivilized insofar as a liberal paternalist neo-civilizing mission is required to remedy the Eastern deficiencies. The key difference, though, is that Keohane's Eurocentrism is subliminal while Angell's was manifest. The final upshot of all this is that Keohane does *not* bracket or abstract Western norms and conceptions of interest but *front-loads* them into the core of his theory. And this necessarily means that his Eurocentrism subverts the positivist fact/value distinction that he claims to uphold (see 1984: 10). The irony here is that there is surely no other IR theorist who has so clearly staked his reputation on the need to develop a rigorous, value-free, positivist social science.[183] Indeed his rationalist statement that states can learn to cooperate in the absence of 'idealistic concerns for the common good or by ideological commitments to a certain pattern of IR' (1984: 78) abrades with his major claim that international regimes and institutions were constructed precisely along ideological lines in order to construct a certain *Western* pattern of IR (1984: ch. 8). Moreover, as I note in Chapter 12 (p. 309), this subliminal neo-imperialist posture becomes upgraded into an *explicit* or manifest expression of paternalist Eurocentrism in the post-Cold War era when Keohane openly advocates a revitalized

---

[183] See especially Keohane (1998); King, Keohane and Verba (1994).

222 CHAPTER 9: ORTHODOX SUBLIMINAL EUROCENTRISM

imperial form of Western intervention and humanitarian intervention in failed Eastern states (Keohane 2003: esp. 295–7).

The classical English School and the 'hierarchical society': between an imperialist rock and an anti-imperialist hard place

At first sight it might seem curious to some readers that the ES is included in this chapter given that in the United States it is often referred to as 'English School realism'. But, in fact, it rests on fundamental liberal foundations comprising Lockean or Grotian liberalism (as in the 'pluralist' wing) and cosmopolitan liberalism (as in the 'solidarist' wing).[184] Moreover, ES pluralism shares with NLI the assumption that anarchy can be mitigated and inter-state cooperation and order can be realized through conforming to (albeit informal) international institutions/conventions (see Hobson 2000: 89–104). Because this chapter is concerned with the 1966–89 era I shall focus here on the Eurocentrism of the 'classical' *pluralist* ES, including Martin Wight, Gerrit Gong and above all Hedley Bull and Adam Watson (with a brief discussion of 'solidarism' reserved for Chapter 12).[185]

A key part of my argument is that classical ES theory has been informed by a subliminal Eurocentrism that involves a self-contradictory and schizophrenic stance vis-à-vis imperialism. A number of scholars have rightly drawn out the imperialist side of the classical pluralist ES and subjected this to critique.[186] However, I want to argue that the classical pluralist ES is of particular note because it constitutes a theory which reveals the problems with the monolithic conflation of Eurocentrism and imperialism, precisely because it oscillates between pro- and anti-imperialist postures. And it turns out to be a considerable irony that the issue of imperialism has been sidelined by the current ES writers' preoccupation with the tension between solidarism and pluralism in the classical school,[187] precisely because this contradictory stance vis-à-vis imperialism emerges within the context of the

---

[184] Though even this division is problematized by the point that there are solidarist cues in Grotius (Linklater 2009: 95).
[185] For an excellent summary of the broad church of the ES see Linklater (2009). And for two very interesting and penetrating book-length takes on the ES see: Buzan (2004); Linklater and Suganami (2006).
[186] Excellent discussions of this are found in: Callahan (2004); Kayaoglu (2010); Seth (2011b); Zarakol (2011).
[187] See especially Wheeler (1992); Dunne (1998: 142–54); Dunne and Wheeler (1996); Alderson and Hurrell (2000: ch. 1); cf. Williams (2005).

pluralist/solidarist debate. Still, this is not to denigrate or ignore the point that in recent years a significant group of ES scholars has begun to develop non-Eurocentric sensibilities and analyses.[188]

This section is broken down into four subsections. The first two consider the Eurocentric big-bang theory of modern world politics that I broached in the last chapter. I then turn in the third section to consider Bull's analysis of what I am taking the liberty of calling the 'Eastern problem', which brings to the fore the key contradiction in Bull's pluralist approach while simultaneously shedding fresh light on the status of solidarist versus pluralist tendencies in Bull's *oeuvre*. And I conclude by rethinking Bull's stance on history and historicism. Partly because of the range of issues to be covered as well as in part because the ES is enjoying a renaissance (mainly in Britain and Australia), this discussion will be a slightly extended one.

The 'Westphilian' origins of Westphalian European international society

The Eurocentric big-bang theory is announced in the opening sentence of the key edited volume, *The Expansion of International Society*:

> The purpose of this book is to explore the expansion of the international society of European states across the rest of the globe, and its transformation from a society fashioned in Europe and dominated by Europeans into the global international society of today (Bull and Watson 1984b: 1).

In one respect, however, their account does not quite fit the implied chronology of the two-step big-bang theory owing to their claim that European international society 'did not first evolve its rules and institutions and then [subsequently] export them to the rest of the world'. Rather the evolution of the European society and its expansion occurred simultaneously (Bull and Watson 1984b: 6; Watson 1992/2009: 214). Nevertheless this chronological vision serves only to qualify rather than undermine the big-bang trope, given that it still rests on the fundamental monological proposition that Europe made itself through the *endogenous logic of immanence* and projected itself outwards to universalize its own institutions through the creation of a global international society. This is developed in some detail by Watson in various places.

---

[188] Cf. Dunne (1997); Keene (2002); Keal (2003); Suzuki (2009); Buzan (2010).

CHAPTER 9: ORTHODOX SUBLIMINAL EUROCENTRISM

In his chapter, 'European international society and its expansion', a key aspect of Watson's analysis is his emphasis on the *uniqueness* of 'European rational restlessness'. Here Europe in its formative stage appears as 'exceptionally turbulent, dynamic, and enterprising', and in strong contrast to the closed or isolated worlds of Asian cultures, Europe was 'innovative and expansionary [filling] out the uncultivated spaces within its boundaries and [starting] to push back its geographical limits in many directions' (Watson 1984: 13). Moreover, the internal competitive dynamic between states underpins the rise of Europe, thereby dovetailing precisely with Eurocentric historical sociological and world historical accounts of the rise of the West that are found in neo-Weberianism, liberalism, neorealism and Marxism. This argument is advanced in detail in Watson's pioneering book, *The Evolution of International Society* (1992/2009: chs. 13–21), though this is focused primarily on the rise of the European states system/international society of states.[189] Here we return to the Eurocentric logic of immanence, which recounts the rise of the modern European state system/international society of states by focusing on the endogenous journey that passes through a linear series of the familiar European way-stations. The journey Watson takes us on begins with the Italian city-state system and then proceeds on to the emergence of sovereignty at Westphalia by way of the Renaissance and Reformation, to arrive in 1713 with the institutionalization of the balance of power at Utrecht.[190] And while it is true that a handful of Eastern developments are mentioned as reacting back on Europe in dialogical fashion, these are very much the exceptions that prove the Eurocentric rule given that they turn out to have been only inconsequential.[191]

Of course, it might be responded that this analysis of the rise of European international society seems entirely reasonable and that accusing it of Western bias seems entirely unreasonable. As Bull and Watson put it: '[b]ecause it was in fact Europe and not America, Asia or Africa that first dominated and in so doing, unified the world, it is not our perspective but the historical record itself that can be called Eurocentric' (Bull and Watson 1984b: 2). But the immediate problem here is that the

---

[189] Note that while Watson's 1992 book, *The Evolution of International Society*, falls outside the temporal confines of this chapter (1966–1989), I feel it legitimate to draw on it here because the book's ideas were formulated over a period that can be traced back to the mid-1960s (see Watson 1992/2009: 4–5).
[190] Watson (1992/2009: chs. 13–18); also Bull (1977: ch. 4); Bull (1980/2000).
[191] Watson (1992/2009: 177–81, 216–18); Wight (1977: 34; 1992: 52, 69–70).

'historical record' that they have chosen to consult excludes almost all Eastern contributions to the rise of Europe and to globalization.[192] Thus they prefer to treat Europe as a self-constituting and exceptional entity that self-generated through the logic of immanence, thereby denying the dialogical notions of an 'other-generated Europe' and the poly-civilizational 'logic of confluence' that a non-Eurocentric approach would focus upon (e.g., Hobson 2004).

Many examples could be drawn upon in order to produce an alternative dialogical narrative, a few of which are worth mentioning so as to consolidate my claim. Thus, for example, while the Italian city-state system was heavily reliant on Eastern trade – a point conceded by Watson (1992/2009: 221) – it was no less reliant on the financial institutions such as cheques, bills of exchange, banks and commenda partnerships which had been pioneered in the Islamic and pre-Islamic Middle East (Hobson 2004: ch. 6). Moreover, it could be argued that the Renaissance and scientific revolution were significantly enabled by Eastern ideas – Indian, Chinese and, above all, Islamic.[193] Or again, the overseas expansion that began in 1492 was only made possible by navigational and nautical techniques that were pioneered by the Chinese and especially the Muslims, in the absence of which the Age of Discovery might never have happened and certainly not when it did (Hobson 2004: chs. 6–7). In any case, though, the Europeans did not 'discover' the East since Eastern traders had been in contact with each other many hundreds of years before Columbus and da Gama were born.[194] Or the role of industrialization, supposedly the leitmotif of British genius, was significantly enabled by Chinese innovations that stem back several millennia (Hobson 2004: ch. 9). And I would add to this the significant Eastern inputs in the rise of the sovereign state within Europe, none of which – with the single exception of Ottoman consulates – are considered by classical ES history (see Hobson 2009).

Another way to express all this is to say that non-Eurocentrism focuses on the constant interactions between civilizations through the dialogical idea of the 'logic of confluence', whereas classical English School pluralism focuses on the exceptional rise of the West in isolation of other civilizations through the monological idiom of the Eurocentric 'logic of immanence'.[195]

---

[192] And for a discussion of the Eastern origins of globalization see Hobson (2004: chs. 2–4).
[193] E.g., Goonatilake (1998); Hobson (2004: 173–83); Goody (2004: 56–83); Bala (2006: chs. 6, 8); Ghazanfar (2006); Raju (2007).
[194] Abu-Lughod (1989); Wink (1990); Hobson (2004: chs. 2–4); Frank and Gills (1996).
[195] And for more on this, conceptualized in more philosophical terms, see the pioneering analyses of Harding (1998) and Al-Rodhan (2009).

Moreover, this alternative analysis replaces the Eurocentric idiom of 'first the West, then the Rest' with 'without the Rest there might be no West'. Ultimately, though, the point is that Bull and his colleagues are of course entitled to their particular historical account, but it should be recognized as a Eurocentric one that reflects the values and interests, or standpoint, of the West rather than the so-called 'real historical record' that Bull and Watson proclaim it to be.

The paternalist defence of imperialism: remedying the 'Eastern problem' in the rise of global international society

Having discussed the first step of the Eurocentric big-bang narrative, I now turn to consider the second step concerning the expansion of European international society. Echoing the opening statement to the edited volume on *The Expansion of International Society*, Watson later asserted that:

> In the [nineteenth century] the Europeans created the first international system to span the whole globe, and established everywhere a universalized version of the rules and institutions and the basic assumptions of the European society of states. Our present international society is directly descended from that universalized European system (Watson 1992/2009: 214).

Critically, the notion of a paternalist civilizing mission underpins Bull's narrative of Europe's initial expansionist phase. In his chapter 'The Emergence of Universal International Society' Bull certainly recognizes that non-Western states had to meet the criteria of the standard of civilization that Europe imposed as condition of entry into international society. But, he argues, the imposition of the European standard of civilization as the normative gatekeeper of membership was not a vehicle of imperial domination but was an entirely reasonable construct. For 'it could hardly have been expected that European states could have extended the full benefits of membership . . . to political entities that were [unable] to enter into relationships on a basis of reciprocity' (Bull 1984a: 122). Taking on the charge that such expansion is a form of European imperialism he asserts that

> the most central rules of international intercourse do not depend for their validity on the special interests of one side but on reciprocal interests. The rules that treaties should be observed, that sovereignty should be respected, that states should not interfere in one another's internal agreed frontiers, of immunity or inviolability of diplomatists . . . can in no sense be viewed simply as instruments of the special interests of a particular

group. This, indeed, is why the Third World countries have sought actually to become part of the international order, even while sometimes purporting to denounce it. It is also what makes nonsense of the attempt to account for international law in terms of a class [i.e., 'exploitative'] theory (1980/2000: 181).

That the East positively and consensually embraced many Western ideas and institutions is reiterated time and again throughout Bull's writings on the topic.[196]

This justification and naturalization of imperialism here is pointed up by Adam Watson, when he notes albeit in passing, that '[t]he insistence on Western values ... can reasonably be considered a form of cultural imperialism. It played an important part in the integrating process which established a European-dominated global international society' (Watson 1992/2009: 273–4). Ultimately, though, whether Bull or Watson rejected the moral sanctioning of Western imperialism is not the key issue here. For both accorded it 'progressive functional sanction' as a means to provide the global 'political good', insofar as it served to spread the 'benefits' of European international society to the non-Western world.[197] Thus the point that Third World countries sought to acquire these institutions not as a means to promote world order but as protections, pure and simple, against an imperialist and marauding West is conspicuous only for its absence, with any sensitivity to the coercive actions of the West all but absent (see Keene 2002; Kayaoglu 2011; Seth 2011b). And it is here where William Callahan's important discussion of the Chinese 'century of humiliation' (c. 1839–1949) is apposite. For this imperialist engagement with China 'did not lead to order but to massive social dislocation, and ultimately violent revolution' (Callahan 2004: 313). Indeed, the various Chinese revolutions were in part stimulated by a reaction against the encounter with the West, with Mao's communism being the final outcome. In this way Bull's disapproval of Third World socialism is oblivious to the part that European coercion played in stimulating its formation, at least in China (and no doubt elsewhere). And thus Bull's silence on such issues has the effect of naturalizing the imperial expansion of European international society.

Nevertheless, it is certainly the case that the classical ES scholar, Gerrit Gong, emphasizes the imperialist notion of the standard of civilization and reveals, often in genuinely sympathetic fashion, the many ways in which its

---

[196] E.g., Bull (1984a: 122–4; 1984/2000: 212–13, 231–3); Bull and Watson (1984c: 429).
[197] And for an extended discussion see Keene (2002); Kayaoglu (2010).

imposition was resisted by non-Western states and was viewed as an affront to their dignity. He also articulates the story of the expansion of the West into China in ways reminiscent of Callahan's analysis. But in the end he invokes Bull and Watson's functionalist-imperial argument, arguing that China's resistance to Europe's impositions of unequal territories and extraterritoriality led her to challenge them 'in international legal terms [which thereby] underscored the extent to which [China] had accepted the principles and practices of the European international society' (Gong 1984: 183). And, of note too is his claim that since 1945 the standard of civilization has declined significantly and has been replaced by the universal human rights regime (Gong 1984: 69).

All in all, this points to a *bipolar* construction of hierarchy in international society, where the 'liberal principle' of non-interventionism applied only to relations between civilized states (i.e., within Europe). Thus imperialist intervention in the East was not only permissible but was positively embraced as a means to civilize Eastern polities and thereby correct the deviancy of the 'Eastern problem' (see also Keene 2002). It is this move, therefore, that serves to convert the focus of the ES from the 'anarchical society' within Europe to the 'hierarchical society' within the global realm. Nevertheless, if the classical ES provided a strong justification or rationale for Western imperialism between c. 1800 and 1960 it performed a *volta face* thereafter, drawing back into a Eurocentric anti-paternalist rejection of imperial intervention, to a consideration of which I now turn.

The anti-paternalist critique of neo-imperialism: lamenting the 'Eastern problem' in contemporary global international society

The contemporary 'Eastern problem' that so concerns Bull emerges in the context of the 'revolt against the West'. The 'revolt' occurs in five key phases, the first four of which produce a highly consensual image of East–West relations (Bull 1984b; 1984/2000). Here he narrates decolonization in terms of the 'triumph of the West' and the notion of emulative or 'conditional' Eastern agency, wherein Western political values and institutions are embraced voluntarily and copied by non-Western states. Thus the

> right of all nations to self-determination, the right of all states equally to sovereignty, racial equality, the duty of rich nations to assist poor, were all ideas present, or at least implicit, in the liberal political tradition of the Western countries, and indeed it was the impact of this tradition on the beliefs of Western-educated leaders of Asian and African countries that

was a major cause, along with [Western] Marxist-Leninist influences, of their struggle against the old [colonial] era (Bull and Watson 1984c: 429).

Moreover, in this vision all the institutions of international society, which were pioneered in Europe, were not only accepted voluntarily by non-Western states but were actively fought for so that they too could come to enjoy the benefits of Western institutions as equal members in international society (e.g., Watson 1992/2009: 300–1). In short, the first four phases were conducted 'in the name of ideas or values that are themselves Western' (Bull 1984b: 222–3), thereby in effect transforming 'the Eastern revolt against the West' into 'the Eastern embrace of the West'.

However, the 'Eastern problem' emerges in the fifth revolt against the West. And it is here where Bull shifts to a conception of 'predatory Eastern agency'; a notion that returns us directly to the conception constructed by the racist-realists such as Mahan and Mackinder, as well as the racist cultural realists such as Charles Pearson and Lothrop Stoddard. To recall my discussion in Chapters 5 and 6, these racists argued that the recalcitrant barbaric East was a threat both to world order and to Western civilization. Analogously, Bull emphasizes that the fifth revolt against the West constitutes a challenge to Western civilization and global international society, such that this might also be termed 'the revolt against civilization'. There are two aspects here, the first of which concerns the point that as Third World states have become formally independent so they 'have been freer to adopt a different rhetoric that sets Western values aside ... Today, there is legitimate doubt as to how far the demands from the Third World coalition are comparable with the moral ideas of the West' (Bull 1984/2000: 213; also 1984b: 224). Here he is referring to the Third World desire for cultural liberation from 'so-called' Western neo-imperialism.

The second aspect of the Eastern problem concerns the point that many Third World states are either despotic, or are simply too weak in an institutional sense to provide order (i.e., 'failed states' or 'quasi-states'), thereby posing a further challenge to the successful reproduction of global international society. Here Bull and Watson in fact rehabilitate the idea of the 'standard of civilization' for assessing contemporary global international society (as do the solidarists), with its discourse of the three worlds of Western liberal civilization, Eastern despotic barbarism and Eastern anarchic savagery. Thus they argue that the idea of equal sovereignty today is a myth, to wit: 'A number of Asian and African states are more like the nascent or quasi-states that existed in Europe before the Age of Richlieu than they are like the modern Western ... states of today' (Bull and Watson 1984c: 430). Indeed, such quasi-states

> still share some of the characteristics that led European statesmen in the last [i.e., nineteenth] century to conclude that they could not be brought into international society because they were not capable of entering into the kinds of relationship that European states had with one another (Bull and Watson 1984c: 430).[198]

The essential claim is that the contemporary existence of Eastern quasi-states and modern day Oriental despotisms serve only to undermine international cohesion through endemic conflict, thereby serving to weaken global international society – much as the racist-realists and racist cultural realists had argued in the late-nineteenth and early twentieth centuries.

The Eurocentric cue lies in Bull and Watson's point that the postcolonial Third World generates the 'Eastern problem' as *the* obstacle to the successful reproduction of contemporary global international society. Blaming the Third World, not least for seeking to preserve its own identity in the face of Western neo-imperial assimilation, is a typical symptom of Eurocentrism for two reasons: first, because it presumes that the East should naturally discard its cultural identity in favour of a Western one given that the latter is deemed to be inherently superior and more conducive to the promotion of world order; and second, because blaming the West for putting the Third World in this defensive predicament never occurs to Bull. This becomes most clearly apparent when he described the revolt against the West as governed by 'tawdry rhetoric' behind which lay

> envy and self-pity ... false and shallow charges levelled against the historical role of the West, the vast gap between aspiration and achievement in the Third World, the bitter ironies of decay in the place of development, tyranny in the place of liberty, [and] the cases of reversion to superstition and barbarism (Bull 1984/2000: 244).

In essence, the contemporary 'Eastern problem' boils down to the proposition that the recalcitrant East, which is not prepared to become fully Westernized, constitutes the key blockage to the fulfilment of Bull's normative aspirations for an orderly global international society.

It is noteworthy here that the attempt to paint the Third World as the obstacle to global progress was a standard stock-in-trade of those thinkers who sought to defend Europe's imperialist past during the anxiety-ridden

---

[198] An argument that Robert Jackson (1990) developed in detail.

THE CLASSICAL ENGLISH SCHOOL   231

era of decolonization. Bull's critique of the Eastern problem certainly dovetails with Frank Füredi's characterization of the post-1945 defenders of the imperial past:

> The negative comparisons with the Third World were complemented by studies which suggested that it was the internal weakness of [Eastern] societies rather than colonialism which constituted the real problem. The substance of the argument was that the Third World was congenitally incapable of looking after its own internal affairs. Chaos, decay and corruption were the characteristics associated with independent post-colonial states. Typically, the colonial era was presented as something of a golden age. Problems were always portrayed as the fault of Third World societies. The evidence that imperialism had left behind a legacy of difficulties was invariably rejected (Füredi 1994: 94).

So what solution does Bull prescribe? The key dilemma that confronted Bull was that his problem-solving politics committed him to finding ways of making global international society work smoothly while his analysis of the 'Eastern problem' as a destabilizing factor in contemporary global international society presented a major challenge to his non-interventionist pluralist approach. For his pluralism required him to tolerate cultural or civilizational heterogeneity across the world while his Eurocentric analysis of the 'Eastern problem' logically required a Western interventionist role in the East in order to remedy this 'cultural deviancy'. Thus Bull found himself, to paraphrase an old Australian saying, 'between an imperialist rock and an anti-paternalist Eurocentric hard place'. And it was this, I believe, that led him to flirt with solidarism, particularly in his Hagey Lecture on 'Justice in International Relations' (Bull 1984/2000), even though in the end he pulled back from the solidarist neo-imperial precipice.

To be specific, the problem of socialism in the Third World that Bull complained of could be overcome by its cultural conversion along liberal lines; something which could be promoted by the institutions that curiously remain outside of the ES list of usual suspects – the GATT/WTO, IMF and World Bank. Moreover, these institutions could help solve the 'social efficiency' problem that Bull also highlights, given that they stand for free access to all countries. Although such forms of intervention by such institutions are not usually associated with the ES – which one ES scholar perceptively points out is unnecessarily confined to the political issue of human rights (Buzan 2004: chs. 1, 2 and 5) – nevertheless in their absence Bull's identification of the 'Eastern problem' has no means of resolution within his anti-paternalist Eurocentric framework. And given that Bull ultimately rejected 'interventionist solidarism' on the grounds that it would only further destabilize global international society, so he found himself in the catch-22 position of being unable to realize his political aims.

It might be argued that Bull's ultimate siding with non-interventionism as against solidarist interventionism at least enabled him to remain consistent to his pluralism. But this obscures the point that Bull's definition of pluralism is deployed inconsistently in his own writings. The first contradiction lies in the point that the *historical* 'Eastern problem' was 'solved' by Western imperial intervention (i.e., paternalist Eurocentrism) while the *contemporary* 'Eastern problem' was to be left uncorrected through the rejection of Western neo-imperial intervention (i.e., anti-paternalist Eurocentrism). This in turn opens up a second contradiction, for while the success of European international society in the eighteenth and nineteenth centuries was premised on a homogeneous civilizational base, nevertheless the fundamental property of his pluralism is that shared thick cultural values are *not* supposed to be required for the reproduction of contemporary global international society. And given that in his analysis modern global international society is undermined by cultural heterogeneity then his 'culturally tolerant' pluralism is once again contradicted.

Concluding the classical English School: the problem of ahistorical Eurocentrism

Bull, Watson and Wight are, of course, known for their interest in *historical* forms of IR, while Bull is famous for his stance within the Second Great Debate in which he criticized US IR for its barren and ahistorical nature. Moreover, in recent years various leading lights have argued that the ES offers up a strong approach for drawing out the very long-run historical origins of the international system (e.g., Buzan and Little 2000; Buzan 2004). But the problem with the 'historical' analyses of Bull, Wight and Watson is that they in effect consign the pre-1648 era to the dustbin of history by arguing that 'IR proper' cannot exist in the absence of (modern) sovereign states. As Bull put it, in 'parts of Africa, Australia, and Oceania before European intervention there were independent political communities that had no institutions of government [and accordingly] such entities fall outside the purview of "international relations"' (1977: 9). Wight expressed it thus: 'one cannot talk about international relations before the advent of the sovereign state' (1992: 1). It is certainly true that Watson analyses in considerable detail many non-Western political formations prior to 1648 in what is in so many ways an undeniably impressive book.[199] But his Eurocentrism leads to the conclusion that such non-Western systems ultimately perform the task of reinforcing the exceptionalism of modern European international society and contemporary European-created global international society, while simultaneously pointing to why the big bang of modern progressive international relations could only have exploded within Westphalian Europe. All in all, the irony is that the Eurocentrism of the classical pluralists undermines their claims to have gone beyond ahistorical IR theory.

This in turn has direct ramifications for Bull's claims about the status and nature of history in IR theory. In particular, he notes that 'theory itself has a history, and understanding of the theorist's historical position is essential to criticism of him and self-criticism by him' (Bull 1972/2009: 254). As Alderson and Hurrell (2000: 40) point out, this conceptual self-consciousness was deployed by Bull as a critique of post-1945 'scientific' American IR theory, where the pursuit of general theory had been hijacked or distorted by the interests and values of the United States (Bull 1966, 1972/2000). This leads Bull to complain that such an unreflexive position tarnishes US IR theory with a 'stifling ... political conformism ... from which the subject is in great need of liberation' (1972/2000: 262). But in the light of my analysis it could be concluded that Bull's Eurocentric provincialism leads him equally into a 'stifling political conformism from which the subject is in great need of liberation'. Even so, in the end Bull would most likely reject such advice, to wit his claim in the Hagey Lectures that:

> Truth is absolute, not relative, and what happened in history is independent of perspectives of time and place. But in choosing what parts of the historical past we examine we quite legitimately allow ourselves to be affected by our interest in the antecedents of events and issues that are important here and now. God forbid that we should turn away from Eurocentric international and imperial history towards so-called anti-imperialist or national liberation accounts of the past (Bull 1980/2000: 175).

---

[199] See Watson (1992/2009: chs. 2–4, 6–8, 11).

10

Critical subliminal Eurocentrism: Gramscianism and world-systems theory, c. 1967–1989

Introduction: critiquing capitalist imperialism, naturalizing Western domination

For many, the claim that much of neo-Marxist IR is Eurocentric will appear as entirely counter-intuitive given its association with the critique of imperialism on the one hand and Western capitalism on the other. But, as I noted in my earlier discussions of Karl Marx (pp. 52–8) and Vladimir Lenin (pp. 136–42), it is perfectly possible to be Eurocentric while at the same time being highly critical of the West. Modern neo-Marxist IR follows closely in the wake of Lenin's brand of critical subliminal Eurocentrism, wherein the West is viewed as the supreme agent of world politics/economics that lies at the very centre of all things, while the East is denied progressive agency of any sort and is portrayed as a hapless down-and-out, condemned for the foreseeable future, if not for all eternity, to eke out a miserable existence in the ghetto of the periphery. And despite the different stances vis-à-vis imperialism nevertheless Marx's paternalist Eurocentrism presents the East as a *passive beneficiary* of Western imperialism while modern neo-Marxist subliminal anti-paternalist Eurocentrism presents it as the *passive victim* of Western domination (as did Lenin).[200]

My focus in this chapter is on world-systems theory (WST) and the 'orthodox' Marxism of Gramscianism, on the grounds that these were the dominant Marxist theories of IR and IPE before 1989. And, just as various orthodox Marxists in the 1970s critiqued dependency theory and WST for its alleged 'bourgeois' and hyper-structuralist properties (Laclau 1971; Brenner 1977), so Robert Cox differentiates his Gramscian

---

[200] The clear exception here is Bill Warren (1980), who returns us directly to Marx's paternalist vision of imperialism as a progressive force.

INTRODUCTION: CRITIQUING CAPITALIST IMPERIALISM   235

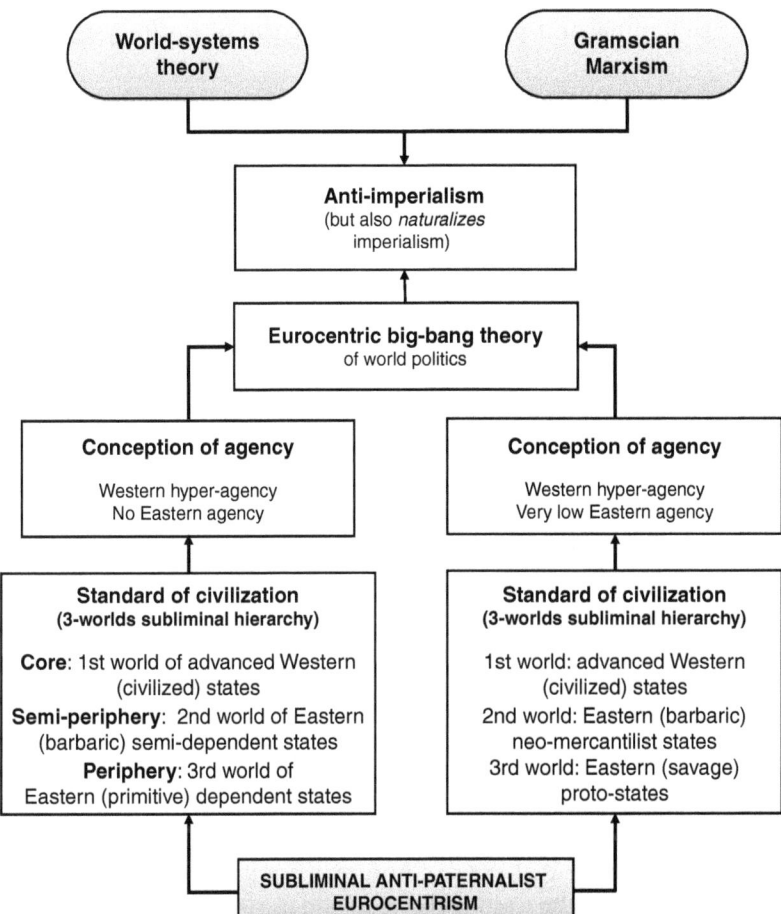

Figure 10.1   Subliminal anti-paternalist Eurocentrism in neo-Marxist IR theory, c. 1967–2010

theory from WST in not dissimilar terms.[201] But the claim of this chapter is that while Gramscianism and WST are generically thought of as very different approaches, nevertheless when viewed through a non-Eurocentric lens they (re)appear as minor variations on a consistent anti-paternalist Eurocentric theme (as shown in Figure 10.1). In what follows I shall reveal how these Eurocentric categories infect both of these major Marxist theories.

[201] E.g., Cox (1981/1986: 206, 214–15; 1987: 108–9, 357–8; 1996: 125, 141 n. 3, 404–5).

The subliminal anti-paternalist Eurocentrism of world-systems theory

It is important to recognize at the outset that not all scholars associated with the broad church of WST are Eurocentric. To prevent confusion it helps to distinguish between *classical* world-systems theory that is most clearly associated with Immanuel Wallerstein, and *neoclassical* world system theory that encapsulates Frank and Gills (1996), Frank (1998), Denemark *et al.* (2000) and Abu-Lughod (1989). While the former is highly Eurocentric, the latter breaks with Eurocentrism in many key ways, making it a significant voice in the development of non-Eurocentric IR/world history. Poignantly, while Andre Gunder Frank was one of the original voices of dependency theory,[202] nevertheless the 'mature' Frank later recanted on his earlier approach and pronounced WST/dependency theory as Eurocentric. Other world-systems theorists have also critiqued Eurocentrism.[203] In what follows, however, I shall focus on Wallerstein's extensive work, not least because he is the figure whom IR scholars associate most closely with WST.

The two-step Eurocentric big-bang theory of world politics/economics

It is a staple of the received wisdom that Wallerstein's theory focuses on *exogenous* global factors. Accordingly, it might immediately be anticipated that his approach would dispense with the Eurocentric logic of immanence outright. But, in fact, Wallerstein's Eurocentrism leads him to contradict this 'global' approach by treating the West and its rise as a largely *endogenous* affair that is self-generated on the back of Europe's exceptionalist properties. Thus, in standard Eurocentric fashion, Wallerstein in effect separates out the East from the West, and then privileges the latter as the pioneering creator of modernity while simultaneously demoting the former to a regressive and unexceptional entity that is incapable of capitalist self-generation. To this end Wallerstein characterizes the world around 1500 through the familiar Eurocentric league table construct. Thus the West occupies division 1 – the civilized first world (civilized, that is, not in a moral but in a materialist sense); division 2 is occupied by the regressive 'redistributive/tributary world-empires' in Asia (or what is akin to the

---

[202] E.g., Frank (1967).
[203] E.g., Wolf (1982); Amin (1989); cf. Braudel (1981, 1982/2002, 1992).

nineteenth-century Eurocentric trope of barbaric Oriental despotisms); and division 3 is occupied by primitive 'reciprocal mini-systems' found in North America, parts of Africa and Australasia (or what is akin to the nineteenth century Eurocentric idiom of savage societies).

Key here is that these Eastern systems were deemed to be incapable of developing into capitalism, such that only the West was capable of making the breakthrough all by itself (1974b: 390–1; 1984: 147–55). Reciprocal mini-systems (or primitive savage societies) existed at very low levels of technological development and were therefore unable to generate productive surpluses. And because they were very weak societies, economically and militarily, they rarely lasted more than 150 years given that most were swallowed up by acquisitive/atavistic Oriental despotic world-empires. By the mid-sixteenth century 'redistributive world-empires' – or single Oriental-despotic state systems – were the common mode of political domination in Asia. As such, they chose not to intensively develop their economies because this would promote strong social actors who might later challenge the state, but instead expanded outwards in order to extract tribute to maintain despotic state power. Nevertheless, in the long run they suffered from geopolitical overstretch given that they could not generate sufficient domestic revenues to support such expansion. And once the inevitable decline had set in it was just a matter of time before a new elite or dynasty would take the reins of state power, only to begin the whole cycle anew. Hence world-empires were confined ultimately to a static developmental 'holding pattern', being unable to break through to an economy that could generate sustained surpluses.

Finally, around 1500 a capitalist world-economy emerged within Europe and broke the hitherto historical rule of long-term stasis. Although Wallerstein is always thought to have emphasized the role of extra-European long-distance trade as the prime factor in the rise of European capitalism,[204] it was in fact largely a series of exceptional *intra*-European developments that he focused upon. First among these was the fact that the European capitalist world-economy was characterized by more than one political centre, enjoying a multiplicity of competing states within a regional subsystemic anarchy. It was this that primarily differentiated Europe from the Eastern empires. Sustained, as well as driven forward, by the balance of power, this anarchic multi-state system dictated that European rulers

---

[204] As was argued in the principal critiques of WST; see Skocpol (1977); Brenner (1977); Giddens (1985).

respect the needs of capital given the constant need to fund their escalating military activities or else suffer the inevitable dire consequences (see esp. 1974a: ch. 3). Strikingly, though, long-distance trade beyond Europe is significantly downgraded. Some have argued that the main hub of world trade at that time comprised the Afro-Eurasian trading system that centred on the Indian Ocean.[205] But Wallerstein rejects this claim and, explicitly confronting Paul Sweezy and Henri Pirenne (with whom he is usually associated) he asserts that 'I am skeptical ... that the exchange of [Asian goods] ... could have sustained so colossal an enterprise as the expansion of the Atlantic world, much less accounted for the creation of a European world-economy' (1974a: 41–2). Focusing instead on intra-European variables he singles out the flight of the peasantry from the land owing to the higher rates of exploitation that were imposed by the nobility in the aftermath of the Black Death; the rise of the towns as nodal points in long-distance intra-European trading circuits and as, above all, refuge harbours for the over-exploited peasantry; the primitive accumulation of capital through the beginning of the enclosure movement; and technological innovations that enhanced agrarian production. Interestingly, if nothing else, this list reveals the many shared overlaps between Wallerstein and Brenner (1977, 1982)! Moreover, the one extra-European dimension that he includes concerns the role of the neo-European empires in the Americas which supplied high calorific foods and fuel. But even this turns out to prove the Eurocentric rule given that it is relegated to only a very minor footnote in his story of the rise of Europe.

Having risen to the top of the world economic hierarchy by the mid-sixteenth century, the second step of the Eurocentric big-bang narrative cuts in immediately, to wit: '[i]n the sixteenth century, in Europe, a capitalist world-economy came into existence which eventually expanded to cover the entire globe, eliminating in the process all remaining redistributive world-economies and reciprocal mini-systems' (1984: 153, also 6, 29, 37). This imperialist expansion is inherent to the process of capital accumulation. Here we confront the opposite problem to that which we encountered with the English School in the last chapter. For while much of the ES presents the expansion of Europe in highly consensual terms, thereby eliding the process of Western coercive imperialism, WST corrects for this deficiency but in the process bends the polemical stick to the opposite extreme to produce a vision of a Leviathanesque, hyper-agential West and a victimized agency-less East.

---

[205] E.g., Frank (1998); Barendse (2002); Hobson (2004); cf. Abu-Lughod (1989).

Wallerstein presents the process of Western imperialism as an overwhelming force that rapaciously converts the Eastern systems into new units that are functional to capitalist exploitation and domination by the West (1984: ch. 8). Thus world-empires, mainly in Asia, saw their state structures weakened while their boundaries underwent a forced contraction; and the surviving mini-systems of North America, the Caribbean and Australia, underwent a wholesale destruction so that they could be rebuilt from scratch along Western lines. Once the whole of the East had been 'restructured' to suit the needs of Western capital, so it was incorporated into the inter-state system which 'operated to facilitate the peripheralization of the production processes in the region and the flows of surplus to core regions via unequal exchange' (1984: 82). This imperialist drive, then, served to set up the key dynamic of the global capitalist world economy (CWE): specifically the sucking of resources and profit from the Eastern periphery to the Western core. And it is precisely here where the next major component of Wallerstein's Eurocentrism emerges; for in conjuring up an image of a Western vampire that sucks the life-blood out of its entrapped Eastern victim, Wallerstein effectively consigns all traces of Eastern agency to the dustbin of history – past, present and future. However, before I examine this aspect in more detail, it is necessary to complete the second step of the Eurocentric BBT by considering very briefly Wallerstein's structural-Eurofunctionalist account of Western hegemony.

The key point to note here is that if the structure of the CWE functions to reproduce Western supremacy, then the existence of Western hegemons serves only to reinforce this given that they constitute the *optimal* political vehicles for reproducing both the CWE and Western supremacy. Thus Wallerstein argues that capital accumulation is maximized when the inter-state structure veers neither towards the extreme end of a world-empire nor towards the opposite extreme of a pure anarchy comprising multiple great powers of roughly equal strength. Rather, '[t]he ideal situation in terms of capital accumulation for the system as a whole is the existence of a hegemonic power, strong enough to define the rules of the game and to see that they are followed ... almost all of the time' (Wallerstein 1996: 98). And, moreover, he argues that: '[i]t has been the cyclical rise and fall of hegemonic powers that has provided the crucial degree of equilibrium to the inter-state politics of the modern world-system, thereby enabling the process of capitalist accumulation [in favour of the Western core] to proceed without serious hindrance' (1996: 102). Wallerstein notes that hegemony has never lasted long and is subject to a rapidly self-liquidating process. But even this turns out to be functionally optimal to both the reproduction of the CWE and Western supremacy, to wit: '[a] hegemony that lasted too long would have pulled the system towards its transformation into a world-empire. And a system that never saw the emergence of a hegemonic power would not have had the possibility of creating the stable interim orders needed to maximize accumulation' (1996: 102). In short, Wallerstein deploys classic structural-functionalist language when he concludes in Althusserian terms that Western hegemony acts as the factor of 'social cohesion of the system as a whole' (1996: 102), thereby sealing his 'Eurofunctionalism'.

Eurofetishism and the elision of Eastern agency

What converts Wallerstein's structural-Eurofunctionalism into 'Eurofetishism' – that is, the eternalizing of Western domination – is his elision of Eastern agency. Where he focuses in some detail on the issue of Eastern agency in *The Politics of the World-Economy* (1984: chs. 9–13), the conclusion is that the structuralist logic of the system prevents any Eastern challenge from being successful, while the Eurofunctionalist logic serves to channel any Eastern resistance that does occur into the unintended *strengthening* of the CWE and the inter-state system which functions on behalf, or at the behest, of the West. This conclusion emerges from three clear points. First, the Eastern national-liberation movements that pushed for decolonization were led by elites who were more interested in their own power than that of their nation. Socialist strategies of delinking involved a 'major economic sacrifice . . . of . . . the very cadres of the revolutionary movement. Their objective class interests work against such self-abnegation' (1984: 84). But in any case, socialist attempts to delink from the capitalist inter-state structure inevitably failed because in every case (e.g., China, Vietnam, Russia) they found that they simply had no choice but to join the inter-state system precisely because the price of ensuring the organizational survival of the socialist state was the acceptance of the rules of the capitalist inter-state system (1984: ch. 9). Thus the unintended effect of Eastern resistance was not the undermining but the *reinforcement* of the system,[206] leading to the 'historic fact of the twentieth century that communist parties in power in socialist states have done at least as much as transnational

---

[206] Here the parallels between Wallerstein's and Waltz's structuralism are striking (cf. Wendt 1987; Hobson 2000: 133–43).

corporations to extend the domination of the [capitalist] law of value' (1984: 93 and 105-7).

The second denial of Eastern agency flows on from the first, which concerns Wallerstein's Eurocentric discussion of decolonization. Rather than focus on the modalities of Eastern agency that were deployed to bring down the empire, the story is recounted instead in terms of the passing of the global hegemonic baton of power from Europe to the United States, which was 'functionally required' both for the continuation of Western hegemonic domination and the maximization of capitalist profits. Thus the East 'had to be decolonized in order to mobilize productive potential in a way that had never been achieved in the colonial era. Colonial rule after all had been an *inferior* mode of relationship of core and periphery, one [that was] no longer desirable from the point of view of the new [American] hegemonic power' (1974b: 412). In the process then, even such a significant moment of Eastern agency is converted into another chapter in the ongoing Eurocentric saga of the 'triumph of the West'.

Finally, the third denial of Eastern agency derives from the structural Eurofunctionalist definition of the CWE. For on the one hand the Eastern periphery is systematically under-developed by the Western core and is deemed to be unable to break out of the iron cage that it has been imprisoned within and, on the other hand, the semi-periphery is deemed to be functional to maintaining the unequal distribution of power between the Northern core and the Southern periphery. Thus the semi-periphery is 'assigned ... a specific economic role but the reason is less economic than political ... [That is] its existence ... means precisely that the upper stratum [the core] is not faced with a unified opposition of all the others because the middle stratum is both exploited and exploiter' (1974b: 405; also 1974a: 350; 1974c: 4-8). Wallerstein then cements this Eurofunctionalism in place by arguing that the division of the world into three zones is vital for systems maintenance because if all states were equally strong, then 'they would be in the position of blocking the effective operation of transnational economic entities whose locus were in another state. It would then follow that the world division of labor would be impeded, the world economy decline, and eventually the world-system fall apart' (Wallerstein 1974a: 355).

All in all, then, while Wallerstein not infrequently argues that the present world-system has entered a long period of crisis and will be replaced by a new one possibly in another 150 years' time, this is contradicted by the logic of his theory which points to an immutable structure alongside a denial of Eastern agency. It was not entirely surprising, therefore, to find that it was the agential power of the East Asian NICs to break out of the periphery that delivered a considerable blow to the integrity of WST at the end of the 1980s. Orthodox Marxist critiques of WST denounce it for its *bourgeois fetishism* and the accompanying tendency to naturalize, reify and hence eternalize capitalism, given that it ignores the underlying social relations of production and thereby obscures working class resistance agency (Laclau 1971; Brenner 1977). Equally, though, when viewed through a non-Eurocentric lens Wallerstein's argument falls into the trap of Eurofetishism insofar as it tends to naturalize, reify and hence eternalize Western domination, given that it ignores inter-civilizational relations and thereby obscures Eastern resistance agency. Given this, it seems a particular irony that a further reason for the theory's demise lay in the attack delivered by right-wing liberals,[207] given their perception of it as a voice of the Third World!

The subliminal anti-paternalist Eurocentrism of Gramscian IR

With the demise of WST in the early 1990s, Marxist IR theory did not wither on the vine but was revitalized as the baton of intellectual power was passed on to Gramscianism. As I noted with respect to WST in the last section, not all Gramscians in IR produce Eurocentric approaches, with a minority seeking to develop non-Eurocentric theories.[208] Nevertheless, that more Gramscians have not taken up the non-Eurocentric challenge is surprising not least because Edward Said drew much from Gramsci (Said 1978/2003). Significant too is that Robert Cox, who provides much of the focus of this section, has recently turned to inter-civilizational analysis, part of which contains various non-Eurocentric cues (e.g., Cox 2001). Nevertheless, here I focus on the Coxian theory of hegemony because this is the variant that is most closely associated with *the* Gramscian theory of IR/IPE. Note that while I shall refer to various post-1989 Gramscian works, thereby breaking with the 1989 watershed of Part II of this book, I feel it to be legitimate because this brand of Eurocentrism continues to mark much of the Gramscian *oeuvre* right down to the present day.

---

[207] See Blaney and Inayatullah (2008).
[208] See especially Gills (1993); Persaud (2001); Slater (2004); Pasha (2006); Morton (2007: ch. 3).

I begin with Cox's well-known distinction between 'critical theory' and 'problem-solving theory'. By noting how neoliberal institutionalism and neorealism work to make the present system run more smoothly he delivers a challenge to their shared claim to stand for positivism and value-free analysis; to wit his claim that mainstream IR theory is 'value-bound by virtue of the fact that it implicitly accepts the prevailing order as it own framework' (1981/1986: 209). Cox's antidote to problem-solving theory is to trace the historical origins of the present international system in order to reveal it as something which is historically contingent rather than natural and eternal. Thus in de-naturalizing the present system he seeks to develop a theory of the world that does *not* reflect and legitimize the interests of the powerful. However, my claim in this section is that Cox's Eurocentrism delivers Gramscianism into the same Eurofetishist trap that WST ends up in, thereby converting his critical theory into a problem-solving theory. This becomes apparent through an examination of his theory of Western hyper-agential hegemony, Western-dominated globalization and the elision of Eastern agency.

Hyper-agential hegemons as the Western imperial controllers of the passive East

While the Gramscian approach to hegemony shares various similarities with neorealist hegemonic stability theory (HST), nevertheless a key difference is that Gramscianism is a critical theory which views the hegemon as an exploiter of others rather than as a self-sacrificial provider of genuine public goods. This much is generally well-known. But when viewed through my non-Eurocentric lens the key difference between neorealist HST and the Gramscian theory of hegemony is that they reflect not a great divide between problem-solving theory and critical theory but a subliminal Eurocentric paternalist/anti-paternalist divide. And the deepest paradox that flows on from this is that Gramscianism's subliminal anti-paternalist Eurocentrism, as with WST, has the unintended effect of naturalizing both Western domination and Western imperialism, which in turn leads us back into problem-solving theory and thereby further reducing the gap between Gramscianism and HST.

The Eurocentric underpinnings of the Gramscian theory of hegemony manifest themselves at numerous levels. First, Gramscianism – like HST and WST – in effect relates the rise and decline of hegemony through the

Eurocentric idiom of the Western relay race. For some the race begins with The United Provinces in the seventeenth century,[209] before the baton of global hegemonic power is handed over to the British in the nineteenth century only to be passed on to the American anchor-man in the mid-twentieth century, who ran the final leg in record time (Cox 1987: 105–267). As with WST and HST the Eastern great powers in the 1400–1800 period are conspicuous only for their absence, the inclusion of which would, of course, break with this Western linearity. Moreover, Gramscianism not only focuses exclusively on Western powers but defines hegemony through a provincial reading of *Western* hegemons. Had Cox focused on the properties of say China and its historical international tribute system then a different conception of hegemony might have emerged (but see Gills 1993).

Second, reminiscent once more of HST and WST, the Gramscian analysis of hegemony works within the 2-step Eurocentric big-bang theory. Thus the first step entails the rise of the West in general and the rise of hegemons in particular, all of which is related through the standard Eurocentric logic of immanence (Cox 1987: 105–267). The second step of the big-bang theory flows on immediately, given that once a leading hegemon emerges at the top, so it naturally expands its power outwards acting as the central director of the world-economy in general and of the *passive* East in particular. Thus hegemons are

> founded by powerful states which have undergone a thorough social and economic revolution. The revolution not only modifies the internal economic and political structures of the state in question but also unleashes energies which expand beyond the state's boundaries. A world hegemony is thus in its beginnings an outward expansion of the internal [national] hegemony established by a dominant class (1996: 136–7, also 134; and 1987: 149–50).

Important here are a number of inter-linked concepts that are borrowed from Gramsci: passive revolution, hegemonic/non-hegemonic national orders, Caesarism and *trasformismo* (Cox 1996: ch. 7).[210]

Hegemony refers to a situation where a particular national society has achieved a thorough social revolution domestically, such that the legitimacy of the dominant bourgeois class is accepted in broadly consensual terms by the masses. By contrast, a non-hegemonic social order goes hand-in-hand with *passive revolution*. Initially, such a situation existed

---
[209] Though Arrighi (1994) traces it all the way back to Venice.
[210] Note that this vital essay was first published in 1983.

within the Eastern states of Europe in the nineteenth century. The key point is that such non-hegemonic societies 'had so to speak imported or had thrust upon them aspects of a new order created abroad without the old order having been displaced. In such societies the new industrial bourgeoisie failed to achieve hegemony. It was blocked by the old forces' (1996: 129). Passive revolution is often accompanied by *Caesarism*, whereby a strong ruler seeks to conform to external dictates but cannot overcome the stalemate between the old agrarian and new bourgeois classes, thereby blocking the modernization of the economy. Finally, *trasformismo* works to assimilate and domesticate 'potentially dangerous [external] ideas by adjusting them to the policies of the dominant coalition and can thereby obstruct the formation of class-based organizational opposition to established social and political power' (1996: 130). Each of these concepts is applied specifically to the Third World: the 'notion of passive revolution, together with its components, Caesarism and trasformismo, is particularly apposite to industrializing third world countries' (1996: 130–1).

It is here where we encounter Cox's Eurocentric approach to the Third World. Thus once hegemony spills out beyond the boundaries of the leading Western hegemonic society in the world we find that

> other [peripheral] countries have received the impact of these [processes] in a passive way, an instance of what Gramsci described at the national level as a passive revolution. This effect comes when the impetus to change does not arise out of a 'vast local economic development ... but is instead the reflection of [external] international developments which transmit their ideological currents to the periphery' (Gramsci cited in Cox 1996: 134).

Critically, in the process of hegemonic expansion

> the economic and social institutions, the culture, the technology associated with this national hegemon become *patterns for emulation abroad*. Such an expansive hegemony impinges on the more peripheral countries as a passive revolution. These countries have not undergone the same thorough [hegemonic] social revolution, nor have their economies developed in the same way, but they try to incorporate elements from the hegemonic model without disturbing old power structures (Cox 1996: 137, my emphasis; see also Gill 1990: 76).

Thus the, albeit muted, process of change in non-hegemonic Eastern societies is generated not through internal processes but is 'thrust upon them' from the outside by Western hegemons (and, as we shall see shortly, by Western-led globalization). Here the Eurocentric cue emerges in the point that Eastern societies are denied the privilege of self-generation, such that any change that does occur is only made possible by the external influences or dictates of Western forces.

Following on from this a further Eurocentric cue emerges in the point that hegemony sets up international institutions that surveil and control the destinies of third world states. The GATT/WTO, as well as the World Bank and the IMF, seek to convert all non-Western states to neoliberalism. While such a point can be incorporated within a non-Eurocentric theory (as I have noted in the previous two chapters), the Eurocentric cue here lies in the point that such an analysis allows no room for Eastern agency. While I shall deal with this issue in a later subsection, it is worth noting that in presenting hegemonic institutions as stifling any potential Eastern resistance agency so we return to Wallerstein's structural-Eurofunctionalism. In this way, for example, Cox argues that *trasformismo* serves to co-opt those individuals from the Third World who initially joined international organizations in order to try and radically transform the system from within. Indeed '[a]t best [such individuals] will help transfer elements of "modernization" to the peripheries' (1996: 139). Moreover, IMF and World Bank stabilization programmes reinforce Western supremacy by preventing the weakest states from becoming so poor that they become a political threat to the Western-led global capitalist system (1987: 218–19). All in all, 'trasformismo ... absorbs potentially counterhegemonic ideas and makes these ideas consistent with hegemonic doctrine' (1996: 139), thereby leading him to conclude that '[h]egemony is like a pillow: it absorbs blows and sooner or later the would-be-assailant will find it comfortable to rest upon' (1996: 139).

Importantly, it is here in particular where we encounter the subliminal three-worlds construction of the world. In the last section I argued that Wallerstein's theory in effect conceptualizes the core of the civilized West, the semi-periphery of barbaric (Oriental Despotic) states and the periphery of Eastern savage societies. But Gramscian IR theory does likewise, counterposing (implicitly civilized) Western states with the (implicitly barbaric) *neomercantilist* Eastern states and the (implicitly savage) primitive Eastern *proto-states* (Cox 1987: ch. 7).

Nevertheless, hegemony is not the only medium or vehicle by which the West dominates the East. For the practice of American hegemony, which went into decline in the late-1960s, has been replaced by a new master-socialization process or Western cultural conversion vehicle – capitalist globalization. And while this was born through the actions of successive Western hegemons, by the 1990s it had taken on a life of its own.

Globalization as the latest vehicle of Western control of the passive East

While Gramscianism is generally thought to replace inter-*national* relations with *global*-relations such that globalization is held to be a core analytical focus, this is at the least mitigated and at the most contradicted by an underlying Eurocentrism in that the 'global' turns out to be the expression of the 'provincial West writ large'. This Eurocentrism is revealed in a number of crucial ways. First, Cox reiterates the Eurocentric logic of immanence treating the rise of globalization as the pure product of endogenous Western developments; a narrative that returns us to the idiom of the Western relay race described in the last subsection. Nevertheless it is the final leg run by the American anchor man that is accorded predominant focus: 'the new [global] economy grew very largely as the consequence of the US hegemonic role and the global expansion of US-based corporations' (Cox 1987: 216). Critically, the West (specifically the US) is represented as the subject of globalization while the East is viewed as its passive object. Moreover, this formative stage constitutes the first step in Cox's Eurocentric big-bang theory of globalization. And in turn, this leads ineluctably into the second stage.

Thus having been 'made in the West' capitalism then expands outwards in the form of globalization, imposing Western capitalist and civilizational dictates upon the East in the process. A key aspect of this process concerns the reconstituting or restructuring of Eastern states according to a Western civilizational logic. Again, while it is certainly the case that the West has sought to culturally convert the East to its own cultural foundations, nevertheless the two scenarios painted by Gramscians are fundamentally Eurocentric. These two scenarios have been aptly captured by Ulf Hannerz (1991) as the 'peripheral corruption scenario' and the 'global homogenization scenario'.

The peripheral corruption scenario is one where the peripheral states adopt Western practices but then corrupt or pervert them to morally regressive ends (Hannerz 1991: 108). In Cox's analysis, Southern states corrupt and pervert incoming Western influences. Thus in his words, 'internationalized' Third World neomercantilist states, which frequently take the form of *military-bureaucratic regimes*

> sought to encourage export-oriented development together with the enforcement as necessary of domestic austerity upon the politically excluded elements of society. Physical repression, ranging from

widespread violations of human rights to open civil wars, generates the 'refugee problem'. In part, it may be explained by a political psychology of authoritarianism but in its broadest terms, the refugee problem has to be understood as a systematic consequence of the globalization trend (Cox 1996: 195–6).

Here there are clear shades of the old Eurocentric Oriental Despotism argument, for it is the political irrationality/immaturity of Third World 'barbaric' state forms that blunts the pure Westernization thrust, perverting and morally degenerating it in the process. Similarly Stephen Gill argues that globalization is often distorted through the prism of Third World authoritarian/military bureaucratic regimes, which entails a 'brutalizing and criminal phase' (Gill 1995b: 70, 95). Of such a portrayal, Hannerz's description is worth quoting:

> The peripheral corruption scenario ... is deeply ethnocentric, in that it posits a very uneven distribution of virtue, and in that it denies the validity and worth of any transformations at the periphery of what was originally drawn from the center. There is little question of cultural difference here, but rather of a difference between culture and non-culture, between civilization and savagery (Hannerz 1991: 109).

For Cox, such regimes are subjected to external Western global dictates under domestic conditions of passive revolution (1987: esp. 218, 238). Overall, though, this scenario envisages a *partial* Westernization/homogenization process, since the regressive nature of Third World states under conditions of passive revolution prevents a full assimilation. Moreover, the primitive Eastern proto-states, though subjected to Western capitalist dictates, are nevertheless insufficiently robust to be completely assimilated.

However, the second variant of the globalization argument takes the form of the 'global homogenization scenario'. This scenario envisages a full assimilation of the East along Western civilizational lines; that is, globalization-as-Westernization entails the West remaking the East in its own image (see also Robinson 2004; but see Morton 2007: ch. 5). Here we encounter what Cox calls the 'internationalization of the state' or what Stephen Gill calls the 'transnationalization of the state' (Cox 1987: 253–65; Gill 1990: 94). The Eurocentric cue lies in the point that the internationalized state acts as a passive conveyor belt or valve, through which dominant Western capitalist practices and norms are transmitted from the Western core via globalization into the non-Western periphery.[211] For as Cox puts it:

> The domestic-oriented agencies of the state are now more and more to be seen as transmission belts from world-economy trends and decision making into the domestic economy, as agencies to promote the carrying out of tasks they had no part in deciding (1996: 193; also 302).

In Stephen Gill's argument globalization is linked to the process of the New Constitutionalism. This envisages a strong socializing process whereby Western neoliberalism disciplines the Third World in order to create a single neo-empire of 'market civilization' (Gill 1995a, 1995b, 1995c). Thus in addition to the role of the Western IFIs, the most important socializing process lies with the enhanced structural power of transnational capital. Adam Morton neatly summarizes this argument accordingly:

> [T]here has been a rise in the structural power of transnational capital supported and promoted by forms of elite interactions that have forged common perspectives, or as 'emulative uniformity', between business, state officials, and representatives of international organizations, favouring the logic of capitalist market relations (Morton 2007: 124).

Thus with the development of the transnational ruling class that links up with the bourgeoisies in the Third World, the way is opened up for the full universalization of Western neoliberal capitalism. In sum, although it is unclear which of these scenarios is the dominant one within Gramscianism particularly as they are mutually exclusive, either way, though, both are clearly Eurocentric.

The Eurocentric denial of Eastern agency

However, this Eurocentric rendition of a *passive* East might be resolved through an analysis of one of Gramscianism's key concepts: that of *counter-hegemony*. Indeed for many Gramscians this is coupled with a Polanyian emphasis on the *double movement*, where the first movement, which entails a restructuring of economies along Western neoliberal lines, necessarily gives rise to a subsequent counter-movement that seeks to rein in the disruptive aspects of the first through social resistance. The key question then is: how strong is Third World resistance agency within the Gramscian

---

[211] But for a Gramscian critique of the transmission belt metaphor see Bieler and Morton (2006) and Morton (2007: ch. 6).

vision? Much is at stake here since a positive answer would go a long way towards overcoming Eurocentrism. And given that counter-hegemony is supposed to be as important to Gramscianism as working class struggle is to Marx, one would anticipate a sustained analysis of this, particularly in the context of the dominated East.

But one of the principal complaints that postcolonial-inspired Gramscians make of mainstream Gramscianism is that it has failed to explore the agency of Eastern actors. Thus Randolph Persaud rightly notes of the dominant Gramscian approach that 'while there is rigorous analysis of the dialectics of hegemony, there is not sufficient incorporation of resistance and counter-hegemony in the *theorization* of hegemonic practices (Persaud 2001: 48–9). Indeed, he claims,

> resistance and counter-hegemony are too often seen as *responses* to ... interests already formed, rather than theorized as dialectically defining the conditions which make hegemonic practices historically 'necessary' in the first place.... As such, counter-hegemonic practices must be seen as a fluid and unstable *engagement*, rather than a settled response to hegemony (Persaud 2001: 49, his emphases).

This conception usefully meshes with Mustapha Kamal Pasha's important idea of 'elective chains of affinities' (Pasha 2006: 153). Both of these interventions reinforce my own argument that East and West dialogically and dialectically engage and intertwine to thereby reconstitute their inner dynamics and retrack their outward trajectories. But when one scans Cox's major writings there is surprisingly little discussion of counter-movements and, when there is, the prospect for counter-hegemony is portrayed as very poor given the general representation of the (Western) working class as overwhelmed by the structural power of global capital.[212] And nowhere is there the critical notion that counter-hegemonic resistance can dialectically constitute and re-track Western hegemony.

In this respect, the predominantly Gramscian essays in the volume edited by Bjorn Hettne (1995) are particularly telling. One of the key theoretical objectives of Hettne's edited volume is to reveal the Polanyian *double movement* in world politics at the end of the twentieth century. One would anticipate, therefore, a significant discussion of counter-hegemony not merely as a counter-response to (the well-substantiated analysis) of the first movement concerning the imposition of Western market civilization on the whole world, but also as a vehicle that redefines and re-tracks

---

[212] Cox (1987: 368–91; 1996: 191–207, 364–6, 471–90).

Western hegemony. However in the 34-page chapter by Gill, we find a mere 1-page discussion of counter-hegemony in the Third World tacked on at the very end. There he references James Scott's (1993) important argument concerning 'everyday forms of resistance agency', even though the example he quotes turns out to bear no relation to Third World resistance vis-à-vis the West (Gill 1995b: 95-6). Similarly, while we learn all about Western globalization and its domination of the East in Yoshikazu Sakomoto's chapter, the discussion of Eastern counter-hegemony is tacked on at the end in a short 2-page discussion (Sakomoto 1995: 141-2). There he talks of Southern grass-roots movements that articulate the voice of the poor and represent a 'silent revolution from below'. The one example he provides is that of the Grameen Bank in Bangladesh, which has lent finance to the poorest women and has thereby helped empower them. While I have also argued that the Grameen Bank is indeed an important expression of bottom-up Eastern agency (Hobson and Seabrooke 2007), nevertheless this appears as too little, too late.

The key problem is that such minimalist assertions of Eastern agency do little or nothing to counter the Gramscian presentation of a reified West that has effectively locked the East within an iron cage of domination. Accordingly, oblique mentions of bottom-up agency have the scent of auxiliary hypotheses dredged up to save the theory from accusations of structural determinism or equally against the charge of Eurocentrism. In the end, then, we are essentially offered top-down structuralist analyses of world politics, which reify the power of the Western transnational capitalist classes, or Western hegemonic domination, or globalization-as-Western domination, while simultaneously writing Eastern agency out of the script. Part of the problem here is that Gramscianism looks in the wrong place for signs of Eastern agency, looking only to the prospects of a unified anti-Western Third World movement (which is deemed to be further way than ever at present), thereby returning us to the problems of Eurocentric monologism.[213] Thus the acute paradox here is that Cox's Eurocentrism has precisely the same effect as that of Wallerstein's, presenting Eastern states/societies as little more than *Träger* – i.e., as 'passive bearers' of anthropomorphic Western hegemonic structural forces.

---

[213] In *Everyday Politics of the World Economy* I have developed alternative conceptions of bottom-up agency, both Western and Eastern (Hobson and Seabrooke 2007). Paradoxically, the key influence that informed this book was *The New International Political Economy* that was co-edited by two prominent neo-Gramscians – Craig Murphy and Roger Tooze (1991).

It is, of course, the deepest irony that Gramscian theory ends up in this Eurocentric cul-de-sac given that it is at least conceptually better attuned to the issues of bottom-up agency and counter-hegemony than any other major theory in IR. But, like so much of contemporary Marxist IR, Gramscianism seems much more at home in talking of the power of Western capitalist forces than the power of Eastern, or even for that matter Western, subaltern agents; a point that some Marxist IR scholars have conceded (Colás 2002; Morton 2007).

Conclusion: WST and Gramscianism in the subliminal anti-paternalist Eurocentric mirror

To conclude it is useful to reveal how Gramscianism and WST converge as a function of their shared subliminal Eurocentrism and in the process contradict much of what they stand for. Two inter-related contradictions stand out. First, while both theories are clearly critical of Western imperialism, nevertheless their subliminal Eurocentrism leads them unwittingly to naturalize this process of Western domination. And when coupled with their elision of Eastern agency, so they undermine the prospects for its overthrow and thereby unwittingly reconvene the old British imperialist idiom that 'resistance is futile'. In the process, then, we are led full square into the twin traps of structural Eurofunctionalism on the one hand and 'Eurofetishism' with its concomitant eternalization of the Western world order on the other. It is noteworthy here that WST awards the East yet lower levels of agency to that found in all the Eurocentric institutionalist theories, and even many of the scientific racist theories, prior to 1945. In this crucial respect, it might be argued that despite its genuine antipathy towards imperialism and Western capitalism, WST is in this key regard one of the most Eurocentric international theories that have been formulated in the last 250 years!

The second major contradiction, which flows on directly from the first, concerns the unwitting deployment of an ahistorical approach. The received view, of course, is that Cox's 'critical theory' is differentiated from orthodox 'problem-solving theory' on the grounds that it denaturalizes Western capitalism in substantial part by enquiring into its *historical origins*, which in turn reveals it not as an immutable or eternal system but one that is contingent and subject to change and transcendence (Cox 1981/1986). But the problem here is that Cox's Eurocentrism, which conceives the rise of the West as self-generating through the logic of immanence, imputes an inevitability to, and thereby ahistorically rationalizes, the rise of the West and the processes by which it universalizes its power over the East.

The most acute irony is that in reproducing Eurocentrism Gramscian IR necessarily draws very close to the neorealist 'ahistorical problem-solving Other' against which it is defined. Interestingly, in the 1985 Postscript to his celebrated 1981 article Cox states that:

> I accept that my own thought is grounded in a particular perspective . . . The troublesome part comes when scientific enterprise claims to transcend history and to propound some universally valid form of knowledge. Positivism, by its pretensions to escape from history, runs the greater risk of falling into the trap of unconscious ideology (Cox 1981/1986: 247).

But the troublesome part of much of Gramscian IR is that it has effectively transcended history by propounding an *ahistorical Eurocentric provincialism written backwards*, thereby leading it into 'the trap of unconscious ideology' (i.e., subliminal Eurocentrism). The logical upshot of all this is that such an ahistorical structuralism, which creeps in through the subliminal Eurocentric backdoor, ultimately transforms Critical Gramscianism into a 'problem-solving theory'. And while Cox criticizes much of modern American IR theory for defending US power in the world,[214] the irony is that his own Eurocentrism generates, albeit *unwittingly*, a defence of the Western interest in general and the American interest in particular.

Likewise, in reproducing ahistorical Eurocentrism, WST necessarily draws close to the 'bourgeois' liberal-modernization theoretical Other against which it is defined. For the upshot of my analysis is that Wallerstein commits the very same error that he accuses liberals (and some Marxists) of. Thus while he asserts that 'the fundamental error of ahistorical social science . . . is to reify part of the totality into . . . units and then compare these reified structures' (Wallerstein 1974b: 387), Wallerstein's Eurocentric ahistoricism leads him to reify one part of the totality, the West, which is then compared to the passive and inert Eastern regions. Or, as one 'orthodox' neo-Marxist put it:

> In a way [WST/dependency theory] . . . has constructed a model which is the mirror opposite of the modernization theories: the dichotomies of rich/poor, traditional/modern are replaced by those of dominant/

---

[214] E.g., Cox (1981/1986: 240–1).

dependent, and centre/periphery. The latter are equally static, and totally impoverish the real process of history (Munck 1984: 14).

Most significantly, while one critic concludes that the Eurocentric perspective of liberal development theory has 'served as a manual for [the] imperial management of [Eastern] societies', the same conclusion could be said to apply to WST.[215] For Wallerstein's theory reveals the many ways in which the West has so successfully and naturally tamed the East while failing to offer the East any cues for expressing agency of any kind. And given that for WST Eastern 'resistance is futile' so, in conclusion, it might be more aptly termed *Western-systems theory*, or perhaps *Western stability theory*. Thus in contrast to Marx and Engels' famous mantra, that the proletariat 'has nothing to lose but its chains', so in WST we receive the mantra that the East has everything to lose but its chains.

Still, none of this is to deny the point that there is some excellent Marxist scholarship in IR – especially within Gramscianism including the work of Cox and Gill – much of which has emerged in recent years.[216] But in the light of the argument made in this chapter I want to close by posing two specific challenges to neo-Gramscians. First, while contemporary Gramscians are often pre-occupied with defending their approach against the charge of economic reductionism,[217] a more urgent challenge concerns the Eurocentric charge for this threatens the existential integrity of Gramscianism on its own terms. And second, while some key Gramscian and Marxist IR theorists have injected a significant element of non-Eurocentrism into their framework,[218] the key question is whether the majority of Marxist IR scholars are prepared to take up the non-Eurocentric challenge that some are already engaging with.

---

[215] Pieterse (1991: 8).
[216] See, for example: Augelli and Murphy (1988); Murphy and Tooze (1991); Denemark et al. (2000); Teschke (2003); Gruffydd-Jones (2006); Bieler and Morton (2006); Van der Pijl (2007, 2010); Rosenberg (2008); Matin (2007, 2011); Morton (2007); Bruff (2008); Shields (2009); Shilliam (2009, 2011); Anievas (2010, 2012); Seth (2011b); and see the references in footnote 218.
[217] See especially Morton (2007); Bieler and Morton (2008); Bruff (2008).
[218] In the Gramscian context see the excellent works by Persaud (2001); Slater (2004); Pasha (2006); cf. Morton (2007: ch. 3); Murphy and Tooze (1991); Augelli and Murphy (1988).

PART IV

1989–2010
Back to the future of manifest 'Eurocentrism' in mainstream international theory

11

Imperialist and anti-imperialist Eurocentrism: post-1989 'Western realism' and the spiritual return to post-1889 racist-realism

Introduction: 'things can only get bitter'

In recent years a number of important postcolonial-inspired readings of post-Cold War IR theory have emerged, arguing that the mainstream has promoted an imperialist vision of world politics.[219] In this and the next chapter I want to push this reading along several notches. Three points are of immediate significance. First, I argue that a significant strand of Western-realism also exhibits an anti-imperialist politics, specifically the cultural realism of Huntington and Lind that I examine at the end of this chapter. Second, in focusing on what I call 'Western-realism' in this chapter and 'Western-liberalism' in the next – two generic theoretical conglomerates that comprise a variety of component theories – I reveal how they rest on different, albeit complementary, Eurocentric metanarratives, thereby providing a more nuanced picture of mainstream Western neo-imperialist international theory. And third, I argue that whereas Eurocentrism was subliminal and hidden away in the 1945–89 era, it returns in its manifest version after the end of the Cold War.

The Western-liberal wing of mainstream international theory relies on a *paternalist* Eurocentrism that sings the world into existence with the idiom that 'things can only get better', and that through paternalist interventionism the East can be culturally converted along Western civilizational lines in order to make the world a better place for *all* peoples (as I explain in the next chapter). This optimistic and 'progressive' vision is countered by Western-realism which sings the world into existence with the idiom that 'things can only get bitter', such that the West's only option is to *imperially contain* the 'new barbaric threat' to civilization and world order. This approach is fuelled and galvanized by a

[219] Füredi (1994: ch. 6): Salter (2007, 2002: ch. 7); Bowden (2009: chs. 7–8).

pronounced degree of Western angst and relative degrees of pessimism concerning the challenges allegedly confronting Western civilization. This sensibility is characterized by Samuel Huntington: that 'this new world is a fearful world and Americans have no choice but to live *with* fear if not *in* fear' (Huntington 2004: 341). Moreover, the title of a significant piece by Daniel Pipes relayed this angst into the Western imagination: 'The Muslims are Coming! The Muslims are Coming!' (Pipes 1990).[220] These statements and many others like them reflect the politics of Western anxiety and insecurity that underpin 'offensive Eurocentric' and 'defensive Eurocentric' international theory.

Nevertheless, that Western-realism and Western-liberalism often share much in common is revealed by the interstitial category of 'Western-liberal realism', which is represented most famously by American neo-Conservatism, as well as 'Western realist-liberalism' that is represented by the likes of Robert Cooper, John Ikenberry and Anne-Marie Slaughter. Echoing the Western-liberals, the liberal-realists interpret the end of the Soviet Union as offering up a grand opportunity for the progressive universalization of Western, and especially, American values (Kagan and Kristol 2000). More specifically, liberal-realism displays a conditional optimism, such that when the United States embraces the neo-imperial mandate its proponents revert to singing 'things can only get better', while in its absence they rue that 'things can only get bitter'. Ultimately their theme song is that 'things could get better or bitter' (even if it's not quite so catchy!)

Interestingly, such a label dovetails with the notion of 'Wilsonian realism', which signifies a commitment to Wilson's so-called liberal internationalist vision, albeit with coercive 'neo-imperialist' unilateral teeth.[221] This is interesting in the light of my argument made in Chapter 7, where I claimed that Wilson was not an internationalist who advocated universal self-determination, but was a racist liberal who denied sovereignty to Eastern societies and called for the need to imperially convert them along Western lines according to the provincial logic of other-determination. While neo-Conservatism rejects scientific racism, nevertheless my reading of Wilson dovetails much more closely with post-1989 liberal-realism than even the label 'Wilsonian realism' conveys at first sight. This is also interesting because Francis Fukuyama's (2006) recent disenchantment with

---

[220] Though it is significant to note that Pipes questioned the alarmist perception of the Muslim threat that other 'Western-realists' voiced, and even disavowed the title of the article that was in fact attributed by the editors of the journal, *National Review*.

[221] Or equally, what Max Boot calls 'hard Wilsonianism' (cited in Lawson 2008: 899).

INTRODUCTION: 'THINGS CAN ONLY GET BITTER'

neo-Conservative 'Wilsonian realism', which led him to embrace a so-called 'realistic Wilsonianism', turns out in the light of my argument to comprise but a very minor variation on a common offensive/neo-imperialist Eurocentric theme. At the same time, this overlap is rendered all the more clear by what I am calling Western realist-liberalism. Thus in order to draw out these similarities I shall also consider in this chapter the realist-liberal theory of US hegemony which overlaps often indiscernibly with liberal-realism.

The further major objective of this and the next chapter is to complete my account of the changing architecture of Eurocentrism. In this Chapter I shall argue that the post-Cold War era has witnessed a *return* to the key themes that were articulated within post-1889 racist-realism, even if such arguments are expressed in Eurocentric institutional terms; hence my claim that this exhibits a 'spiritual' return. Indeed it is striking just how many of the arguments made by various defensive and offensive racists (as were discussed in Chapters 4–7) have been directly replaced by contemporary defensive and offensive Eurocentric institutional international theory. The parallels between some of the relevant thinkers are drawn in Table 11.1.

Table 11.1 *Back to the future of post-1889 racist-realism/racist cultural-realism*

		Western-realism	Western liberal-realism/realist-liberalism
Pro-imperialist		Offensive Eurocentrism/ Offensive racism	Part-paternalist Eurocentrism/ part-offensive Eurocentrism
	Post-1889	Mahan, Mackinder, Giddings, Powers	J. S. Mill
	Post-1989	Kaplan, Kennedy, Pfaff, Brzezinski, Ferguson, Krasner	Kagan, Krauthammer, Cooper Fukuyama, Ignatieff, Rieff, Rothkopf, Ikenberry, Slaughter
Anti-imperialist		Defensive Eurocentrism/ defensive racism	
	Post-1889	C. H. Pearson, Putnam Weale, Stoddard	
	Post-1989	Huntington, Lind	

260 CHAPTER 11: WESTERN-REALISM (POST-1989)

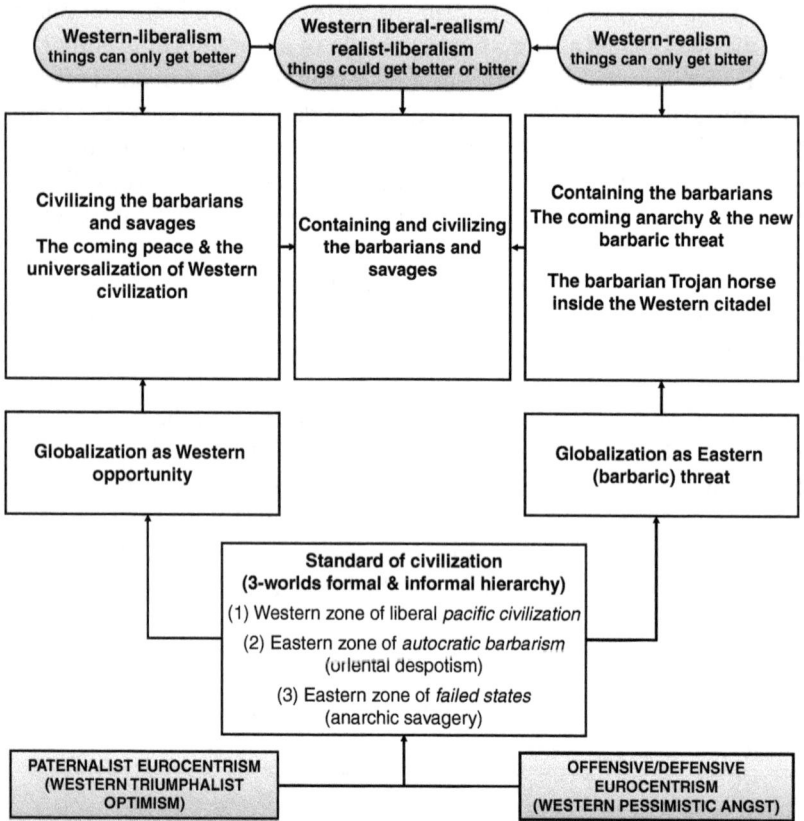

Figure 11.1 Post-1989 IR theory as promoter and defender of Western civilization

Figure 11.1 above presents a summary of the two broad streams of international theory, as well as the overlapping interstitial categories of liberal-realism and realist-liberalism, as they emerged in the post-Cold War era. This chapter shall consider the right-hand side while the following chapter considers the left-hand side. Note that I shall discuss the interstitial category in the relevant places in each of these two chapters.

The base categories of offensive Eurocentrism in Western-realism

Reconstructing a tripartite Eurocentric global hierarchy

Starting at the bottom-right of Figure 11.1, we can see that the base of post-1989 Western-realism comprises an *offensive* conception of Eurocentric institutionalism, wherein difference resides principally in *institutional factors* rather than the racial ethnology of its nineteenth century ancestor. Having conceptually separated the West from the Rest, Western-realism overlays upon this a formal hierarchical three-worlds construction. Here the West is privileged as the realm of civilization, while the Rest is situated within the realms of autocratic barbarism (the Second World) and anarchic savagery (the Third World).

Although the standard of civilization/standard of statehood no longer underpins international law, having ended in 1945, it has nevertheless been deployed as a socio-ideological template at the subliminal level during the era of decolonization and at the explicit or manifest level since 1989. It is this that guides the construction of the world and in turn the prescriptive policies required in the 'treatment' of the deviant, uncivilized societies.[222] There is, however, one twist that is significant. In the nineteenth century the standard of civilization was based only in part on the nature of the polity. Rather, what was crucial was the nature of *all* institutions, which were judged to be rational in Europe and irrational beyond Europe. Such a binary construction, for example, pitted barbarous Eastern irrational mystic religions against rational Western civilized religions/science, or Eastern barbarous/savage collectivism against rational Western civilized individualism, and so on. By contrast, today the revitalized standard of civilization rests significantly on the standard of statehood – specifically the degree to which a centralized state attains rational-bureaucracy and democracy – even though 'irrational' societal criteria such as Islamic fundamentalism retain a place.[223]

This three-worlds formal hierarchical conception of world politics is most clearly represented within the Western-realist liberalism of Robert Cooper's work (2002, 2004). Cooper differentiates European *postmodern states* – which have created a civilized zone of peace – from 'the Rest'. European states owe their peaceful relations to an 'honest' and civilized 'moral consciousness' that rejects war (or more specifically, war between civilized states); a position which was articulated previously by the liberal scholar, John Mueller, in his well-known book *Retreat from Doomsday* (Mueller 1990). The second world comprises *modern states* (located principally in Asia) that engage in old-style

---

[222] See also Fidler (2000); Bowden and Seabrooke (2006); Bowden (2009). And for a Eurocentric take on this see Donnelly (1998).
[223] For example, one writer asserts that 'nationalism, non-alignment and religious fundamentalism have proved to be of more transcendant importance in the Third World than communism' (Layne 1989: 22).

relations involving Machiavellian principles of *raison d'état* and warfare. This approximates with the barbaric category, incorporating autocratic China and Middle Eastern despotic-Islam (i.e., the revived conception of the Oriental despotisms of the nineteenth century). And finally, he delineates a third world of *pre-modern* states – specifically failed/collapsed states – which are reduced to an anarchic state of nature torn apart by a Hobbesian war of all against all (i.e., the third world of savage societies in nineteenth century parlance). But critically, this is not simply an innocent description since it is politically loaded, as I now explain.

Eurocentric double standards and the bipolar/schizophrenic international

This three-worlds construction runs in tandem with the Eurocentric double standard that emerges through the bipolar or schizophrenic formal hierarchical construction of the international, wherein Western states treat each other differently to the way that they treat non-Western polities/societies. Because Western states are deemed to be civilized, so they are rewarded with dignity (i.e., sovereignty). Conversely, non-Western polities are deemed barbaric or savage and are therefore unworthy of dignity (i.e., sovereignty is withdrawn). And this neo-imperialist conception was, of course, an idiom of nineteenth century Eurocentrism in all its imperialist guises (as I explained in Chapters 2, 5 and 7).

In particular, nineteenth century Western-racist realism – expressed in the racist geopolitical writings of the likes of Mahan, Mackinder, Giddings and Powers – asserted the right of Western states to colonize Eastern polities and societies in order to contain and punish the barbarian/savage threat. Significantly, as I explained in the first two parts of this book, the accompanying nineteenth century idiom of 'social efficiency' carried a great deal of weight. This idea stipulated that all societies had a duty to develop their lands productively. Should they fail, then paternalist Eurocentric and racist-imperialist Western thinkers believed that they had to make way for Western imperialists to perform this necessary task. And in the extreme offensive racist-Eugenicist vision, it was deemed legitimate to directly exterminate the recalcitrant natives who resisted this 'legitimate' Western incursion (as in Karl Pearson). Of course, these extreme measures are no longer valid: genocide is no longer advocated; since 1945 sovereignty has become enshrined as a right of all states, notwithstanding the idea of conditional-sovereignty that underpinned the UN Universal Declaration of Human Rights (1948); formal

THE BASE CATEGORIES OF OFFENSIVE EUROCENTRISM 263

colonialism has been disavowed both legally and normatively, and scientific racism has been discarded in international theory/politics. But the key point is that contemporary offensive Eurocentrism has modified rather than abolished the nineteenth century posture. Thus contemporary offensive Eurocentrics argue that Eastern polities forfeit the right to sovereignty in those instances where such states are unable to bring order or democracy to their societies. Above all, non-Western polities are not recognized as sovereign if their instability poses a clear and present danger to Western states, as is congruent with the imperialist discourse of the standard of civilization/standard of statehood. Accordingly, such thinkers argue that Eastern polities/societies need to be punished through various forms of Western neo-imperial intervention.

All in all, the nineteenth-century imperial mantra of Western *hyper-sovereignty* and the denial of Eastern sovereignty has been reinstated by Western neo-imperialist international theory following the 'exceptional period' of decolonization (though, of course, today we witness the concept of Eastern state *conditional* sovereignty). Notably, this hyper-sovereign conception is one that has been generally obscured in peoples' minds by the popular headlining argument that globalization undermines the sovereignty of *all* states; an argument that is reinforced by the idea of 'postmodern' European states which sacrifice aspects of their sovereignty within the EU more specifically.

Reconstructing globalization-as-Eastern threat

Moving up to the next level in Figure 11.1, Western-realism interprets globalization as posing an Eastern threat to Western civilization. Once again, such a conception was fundamental to much of nineteenth-century Western racist-realism after 1889. As I explained in Chapters 4, 5 and 6 the most well-known exemplars of this genre were Alfred Mahan (1897) and Halford Mackinder (1904), though it is found in its most acute form in the cultural-realist racist works of Charles Henry Pearson (1894), B. L. Putnam Weale (1910) and Lothrop Stoddard (1920). These thinkers were especially concerned by what was often called the 'closing of the world' – or what we today call global interdependence. This was a central source of anxiety because it brought Eastern peoples right onto the doorstep of the West via the revolution of transport and communications. For the racist-realists and racist-cultural realists the resulting projection of the East out of so-called isolation was an omen for the West, given their perception that the East was not merely hungry but keen to dethrone Western hegemony and undermine civilization.

Likewise, we return to this post-1889 angst-ridden vision in the writings of Western-realists after 1989. In general, contemporary Western-realists point to technological mobility, especially through transnational weapons-movements, which enables non-Western – especially Islamic – terrorists to strike at the heart of the West, while the rise of non-Western great powers such as China and the disintegration of third world societies into savage anarchies under global interdependence brings the Eastern threat directly onto the doorstep of Western civilization (as noted above). As the Western-realist liberal writer, Michael Ignatieff, put it succinctly: 'terror has collapsed distance, and with this collapse has come a sharpened American focus on the necessity of bringing order to the frontier zones. Bringing order is the paradigmatic imperial task' (Ignatieff 2003a). And when Robert Cooper (2002) proclaims that 'Usama bin Laden has now demonstrated for those who had already not realized that today all the world is, potentially at least, our neighbour', he means that under globalization the Eastern threat is now barracking at the gates of the Western citadel. Or as he put it in his book *The Breaking of Nations*, globalization's ability to deliver terrorism and the dirty bomb 'could bring a nightmare in which states lose control of the means of violence and people lose control of their futures. Civilization and order rests on the control of violence: if it becomes uncontrollable there will be no order or civilization' (Cooper 2004: ix, see also x, 6, 55).

Huntington also displays a similarly deep-seated fear of a globalized world (as I explain later). But also of note here is his point that since 1989 the impact of globalization has ushered in a profound identity crisis within the West (2004: 13). Like other Western-realists Huntington laments the end of the Cold War since this has robbed the West in general and the United States in particular of an Other against which the identity of the Western self can be maintained; hence the need to look once again to the East for a new Other (see esp. Salter 2007). As he put it:

> the collapse of the Soviet Union and of communism left America not only with no enemy, but also for the first time in its history without any clear 'other' against which to define itself. . . . With the evil empire gone, how was America to define itself? Or, as John Updike put it, 'Without the cold war, what's the point of being an American?' (Huntington 2004: 261, 263).

Such an anxiety was wryly parodied by the Greek poet, Konstantinos Kavaphes, who finished his poem 'Waiting for the Barbarians' with the words:[224]

Why is everybody beginning to be so uneasy?
Why so disordered? (See how grave all the faces have become!)
Why do the streets and the squares empty so quickly, and they are all anxiously going home to their houses?
Because it is night, and the barbarians have not got here,
and some people have come in from the frontier and say that there aren't any more barbarians.
What are we going to do now without the barbarians?
In a way, those people were a solution.

Barbarians at the gates of the Western citadel and the barbarian Trojan horse inside the citadel

Moving up another level of Figure 11.1, we encounter the normative arguments that underpin the construction of the 'new barbaric threat' to Western civilization. This new post-1989 threat returns us to the spirit of the Western racist-realist and racist cultural realist perception of the yellow peril after 1889. In this section I shall focus on Western-realism reserving my discussion of cultural realism for the final section of this chapter. In essence, in going back to the future of post-1889 racist-realism, contemporary Western-realism exhibits an acute sense of anxiety. This translates into a *siege mentality* wherein the West is imagined as a citadel under attack from the Eastern barbarians and savages, who now stand either barracking at the gates or who are slipping their way inside them to gnaw at the citadel's foundations like an army of teaming woodworm. This mentality might best be summed up by two inter-related idioms: 'barbarians at the gates of the Western citadel' and the 'barbarian Trojan horse inside the Western citadel' (cf. Salter 2002: ch. 7). Thus when Daniel Pipes warns that 'the Muslims are coming! The Muslims are coming!', he is in effect reinvoking the central trope of nineteenth-century Western racist-realism, found in Mahan, Mackinder, Giddings and Powers, and in yet more acute form in the work of the racist cultural-realists, C. H. Pearson (1894) and Lothrop Stoddard (1920), all of whom constructed the idiom of 'The barbarians are coming! The barbarians are coming!' In essence, the central idiom of contemporary Western realism is the perception or construction of 'the coming anarchy and the new barbarism'.

---

[224] The poem was translated into English in 1955. The full version is posted at: www.kenyonreview.org/programs-resources-kavaphes.php

While this view was developed in books such as Zbigniew Brzezinski's *Out of Control* (1993) and Daniel Patrick Moynihan's *Pandaemonium* (1993), nevertheless this alarmist message hit the headlines in Robert Kaplan's article, 'The Coming Anarchy' (1994). Kaplan provides a snapshot of West Africa, a region he views as a microcosm of all that is wrong with the Third World. The result is a desperate picture of deprivation and depravity: of rampaging crime, disease, poverty, corruption, drug-trafficking, tribal conflict, ecological disaster, the explosion of population growth and an exodus of refugees that washes into the West like a human tsunami. Kaplan points to a 'criminal anarchy' in the context of failed and collapsed states that, in turn, poses a threat to the West. Interestingly, he draws explicit links to the Victorian era, insisting that West Africa 'is again becoming, as Graham Greene once observed "black" and "unexplored"'. He also deploys neo-Malthusian logic in predicting a demographic doomsday scenario for the East. Invoking images of the 'teeming hordes' in what might be dubbed the coming 'Black Peril' that the West now faces, Kaplan argues that the breakdown of African societies 'will prompt mass migrations and, in turn, innate group conflicts ... will be the core foreign policy challenge from which most others will ultimately emanate'. Thus '[w]e are entering a bifurcated world. Part of the globe [the West] is inhabited by Hegel's and Fukuyama's last man, healthy, well-fed and pampered by technology. The other, larger, part [the East] is inhabited by Hobbes's first man, condemned to a life that is "poor, nasty, brutish and short"'. As a result of this desperate condition, war between East and West is inevitable: 'there is a large number of people on this planet, to whom the comfort and stability of a middle-class life is utterly unknown [and therefore] find war and a barracks existence a step up rather than a step down'.

Kaplan concludes by issuing a word of warning to his fellow-Americans, much as did his predecessors Mahan and Mackinder, Giddings and Powers. For in this 'age of cultural and racial clashes, when national defense is increasingly local, Africa's distress will exert a destabilizing influence on the United States ... But Afrocentrists are right in one respect; we [Americans] ignore this dying region at our own risk' (Kaplan 1994). And it turns out, he argues, that the real threat to the West is not what was going on between Europeans in Yugoslavia in the 1990s, but that which would be spewed out by an inverted African black hole in the coming years.

One of the principal influences behind Kaplan's analysis is found in the neo-Malthusian analysis presented in Paul Kennedy's book

THE BASE CATEGORIES OF OFFENSIVE EUROCENTRISM   267

Preparing for the Twenty-First Century (1993).[225] This is worth considering in some detail not least because it provides a clear link between neo-Malthusianism and the new barbarism thesis. Here he advances the core claim that the greatest challenge to world order in the coming century is the rising relative demographic gap between the advanced/civilized West and the backward/uncivilized East. Kennedy explicitly rehabilitates, albeit with an important twist, Thomas Malthus's famous 1798 *Essay on the Principle of Population*. The popular take-home reading of Malthus is his claim that over time population increases outpace food technologies/production, with the result being famine and war. Or put differently, the technological means of food production progress arithmetically whereas population growth develops geometrically.[226] But behind this universalist reading was his focus on *relative* demographics concerning the wealthy and poor classes *within* the advanced European countries, where increases in the size of the poor through state welfare support threatens to undermine the development of these societies in aggregate;[227] an argument which later flourished in much of the social Darwinian and especially Eugenicist literatures later on in the nineteenth century. Moreover, his relativism was apparent in his highly Eurocentric discussion of non-Western societies, whose regressive and irrational institutions above all accounted for the lack of population growth across the vast majority of the East,[228] though China was a clear exception.[229]

The key twist in Kennedy's development of Malthus's argument concerns the transposition of relative class demographic differentials *within* advanced societies into the international sphere, where the relative demographic gap between advanced Western and backward Eastern societies becomes the pivotal concern. This in effect inverts Malthus's international picture. For today the technological explosion is occurring in the advanced West that suffers from a static population trajectory with an increasingly 'high elderly-dependency ratio', while the East suffers a population explosion with a very low elderly dependency ratio under conditions of low technological advancement (i.e., a Malthusian crisis).

---

[225] Nevertheless, although the panic over the Eastern demographic 'explosion' was revived during the Cold War, it is worth noting, as Bonnett (2004: 176) points out, that at the peak of decolonization it was used by some writers to explain the rise of the Third World.
[226] Malthus (1798/1971: Bk I, ch. 1).   [227] Malthus (1798/1971: Bk III, chs. 1–14).
[228] Malthus (1798/1971: Bk I, chs. 3–11).   [229] Malthus (1798/1971: Bk I, ch. 12).

Interestingly, on first reading one might view Kennedy's argument as departing from Malthus's conservative and right-wing approach, producing a left-liberal or even a radical statement; to wit his deep concern with contemporary ecological crisis and his harsh criticisms concerning the greed and irresponsibility of Western multinational corporations, as well as his criticism of the diffusion of inappropriate First World technologies to the South; all of which in aggregate serves only to exacerbate the problem of Third World backwardness and poverty. But it turns out that the chief concern which underpins the book's argument is the negative impact on Western civilization that the relative demographic gap produces. The crux of this threat is expressed thus:

> [I]f the developing world remains caught in its poverty trap, the more developed countries will come under siege from tens of millions of migrants and refugees eager to reside among the prosperous but aging populations of the democracies ... [T]he results are likely to be painful for the richest one-sixth of the earth's population that now enjoys a disproportionate five-sixths of its wealth (Kennedy 1993: 46).

In addition, he argues that there is a strong security threat entwined within the neo-Malthusian crises in the Third World, given that the resulting instabilities

> could take place in regions where the possession of advanced weaponry [including chemical and nuclear weapons] by ambitious and threatened regimes [read autocracies/Oriental despotisms] makes a potentially lethal combination, with implications that would be far from local (Kennedy 1993: 347).

From this one might anticipate a solution whereby Third World development through technological innovation and other factors would be advocated, thereby cutting off the tap-root of the exodus of Third World peoples into the West, as well as relieving the pressures that could trigger a nuclear or chemical weapons strike by a contemporary Oriental despotism. But such a 'solution' turns out to constitute a yet more damaging threat to Western hegemony. For, he argues, 'if the developing world manages to raise its output and standards of living' thereby relieving the Malthusian crisis, then 'the West's proportion of economic output, global power and political influence will decline steadily, simply because of the sheer force of numbers' (Kennedy 1993: 45–6). Worse still, he goes on to argue, such a scenario raises 'the interesting question of whether "Western values" ... will maintain their prevailing position in a world overwhelmingly peopled by societies which did not experience the rational scientific and liberal assumptions of the Enlightenment' (Kennedy 1993: 46). That Kennedy views this potential predicament in the gravest terms is suggested by his earlier Eurocentric claim that while *all* societies are capable of developing, nevertheless this applies only to those that adopt Western institutions *in toto* (Kennedy 1993: 16–17). Or put differently, only when all societies adopt Western values can there be any relief from the Eastern threat. But given that for Kennedy this has not eventuated in the East, then logically this means that a rising East confronting a declining West would constitute the gravest threat to both civilization and world order. Thus in defending Western hegemony and its civilized values and institutions Kennedy returns us directly to the pessimistic and angst-ridden analyses of the racist-realists. While Malthus in his day did not perceive a rising demographic threat to Europe from the East, by the late-nineteenth century/early twentieth century this perception became a staple of much Western racist thought.

The anxiety over failed states is complemented in much of Westernrealism with an equally strong anxiety concerning the second world of 'barbaric' autocratic states, whose rising economic and military success is thought to provide no less of a threat to civilization and world order. For such states constitute a prelude to future imperial expansion (Cooper 2004: 24). Thus in his *Foreign Policy* debate with Thomas Friedman, Robert Kaplan argues that after 1989 the world has 'returned to normal', by which he means that rising Eastern powers are exacerbating geopolitical competition (see Friedman and Kaplan 2002). Likewise for Robert Kagan the challenge today is simple but ominous: 'history has returned, and the [civilized] democracies must come together to shape it, or others will shape it for them' (Kagan 2008: 4). And similarly, Charles Krauthammer (1990/1991: 31) argues that '[t]he current weapons states [Oriental despotisms] have deep grievances against the West ... [and] are therefore subversive of the international status quo, which they see as a residue of colonialism'.

If China already exhibits imperial traits, the problem is multiplied further in the context of Islamic states. 'A successful Islamist state, fired with enthusiasm for bringing the teachings of the Koran to the unbelievers, is more likely to be a threat' that will redound on the West in the long run (Cooper 2004: 25). And as is well-known, it is the rising Sino-Islamic threat that most concerns Lind and especially Huntington (as I explain later). This perception emerged very quickly after 9/11, as Daniel Pipes explains, even though concerns over an emerging Muslim threat stem back to the

1970s (Füredi 2007). Equally, though, this analysis returns us directly to the nineteenth century racist-realist trope of the yellow peril, where high levels of (predatory) Eastern agency struck fear into the hearts of many Westerners. No less significantly, this anxiety invokes the medieval analogy wherein the identity of (Western) Christendom was constructed in defeat, based on a sense of siege vis-à-vis the various Eastern races that flooded into Europe in wave after wave prior to the Columbian epoch (Mackinder 1904; Putnam Weale 1910: ch. 5).

The threat of rising Islamic powers runs ineluctably into the fear of the Islamic terrorist threat. This is associated with the second-world barbarism of Islamic autocratic fundamentalism on the one hand and the conflation of failed states (or savage polities) with terrorism, especially Islamic terrorism on the other. This is based on the notion that the internal anarchy and chaos of failed states in the third world breeds terrorists who then seek to attack the West. And since 9/11 this has been exacerbated by the (problematic) *perception* that failed states are also thought to provide safe havens for global terrorist networks, especially Al-Qaeda.[230] Interestingly, when Western-realists sometimes argue that the response of the West should be to ally with Russia, which guards the West's 'great right flank', in order to defeat the Islamic terrorist threat (as do some cultural realists – e.g., Lind 1991), so we return directly to Mackinder's racist-realism and his argument that Europe and the United States needed to ally with Russia so as to defeat invading Eastern threats as they journeyed to the West through the 'pivot' or 'heartland' of the world (Mackinder 1904).[231]

Western-realism and the resort to neo-imperialism: containing the 'new barbaric threat'

Finally, these offensive Eurocentric analyses culminate in a neo-imperialist containment politics, even though this takes on a range of different forms. Many call for American 'hegemonic/neo-imperial' interventionism in the East;[232] an idea that finds its strongest place in

---

[230] But for excellent critiques see Simons and Tucker (2007); Hehir (2008).
[231] Nevertheless, this is by no means to discount the West's deep concerns about Russia, especially over the recent revival of wars in Chechnya and Georgia; concerns that are more *intra*-civilizational rather than inter-civilizational. Interestingly, Russia is constructed as part friend and part foe, occupying an interstitial zone between East and West, as has in fact long been the case; on this see the excellent discussion in Neumann (1998).
[232] E.g., Kaplan (2003, 2006); Ferguson (2004).

Western liberal-realism,[233] and among various realist-liberals.[234] Note that because these particular realist-liberals are so close to the arguments made by liberal-realists I shall also discuss some of them here.

Interestingly, some of these neo-imperialists deny a commitment to imperialism, or refer to it in all but (sanitized) name, speaking of the United States instead as a 'benevolent hegemon', or as a kind of 'democratic hegemon' (Brzezinski 2004), though equally others refer to it as a 'benevolent empire' and a 'Behometh with a conscience' (Kagan 1998).[235] But whichever label is used cannot detract from the key point that such formulations rest on the idea of 'American exceptionalism'; the idiom that underpinned a series of historical imperialist visions including Thomas Jefferson's 'empire of liberty' and the post-1850 conception of America's 'manifest destiny'. In this imaginary it is vital to note that equating US interests with the universal – a very Eurocentric conflation in itself – can be squared only by deploying another Eurocentric idea: that of 'Eastern false consciousness'. Thus it is assumed that when non-Western states seek to follow their own cultural interests – such as Lee Kuan Yew's 'Asian Way' – so they are merely exhibiting signs of self-delusion and, even worse, self-denial. Better that they realize this and cast aside their own civilizational pride, for in assimilating Western values and institutions they will 'naturally' find themselves, albeit in the long run, freer and more prosperous; an argument that is made explicit by the realist-liberal thinker, David Rothkopf (1997: 49).

The assumption that American interests are the universal implies in the minds of Western-realists and especially Western-liberal realists and realist-liberals that America's high degree of virtue means that other states feel naturally *un*threatened by the US.[236] But only by deploying this Eurocentric idea can the advocacy of US neo-imperialism be presented as benign; to wit the argument of Robert Kagan, that US hegemony after 1989 is not so much selfless but guided by 'the kind of enlightened self-interest that, in practice, comes dangerously close to generosity' (Kagan 1998: 28). Or as Fareed Zakaria (2003) puts it: 'American power

---

[233] E.g., Kristol and Kagan (1996); Kagan (2004, 2008); Krauthammer (1990–91, 2004); Zakaria (2002, 2003).
[234] E.g., Ignatieff (2003a, 2003b); Rieff (1999); Rothkopf (1997); Cooper (2002).
[235] These terms are complemented by a range of others including: 'consensual empire' (Maier), 'empire of invitation' (Lundestad), 'imperial republic' (Aron), 'democratic imperialism' (Kurtz 2003) or 'participatory imperialism' (Feuer 1986: 204–15); and for excellent summary discussions see Cox (2004); Ikenberry (2004: esp. 617–20).
[236] E.g., Krauthammer (1990–91, 2004); Zakaria (2002, 2003).

is not simply good for America; it is good for the world ... Other countries are simply not ready or able, at this point, to take on the challenges and burdens of leadership'. Such a rhetorical move was performed, no doubt unwittingly, by President George W. Bush in November 2003, when he rather innocently asserted that America 'has no territorial ambitions. We don't seek an empire. Our nation is committed to freedom for ourselves and for others' (cited in Ignatieff 2003a); to which Michael Ignatieff responds appropriately:

> Yet what word but 'empire' describes the awesome thing that America is becoming?.... America's empire is not like empire of times past, built on colonies, conquest and the white man's burden. The twenty-first century is a new invention in the annals of political science, an empire lite, a global hegemony whose grace notes are free markets, human rights and democracy, enforced by the most awesome military power the world has ever known (Ignatieff 2003a).

This elision of a neo-imperial mentality is all the more perplexing given Bush's later paternalist statement uttered in 2005, that '[t]he essence of civilization [i.e., the West] is that the strong have a duty to protect the weak' (Bush 2005, cited in Salter 2007: 83).[237] Put simply, to paraphrase von Clausewitz, in this liberal-realist vision US hegemony is the continuation of liberal imperialism by other means. Or as one critic phrases it: 'Mill's characterization of nineteenth-century Britain as a "benevolent despot" is not so different from the neoconservative understanding of the USA today as a "benevolent hegemon"' (McCarthy 2009: 221); though this should hardly be surprising given that the link between Mill's particular conception of imperialism in the nineteenth century and what the United States should be doing today is made increasingly explicit by its contemporary advocates (e.g., Kurtz 2003; Ferguson 2004).

On the realist-liberal side we find official proclamations of this universalist conception of the American interest, found in numerous statements issued by Madeleine Albright. Thus we learn from Albright that '[i]f we [the United States] have to use force, it is because we are Americans. We are the indispensable nation. We stand tall. We see further into the future'; and that '[w]e will behave multilaterally when we can and unilaterally when we must'.[238] And, of course, such an idiom reveals the classic face of paternalist-imperialism that updates the

---

[237] And for an excellent discussion of this issue more generally see Salter (2007); O'Hagan (2007); Bowden (2009).
[238] These came from the NBC *Today* show in 1998 and a 1994 UN Speech respectively.

formula first laid out by Gilpin in his neorealist theory of hegemonic stability (as I discussed in Chapter 8).

That the American interest is the universal, and is therefore inherently good for the world, underpins David Rothkopf's 1997 article 'In Praise of Cultural Imperialism'. American culture, he insists, is not 'relativistic' but comprises

> an amalgam of influences and approaches from around the world, into a social medium that allows individual freedoms and cultures to thrive. Recognizing this, Americans should not shy away from doing that which is so clearly in their economic, political, and security interests – and so clearly in the interests of the world at large. ... Americans should not deny the fact that of all the nations in the history of the world, theirs is the most just, the most tolerant, the most willing to constantly reassess and improve itself, and the best model for the future (Rothkopf 1997: 48–9).

Having exorcized the particularism of the American interest, Rothkopf is emboldened to proselytize the cause of American cultural imperialism, safe in the knowledge that this will naturally be welcomed by all other societies. Thus without even a hint of irony he proclaims that

> It is in the general interest of the United States to engage the development of a world in which the faultlines separating nations can be bridged by shared [universal] interests. And it is in the economic and political interests of the United States to ensure that if the world is moving toward a common language, it be English ... that if the world is becoming linked by television, radio and music, the programming be American; and that if common values are being developed, they be values with which Americans are comfortable (Rothkopf 1997: 45).

Such rhetoric, however, reflects the hubris that is typical of imperial powers at their peak. Indeed it is directly reminiscent of the many self-congratulatory statements that were uttered by leading British imperialists in the late-nineteenth century, typical of which was Joseph Chamberlain's proud boast: 'I believe in this race, the greatest governing race the world has ever seen; in this Anglo-Saxon race, so proud, so tenacious, self-confident and determined, this race which neither climate nor change can degenerate, which will infallibly be the predominant force of future history and universal civilization'. Equally, Lord Curzon no less proudly proclaimed that '[i]n empire, we have found not merely the key to glory and wealth, but the call to duty, and the means of service to mankind'.[239] But, as this very British context reminds us, there is clearly a thin line between hubris and anxiety.

[239] Chamberlain and Curzon, cited in Hobson (2004: 237–8).

More generally, most of the contemporary arguments to justify (neo-imperialist) Western hegemony return us directly to the spirit of the nineteenth-century Western racist-realists such as Mahan (1897), Mackinder (1904), Giddings (1898) and Powers (1898). Moreover, the Western realist-liberals also hark back in some respects to the spirit of the paternalist Eurocentrics such as Cobden (1868a, 1868b), Angell (1913, 1937) and especially Mill (1859/1984, 1861/1998), though they also share many overlaps with the racist-liberals such as Reinsch (1905a, 1905b), Sidgwick (1897), Wilson (1902a, 1902b) and Ireland (1905), but especially Dilke (1868), Strong (1885, 1889) and Fiske (1885). Robert Cooper tells us that '[i]t is precisely because of the death of imperialism that we are now seeing the emergence of the [Eastern threats of the] pre-modern world. ... If they become too dangerous, it is possible to imagine a defensive imperialism ... perhaps even the need for colonization [which] is as great as it ever was in the nineteenth century' (Cooper 2002). In particular, he argues that for the first time since the nineteenth century, we have returned to the idiom of *terra nullius*. Failed states/savage societies provide havens for terrorist networks – a standard Eurocentric trope – which require Western imperial containment. 'If non-state actors, notably drug, crime or terrorist syndicates take to using non-state (that is, pre-modern) bases for attacks on the more orderly parts of the world [i.e., Western civilization], then the organized [Western] states will eventually have to respond (Cooper 2004: 18).

Echoing Michael Ignatieff's argument about 'empire-lite', this imperialism is portrayed in terms reminiscent of the nineteenth century concept of the civilizing mission – 'one [that must be] acceptable to a world of human rights and cosmopolitan values ... an imperialism which, like all imperialism, aims to bring order and organization but which rests today as the voluntary principle ... [based on] the lightest of touches from the centre' (Cooper 2002). And if this requires certain double standards on the part of the West then so be it:

> The postmodern [European] state ... needs to get used to the idea of double standards. Among themselves, the postmodern states operate on the basis of laws and open co-operative security. But when dealing with more old-fashioned kinds of state outside the [European] post-modern limits, Europeans need to revert to the rougher methods of an earlier era – force, preemptive attack, deception, whatever is necessary for those who still live in the nineteenth-century world of every state for itself. In the jungle, one must use the laws of the jungle (Cooper 2004: 61–2).

Interestingly, such an approach echoes not only Mill's paternalist Eurocentric instruction, but equally that of David Hume's a century earlier when he asserted that

> were a civilized nation engaged with barbarians, who observe no rules even of war, the former must also suspend their observance of them, where they no longer serve to any purpose; and must render every action or rencounter as bloody and pernicious as possible to the first aggressor (Hume cited in Whelan 2009: 45).[240]

Ultimately, for Cooper, such imperialism must take the form of expanding postmodern Europe to incorporate the barbaric and savage worlds; for such an expansion turns out to be global humanity's last best hope for reaching civilization in order to terminate the new barbaric threat to civilization and world order. As he asserts: '[i]f this process is a kind of voluntary imperialism, the end state might be described as a cooperative empire. "Commonwealth" might indeed not be a bad name' (Cooper 2002).

Here it deserves reiterating that the nineteenth century bipolar formal hierarchical conception of the international, which inherently issues an imperialist rationale contained within the discourse of Western double standards, has returned in a contemporary *neo*-imperial form. Fukuyama's summary of Kristol's and Kagan's neo-Conservative position exemplifies this point. For as he put it, they 'argued explicitly for regime change as a central component of their neo-Reaganite policy. They asserted that getting tyrannical regimes to play by civilized rules through agreements, international law, or norms was ultimately unworkable' (Fukuyama 2006: 41–2); a sentiment that returns us directly to the statement made by John Stuart Mill (see p. 289 in the next chapter). Echoing Cooper, Robert Kagan explicitly invokes the bipolar concept, asserting that:

> The problem is that the United States must sometimes play by rules of a Hobbesian world, even though in doing so it violates Europe's postmodern norms. It must refuse to abide by certain international conventions that may constrain its ability to fight effectively in Robert Cooper's jungle ... It must live by a double standard. And it must sometimes act unilaterally ... only because, given a weak Europe that has moved beyond power, the United States has no choice *but* to act unilaterally (Kagan 2004: 99).

---

[240] And for an excellent discussion of Hume's imperialist-Eurocentrism see Whelan (2009: 6–47).

Here he insists that the nature of the Eastern threat and Europe's retreat into a 'postmodern paradise' means that the United States has no choice but to discipline and punish, unilaterally if necessary, the savages to the East. Thus rather than criticizing America, as many Europeans have done, Kagan insists that it 'would be better ... if Europeans could move beyond fear and anger at the rogue colossus and remember, again, the vital necessity of having a strong, even predominant America – for the world and especially for Europe. It would seem to be an acceptable price to pay for [Europe's] paradise' (Kagan 2004: 101). Or, put differently, this would be an acceptable price to pay for the maintenance of Western civilization and world order.

To this can be added a string of writers such as Max Boot, who argues that 9/11 was not in fact 'payback' for American imperialism. For such a view

> is exactly backward: The September 11 attack was a result of insufficient American involvement and ambition; the solution is to be more expansive in our goals and more assertive in their implementation. ... Afghanistan and other troubled lands today cry out for the sort of enlightened foreign administration once provided by self-confident Englishmen in jodhpurs and pith helmets (Boot 2001).

William Pfaff, in his Western-realist book *The Wrath of Nations* expressed it thus:

> [t]he immediate future of Africa ... is bleak, and it would be better if the international community would reimpose some form of paternalist neo-colonialism in most of Africa, unpalatable as that may seem. The mechanism of the international mandate, employed by the League of Nations ... might be revived (Pfaff 1993: 158).

Paul Johnson asserted in 1993 that '[m]ost African states are not fit to govern themselves. Their continued existence, and the violence of human degradation they breed, are a threat to stability and peace as well as an affront to our consciences ... [T]he civilized world must ... go to Africa and govern'.[241] And in a similar vein, the Western-realist Robert Kaplan (2006) likens American military engagements in the East to the waging of the war against the American-Indian natives that reached its climax in the nineteenth century. Just as the European immigrants pacified unruly, uncivilized space through wiping out native Indian communities and containing them within reserves, so the extension of this principle into the

---

[241] Johnson cited in Malik (1996: 37).

Eastern world is a necessary tool to protect Western civilization today (though genocide is no longer on the agenda).

This link with nineteenth century imperialism is an explicit focus of Niall Ferguson's 2004 book, *Colossus*, which advances many of the arguments developed in his previous 2002 book *Empire*. Indeed *Colossus* in effect puts into book form the imperial mantra that was sung by Max Boot just after 9/11. In strong contrast to those radicals who seek to purge or decontaminate US hegemony of its imperialist properties, Ferguson's key message is nothing if it is not honest: Americans need to come clean about their imperial role in the world which, he claims, the United States has *always* engaged in.[242] Accordingly they would do much better if they could get over their guilt complex. Taking on the left-liberals he insists that failing to utter the E-word (empire) in the context of US foreign policy serves only to undermine the impetus for US imperialism which, he insists, has a progressive role to play in the world. Thus while Ferguson echoes Ignatieff's explicit pro-imperial stance, his complaint is that US imperialism today is 'not so much "lite" but disposable',[243] by which he means that American empire needs to be made much more robust. The object lesson for America today – and where the parallel with the nineteenth century is made most forcefully – is that the United States needs to develop the kind of staying power that the British had in their imperial heyday, rather than withdrawing once the initial intervention had been completed. Here Ferguson returns us to *some* of the claims made by various racist–imperialists including Giddings, Powers and Kidd (1898), whose key rationale for writing his book *The Control of the Tropics* was to assuage Westerners of their home-grown 'imperialist-guilt syndrome'. For it was precisely this that served to paralyse the West and thereby prevent it from undertaking the necessary imperialist role in world affairs that civilization demands (see pp. 114–16, this volume).

One of the central themes of Ferguson's two books discussed here concerns his celebration of Anglo-Saxon imperialism or 'Anglobalization' – both in its nineteenth-century-British form and its twentieth-century-American guise – as the civilizing force that combats the evil empire of barbarism and chaos. Moreover, he insists that the case for empire today is yet more urgent given the particularly virulent strein

---

[242] See also Mallaby (2002).   [243] Ferguson (2004: 204).

of the *new* barbaric threat (cf. Mallaby 2002). Reminiscent of the racist-realists mentioned earlier, he argues that should the US forfeit the imperial mantle then:

> Waning empires, religious revivals, incipient anarchy, a retreat into fortified cities: These are the Dark Age experiences that a post-imperial world [today] could conceivably find itself reliving... If the United States is to retreat from global hegemony – its fragile self-image dented by minor setbacks on the imperial frontier – its critics at home and abroad must not pretend that they are ushering in a new era of multipolar harmony, or even a return to the good old balance of power. For the alternative... could be apolarity – a global vacuum of power. And far more dangerous forces than rival great powers would benefit from such a not-so-new world disorder (Ferguson 2004: xxvii–xxviii).

Interestingly, just over a century earlier the offensive racist-realist Franklin Giddings warned that the failure of the United States to form an Anglo-Saxon racial alliance with Britain in order to contain the forces of barbarism would surely be punished by 'another thousand years of medieval night [that] will fall upon the Western world' (Giddings 1898: 605). And this in turn feeds directly into the racist-realism of Alfred Mahan and Halford Mackinder, with the latter warning of the need for the West to marshal against the yellow peril at the beginning of the twentieth century, on the basis that the Roman Empire was brought down by barbarians only to leave Europe in the long thousand year night of the Dark Ages, battered and bruised by wave after wave of incoming Eastern barbarians.

But to be clear: none of this is *in any way* to smear Ferguson, or any of the other 'Western-realists' whom I examine in this chapter, as racist. And nor is this to deny the impressiveness of some of this scholarship, Ferguson's in particular. My claim, rather, is that they embody an 'offensive' Eurocentric institutionalism that reconvenes in content and 'spirit' rather than metanarratival form some of the key arguments or themes that illuminated the minds of some, though by no means all, of the racist-realists in the post-1889 era.

Finally, it is noteworthy that other forms of neo-imperial containment are advocated by various Western-realists. Some such as Stephen Krasner advocate 'shared sovereignty', though this complements the general theme of the revival of international trusteeship. Nevertheless, because this is also advocated by various liberals I shall deal with this in one summary discussion in the next chapter.

Addendum. Defensive Eurocentrism: cultural-realism and the critique of imperialism

While the majority of Western realists adopt a containment/imperialist mentality vis-à-vis the new barbaric threat, the cultural realist work of Samuel Huntington and William Lind provides an *anti*-imperialist solution. Thus to complete both the summary of Western-realism as well as the historical analysis of the changing configurations of Eurocentrism, it is worth briefly exploring this example of defensive Eurocentrism. In a thought-provoking article Akira Iriye (1997) makes the case for drawing a close parallel between Huntington and the racist-imperialist thinker, Alfred Mahan. Although I also find evidence of such a link, I want to argue that an even closer link exists between Huntington and the racist cultural realism found in Charles Henry Pearson's *National Life and Character* (1894), Lothrop Stoddard's *The Rising Tide of Color* (1920) and *Clashing Tides of Color* (1935) and, albeit less directly, B. L. Putnam Weale's racist tract, *The Conflict of Colour* (1910).[244] All of these thinkers begin their analyses with the threat that the 'barbaric peril' poses for Western civilization; an argument that runs in stages.

In Huntington's book *The Clash of Civilizations* (1996) the roots of the barbaric threat that the Chinese and Muslims pose for Western civilization are located within a neo-Malthusian framework that begins with the Eastern population explosion (Huntington 1996: chs. 4–5; also Lind 1991: 44). And this surplus population is problematic in part because it will seek to flood into the heartlands of the West (Huntington 1996: ch. 5). Such an emphasis is one that also featured prominently in Stoddard's 1920 book, in which he constructed a vivid image of a besieged Western citadel battered by an incoming tsunami of non-Western immigrants.

Another key shared property exists in the point that at first sight Huntington appears to grant various Eastern societies high levels of agency. As he put it, during the twentieth century, '[f]ar from being simply the objects of Western-made history, non-Western societies were increasingly becoming the movers and shapers of their own history and of Western history'.[245] This refers to their ability to economically develop as well as resist the influence that the West had previously imposed upon Eastern societies via imperialism. Interestingly, this general thrust overlaps with various pre-1945 scientific racist thinkers. Thus Alfred Mahan spoke of 'the

---

[244] For a discussion of Pearson see pp. 87–9; and for Stoddard see pp. 142–9.
[245] Huntington (1993: 53).

stirring of the East' and 'its entrance into the field of Western interests, not merely as a passive something to be impinged upon, but with a vitality of its own, formless yet, but significant' (Mahan 1897: 97). More significantly, Charles Pearson (1894) and Lothrop Stoddard delivered their wake-up call to the hubris of Western civilization when they spoke of the agency of the yellow East Asians (the Japanese and Chinese) and also, in Stoddard's case, the brown Muslims (e.g., Stoddard 1920: 60). There is an obvious parallel here in that Huntington singled out China and Islam as constituting the key contemporary threats to Western civilization. Lind chimes in here too:

> [A] potential threat from Islam may develop if the Soviet Empire breaks up. [If so] the West's great right flank ... will almost certainly be endangered as the Islamic republics seek to join their Muslim brethren ... [such that] the twenty-first century could once again find Islam at the gates of Vienna, as immigrants or terrorists if not as armies (Lind 1991: 45).

Overall the clearest point of overlap between all these thinkers lies with their implicit notion of Eastern predatory/barbaric agency since China and Islam constitute the very antithesis to civilization and world order.

A further shared overlap between Huntington/Lind and Stoddard/ Pearson comprises their construct of 'globalization-as-barbaric threat', since it is globalization that delivers a surplus tide of Eastern peoples to the gates of the Western citadel, or right into its heart via immigration. As Huntington put it, one principal reason for the clash of civilizations since 1989 is that:

> [The] world is becoming a smaller place. Interactions between peoples of different civilizations are increasing; these increasing interactions intensify civilization consciousness and awareness of differences ... North African immigration to France generates hostility among Frenchmen ... Americans react far more negatively to Japanese investment than the larger investments from Canada and European countries (Huntington 1993: 25–6; see also 2004: 14).

And as I explained in Chapters 5 and 6, this was very much a defining feature of Stoddard's and Mahan's lament concerning the 'closing of the world'. Stoddard, though, went a little further than Mahan, for while the latter perceived the incoming threat in military terms, Stoddard was principally concerned with what he called the 'coloured immigration peril'.

But what makes this non-Western immigration peril so dangerous in the minds of Huntington and Lind is its conversion into a highly toxic mix that is made possible by the political virus of home-grown Western multiculturalism. Thus while the exodus of non-white peoples from the non-Western world provides the trigger for the crisis of American civilization, the indigenous growth of multiculturalism within the Western citadel provides the bullet. And just as Western liberal sentimentalism nurtured the immigration peril according to Stoddard, so for Huntington it too constituted the Trojan horse that served to open the citadel's floodgates to the incoming tsunami of non-Western immigrants. Interestingly, James Kurth argues that the 'real clash' is between Western civilization and multiculturalism *within* the West (Kurth 1994). For both Huntington and Lind, maintaining the cultural purity of America in the face of this 'barbaric-cultural invasion' is a vital factor in renewing America as the ultimate defender of Western civilization, much as it was for Stoddard, Grant and many other defensive racists. And much as Stoddard was deeply anxious about declining white unity as a result of domestic factors, so for Huntington and Lind home-grown multiculturalism serves not only to boost the vitality of 'foreign cultures' within the West but simultaneously dilutes the hegemony of Anglo-Saxon Protestant culture.

In turn this gives rise to Huntington's political prescription, wherein the prime responsibility of the United States today is to police the Eurocentric line of civilizational apartheid in order to keep the contaminating influence of non-Western culture at bay, thereby maximizing the distance between Anglo-Saxon and non-Western cultural elements. As Huntington put it in the all-important final chapter:

> The futures of the United States and of the West depend upon Americans reaffirming their commitment to Western civilization. Domestically this means rejecting the divisive siren calls of multiculturalism. Internationally it means rejecting the elusive and illusory calls to identify the United States with Asia ... [For when] Americans look for their cultural roots, they find them in Europe (Huntington 1996: 307, 318).

And from the seed that was planted in his most well-known book grew the subsequent volume, *Who are We?*, where he launched into a critique of multiculturalism at home as well as Latin American immigration and the contaminating influence upon the American Creed that 'Hispanization' entails (Huntington 2004: ch. 9).[246] Critically, such an

---

[246] Note that while Mexico, of course, lies in the same line of longitude to the United States (as does Africa vis-à-vis Europe), nevertheless Mexican culture is seen as inferior to American civilization.

analysis harks back not just to Stoddard and Charles Pearson but also to the arch-Eugenicist and anti-immigrationist, Madison Grant. In this context Grant's complaint is prescient – to wit the

> result of unlimited immigration [into the United States] is showing plainly in the rapid decline in the birth rate of native [white] Americans. ... The native American is too proud to mix socially with [the immigrants] and is gradually withdrawing from the scene, abandoning to these aliens the land which he conquered and developed. The man of the old stock is being crowded out ... by these foreigners. These immigrants adopt the language of the native American, they wear his clothes ... but they seldom adopt his religion or understand his ideals and while he is being elbowed out of his own home the American looks calmly abroad and urges on others the suicidal [multi-cultural or multi-racial] ethics which are exterminating his own race (Grant 1918: 91).

Still, while Huntington calls for strong non-Western immigration controls he also argues that non-Western immigrants must and *can be* fully culturally assimilated to the American Creed. Of course, this might imply that the parallels with the nineteenth- and early twentieth-century racists diverge at this point, where some of the latter were highly critical of non-white immigration for the racial-miscegenation threat that it posed as well as for the fact that inferior non-white races were unable to culturally assimilate. But, while this was certainly the case for Stoddard, Grant and many others, nevertheless many scientific racists believed that even under conditions of non-Western immigration, Western civilizational purity could be maintained through cultural assimilation. This position often emerged as a function of a Lamarckian-racist input. In this particular respect Huntington's argument finds its closest parallel with Lamarckian-inspired racists such as John W. Burgess, who asserted that

> I consider ... the prime mission of the ideal American commonwealth to be the perfection of the Aryan genius for political civilization. ... *We must preserve our Aryan nationality in the state, and admit to its membership only such non-Aryan race-elements as shall have become Aryanized in spirit and in genius by contact with it*, if we would build the superstructure of the ideal American commonwealth (Burgess 1895: 407, my emphasis).

Nevertheless, the parallels between Lind/Huntington and Stoddard as well as Charles Pearson and Grant re-emerge in their anti-imperialist posture. Stoddard rejected Western imperialism in Asia on the grounds that it served only to alienate the yellow and brown races that would then seek to avenge the West,[247] while Pearson believed that the game was up for Western imperialism for a number of reasons that I explained in Chapter 4. Likewise Lind asserts that:

> A defensive stance should facilitate alliances with other cultures. [But] it is important to emphasize that the call for a culturally oriented foreign policy is not a call to revive Western imperialism. Rather it is a call for the West to prepare to defend itself. As such, it need not be threatening to anyone else, and should be carefully presented as nonthreatening (Lind 1991: 48).

Likewise Huntington's anti-imperialist defensive Eurocentric angst leads him to conclude that:

> The belief that non-Western peoples should adopt Western values ... is immoral because of what would be necessary to bring it about. ... Imperialism is the necessary logical consequence of [such a] universalism. ... Western universalism is dangerous to the world because it could lead to a major intercivilizational war between core states and it is dangerous to the West because it could lead to the defeat of the West. ... A multicultural America is impossible because a non-Western America is not American. A multicultural world is unavoidable because global empire is impossible. The preservation of the United States and the West requires the renewal of Western identity (Huntington 1996: 318).

Or as he warned in more succinct terms, it is 'most important ... to recognize that Western intervention in the affairs of other civilizations is probably the single most dangerous source of instability and potential global conflict in a multicivilizational world' (1996: 312).

Critically, this was the exact same logic of Stoddard's argument, in which he concluded that:

> It was typical of the malaise which was overtaking the white world that the close of the nineteenth century should have witnessed an ominous ignoring of white solidarity ... [and that multicultural] internationalists caressed visions of 'human solidarity' culminating in universal race-amalgamation. ... One thing is certain: the white man will have to recognize that the practically absolute world-dominion which he exercised during the nineteenth century can no longer be maintained. Largely because of that very dominion ... [we now witness] a widespread [non-white] ferment ... which is destined to grow more acute in the near future (Stoddard 1920: 170, 228).

---

[247] Though this is not to deny his point that the West must retain its imperial outposts in black Africa and red Latin America in order to block the rising yellow and brown imperialist tide from swamping these continents.

Moreover, the link is reinforced by their calling for the white races/ Western peoples to renew their civilizational purity and huddle together inside the walls of the Western citadel, batten down the hatches, raise the drawbridge and lower the portcullis in the face of this incoming barbarian tsunami. For in the absence of such a defensive strategy, non-white immigration, when combined with the 'Trojan horse' of home-grown multiculturalism and political correctness, will serve only to subvert the underlying structure of Western civilization thereby bringing the citadel's inhabitants to their knees.

Critically, this all culminates in one of the clearest signs of Huntington's Eurocentric approach. For while it is often thought that Huntington specified the existence of seven or eight civilizations so as to transcend the allegedly 'essentialist' East–West divide,[248] his Eurocentric approach leads him to demarcate just such an 'essentialist divide'; to wit his conclusion that

> On a world-wide scale civilization seems in many respects to be yielding to barbarism, generating the image of an unprecedented phenomenon, a global Dark Ages, possibly descending upon humanity . . . In the clash of civilizations, Europe and America will hang together or hang separately. In the greater clash, the global 'real clash' between Civilization and barbarism . . . [the advanced Western countries] will also hang together or hang separately (Huntington 1996: 321).

Thus, in sum, Huntington and Lind share with the racist cultural-realists – Stoddard, Grant and Pearson – an overarching desire to maximize the distance between East and West, especially by curtailing non-white/ non-Western immigrants and by policing and protecting the boundary between white and non-white, Western and non-Western, civilizations.

---

[248] Or seven civilizations if the 'marginal case' of Africa is omitted (1996: 45–7). Interestingly, this compares closely with Stoddard's specification of five main 'civilizations', though these are defined in racial terms. Moreover, while Huntington describes the boundaries of civilizations in cultural terms and as blood-stained, Stoddard talks about the racial frontiers between the white and non-white worlds as marked by flesh and blood (Stoddard 1920: 236).

12

Imperialist Eurocentrism: post-1989 'Western-liberalism' and the return to post-1830 liberal paternalist Eurocentrism

Introduction: 'things can only get better'

Because much of the introduction to this chapter was established in the introduction to Chapter 11, here I shall merely highlight three key points. First and foremost, this chapter focuses on the Eurocentric origins of what I call *Western-liberalism*. This is a conglomeration of theories that can loosely be captured by the umbrella term of 'cosmopolitanism', comprising liberal internationalism, liberal-cosmopolitanism, mainstream 'liberal-constructivism', and solidarist English School theory. I shall also consider some versions of 'realist-liberalism' (having considered the 'realist-liberal' theories of US neo-imperialism in the last chapter). The prime task here is to reveal the paternalist Eurocentrism of Western-liberalism, which provides a complementary but different metanarrative to the offensive Eurocentrism of Western-realism. And, in the process, I shall show how post-1989 Western-liberalism propels us back to the future of the post-1830 phase of *manifest* paternalist Eurocentric liberal international theory.

Second, this point in turn begs the question as to how contemporary Western-liberalism fails to recognize its pre-1945 Eurocentric roots. Here I argue that this is made possible by the performance of a Eurocentric 'temporal othering' sleight of hand. In particular, Western-liberals assume that new progressive and egalitarian values associated with democracy, human rights and multiculturalism have come to the fore after 1989 in ways that have not been witnessed before. Implicitly, and sometimes explicitly, Western-liberals contrast this new progressive humanitarian era with the imperialist and racist values of the nineteenth century. In particular, a kind of 'temporal binary' is constructed whereby the nineteenth century is reimagined as more racially intolerant and imperialist than it was so that the post-1989 era can be portrayed as more culturally tolerant and anti-imperialist than it is (cf. Young 1995). Temporally othering the nineteenth century in this way enables the construction of a pure progressive post-1989 'self' that is strictly demarcated or severed off from its nineteenth-century 'Other' through the construction of a line of temporal apartheid, thereby serving to elide the Eurocentric continuities between contemporary liberalism and its nineteenth-century forefather. Indeed, the irony here is that much of international theory in general and liberalism in particular has become possibly more imperialist since 1989 than it was in the nineteenth century.

Third, while Western-realism is marked by a pronounced degree of anxiety and pessimism and invokes a 'sense of Western siege', Western liberalism is underpinned by a strong degree of optimism and a not infrequent Western triumphalism that is either implicit or explicit, and views the post-1989 era as presenting a paternalist opportunity for universalizing Western civilization so as to 'help and rescue' Eastern societies. Accordingly, while Western-realism sings the world into existence with the theme tune 'things can only get bitter', Western-liberalism chants that 'things can only get better'. Thus despite many shared overlaps, the key difference is that Western-liberals assume that universalizing Western civilization and spreading Western norms is a progressive universal good that will benefit *all* peoples, while Western-realists assume that defending Western civilization against the 'Eastern barbaric threat' is vital so as to maintain civilization and world order. The overlaps between contemporary Western-liberalism and its 1830–1945 predecessors is summarized in Table 12.1.

The narrative of this chapter is related in four sections and will follow the left- and middle columns of Figure 11.1 (see p. 260). Part one fleshes

Table 12.1. *Back to the future of post-1830 paternalist-Eurocentrism*

Post-1830 liberalism	Post-1989 Western-liberalism	Post-1989 Western realist-liberalism
E.g., Cobden, Bright, J. S. Mill, Hobson, Angell, Zimmern, Murray	E.g., Friedman, Wolf, Téson, Rawls, Held, Donnelly, Risse, Finnemore, Nussbaum	E.g., Fukuyama, Cooper, Rieff, Rothkopf, Ikenberry, Slaughter

out the basic paternalist-Eurocentric categories of Western-liberalism, while part two considers two of the seminal liberal-cosmopolitan theories of global politics that are advocated by John Rawls and David Held. Part three hones in on the various liberal, English School and constructivist theories of humanitarian intervention that are embedded within liberal cosmopolitanism. And finally, part four considers a range of theories that are based around the democratic imperative including the 'duty to prevent', the Concert of Democracies, democratic peace theory, and the return to the old imperial idea of international trusteeship.

The base categories of paternalist-Eurocentrism in Western-liberalism

Reconstructing a tripartite Eurocentric global hierarchy

Moving up one level from the bottom of Figure 11.1, like its nineteenth century predecessor contemporary Western-liberalism constructs a three-worlds hierarchical metageography. The first world comprises civilized liberal states, which is contrasted with the second world of autocratic states (Oriental despotism in nineteenth-century parlance) and the third world of collapsed/failed states (savage anarchical societies in nineteenth-century parlance). Once again, as was explained in the last chapter, here we encounter a 'standard of statehood' that reinvokes the old nineteenth century standard of civilization, though one that focuses more on the nature of the state than with the wider set of cultural norms.

However, before proceeding any further, it is necessary to deal with the argument advocated by John Rawls in his key liberal text *The Law of Peoples* (1999), given that he seeks to partially disrupt this three-worlds hierarchical construction. This is particularly significant because Rawls believes that his liberal vision has 'genuinely' universalist criteria that do not offend the cultural sensibilities of non-Western peoples, which forms his main defence against the Eurocentric charge (see esp. Rawls 1999: 60–1, 65, 68, 93, 110–11, 123–4). In his construction we encounter the West as the representative of first world civilization, which is then followed by second world Eastern autocracies ('outlaw states') and third world savage anarchical societies ('burdened societies'). However, the key move he makes is his insertion of an interstitial category that lies between the first and second world constructs. Here he discusses 'decent hierarchical societies', which are Eastern but reside alongside Western liberal societies as 'well-ordered peoples'. The ideal-type example he provides is that of 'Kazanistan', which is an Islamic society that tolerates non-Islamic elements and enters into reciprocal relations with the rational/civilized West (1999: 75–8). In this way he seeks to break with the conflation of civilization and Western societies, allowing for the possibility of non-Western societies within this category. And, as we shall see shortly, he does not so much talk about a unified West but the peoples of *well-ordered societies* (comprising Western liberal societies and non-Western decent hierarchical societies), which need to civilize the non-Western peoples.

This raises the question as to whether Rawls has succeeded in breaking with the Eurocentric three-worlds hierarchy that privileges the West as the sole occupant of civilization. The critical point here is that 'well-ordered' Eastern societies might be more accurately termed 'near-civilized' societies. For it is clear that the highest civilized norm of reference is the liberal West and that overall, decent non-Western hierarchical societies, through moral learning via emulating and cooperating with the West, will and should teleologically evolve into the idealized Western form of liberal society. In other words, the West remains the locus of civilization while well-ordered Eastern societies drop short of this category, the effect of which is to render this already residual interstitial Eastern category into a highly marginal one.

Nevertheless, it is important to concede that while the Second World is represented by the likes of authoritarian Middle Eastern polities and Chinese autocracy, it is also true that there is an intra-Western dimension here, represented by quasi-authoritarian Russia. Accordingly, not all aspects of Western-liberalism can be captured perfectly within the framework that I deploy here.

Reconstructing Western 'hyper-sovereignty'/Eastern 'conditional-sovereignty', and the issue of Eurocentric double standards

As with Western-realism so I note that having separated out East from West and having endowed the latter with superior rational politico-institutional properties, Western-liberalism returns us to the nineteenth century *bipolar* formal hierarchical conception of world politics. It is, of course, conventionally held that classical liberalism stood for non-interventionism/self-determination and peace. But as we saw in Chapter 2, it turns out that for the paternalist Eurocentric liberals such a conception applied only to intra-Western relations. The most well-known expression of this is found in J. S. Mill's statement:

> To suppose that the same international customs, and the same rules of international morality, can obtain between one civilized nation and another, and between civilized nations and barbarians, is a grave error ... In the first place, the rules of ordinary international morality imply reciprocity. But barbarians will not reciprocate. They cannot be depended on for observing any rules ... In the next place, nations which are still barbarous have not got beyond the period during which it is likely to be for their benefit that they should be conquered and held in subjection by foreigners (Mill 1859/1984: 118).

In essence, while 'civilized states' should treat each other with dignity thereby entailing non-intervention (hence they were 'deserving' of sovereignty), barbarian peoples were deemed uncivilized and thus insufficiently advanced to warrant the same degree of respect – hence Eastern polities were denied sovereignty. Moreover, because non-Western peoples were deemed to be immature, citizenship rights were also to be denied. Accordingly, Mill argued in *On Liberty* that 'despotism is a legitimate mode of government in dealing with barbarians, provided the end be their improvement, and the [colonialist] means justified by actually affecting that end' (Mill 1859/1998: 14–15).

Likewise, post-1989 contemporary Western-liberals, as we saw with the Western-realists in the last chapter, insist that Eastern polities should not be granted sovereignty in a once-and-for-all move. Contemporary Western-liberalism is ostensibly motivated by a desire to right the wrongs that Eastern peoples face within their own societies. Rather than seeking to *contain* Eastern societies (as in Western-realism) Western-liberals are more interested in *culturally converting* them along Western lines so that the injustices of the world can be overcome; a point that is shared with Western liberal-realism. Nevertheless, like their Western-realist cousins, they argue that sovereignty in the Third World should have a 'conditional status'; that is, sovereignty should only be recognized when states treat their own populations fairly by respecting human rights contained within a democratic form of governance. And as we saw with respect to Western-realists, conditional sovereignty is a vital pre-requisite or normative trigger for Western neo-imperial intervention, as it was for nineteenth century paternalist-liberalism, in the absence of which the 'abuse of millions of non-Western peoples continues unabated'. Thus they share in the neo-imperial discourse of Western state *hyper-sovereignty*, which legitimizes intervention in 'morally offensive' Eastern states on the basis of their 'conditional sovereignty'. The key difference, though, is that contemporary Western-liberals are living in a time when sovereignty has already been formally granted to the Eastern states following decolonization. Thus the nineteenth century liberals argued that Eastern polities should be denied sovereignty altogether, while contemporary liberals argue that extant Eastern sovereignty should be withdrawn if Eastern polities fail to act in a civilized manner.

Reconstructing globalization-as-Western opportunity

Moving up another level in Figure 11.1, I noted in the last chapter that Western-realists construct *globalization-as-Eastern threat*. While Western-liberals, like the Western-realists, pinpoint various threats ushered in by the dark side of globalization – e.g., ecological crisis, nuclear weapons proliferation, terrorism, the democratic deficit, and the flood of refugees/emigrants from savage polities (i.e., failed states) – their central thrust revolves around the construct of *globalization-as-Western opportunity*. That is, globalization enables the West to diffuse and universalize its civilizational norms (economic, political, cultural and ethical) around the world in order to *culturally convert* all states along Western lines. As we saw in Chapter 2, this construction is precisely the same one that was deployed by paternalist liberal Eurocentrics in the nineteenth century through to 1945.

This parallel is found clearly in the nineteenth century and post-1989 liberal internationalist conceptions of global capitalism. Today the principal International Financial Institutions such as the World Bank and the World Trade Organization are in part founded on the mission to civilize or culturally assimilate Eastern societies along Western neoliberal lines. Many contemporary liberal internationalist Western-liberals also perceive the task of capital mobility as performing a similar mission. In Thomas Friedman's well-known aphorism, globalization forces non-Western polities to don a (Western neoliberal) 'golden straitjacket' (Friedman 1999; see also Wolf 2005). The parallel with the nineteenth century is found in the point that contemporary Western-liberals adopt the arguments of Cobden and Mill, wherein global free trade acts as a 'civilizing force', leading to the adoption of national 'self-help', 'specialization' and 'comparative advantage' on the one hand while incentivizing Eastern peoples to intensively develop or raise their economies towards the peak of liberal capitalism through individualistic self-help and 'hard work' on the other. Moreover, the spread of liberal capitalism and universal Western liberal institutions by the West promotes 'civilizational' norms of development, cooperation and ultimately peace (Friedman 1999: 195–217), to a detailed discussion of which I now turn.

Paternalist liberal neo-imperialism: civilizing the barbarians/savages

Moving up to the final level of Figure 11.1, we encounter a series of Western-liberal theories that advocate the need to 'civilize the barbarian and savage societies' (though, of course, these terms are not explicitly deployed). The impetus to this thrust was in part provided by Francis Fukuyama's (1989, 1992) 'end of history' thesis, which first appeared on the eve of 9/11 and constituted the mid-wife in the birth of post-Cold War Western-liberalism, triumphantly declaring Western capitalist-democracy as the final stage of human history.[249] As he put it on the opening page of his famous article:

> The triumph of the West, of the Western idea, is evident first of all in the total exhaustion of viable systematic alternatives to Western liberalism ... What we are witnessing is not just the end of the Cold War, or the passing of a particular period of postwar history, but the end of history as such: that is, the end point of mankind's ideological evolution and the universalization of Western liberal democracy as the final form of human government (Fukuyama 1989).

The subsequent fall of the Berlin Wall unleashed a wave of euphoria that washed across Western societies, providing a spur for the take-up of Fukuyama's triumphalist sensibility. Still, while it is certainly the case that Fukuyama expressed considerable worries about the final stage of history in the last paragraph of the article (1989: 18) as well as in the final part of his book (1992: 287–339), nevertheless he, not unlike Mill who had expressed certain reservations about the final stage of history (1836/1977), was unequivocal that it was the best one and that 'boredom' at the end of history is a small price to pay for living in an earthly paradise.

---

[249] That this rehabilitation of Hegel entails a Eurocentric move is hardly surprising given his well-known claim in *The Philosophy of History* that '[t]he History of the World travels from East to West, for Europe [i.e., the West] is absolutely the end of history, Asia the beginning' (Hegel 1837/2001: 122). And for Hegel's Eurocentrism see Whelan (2009: ch. 5).

To return to the discussion of Huntington at the end of the last chapter, while it is clear that he invokes a defensive Eurocentrism that contrasts with Fukuyama's paternalist Eurocentrism, nevertheless they both share in the fundamental normative prescription of the need to 'defend Western civilization', thereby problematizing in this key respect the great divide that is usually thought to exist between them. Moreover, the majority of Western liberals implicitly make the argument that liberal-democratic capitalism represents the end of history. Thus they focus on the necessary 'perfectionist' changes that need to be brought about to international society in order to realize this particular liberal conception of the end of history; all of which are to be performed through paternalist neo-imperial interventionism. Overall, then, 1989 represents the greatest opportunity for the West to make the world a better place for all. For as Larry Diamond characterized this sentiment: 'Not since the end of World War I have the Western democracies had such an opportunity to shape the political nature of our world. By promoting democracy abroad, the United States can help bring into being for the first time in history a world composed mainly of stable democracies' (Diamond 1992: 29).

Paternalist liberal-cosmopolitanism and the universalization of Western civilization

John Rawls and the liberal 'law of peoples'

Viewed through a non-Eurocentric lens, I begin with two hard test-cases, the first of which returns us to Rawls' theory found in his *Law of Peoples*. As was noted earlier, Rawls, in effect, seeks to defend his theory against the Eurocentric charge. In particular, he argues for a cultural pluralism such that civilized liberal societies must tolerate the existence of non-Western cultures, by which he basically means 'non-Christian' (see esp. Rawls 1999: 122–5). And, as was noted earlier, he includes 'decent' non-Western societies within the category of 'well-ordered peoples' alongside Western liberal societies. Here I discern five key Eurocentric dimensions to his theory.

First, as noted above, 'decent hierarchical' Eastern peoples are required to move up the civilizational-hierarchy by emulating and assimilating Western political values through moral/civilizational learning. But while there is no compunction for such decent peoples to give up their religion, nevertheless the pertinence of the Islamic state of

Kazanistan is rendered problematic by his claim that all well-ordered hierarchical societies must exhibit a separation of church and state (1999: 124). This either contradicts his 'tolerance' of Islamic decent societies at most, or at the least simply narrows or marginalizes this already 'residual' category even further.

Second, one of the chief means by which cooperation with the West civilizes non-Western and well-ordered Eastern states concerns the *imposition* of free- and hence fair-trade. This is vital, Rawls argues, not just for its civilizing principle but also because it prevents the wealthy Western states from exploiting developing societies (1999: 42–3). But as I noted in the discussion of Keohane in Chapter 9, this claim elides the point that free trade can be the policy of choice for the wealthy Western states which, having industrialized through protectionism then withhold such a benefit to the Eastern developers. And as was also noted, there are clear parallels between contemporary trade policy and the unequal treaties of the nineteenth century. While Rawls' liberalism would lead him to discard this economic containment argument, nevertheless the fact that Eastern societies often perceive such 'cooperative' free trade in precisely these terms means that this 'socializing principle' would serve only to undermine rather than promote cooperation with the West. Either way, though, the conclusion is that Rawls' conflation of free trade with 'fair trade' is problematic (though given that his liberal posture would reject my reasoning here I shall not interrogate this point any further).

Third, and above all, Rawls elicits a paternalist Eurocentrism insofar as well-ordered peoples (which refer mainly to those in the West given the already highly residual nature of decent hierarchical Eastern peoples) must work to bring those Eastern peoples in the second and third worlds into the zone of liberal civilization that is governed by the liberal law of peoples (1999: 91). Outlaw states (second world Oriental despotisms) that abuse human rights must be condemned and subjected to forcible sanction in the first instance and coercive humanitarian intervention in the last (1999: 79–81, 93). Once invaded it is incumbent upon the civilizer to reconstruct the state along Western liberal lines so as to effect a full cultural conversion; a standard principle of the humanitarian interventionist literature (see esp. Keohane 2003). Third world failed (or savage) societies, which he calls 'burdened societies', must be civilized through the 'duty to assist'. This entails a paternalist role of teaching savage societies civilized values as well as providing aid and assistance to build a more robust set of political institutions

(1999: 110–11). Education is also an important means to teach Eastern women to have less babies, thereby solving the problem of demographic/Malthusian crisis. All in all, Rawls advocates paternalist neo-imperial intervention, principally by the West, in second/third world Eastern societies in order to bring them into the liberal fold of Western civilization.

Fourth, the Eurocentric giveaway in Rawls' theory lies in the double standard that underpins the treatment of outlaw states. Here he concedes that Western states can be outlaws, though the examples he provides are mainly confined to the sixteenth and seventeenth centuries, with Nazi Germany being the only modern example (1999: 105–6). Nevertheless he does point out that should Western states today engage in imperial wars, or wars to enhance their territory/wealth/power, so they would qualify as outlaws (1999: 91). But there are several problems here. While many of the wars that the United States has engaged in within the last fifty years or more have been precisely about enhancing American power/wealth/influence, Rawls singles out only one instance of 'outlaw behaviour' by the US.[250] Moreover, the recent Iraq War was sold in the USA and Britain as a means of pre-emptive defence against an outlaw state, presumably satisfying Rawls' criterion of the right of self-defence (1999: 91–2). But clearly one of the rationales for this war was the need to maintain and enhance the West's access to cheap oil supplies, upon which Rawls is once again silent; notwithstanding the point that arguably President Bush, and almost certainly Prime Minister Blair, went to war on a false prospectus. Crucially, materialist power interests are rarely separable from higher level ideational principles; a point that is elided by Rawls' overly abstract philosophical discussion.

The key double standard emerges in the point that while Western liberal states can be outlaws, nevertheless he insists, it is not permissible for other liberal states to punish them. Principle 4 of his 'laws of free and democratic peoples' asserts that liberal states *must refrain* from going to war against, or intervening in, each other (1999: 37–8, 94). Moreover, Rawls insists that well-ordered peoples must 'observe a duty of non-intervention' in each others' affairs (1999: 25); a prohibition that is summarized by one commentator as 'so stern that it excludes even the use of foreign aid by the governments of liberal peoples to create incentives for decent peoples to become more liberal' (Miller 2003: 217;

---

[250] This refers to the firebombings of various Japanese cities and the nuclear strikes on Hiroshima and Nagasaki during WWII (Rawls 1999: 95, 100, 102).

see also Rawls 1999: 62, 85). Crucially, this contrasts strikingly with Rawls' insistence that Western liberal states *must* punish Eastern outlaw states.

Such a double standard returns us to the Eurocentric notion of the bipolar formal hierarchical conception of world politics, whereby civilized Western states treat each other with dignity and therefore respect each other's sovereignty, while Eastern despotic states and failed states (or burdened societies) are deemed uncivilized and are therefore granted only conditional sovereignty. And when coupled with his paternalist Eurocentric desire to see the whole world become liberalized along Western lines, so the West is granted hyper-sovereignty in order to realize this dream. Moreover, it is often the case that those states, most especially the United States, which insist on the conditional sovereignty of others are often the ones that are most resistant in accepting any limits whatsoever to their own sovereignty. Rawls' approach serves to enshrine this double standard on the part of liberal states.

Fifth and finally, though, it is noteworthy that Rawls might defend his theory by claiming that he rejects paternalism (see e.g., 1999: 111–12), arguing that once burdened societies have been helped by the intervention of 'well-ordered societies' to stand on their own feet, so the interveners should withdraw and leave them to be independent. But this rationale is precisely the same as that advanced by nineteenth century liberal imperialists, as well as that which underpinned the trusteeship-based League of Nations Mandate System. Accordingly, Rawls' paternalism is evident in his key claim that 'the long-term goal of (relatively) well-ordered societies should be to bring burdened societies, like outlaw states, into the Society of well-ordered Peoples. Well-ordered peoples have a [paternalist] *duty* to assist burdened societies' (1999: 106).

David Held and cosmopolitan democracy

A second hard-test case is found in the theory of cosmopolitan democracy that was first comprehensively laid out by David Held in his pioneering book *Democracy and the Global Order* (see also Archibugi *et al.* 1998). This is a highly sophisticated version of cosmopolitan liberalism, filled with many nuances, the sum of which positions Held outside the standard triumphalist Western discourse that finds its ultimate expression in Fukuyama's thesis (see esp. Held 1995: 3–4). In particular he focuses on the dark side of globalization, which poses major challenges to the modern liberal-democratic state including those of ecological crisis as well as the global inequality and democratic deficit that is created by global capitalism. Moreover, with respect to the key issue that concerns my discussion here, in an impressive debate Held defends himself against various, though not all, aspects of the Eurocentric charge that Heikki Patomäki levels (Held and Patomäki 2006); a charge that he first developed in an earlier article (Patomäki 2003: 352–6).

My deconstruction of Held's theory is undertaken in two inter-related stages. First I begin by critically discussing Held's response to Patomäki's charge of 'ahistorical-Eurocentrism' and that his approach stands 'outside of history'. Held replies by claiming that his principle of individual autonomy was very much derived from historical processes. However, my central point is that while Held's theory of cosmopolitan governance is indeed derived from history it is, nevertheless, recounted within a traditional Eurocentric narrative. This is worth pursuing not least because on this particular Eurocentric charge that Patomäki levelled (Held and Patomäki 2006: 120), Held remained surprisingly silent. And second, having discussed the Eurocentric features of Held's historical analysis I then proceed to consider briefly how his theory of cosmopolitan democracy is underpinned by Eurocentrism.

The historical story that Held recounts is laid out in the first five chapters, which in aggregate reproduce perfectly the Eurocentric bigbang theory of globalization and world politics (BBT). As I have explained in previous chapters, the BBT rests on a two-step Eurocentric narrative. In the first step the West makes itself through its own *exceptional* properties/virtues, such that the rise of the West can be narrated in terms of the endogenous Eurocentric *logic of immanence*, before first Europe through imperialism and later the United States through globalization expands outwards to remake the world according to its own civilizational standard. Thus in chapter 2 Held tells us that 'the story of the formation of the modern state is in part the story of the formation of modern Europe, and vice versa . . . European expansion and development have had a decisive role in shaping the political map of the modern world' (1995: 31). Or, to paraphrase Charles Tilly's (1990) famous dictum that 'war made the state and the state made war', so in Held's formulation we implicitly encounter the mantra that 'the West made the state and the Western state made the Rest'. Thus Held's theory of the rise of the modern state recounts the usual list of European waystations through which the European developmental train, or Oriental Express, steamed past on its exceptional and immanent journey to the terminus of modernity. The European train began its familiar journey in Ancient Greece, steamed through the Roman Empire on its way to European feudalism and medieval Christendom, before it passed through the Reformation into absolutism whereupon the outlines of the modern state were forged while the inter-state system was born at the Westphalian way-station. Finally, once the sovereign state had been created single-handedly by the Europeans so further endogenous initiatives unfolded culminating in the establishment of the liberal-democratic state by the twentieth century. He produces much the same narrative in chapter 3 concerning the rise of capitalism, which begins with the European medieval agricultural revolution before it was given decisive impetus by the union of rulers and capitalists in the absolutist phase, particularly as the former required new sources of revenue to fund their wars under the exceptional situation of intra-European anarchy.

Turning to the second step of the BBT, in chapter 3 Held's Eurocentrism is made all but explicit when he claims that 'the growth of interconnections between states and societies – that is of [early/thin] globalization – became progressively shaped by the expansion of Europe. Globalization initially meant "European globalization"' (1995: 60); though equally the 'main' phase after 1945 is recounted in terms of 'American globalization'. His account here conforms to the familiar logic of Western immanence found in the Eurocentric Western relay race metaphor, whereupon the baton of global power was passed from the Spanish and Portuguese after 1492 to the Dutch in the seventeenth century, then to the British and French in the eighteenth and nineteenth centuries, before culminating in the final leg that was run in record time by the Pax American anchor man who delivered globalization in its thick form (see especially Held et al. 1999). Furthermore, he argues that the 'emergence of [European] capitalism ushered in a quite fundamental change in the world order: it made possible, for the first time, genuinely global interconnections among states and societies; it penetrated the distant corners of the world and brought far-reaching changes to the dynamics and nature of political rule' (1995: 62).

Of course, to all this Held might offer up the kind of response that we noted vis-à-vis Hedley Bull's defence (see p. 224): that if this narrative is Eurocentric it is because it merely reflects the actual or real historical record which records the 'fact' that the West was first and the Rest was last. Nevertheless, I shall refrain from recounting the many examples of my alternative non-Eurocentric narrative that I mentioned earlier (pp. 224–6) and elsewhere (Hobson 2004), which suggest that the rise of the West was significantly Eastern Other-made rather than purely European Self-made. Thus in place of Held's implicit Eurocentric idioms – 'first the West, then the Rest' and 'the West made globalization, and globalization made the Rest' – I offer the non-Eurocentric formulations that 'without the Rest there might be no West', and that 'without Restern globalization there might be no Western globalization'.

Having established the Eurocentric aspects of Held's historical analysis, I now turn to the second issue concerning the question as to whether Held's theory of cosmopolitan democracy itself contains elements of Eurocentrism; a charge that Held vehemently denies.[251] Much of his defence boils down to the propositions that he supports the interests of global humanity rather than one part of it (namely the Western peoples), and that liberty and the equal worth of each human being are genuinely universal beliefs that would be supported as much by Eastern as by Western peoples. As he put it when answering a question on this issue at a recent talk that he gave at the University of Sheffield: 'Just because my values are Western does not make them wrong; indeed if Amartya Sen was here today he would agree with my political values'. This might be true, though whether Sen speaks for the entire 5 billion Afro-Asian people is, of course, another matter. Either way, though, the question of concern here is: are Held's values genuinely universal or does his normative framework universalize a particular Western conception of liberty and equality? As I have highlighted throughout this book, and especially in my discussion of US hegemony in the last chapter, it is precisely the conflation of Western conceptions of the 'political good' with the universal that constitutes the essence of much of Eurocentric international theory. Or to rephrase the question: is Held's conception of the political good really just pointing to a provincial Western discourse masquerading as the universal?

The answer to this question must, by definition, be made in the affirmative, precisely because Held's notion of the political good is derived purely from the Western historical experience. Poignantly, Held admits as much when he asserts in chapter 7, drawing from Rawls, that his principle of individual autonomy (albeit within a collective setting) is embedded within the public political culture of a democratic society, where *embedded* 'connotes ... that the principle has developed as part of, and has been constructed upon, the conceptual and institutional resources of Western democratic culture' (Held

---

[251] See Held in Held and Patomäki (2006: 117–19, 122, 129).

1995: 148). And in any case, that Held's normative political armoury is founded on a particular Western conception should come as little surprise given that the whole purpose of his (Eurocentric) historical discussion was to extract just such a Western conception of the political good in the first place. It is in this sense that I describe his theory of cosmopolitan democracy, founded as it is on a particularistic reading of the Western experience, as Eurocentric.

Going by the tone of his response to the Eurocentric charge levelled by Patomäki, one might well anticipate a vehement rejection of my argument. But in one important sense, the problem that emerges here is that Held seems to conflate the Eurocentric charge with the assumption that he is defending the West or the Western interest *against* the East, thereby rendering his politics as based on an exploitative imperialism. And given his strong Kantian credentials, such an imperialist charge would appear perplexing if not bewildering, given that Kant was vehemently anti-imperialist (as I explained in Chapter 3). My point, though, is *not* that Held supports the exploitation or coercive domination of the East by the West, for he certainly does not, but rather that his theory of cosmopolitan democracy is derived from a Eurocentric reading of the Western historical experience. All in all, then, that Held believes passionately that his theory of the good is inherently universal and will genuinely benefit *all* peoples is *not* at stake. Rather, I want to point out that his theory exhibits that most seductive property which Eurocentrism offers its believers: that Western provincialism does not simply '*masquerade* as the universal' because it *truly is* the universal. I do not doubt the sincerity or firmness of this Eurocentric self-belief, whether it is expressed by neo-Conservatives, Western-realists or Western-liberals. I merely point out that, for better or worse, their theories are based on the conflation of Western values with the universal and that we will have to take it on face value that all non-Western peoples would inherently agree with the particular set of Western values being offered by whichever theorist we examine here.

The paternalist-Eurocentrism of liberal humanitarian theory

The 'benign' politics of liberal-imperialism: from neoliberal humanitarianism to liberal constructivism via English School solidarism

It is noteworthy that humanitarian interventionism is a hallmark of Western-liberalism in the post-Cold War era, constituting a staple of a range of IR theories, all of which subscribe to liberal-cosmopolitanism in some shape or form. One of the more striking aspects of liberal-cosmopolitanism found in some, though not all, of its proponents lies in its 'born-again' nature, where its advocates unearth an old philosophy, and rather like a miner who has just found a very large golden nugget, euphorically hold it up above their heads and proclaim in triumphant fashion that herein this nugget lies the solution to the world's manifold problems. One such proselytizer is Fernando Téson. Indeed Téson directly confronts the postcolonial relativists by asserting that '[t]he liberal can concede that the views he defends are Western, and still maintain that they are better values' (2003: 101). Moreover, taking on the anti-interventionist statist critique of cosmopolitanism – of which Hedley Bull's pluralism would be a clear example – Téson insists that an international society/system that tolerates the existence of abusive non-liberal states in preference for maintaining world order is simply a system that is not worth defending (2003: 111–13); though this a fundamental trope of humanitarian interventionist theory more generally.

Nevertheless, when viewed through a non-Eurocentric lens a contradiction appears at the heart of Téson's analysis. He begins by advancing a clear paternalist Eurocentric argument asserting that states are only legitimate to the extent that they respect human rights, which in turn is premised on the principle of individual autonomy (2003: 96–7). And given his claim that such a principle does not exist outside of the West so his arguments for humanitarian intervention amount to no more than extending the zone of Western civilization across the world. As he put it: 'Humanitarian intervention is one tool to help move the quantum of political freedom in the continuum of political coercion to the Kantian center of that continuum away ... from the extreme lack of order (anarchy), and ... from governmental suppression of individual freedom (tyranny)' (2003: 97). Or, as the liberal-cosmopolitan feminist scholar, Martha Nussbaum, puts it when speaking of the need to emancipate Eastern women from their oppressive patriarchical societies: 'we would rather risk charges of imperialism ... than to stand around ... waiting for a time when everyone will like what we are going to say' (Nussbaum 1995: 2). In essence then, in this vision all non-Western societies that do not respect and defend the norm of individual autonomy are in effect 'ripe' for Western liberal neo-imperial intervention and cultural conversion.

However, the contradiction emerges later, with Téson in effect retreating from the hard-edged Eurocentric imperialist precipice when he invokes a much higher interventionist threshold, suggesting that humanitarian intervention is legitimate only in 'beyond the pale cases'. These comprise the gross abuse of human rights in cases confined to the likes of genocide, ethnic cleansing, and widespread torture. Thus it would seem that the two thresholds that justify humanitarian intervention co-exist in an indeterminate way at best, and a contradictory way at worst. But Téson's apparent retreat from the Eurocentric precipice unravels through his bottom-line normative position: that because he believes that the only legitimate states are those which respect individual autonomy and that for him these are by definition Western democracies, so he necessarily ends up by supporting a hard-line paternalist Eurocentric position, wherein Western liberal states must convert Eastern societies through humanitarian intervention in order to create a Western liberal 'empire of uniformity' or a global (benign) empire of Western civilization.

Humanitarian-interventionist theory also finds its expression in liberal-constructivism, neoliberalism and English School solidarism. Underpinning these theories is the inherent paternalist-Eurocentrism of its ideational organizing principle – the 'responsibility to protect' (R2P). This idea was first articulated at the official level with the 2001 UN report, even though it had been around during the 1990s. This framework is organized around the notion that Western states have a *duty to intervene* in Eastern failed states (savage societies) and autocratic polities (Oriental despotisms), where the failure to protect strangers' human rights, especially in cases of egregious abuse, is deemed to be intolerable. In certain key respects R2P is reminiscent of the nineteenth century 'white man's burden', requiring not just Western paternalist intervention to rescue Eastern victims, but a subsequent reconstruction of the state along Western lines. In this way R2P reconvenes the conception of Western hyper-sovereignty and conditional Eastern sovereignty. As Robert Keohane argues in relation to 'troubled societies' (which are reminiscent of what Rawls calls *burdened societies*): 'troubled societies may have more or less of it, but the classic idealtype of Westphalian sovereignty should be abandoned even as an aspiration'. Moreover, Keohane insists that even once these troubled societies have been refurbished with a Western form of state, they should still be denied full sovereignty in favour of 'gradations of sovereignty' (Keohane 2003: 276–7), thereby returning us to the nineteenth century imperialist hierarchical conception of a 'procession of sovereignty'.

One clear example of liberal-cosmopolitanism is found in the solidarist wing of the English School, which emerged forcefully after the Cold War. While the pluralist wing supposedly stands for non-interventionism and privileges 'order over justice', solidarism inverts this by privileging humanitarian interventionism over order (e.g., Wheeler 2000). And moreover, solidarism overlaps with much of Western-realism in its belief that repression within savage societies spills out into the international realm in the shape of warfare, terrorism and the exodus of refugees and chaos more generally. Interestingly, Bull and Jackson's so-called 'conservative' defence of order over justice means that paternalist interventionism is rejected in favour of an anti-imperialist politics.[252] Thus while solidarism's preference for 'saving strangers' may appear to move beyond the *conservative* pluralist ethics of state sovereignty – or what the solidarists view as, in effect, the 'politics of malign neglect' – nevertheless they respond by advocating a paternalist-Eurocentric civilizing mission. Moreover, fulfilling its Eurocentric cosmopolitan-liberal brief, solidarism holds that international society only properly exists when all societies are governed by the shared thick norms of Western societies.

This analysis of Eurocentric-paternalism can be advanced by considering the liberal-constructivist approach to humanitarian interventionism. Here it is possible to detect two main Eurocentric dimensions – one explicit and the other implicit. The explicit Eurocentric formulation takes the form of a triumphalist return to the nineteenth century civilizing mission. As Belloni aptly conveys this, the constructivist 'pro-interventionist attitude ... is often focused on the diffusion of human rights norms from the international [the West] to the domestic level [within the East], and brimming with notions of their [Western] success in the betterment of the human condition' (Belloni 2007: 453). Because I have in effect discussed this above, I shall move on to the second Eurocentric aspect which emerges at an implicit level. Key here is the assumption that while 'progressive' humanitarian intervention was subverted by a racist-imperialist discourse in the nineteenth century, today it takes a sincere and empathic form that is free of racist and imperialist

---

[252] Notable here is that in his excellent book, *The Global Covenant*, Jackson argues that postcolonial international society is constituted by a 'global covenant' that tolerates cultural diversity. It is 'horizontal rather than hierarchical, inclusive rather than exclusive, and is based expressly on the pluralist ethics of equal state sovereignty, self-determination, and non-intervention' (Jackson 2000: 14).

bias. Such a claim provides an excellent example of the ahistorical temporal-othering construct that I described earlier. One prominent constructivist scholar characterizes the new civilizing process as one 'by which non-white, non-Christian populations became "humanized" for the West' (Finnemore 2003b: 157). But this serves unwittingly to 'naturalize' humanitarianism, thereby obscuring some of the underlying continuities between contemporary intervention and its nineteenth century paternalist-Eurocentric (and on occasion offensive racist) imperial predecessor.[253]

Moreover, Finnemore claims that this new 'non-Eurocentric' humanitarian discourse has trumped warfare whereas in the eighteenth century war was glorified and 'progressive' intervention shunned (2003b: 135). But this could hold only if we confine our remit to *intra-Western* state relations, given that warfare between Western and Eastern states has been a commonplace since 1947. And, of course, nineteenth-century Western liberal imperialism was often called the 'civilizing mission' precisely because in theory its prime mandate was to rescue Eastern victims of repressive autocratic and savage societies by civilizing their institutions in order to deliver individualist/human rights to strangers as well as to ex-pat whites. Significantly, as we saw in the last chapter, certain Western realist-liberals explicitly recover this recessive imperial dimension in contemporary humanitarian interventionism, proclaiming it as a fundamental component of a benign US neo-imperialism, to wit: 'what is exceptional about American [humanitarian] messianism is that it is the last imperial ideology left standing in the world, the sole survivor of imperial claims to universal significance' (Ignatieff 2005: 16).

But to close this discussion of constructivism, it is worth noting at a more general level that the dominant liberal variant reproduces paternalist Eurocentrism in various ways, even if some of the more critical variants offer a wealth of non-Eurocentric insight.[254] An excellent example of this is found in Finnemore's seminal and influential book, *National Interests in International Society*. There she concludes by asserting that there are three

---

[253] As I noted in Chapter 4, Paul Reinsch (1905a, 1905b) is one liberal racist who advocated a benign civilizing mission that complemented paternalist Eurocentric conceptions. Moreover, Woodrow Wilson and Raymond Buell, who also embraced racism, argued for the civilizing mission, albeit under the auspices of the League of Nations Mandate System (see Chapter 7, this volume).

[254] See especially Ling (2002); Price and Tannenwald (2003); Katzenstein (2009); Zarakol (2011).

dominant 'benign' norms in international society. These comprise the norms of liberal capitalism, bureaucratic states and human rights, all of which define the most appropriate behaviour that states *should* conform to if they want to be seen as civilized (Finnemore 1996a: ch. 6). Two Eurocentric moves are made here. First, her story in effect portrays the various UN agencies and other international non-state actors as paternalist-Eurocentric vehicles that socialize or 'civilize' states around the world to assimilate Western civilizational norms. In other words, this is a story of an informal Western civilizing mission, particularly given her belief that such norms are progressive, in contrast to the 'bad norms' of the 'racist nineteenth-century imperial mission'. Accordingly, she elides the point that both the 'good norms' of contemporary international society and the 'bad norms' of the nineteenth century have in their respective periods underpinned the Western civilizing mission.

Second, Finnemore's approach serves unwittingly to naturalize hierarchical relations between the East and West. For in her quest to quarantine power interests from norms she is unable to reveal how the latter are propagated often by and for the West. Indeed the norms that she focuses on, especially in her final chapter, are clearly Western-framed norms. The result of this is to lead the argument into the trap of *Eurofetishism*, which naturalizes and eternalizes the global hierarchy of West over East. Accordingly, it is a particular irony that Finnemore chastises the highly Eurocentric 'world-polity theory', associated with John Boli, John Meyer and others,[255] on the grounds that it marginalizes power in the process of norm-diffusion (see Finnemore 1996b: 339). All in all, David Fidler goes so far as to say that 'even the many reflectivist and constructivist challenges to the liberal hegemony in international law and relations . . . are merely searches for different forms of Western-led civilizational harmony' (Fidler 2000: 413).[256]

The upshot of this analysis is the point that much of liberal cosmopolitanism and humanitarian interventionist theory returns us to the nineteenth-century paternalist discourse of the civilizing mission. Contemporary liberal scholars elide this connection on the grounds that the West views the Eastern peoples as equals and that interventionism is motivated only by the purest and noblest of intentions; as when the Labour Party chairman, John Reid, announced that 'We not only have

---

[255] See, for example, Meyer *et al.* (1997); Boli and Thomas (1998).
[256] Though this is to obscure a range of constructivist theorists who do not subscribe to Eurocentrism. For some of these see the references in footnote 254, p. 303, this volume.

rights to defend in the world, but we also have responsibilities to discharge; we are in a sense our brother's keeper globally' (cited in Chandler 2004: 75). In such ways, the old realist maxim, that 'might equals right', is inverted into the formula that 'right equals might' (Chandler 2004: 76). But in the light of this chapter's argument the more accurate maxim would be that 'Western right equals might'. And, in any case, the whole discourse of being 'our brother's keeper' through benign intervention constitutes the essence of the liberal civilizing mission (as I explained in Chapter 1, pp. 23–30).

But I want to close this section by noting a particular irony. Since 1989 it has become a commonplace of mainstream Western-liberals to claim that the defence of sovereignty, which found strong institutional support in the UN Charter, is really tantamount to an Eastern 'tyrant's charter', enabling Eastern despots to carry on gross human rights abuse untouched by the 'international community'. Nevertheless, the deep irony here is that it was the United States that was in large part responsible for this problem as it insisted on protecting sovereignty precisely so that it could maintain its racist policies at home. For as John Foster Dulles complained at the time, it would create significant difficulties concerning the 'negro problem in the South'. To rectify this potential race problem, Article 2, paragraph 7 was inserted which stated that: 'Nothing contained within the present Charter shall authorize the United Nations to intervene in matters which are essentially within the domestic jurisdiction of any state or shall require the members to submit such matters to settlement' (cited in Lauren 1996: 167). And yet the further irony is that it was various Eastern representatives at the United Nations who fought hard for human rights legislation, usually in the face of Western resistance (Lauren 1996).

Paternalist-Eurocentrism and the 'democratic imperative'

From the duty to protect to the duty to prevent and the duty to democratize

The idea of humanitarian intervention and the 'duty/responsibility to protect' has been extended within the realist-liberal wing into a proactive military 'preventionist' discourse termed the 'duty to prevent'. Indeed, Slaughter and Feinstein (2004) developed this concept as a direct corollary of 'the duty to protect'. The duty to prevent refers to the problem of the proliferation of weapons of mass destruction (WMD). Slaughter and

Feinstein are particularly critical of the NPT regime on the grounds that it is concerned only with the presence of WMD rather than that state's particular regime-form. As they put it, '[t]he problem with the [NPT's] approach is that its opening proposition is to treat North Korea as if it were Norway. This flaw has exposed the non-proliferation regime to abuse by determined and defiant regimes, especially those headed by dictatorial rulers' (2004: 143–4). Accordingly, they conclude that the non-proliferation campaign 'must be based ... on the recognition that leaders without internal checks on their power, or who are sponsors of terror, and who seek to acquire WMD are a unique threat' (2004: 145). In this discourse, Eastern autocracies are broadly akin to the 'barbaric' Oriental Despotisms of the nineteenth century, which must be contained for the barbaric threat that they pose. Indeed, Western states have a duty to prevent such dictatorships threatening the world, most obviously by undertaking neo-imperial interventionist measures. Thus prior to the acquisition of WMD, Western states should apply a range of measures such as sanctions and, if necessary, military force. More generally, this argument overlaps clearly with the neo-Conservative pre-emptive defence argument that was enshrined within the 2002 Bush Doctrine. Of note too is that this theoretical position was pre-empted in a 1995 article, in which Slaughter asserts that 'Liberal theory permits more general distinctions among different categories of States based on domestic regime-type' (1995: 509).

Recently, this approach has been extended further within the Western-realist liberal camp through the idea of a 'Concert of Democracies' (CoD). Here the various realist-liberals converge with the liberal-realist conception of the League of Democracies called for by Robert Kagan (2008: 97–105), though various liberals also point to this idea (e.g., Held 1995: 232; cf. Rawls 1999: 93). In essence, the CoD thesis entails a proactive Western posture vis-à-vis non-Western autocratic polities (as well as Russia).[257] In the seminal statement of this realist-liberal position, John Ikenberry and Anne-Marie Slaughter (2006) argue that current international institutions (especially the key IFIs and the UN) are no longer fit for purpose. While they call for reform of the UN, Ikenberry and Slaughter also suggest the need for a CoD that

---

[257] Nevertheless, while there is clear unease over post-1991 Russian authoritarianism it would be fair to say that the 'Oriental despotisms' of North Korea and Iran are viewed with particular suspicion as, of course, was Iraq. Notably these three countries constitute Bush's 'axis of evil' and supersede the Evil Empire of the Soviet Union.

can ratify and institutionalize the democratic peace. If the UN cannot be sufficiently reformed, they suggest that the CoD trumps the UN and 'authorizes collective action [and the] use of force by super-majority vote' (Ikenberry and Slaughter 2006: 8). The new CoD approach incorporates interventionism in the non-Western world in order to extend the civilized democratic zone of peace.

The CoD approach also evolved out of democratic peace theory (DPT). Here the civilized world of democratic states forms a zone of peace, while the barbaric world of autocratic states forms a zone of war, reflecting an underlying discourse of the standard of civilization (based principally on the standard of statehood). DP theorists do not claim that liberal states are inherently pacific; merely that they do not go to war with each other. Thus they invoke Immanuel Kant's thesis that liberal states go to war with autocracies since the latter are inherently war-prone and cannot be trusted to act in a civilized or rational manner.[258] This much is repeated in standard secondary summaries within the IR literature. But two points that are not mentioned are particularly noteworthy. First, even the standard mantra is problematic insofar as the roots of DPT do *not* lie wholly in Kant's theory. For while it is clearly the case that for Kant republican-democratic states are less likely to go to war with each other, nevertheless even if all states in the world comprised republican regimes, the continuity of international anarchy means that war would still break out. For Kant, the solution to the problem of international anarchy is for states to renounce such anarchy by collectively establishing a set of international legal norms that could guarantee perpetual peace. And to the extent that many DP theorists invoke a proactive Western interventionist stance so they share far more in common with the paternalist Eurocentric thinker, John Stuart Mill, than they do the anti-paternalist Eurocentric scholar, Immanuel Kant (see especially Jahn 2006b).

Second, when viewed through a non-Eurocentric lens a series of crucial issues emerge which are generally not considered, even though they are components of DPT. In the first instance DPT constructs a dividing line between East and West or, to use nineteenth-century language, a frontier between civilization and barbarism/savagery. For many DP theorists autocratic states 'are viewed *prima-facie* as unreasonable, unpredictable and potentially dangerous. These are states either

---

[258] E.g., Doyle (1983a, 1983b); Russett (1990); Owen (1994); Rawls (1999: 44–54); cf. Mueller (1990).

ruled by despots, or with unenlightened citizenries' (Owen 1994: 96); a formulation that returns us directly to the nineteenth-century theory of Oriental despotism. In its extreme form, as David Blaney perceptively points out,

> nonliberal states are constructed as sites of legitimate intervention for liberal purposes and perhaps as objects of violent moral crusades – both paradigmatic forms of ... 'liberal favoritism' in Owen's [term], democratic 'xenophobia' in Russett's, and liberal bellicosity in mine (Blaney 2001: 35).

In this conception we return to the bipolar formal hierarchical conception of world politics, wherein Western states are rewarded with civilizational status and thus enjoy the privilege of *hyper*-sovereignty, while Eastern polities are demoted to the status of *conditional*-sovereignty (connoting the withdrawal of sovereignty such that they are constructed as 'ripe' for Western intervention).

In sum, while advocates of DPT differ in tone on this point, the logical extension of DPT is the assimilation of non-liberal states into the universe of the civilized West. One clear exception to this interventionist stance is provided by Michael Doyle,[259] who is most faithful to Kant's anti-imperialist legacy (see my discussion of Kant on pp. 62–74). This suggests that not all DPT rests on a paternalism, even if all of it reflects a Eurocentric metanarrative. Nevertheless, this qualification aside, the continuation of civilized Western democratic states and barbaric Eastern autocracies serves as a means to define and reproduce the Western self against the Eastern other.[260]

The return of international trusteeship

Last, but not least, these Eurocentric themes are echoed in the literature on protectorates/international trusteeship/shared sovereignty. And, as I mentioned in the last chapter, in this literature we encounter a convergence of Western liberal-realists and realist-liberals.[261] Significantly, the idea of international trusteeship was eclipsed in the revolt against Western empire in the aftermath of WWII. Kwame Nkrumah, for example, denounced trusteeship as 'nothing but deception, hypocrisy, oppression, and exploitation' (Nkrumah cited in Bain 2003: 65).

---

[259] Doyle (1983a, 1983b). [260] Blaney (2001: 40–1).
[261] Cf. Helman and Ratner (1992–3); Lyon (1993); Keohane (2003); Krasner (2004); Fearon and Laitin (2004); Herbst (2004); Fukuyama (2005); Søbjerg (2007).

Moreover, as William Bain points out, 'the right of self-determination transformed trusteeship into nothing less than a crime against humanity' (Bain 2003: 66). But as I have argued throughout this and the last chapter, since the end of the Cold War most of mainstream Western international theory has gone back to the future of the 1830–1945 era. And it is precisely this revivified paternalist Eurocentrism and offensive Eurocentrism that is responsible for the reinvoking of protectorates/trusteeship.

Modern conceptions of international trusteeship involve a virtual return to the League of Nations Mandate System where Western powers 'come to the aid' of failed states and 'help' them govern their own jurisdictions in order to prepare them for future self-governance. Such a form of direct interventionism, as in the B and C Mandates, is envisaged in terms of decades and 'quasi-permanence'. Moreover, such a conception returns us to the nineteenth century, particularly Lord Lugard's concept of 'indirect rule'. And directly echoing this nineteenth-century approach, Jeffrey Herbst (2004) asks rhetorically why contemporary failed states that behave irresponsibly and repressively towards their own populations should be recognized as sovereign by the international community (read 'the West'). Given the conditional nature of their sovereignty so Herbst advocates a 'decertification process' for collapsed states or chronically failed states, which strips them of their sovereignty and thereby opens them up to neo-imperial Western interventionism so as to culturally convert them along Western liberal lines. Or in Keohane's paternalist normative vision, such intervention 'creates a quasi-imperial situation in which outsiders rule [as a trusteeship] by virtue of force, legitimated by their supposed good intentions'; and that even once state reconstruction has been effected, he insists, there should be 'no opening for Westphalian sovereignty' (Keohane 2003: 296, 297).

Such Western realist-liberals and Western-realists share in the point that there is no viable alternative to trusteeship, on the grounds that in its absence the new barbaric threat would arrive unimpeded on the doorstep of the West. Richard Caplan expresses it thus:

> it is no longer possible to assume that states can necessarily insulate themselves from the effects of chronic state weakness or collapse even in remote parts of the world. As a consequence of globalization, 'zones of chaos' – to use Robert Cooper's term – today are fertile grounds for the establishment of drug, crime and terrorist syndicates from which no country can be immune (Caplan 2007: 238).

Ultimately, the lowest common denominator of contemporary and past international trusteeship is a paternalist mentality which denies the free-will and agency of Eastern peoples on the grounds that they are incapable of full self-determination, such that only the civilized West is capable of delivering the rational institutions that can enable the backward societies to eventually progress into civilization. All in all, though, 'no matter how enlightened or well-intentioned [international trusteeship is it] cannot escape by nature its imperial past because it belongs to a mode of conduct that is imperial' (Bain 2003: 75).

As I noted in the last chapter, perhaps the key conclusion here is that the standard of civilization/statehood has been revived in the post-Cold War era, such that states can only be treated with sovereign dignity if they conform to democracy and enable the progressive development of their citizenry. And it is here where we encounter perhaps the profoundest paradox or contradiction that lies at the core of Western-liberalism. For at its core is the axiom that the racist and Eurocentric imperial 'standard of civilization' that underpinned European international law from the nineteenth century down to 1945 came to an end after World War II, and was replaced by a so-called *anti-imperialist* and anti-racist humanitarian principle that protects *all* individuals equally across international society over and above the particular interests of 'repressive' states (e.g., Vincent 1984). This is indeed the corollary argument to the claim that racism is no longer tolerated in the international system and that, therefore, racial equality prevails. But it should be apparent by now that the informal paternalist-Eurocentric discourse of the standard of civilization has very much been resurrected, in part through the very conception of international law that was supposed to represent its nemesis: namely the law pertaining to humanitarianism.

Such a position is rarely conceded by Western-liberals, though Jack Donnelly provides a bold exception:

> European human rights initiatives have been missionary in the best sense of the term, seeking to spread the benefits of (universal) values enjoyed at home. Fear ... should not immobilize us in the face of abuses of power by dictators hiding behind the legal norm of sovereignty or a claim to radical cultural difference. Something like a standard of civilization is needed to save us from the barbarism of a pristine sovereignty that would consign countless millions of individuals and entire peoples to international neglect. At the present historical juncture, only the idea of internationally recognized human rights ... seems capable of playing such a role (Donnelly 1998: 15–16).

PART V

Conclusion
Mapping the promiscuous architecture of
Eurocentrism in international theory,
1760–2010

13

Constructing civilization: global hierarchy, 'gradated sovereignty' and globalization in international theory, 1760–2010

Introduction

While the focus of Chapters 2–12 zoomed in to unearth the details of the different variants of Eurocentrism and scientific racism, this chapter's first section zooms out so as to provide an overview of the changing architecture of 'Eurocentrism' in international theory in the 1760–2010 period. The second section provides a very quick overview of the 'polymorphous careers' of the three key theories of IR – Realism, Liberalism and Marxism – while the third section considers how international theorists have always developed *hierarchical* conceptions of world politics alongside their associated notions of *gradated* sovereignty.

Constructing 'Eurocentrism' in international theory, 1760–2010

Table 13.1 provides an overview of the changing architecture of 'generic Eurocentrism' in the last quarter millennium. Note that if we divide it into its four component periods, the architecture exhibits a 4×4×2×4 formation.

1760–1914: two modes of manifest Eurocentrism, two modes of scientific racism

Beginning at the bottom box of Table 13.1 that covers the 1760–1914 era, it is noteworthy that these four discourses emerged at different times. Thus the anti-paternalism associated with the likes of Smith and Kant emerged in the second half of the eighteenth century, while paternalist Eurocentrism was consolidated as a key variant after about 1830 (though its distant and tentative origins stem back to the Spanish attempts at

Table 13.1 *Mapping the changing architecture of 'Eurocentrism' in international theory in the four key eras, 1760–2010*

	Pro-imperialist	Anti-imperialist
1989–2010 Manifest Eurocentrism	**Paternalism** Rawls, Held, Téson, Nussbaum, Fukuyama **Offensive Eurocentrism** Kagan, Cooper, Ferguson	**Anti-paternalism** (subliminal Eurocentrism) Neo-Marxism, **Defensive Eurocentrism** S. P. Huntington, Lind
1945–1989 Subliminal Eurocentrism	**Paternalism** Gilpin, Keohane, (Waltz, Bull, Watson)	**Anti-paternalism** Carr, Morgenthau, (Waltz, Bull, Watson)
1914–1945 Manifest Eurocentrism	**Paternalism** Woolf, Zimmern, Murray, Angell	**Anti-paternalism** (Subliminal Eurocentrism) Laski/Brailsford, Lenin/Bukharin
Scientific racism	**Offensive racism** Wilson, Buell, Kjellén, Spykman, Haushofer, Hitler	**Defensive racism** Stoddard, Grant, E. Huntington
1760–1914 Manifest Eurocentrism	**Paternalism** Cobden/Bright, Angell, Hobson, Mill, Marx	**Anti-paternalism** Smith, Kant
Scientific racism	**Offensive racism** Ward, Reinsch, Kidd, Mahan, Mackinder, von Treitschke	**Defensive racism** Spencer, Sumner, Blair, Jordan, C. H. Pearson, Ripley, Brinton

Notes:
1. All references to Eurocentrism are to 'Eurocentric institutionalism'.
2. I have not included all the thinkers I consider in this book so as not to clutter the table.
3. Those who fit in more than one box have been placed in brackets.

'reading' the 'Indian natives', particularly that of Francisco di Vitoria's (1539/1991), in the wake of the 'discovery' of the Americas).[262] Although scientific racism emerged gradually during the eighteenth century, it only became a significant discourse in Britain, for example, after 1850. Indeed, it was only in the second half of the nineteenth century when scientific racism became a major epistemic force, and only after 1889 when racist-realism emerged.

Zooming in further it is instructive to consider the similarities and differences between the four variants on the vertical and horizontal axes. Turning to the imperialist discourses on the vertical axis, it is important to note that paternalist Eurocentrism for the most part entails a highly optimistic, and frequently triumphalist, 'progressive' politics. That is, such thinkers, who include Cobden and Bright, Angell, Hobson, MacDonald, Robertson, Mill and Marx, envisage imperialism as a civilizing mission. For these thinkers the *pioneering* agency of the Europeans in conjunction with *conditional* Eastern agency means that not only can the former promote the development of Eastern societies through the civilizing mission, but they have a 'moral duty' to do so (i.e., the 'white man's burden'). Although Mill and Marx envisage the process as requiring a certain amount of despotism (Mill) or coercion (Marx), others such as Hobson advocate the need for the Europeans to empathize with the non-European peoples and as far as possible to construct a system that will 'genuinely' help them.

By contrast, the offensive racist-realism of Mahan and Mackinder, as well as Giddings and Powers, is founded on a strong sense of Western anxiety. The idiom of the yellow peril is paramount in their thought and requires the Americans and Europeans to defend against this – principally through an Anglo-Saxon racial alliance. Such a defence takes the form of an imperialist offensive (on the basis that the best form of defence is attack). This approach grants the yellow races in particular high or very high degrees of agency, albeit of a regressive and predatory kind. However, another strand of racist-realism downplayed the barbaric threat and indulged in an unmitigated white racial triumphalism which effectively denied non-white racial agency altogether (e.g., Theodore Roosevelt, von Treitschke, von Bernhardi). But for the various differences it is important to note that some offensive racists drew close

---

[262] See especially: Pieterse (1992); Pagden (1995); Jahn (2000); Inayatullah and Blaney (2004); Anghie (2005); Pateman and Mills (2007); Bowden (2009); Blaney and Inayatullah (2010).

to the conception of the 'benign civilizing mission' of paternalist-Eurocentrism, most of whom were liberals (cf. Ireland, Sidgwick, Reinsch, Wilson). Moreover a good number of liberal racists, like the racist-realists, pronounced a triumphalist vision in which the natural expansion of the white race would deliver civilization to the dark places of the world (e.g., Strong, Fiske, Dilke, Seeley). Nevertheless, some liberal-racists, as did various racist-realists, advocated either an indirect exterminism (e.g., Kidd) or a 'direct exterminist' conception of imperialism (e.g., Ward) – as did various socialist-racists (e.g., Karl Pearson). And nor should we ignore the various socialist racists and paternalist Eurocentrics who embraced imperialism as a means to civilize the inferior Eastern societies (cf. Sidney Webb, Ramsay MacDonald, H. G. Wells and many, if not hundreds, more).

The ultimate upshot of this is to say that while there are clear differences between the offensive racist and paternalist Eurocentric approaches to imperialism, nevertheless the borderline between them is at times extremely fuzzy with a significant degree of overlap at the margins between liberal/socialist racist- and paternalist Eurocentric-imperialists. Moreover, we cannot simply assume that liberal or socialist imperial thought necessarily provides a softer conception of imperialism to racist-realism.

Turning now to explore some of the horizontal relationships between offensive and defensive racism on the one hand and between paternalist- and anti-paternalist Eurocentrism on the other, a series of similarities and differences become apparent. The conventional or popular assumption that scientific racism imposes fixed essences to the various races is, as I have argued in various chapters, highly problematic. In the 'universalist' strand of defensive racism, which I examined in Chapter 4, Spencer believed that all races – including the negroes – were capable of auto-development such that they would break through to modernity of their own accord at some point in the future (even if this would take a matter of centuries in the case of the blacks). In this respect, Spencer and Sumner's defensive racism overlaps very clearly with the anti-paternalist Eurocentrism of Smith and Kant, insofar as both variants award 'derivative agency' to the non-European peoples. Moreover, Spencer and Sumner also shared with Smith and Kant an aversion to Western imperialist paternalism on the grounds that this would disturb the natural developmental trajectories of both the European and non-European worlds. But where Spencer and Sumner depart from the anti-paternalist Eurocentrics and overlap directly with the offensive racists is in their belief that races are best kept apart on the grounds that race-mixing (miscegenation) and the climate of the tropics leads only to white racial degeneration.[263] Interestingly, it was this problem that forced the offensive racists to find ways round the problem of tropical climatic trauma in order to justify and maintain their imperialist stance.[264] Moreover, the anti-miscegenationist rationale that underpinned anti-imperialism was taken further by Charles Henry Pearson and Lothrop Stoddard; while the climatic trauma rationale of anti-imperialism was advanced by the likes of Daniel Brinton, William Z. Ripley, Comte Arthur de Gobineau, Robert Knox, Ellsworth Huntington and Madison Grant (as well as Charles Henry Pearson).

The final comparison is that between paternalist and anti-paternalist Eurocentrism. The key difference lies in their conceptions of Eastern agency, where in contrast to the anti-imperialist conception of *derivative* agency, the paternalists awarded the East lower levels of agency (specifically 'conditional' agency). It is this difference which leads to the opposing claims that imperialism is either *not* required because the Eastern peoples will auto-generate (anti-paternalism), or *is* required because only in this way can the necessary rational institutions be delivered so as to kick-start Eastern development (paternalism).

1914–1945: Two modes of manifest Eurocentrism, two modes of scientific racism

Because much of the generic Eurocentric international theory in the period from 1914 to 1945 carries forward the story that marks the pre-1914 era I shall move quickly here. The paternalist-Eurocentrics were, for the most part, liberals as well as Fabians, who argued for the 'benign' civilizing mission. The key contrast with most of the pre-1914 thinkers of this category was that most embraced a conception of *international imperialism*; a formula that was, ironically, born in the 1902 work of J. A. Hobson via his concept of 'sane imperialism'. Thus Zimmern, Angell, Murray and Woolf argued that the imperial civilizing mission should continue but that it needed to be supervised by an impartial independent government – i.e., the League of Nations Mandate System. That said, though, some became highly critical of the League's

---

[263] Notwithstanding the point that Kant's anthropological and geographical writings – as opposed to his political writings – exhibited a similar racist predisposition.
[264] Cf. Giddings (1898); Kidd (1898); Pearson (1905).

workings,[265] thereby qualifying Carr's assumption that liberal 'idealists' staked all their political chips on the roulette wheel of the League. And, moreover as I explained in Chapter 7 a number of these thinkers argued that the British Empire had to be maintained alongside the League if the latter was to operate effectively.[266] Accordingly, these thinkers maintained the paternalist-imperialism of their pre-1914 predecessors, even if the *form* of their prescription was different.

But once again, there is a notable overlap between the aforementioned paternalist Eurocentric thinkers and some liberal-imperialist racists, who included Wilson, Buell, and intriguingly, David Starr Jordan (1919) who had been a racist anti-imperialist before the war but joined the 'liberal-progressive' cause of international imperialism in its aftermath. Interestingly, a further overlap exists here with the racist-realist, Halford Mackinder (1919), who also embraced the idea of international imperialism and the League of Nations. Nevertheless, the majority of the racist-realists differed substantially to the liberals, all of whom advocated national imperialism as a means to enhance the power of a particular nation-state. Thus the American geopolitician, Nicholas Spykman, advocated American colonialism while the German racist-realists – especially Karl Haushofer, Richard Hennig, Heinrich von Treitschke, Friedrich von Bernhardi, Friedrich Ratzel and Adolf Hitler – advocated the expansion of German colonialism. Critically, though, the school of geopolitics embraced a brand of racism that differed to the genetic-determinist Eugenics of Hitler. Moreover, in the writings of Houston Stewart Chamberlain, von Treitschke, Hitler and, of course, the German racial hygienists, the Jews feature prominently and were awarded only moderate levels of agency that were inversely proportional to the size of the racial threat that they posed to the Aryan race.

Significantly, some of the defensive racists shared in common with Hitler a Eugenicist racism, though this was deployed to support a largely anti-imperialist politics (as in Madison Grant and Lothrop Stoddard). For the paradox was that Stoddard was highly critical not just of liberal internationalists and European imperialist movements but, above all, of the 'Prussian plotters of Weltmacht' who had committed one of the greatest disservices to the cause of white racial unity and had served only to enhance 'race suicide' (a term that was coined by the American racist, Edward Ross, in 1899). And Stoddard's arguments to an

---

[265] E.g., Hobson (1921, 1932); Woolf (1933); Angell (1933); Laski (1933, 1940).
[266] Cf. Zimmern (1934); Angell (1931, 1937); Muir (1917).

important extent provided the counter-position to the Nazi imperialist cause, given that his principal normative-political strategy was to batten down the hatches of the white 'inner dikes' and erect high walls around the white citadel so as to keep the contaminating virus of the non-white races out. Thus while the Jewish racial threat reached extreme proportions in Hitler's mind, it was the 'yellow–brown racial threat' that exercised Stoddard's anxious imagination. But the paradox was that the racist-Eugenics of Grant and Stoddard remained far closer to Hitler's approach than the latter did with the German imperialist geopolitikers.

Finally, the fourth perspective – that of subliminal anti-paternalist Eurocentrism – though complementing the likes of Smith and Kant in the critique of imperialism, nevertheless heralded a new form of Eurocentrism that would take off after 1945. This subliminal Eurocentrism underpinned the Marxism of Lenin, Bukharin, Luxemburg and Hilferding,[267] as well as the socialism of Brailsford and Laski. Though highly critical of imperialism, nevertheless these thinkers departed from Smith and Kant insofar as they reified Western agency but eradicated almost all traces of Eastern agency. But the paradox here, as I noted with respect to world-systems theory in Chapter 10, is that this mode of Eurocentrism advances one of the lowest degrees of Eastern agency found anywhere, including many of the scientific racist theories.

1945–1989: Two modes of subliminal Eurocentrism

One obvious counter-response to my argument thus far might well be that even if Eurocentrism and scientific racism had been present in international theory in the period running up to 1945 – though notably this has not been conventionally recognized or accepted – nevertheless the discipline as well as the practice of world politics has moved away from such discourses since then. It is certainly the case, as I shall explain below, that by 1945 scientific racism had been discarded within IR theory, but this should not be taken to mean that the subsequent era of decolonization witnessed the replacement of racial intolerance with a more tolerant and benign discourse of racial equality, as many IR theorists assume.[268] For while such a claim presupposes a binary

---

[267] Nevertheless, though I see Trotsky's work as largely Eurocentric there are potential non-Eurocentric cues.
[268] See for example: Alexandrowicz (1967); Vincent (1984); Gong (1984); Klotz (1995); Finnemore (2003a, 2003b).

construction, where the alternative to racism is racial tolerance, this necessarily obscures the presence of a third discourse: subliminal Eurocentric intolerance. And it is precisely this, I argue, that came to underpin IR theory during the era of decolonization (1945–89).

The principal reason for the emergence of subliminal Eurocentrism lies with the West's 'colonial-racist guilt syndrome', or what has been termed 'post-imperial cringe'.[269] In turn, the emergence of this syndrome was due in part to a series of intra-Western developments, which comprised the internalist critique of scientific racism within the Academy,[270] as well as the revulsion that the Nazi atrocities invoked in the Western mind. But it also emerged as a response to the successful strategy of rhetorical entrapment that was deployed by the anti-colonialist nationalist movements, as they managed to discredit both scientific racism and formal empire.[271] Here it is noteworthy that characterizing the 1947–89 era as that of the Cold War, which was essentially an intra-Western civil war, deflects attention or focus away from the battle for decolonization between East and West. For it was this battle in particular that comprised an important milieu or backdrop in the development of subliminal Eurocentric international theory. In general, the upshot of the emergent Western racist-imperialist guilt complex was not so much a turn away from imperialism in practice, given that both the Western superpowers continued it in a variety of ways between 1945 and 1989 – even if it reined in Europe's imperialist ambitions – but a desire to hide or obscure imperialism from view in the body of international theory. Indeed in subliminal Eurocentrism all the monikers of manifest Eurocentrism are present but are obscured or hidden from immediate view. In essence, all talk of 'civilization versus barbarism' or of 'whites versus non-whites' was given a wide berth on the grounds that it smacked of the old racist idea of Western racial and imperial supremacy.

An excellent example of the elision of imperialism lies in Hans Morgenthau's principal work, *Politics Among Nations* (1948/1967) in which imperialism is reimagined not as a policy that the West had long deployed vis-à-vis the East but as a *normal* universal strategy of aspiring great powers in relation to each other. This process of what Frank Füredi

---

[269] Sandbrook (2010).
[270] See Gossett (1997: ch. 16); Stocking (1982: ch. 11); Barkan (1992); Hannaford (1996: ch. 11).
[271] Tinker (1977: ch. 6); Hunt (1987); Füredi (1998a, 1998b); Lauren (1996); Abernethy (2000).

(1994: ch. 5) calls the 'whitewashing of imperialism' also finds its expression in Hedley Bull's pluralist English School theory, where we encounter a retrospective justification of pre-1945 imperialism as a benign process that diffused civilization across the world. A further subliminal strategy that was often deployed was the advancing of a 'benign' *neo*-imperial politics that went by a whitewashed or sanitized name. Thus neorealism elevated the exercise of (Anglo-Saxon) *hegemony* to the implicit status of a civilizing mission, while neoliberal institutionalism did much the same with respect to the role played by Western international institutions, especially the IFIs. In both visions, the prime rationale of Western hegemons and their international institutions is to culturally convert third world states along Western civilizational lines; the very essence of the liberal civilizing mission. And both approaches echo the manifest paternalist Eurocentric formula of awarding pioneering, progressive agency to the West and conditional agency to the East, though Gilpin adds into this mix the notion of predatory Eastern agency in his discussion of the decline of (Anglo-Saxon) hegemony.

Another generic property of subliminal Eurocentric IR theory in the post-1945 era is to shift focus away from direct attention to North–South relations, or what I have preferred to call East–West relations, in favour of a near-exclusive focus on intra-Western relations. In this vision the West is once again granted hyper-agency while Eastern agency is downgraded, if not erased altogether. That is, all developments within world politics are explained through Western hyper-agency, with the West being presented as the universal. This is a typical feature of classical realism and Waltzian neorealism, and is to an important extent reproduced in neorealist hegemonic stability theory. Indeed HST effectively instructs the student that she can learn all she needs to know about world politics/economics simply by focusing all her attention on the actions of the Anglo-Saxon hegemons. And as noted in Chapter 9, Keohane's neoliberal institutionalism explicitly focuses on intra-Western relations, even though East–West relations slip in through the subliminal Eurocentric backdoor, as noted a moment ago.

At this point, though, the sceptical reader might well object to my claim by offering up liberal modernization theory and dependency/world-systems theory as examples of theories that focus *explicitly* on North–South or East–West relations. But they, too, turn out to be the exceptions that prove the subliminal Eurocentric rule. The Eurocentric cues are found either in the guise of the reification of Western agency and the erasure of Eastern agency (as in WST), or in the point that the East is awarded derivative agency insofar as it will replicate the Western development path, the five stages of which weave a linear line that begins with replicating British industrialization only to culminate with the age of high-mass consumption, US-style.[272] Moreover, the old explicit Eurocentric trope of 'civilization versus barbarism' effectively became replaced by the subliminal Eurocentric tropes of 'tradition versus modernity' and 'core versus periphery'.

One particularly interesting aspect of post-1945 international theory involves the whitewashing of traditional pre-1945 racist thinkers. Thus Herbert Spencer's theory is (re)presented (mainly by sociologists) as a universal theory of the rise of industrial society out of militant society shorn of all its racist aspects, while Mahan and Mackinder are (re)presented as geopoliticians whose leitmotif was 'national realpolitik', with any sign of their underlying 'racist-realpolitik' having all but magically disappeared through the performance of a Eurocentric sleight of hand. But the most egregious example of this was the recasting of Woodrow Wilson within the popular IR imagination. For he suddenly became the founding father of twentieth-century liberal internationalism, based as 'it is' on anti-imperialism and self-determination rather than on what 'it was': an 'offensive racist' vision based on the denial of Eastern state sovereignty and a pro-imperialist stance abroad coupled with strong racial immigration controls at home. And the same 'sanitizing process' has been applied to all the significant racist and Eurocentric international theorists of the pre-1945 era which, of course, provides a good deal of the rationale that motivated me to write the first half of this book.

All of which brings me to a particularly controversial issue; notably, that while Eurocentric readers will most likely reject my claims here, so too from the opposite extreme would a good number of 'critical race scholars'. For these latter thinkers would most probably reject my claim that post-1945 international thought has taken a subliminal Eurocentric-institutionalist form, while simultaneously rejecting my more general claim that Eurocentric institutionalism and scientific racism can be significantly differentiated. Thus they argue that Eurocentric institutionalism or cultural Eurocentrism is merely racism masquerading as a more tolerant 'culturalism' – i.e., as 'racism in disguise'.[273] Thus when

---

[272] Though Rostow (1960) notes that the replication process is not one of photocopying Britain's industrialization given the role of state intervention in late-development.
[273] See especially: Barker (1981); Hunt (1987); Balibar (1991); Miles (1993); Malik (1996); Füredi (1998a); MacMaster (2001); Perry (2007); McCarthy (2009).

speaking of the post-1945 substitution of cultural difference for racial difference, one such thinker concludes that '[t]he terms may change, perhaps giving the impression that the old [racial] problems have disappeared, when in fact they have merely acquired protective coloration through semantic camouflage' (Perry 2007: 216). Or as Thomas McCarthy expresses it in his excellent book, *Race, Empire, and the Idea of Human Development*: 'the demise of scientific racism in its evolutionary-biological form did not mean the end of racist thinking in scholarly discourse altogether. A new, post-biological modality of neo-racism is now widespread in social science' (2009: 91). Much is at stake, politically and analytically, in determining whether 'institutional Eurocentrism', let alone its subliminal form, is merely semantic camouflage for racism.

While Eurocentric institutionalism often echoes many of the prejudices of scientific racism and at times performs similar political tasks – as indeed I explained earlier – nevertheless to reduce them one to the other is problematic. Indeed it is my rejection of this conflation that comprises a key rationale of this book, and much of the justification for my claim has also been substantiated implicitly in this chapter. Nevertheless a few key points are worth emphasizing to consolidate my pivotal claim. In the first instance Eurocentric institutionalism contains no references to genetic/biological properties as a marker of ethnological difference. To conflate these would, I believe, constitute not merely an analytical but also a tactical mistake from a critical-emancipatory perspective, given that none of the post-1945 Eurocentrics, not even Samuel Huntington, would argue for non-white inferiority on racial/genetic grounds,[274] and would therefore dismiss outright the Eurocentric-cum-racist charge. It is also analytically problematic because Eurocentric institutionalism outside of the narrow genre that invokes a climatic determinism (i.e., List and Montesquieu), posits that *all* races and peoples are capable of developing, either spontaneously (as in liberal anti-paternalist Eurocentrism) or once the rational institutions have been delivered courtesy of the Western civilizing mission (as in paternalist Eurocentrism). By contrast many scientific racists are far more ambivalent in this respect with the majority denying black agency altogether, while equally many view yellow and sometimes brown agency

---

[274] Though of course his namesake, Ellsworth Huntington, made exactly this racist claim!

as particularly strong, albeit inherently regressive or predatory.[275] Moreover, as I also noted earlier, for the most part the imperialist visions differ substantially such that many paternalist Eurocentrics talk of the non-coercive civilizing mission while many offensive racists seek either to contain/exploit the barbaric Eastern menace or, at the extreme, to exterminate it. That said, though, as I noted earlier, various racists such as Reinsch, Ireland, Sidgwick, Wilson, and Buell echoed the paternalist Eurocentrics by arguing for a 'benign' civilizing mission. But when seen in the round, although there are clearly some significant overlaps between Eurocentric institutionalism and scientific racism, there are also some significant, irreducible differences.

One unequivocal difference, however, concerns the point that unlike the vast majority of scientific racists, Eurocentric institutionalists have no problem with blood-mixing.[276] Inter-relatedly, many racist theorists viewed non-whites, especially blacks, as virtual animals, with Comte de Buffon claiming that it was the Hottentot (the Khoi-Khoi of south-western Africa) who constituted the missing link between apes and humans. Indeed, no Eurocentric institutionalist would have thought it appropriate to exhibit a Black African pygmy alongside an ape, as happened to Ota Benga in the Bronx Zoo in 1906 at the ultimate behest of the arch-Eugenicist, Madison Grant. Moreover, Buffon's argument meshed neatly with Edward Long's racist claim that: 'Ludicrous as the opinion may seem, I do not think that an orang-outang husband would be any dishonour to a Hottentot female' (Long cited in Bhabha 1994: 91). While most of us today would find little with which to quibble concerning the first part of Long's statement, certainly no Eurocentric institutionalist covered in this book would agree with the latter part. Nevertheless, the critical race theorists' response would most likely be that cutting the Gordian Knot which links Eurocentric institutionalism with scientific racism lets the former off the moral hook. But this necessarily downplays the extent to which Eurocentric institutionalism, as well as subliminal Eurocentrism, are no lesser forms of bias.

---

[275] Even so, I readily concede that many offensive Eurocentric writers after 1989 make a similar claim – a point I made in Chapter 11.

[276] And even when a few scientific racists approved of miscegenation it was supported as a means for the superior white race to conquer and eradicate the inferior non-white races (eg., Gumplowicz, Ratzenhofer and Ward).

1989–2010: Back to the future of manifest Eurocentrism

One of the most profound paradoxes to emerge in this book concerns the point that the contemporary politics of Eurocentrism is whitewashed and consigned to history, removing it from the present and quarantining it alongside the racism of the nineteenth century. As I explained in Chapter 12, this very Eurocentric sleight of hand is performed through the construction of a temporal binary, where the nineteenth century is (re)presented as more racially intolerant and imperialist than it was so that the post-1989 era could be portrayed as more tolerant, culturally pluralist and anti-imperialist than it is. For the contemporary era, much of international theory is no less intolerant than was its nineteenth-century ancestor and certainly no less imperialist. Indeed one of the more striking developments that I have examined in this book concerns the way in which international theory after 1989 has in fact returned almost directly to the manifest 'Eurocentric' forms that it took in the nineteenth century and first half of the twentieth (see Table 13.1). While the discursive *form* of scientific racism has not re-appeared in international theory, it is nevertheless striking how much of its *content* finds its contemporary voice in offensive and defensive Eurocentric institutionalism.

Not only do we find a direct return to manifest Eurocentrism, but equally much of mainstream international theory has explicitly resuscitated the E-Words – 'Eurocentric Empire'. As one critical commentator puts it, '[o]ne way of dealing with the current return of civilization ... is to show that it is indeed an embarrassing anachronism, harking back to a time when "civilization" was one of colonialism's most powerful ideological tools' (Neocleous 2011: 145). Indeed, as I explained in the previous two chapters, the Eurocentric standard of civilization is explicitly utilized by international theorists such that 'failed states' in the East find their nineteenth-century Eurocentric equivalent in 'savage anarchic societies', no less than the construction of contemporary Eastern autocratic states – often going by the euphemisms of 'rogue' and 'pariah', though sometimes grouped together into the collective term of the 'axis of evil' – reconvenes the nineteenth-century idiom of barbaric Oriental despotism. Moreover, the modern push to spread Western state forms via IMF programmes that impose 'good governance' models on Eastern debtors finds its nineteenth-century equivalent in the civilizing mission that sought to impose rational bureaucratic structures. Also noteworthy is that while Britain imposed free trade upon Eastern states in the nineteenth century along with the unequal treaties, so after 1989 the Western free trade regime that imposes cultural conversion to Western civilizational principles was intensified as the hole-riddled GATT was replaced in 1995 with the more watertight and highly disciplinary WTO. And as I noted in Chapter 8, the nineteenth-century system of 'capitulations' finds its modern equivalent in IFI structural adjustment programmes that require Eastern states to harmonize their domestic legal systems according to Western principles. Last, but not least, the push to humanitarian intervention followed by state reconstruction along Western lines echoes in spirit the essence of the nineteenth-century civilizing mission conception that liberal imperialists advocated.

What explains this shift to manifest Eurocentrism after 1989 and its simultaneous move back to the future of the pre-1945 era? I noted earlier that international theory shifted from manifest Eurocentrism and scientific racism to subliminal Eurocentrism after 1945 as a function of the emergent 'colonial-racist guilt syndrome'. Moving forward in time I argue that after the end of the Cold War, Western international thinkers began to release themselves from the socio-psychological confines of this syndrome and began to proclaim in increasingly strident terms the inherent superiority of Western civilization once more. The awarding of sovereignty to the Eastern polities during the era of decolonization rested extremely awkwardly for many Western imperialist international thinkers who viewed this concession as a giant affront to the hyper-sovereign status of Western states. Nevertheless, the end of the Soviet Union and the simultaneous termination of the West's third civil war of the twentieth century constituted an 'intervening variable' insofar as it furnished Western imperialist thinkers with the opportunity to openly reassert the West as the prime neo-imperial mover of world politics. And this in turn led much of mainstream international theory to effectively roll forward the conception of Western sovereignty so as to restore its imperial hyper-sovereign status, while simultaneously rolling back Eastern sovereignty into the neo-imperial conception of 'conditional sovereignty'. In this way, the West could relegate in triumphalist fashion the 'postcolonial interlude' to a minor footnote in what was now portrayed as the long, normal Eurocentric history of Western supremacy.[277] Accordingly, post-1989 imperialist international theory returns us back to the pre-1945 conception of world politics as governed by formal

---

[277] See also Füredi (1994: 103).

hierarchy and gradated sovereignty, with the era of decolonization now happily but a faded memory.

However, that much of mainstream international theory has returned to the imperialist themes of pre-1945 thought should not obscure the anti-imperialist voices. Notable here, as I explained at the end of Chapter 11, is the anti-imperialism of racist cultural-realism associated with Charles Pearson and Lothrop Stoddard that finds its contemporary expression in Huntington and Lind's defensive Eurocentric theory, albeit stripped of its scientific racist properties. For these latter thinkers, the end of the Cold War did not present itself as an opportunity to reassert Western hyper-sovereignty but instead led them to rue the good old days of the Cold War. For as I noted in Chapter 11, now that the Soviet Other had gone so the West in general and America in particular had to find new enemies to construct so as to shore up Western identity. The result was a (re)turn to the East such that the Muslims and the Chinese were now constructed as the not-so-new Others against which American identity could be defined and defended.

Mapping the polymorphous/protean careers of liberal, realist and Marxist international theory, 1760–2010

I now turn to provide a potted summary of the 'protean careers' of liberal, realist and Marxist international theory, the details of which were examined in Chapters 2–12. As I explained in Chapter 1, IR theory is conceptualized in much of conventional IR historiography through the ahistorical lens of the 'great tradition' narrative.[278] This takes a snapshot of the present and then extrapolates this picture back in time to an imaginary originary point. And from there we move forward in time along a uniform linear path upon which the various 'great theorists' are located. This produces an ahistorical take on each of the great theories, smoothing out any *major* differences or discontinuities to manufacture a pristine linear image whereby each member of the tradition is represented in isomorphic terms. This is not to deny the point that conventional narratives accept that there are different variants within each 'great tradition'. Liberalism, for example, is subdivided into liberal internationalism, liberal/neoliberal institutionalism, interdependence theory and cosmopolitanism. But in all cases, the conventional axiom posits that liberalism is committed to individualism, free trade, democracy,

---

[278] See especially Schmidt (1998a: ch. 1); Keene (2005: ch. 1).

328 CHAPTER 13: CONSTRUCTING CIVILIZATION: 1760–2010

self-determination, and peace and prosperity for all, with differences appearing only in terms of the *means* by which these outcomes or goals can be achieved. Put differently, this conventional narrative pays attention only to differences in *surface-type* forms.

By contrast, my objective is to explore each theory's 'polymorphous' or 'protean' career such that focusing on changes in *deep content* – specifically the relevant Eurocentric and racist metanarratives – necessarily disturbs the linear trajectory of the conventional ahistorical 'great tradition' approach. And thus by focusing on how each theory crystallizes in radically *different forms* over time as different imperialist and anti-imperialist 'Eurocentric' metanarratives cut in and out, so this necessarily reveals each international theory as highly promiscuous and multivalent.

The polymorphous career of liberal international theory

Figure 13.1 presents the conventional linear narrative of the liberal 'great tradition' which, though taking different forms through time, is grounded on a consistent anti-imperialist base in which individual autonomy, democracy and internationalism are vital baseline components. Distilling my claims made in Chapters 2–5, 7, 9, 11 and 12, I forward two alternative polymorphous liberal careers – the anti-imperialist tradition (Figure 13.2) and the imperialist tradition (Figure 13.3). Two key points are noteworthy. First, different Eurocentric metanarratives are situated not merely between the two trajectories but also within each of them. For if we combined the two

c. 1760–1816	c. 1830–1913	c. 1900–1945	c. 1968–2000s	1989–2010
Smith, Kant, Ricardo	Cobden, Bright, Mill, Angell	Hobson, Wilson, Zimmern, Murray, Mitrany, Angell	Keohane/Nye Cooper, Morse; Keohane, Powell Rittberger	Fukuyama, Doyle, Held, Rawls, Téson
Classical liberal internationalism	Classical liberal institutionalism		Interdependence theory/neoliberal institutionalism	Liberal cosmopolitanism

⟶ Linear trajectory ⟶

Figure 13.1 The conventional ahistorical 'great narrative' of liberal international theory

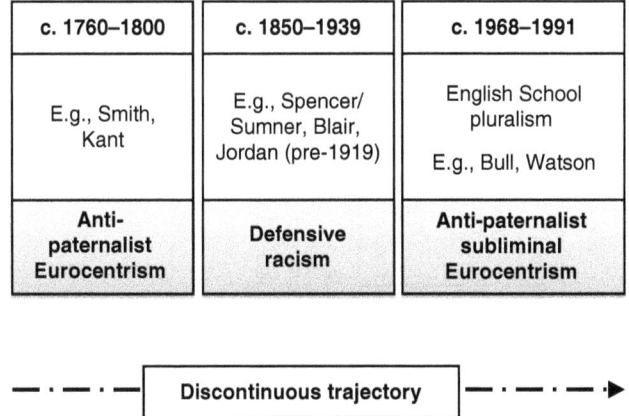

Figure 13.2 Alternative 'polymorphous/protean' career of anti-imperialist liberalism

in a single table, the discontinuities and ruptures would become yet more apparent. And second, while the imperialist tradition, based as it is on different 'Eurocentric' discourses, clearly undermines the notion of cultural pluralism, so the same is true of the anti-imperialist tradition. That is, even when liberals conform to anti-imperialism they do so for reasons that derive from their commitment either to Eurocentric institutionalism or to scientific racism.

Here it is interesting to note that within IPE it is commonly assumed that the Manchester School of liberal internationalism stood not merely for anti-imperialism but also for a cultural pluralism and cosmopolitanism. The paradox of my revisionist analysis is that Manchester liberalism reflected either a paternalist Eurocentrism (e.g., Cobden and Bright), or an offensive racist social Darwinism (Bagehot),[279] or equally an anti-paternalist Eurocentrism if we include Smith in this umbrella category. Finally, though, it is important to recognize that within the English School a non-Eurocentric approach has begun to emerge mainly since 2000 as I noted in Chapters 1 and 9.

---

[279] Walter Bagehot, who was editor of *The Economist* (1861–77), was an important social Darwinian. And as I noted in Chapter 5 in other writings he appeared to support British imperialism.

c. 1830–1919	c. 1860–1919	c. 1900–1939	c. 1914–1939	c. 1960–1989	c. 1989–2010	
Liberal imperialists	*Liberal imperialists*	*International imperialists*	*International imperialists*	*Statist liberals*	*Liberal cosmopolitans*	*'Realist-liberals'*
E.g., Cobden, Bright, Mill, Angell, Robertson	E.g., Dike, Seeley, Ritchie, Reinsch, Ireland, Bagehot	E.g., Wilson, Reinsch, Buell, Jordan (1919)	E.g., Hobson, Zimmern, Angell, Murray	E.g., Bull, Watson, Wight, Keohane	E.g., Rawls, Fukuyama, Held, Wheeler, Téson, Nussbaum	E.g., Ikenberry/ Slaughter, Rothkopf, Cooper, Ignatieff
(MANIFEST) PATERNALIST EUROCENTRISM	OFFENSIVE RACISM	OFFENSIVE RACISM	(MANIFEST) PATERNALIST EUROCENTRISM	SUBLIMINAL PATERNALIST EUROCENTRISM	(MANIFEST) PATERNALIST EUROCENTRISM	

– – – – – – – – – – | Discontinuous trajectory | – – – – – – – – →

Figure 13.3 Alternative 'polymorphous/protean' career of paternalist-imperial liberalism

The polymorphous career of realism, c. 1889–2010

The conventional 'great tradition' narrative of realism is one that stems back to Thucydides in 431 BCE, and then moves forwards via Hobbes and Machiavelli in the sixteenth century, before re-appearing in its 'classical' guise in the aftermath of WWII, with Carr and Morgenthau, then proceeds on into its neorealist phase beginning with hegemonic stability theory in the 1970s and Waltzian neorealism after 1979, before culminating in the post-Cold War era with the likes of Mearsheimer, Grieco and Krasner. To this we might add the liberal-realists (especially the US neo-Conservatives) as well as, perhaps, the cultural-realists (Huntington and Lind). However, on the basis of the claims made in Chapters 5–8 and 11, Figure 13.4 presents my alternative discontinuous narrative of the development of realist international theory in the post-1889 period.

The polymorphous/protean career of Marxist international theory, c. 1840–2010

The conventional assumption holds that Marxism is anti-imperialist and anti-Eurocentric, given its inherent critique of Western capitalist imperialism. But distilling my claims made in Chapters 2, 6 and 10, Figure 13.5 produces my alternative reading of the polymorphous career of Marxist international theory.

Two key points are noteworthy here. First, while the anti-imperialist tradition within Marxism (Marx and Engels excepted) is clearly very strong, nevertheless the Eurocentric reification of the West as the supreme controlling subject of world politics coupled with the virtual denial of Eastern agency leads, albeit unwittingly, into an approach that *naturalizes* Western imperialism/neo-imperialism (see Chapter 10). And second, unlike liberalism and realism, since 1989 postcolonial and non-Eurocentric frameworks have certainly begun to emerge within neo-Marxism, as they have within the English School, thereby providing the exception to my general claim that IR theory seeks to promote and defend Western civilization (see the far right-hand box of Figure 13.5).

Constructing civilization: deriving global hierarchy, 'gradated sovereignty' and globalization, 1760–2010

Finally, to close this chapter and the book more generally I want to reveal how my arguments serve to produce a radically different take

	1889–1945		Post-1945	Post-1973	Post-1989		
	Racist-realism	*Racist cultural-realism*	*Classical realism*	*Neorealism*	*'Western-realism'*	*'Western liberal-realism'*	*Cultural-realism*
	E.g., Mahan/ Mackinder von Treitschke, Spykman, Haushofer, Hitler	C. H. Pearson, Stoddard, Grant	E.g., Carr, Morgenthau	E.g., Gilpin/ Kindleberger, Kennedy, Krasner, (Waltz)	E.g., Kaplan, Brzezinski, Ferguson	E.g., Kagan, Krauthammer, Boot	E.g., Lind, Huntington
	EXPLICIT IMPERIALISM OFFENSIVE RACISM	ANTI-IMPERIALISM DEFENSIVE RACISM	ANTI-IMPERIALISM? SUBLIMINAL EUROCENTRISM	IMPLICIT NEO-IMPERIALISM SUBLIMINAL PATERNALIST EUROCENTRISM	EXPLICIT NEO-IMPERIALISM OFFENSIVE EUROCENTRISM	EXPLICIT NEO-IMPERIALISM PART PATERNALIST/ PART OFFENSIVE EUROCENTRISM	EXPLICIT ANTI-IMPERIALISM DEFENSIVE EUROCENTRISM

─ ─ ─ ─ ─ ─ ─ ─ ─ ─ Discontinuous trajectory ─ ─ ─ ─ ─ ─ ─ ─ ─ ─ →

Figure 13.4 Alternative 'polymorphous/protean' career of realism

GLOBAL HIERARCHIES AND GRADED SOVEREIGNTY 333

c. 1840–1895	c. 1910–1920s	c. 1967– c. 1989	Post-1989	
Classical Marxism I:	*Classical Marxism II:*	*Neo-Marxism (world-systems theory/ Gramscianism)*	*Neo-Marxism (Gramscianism & other variants)*	*Postcolonial Marxism*
Marx & Engels	Lenin, Luxemburg, Hilferding, Bukharin	E.g., Wallerstein/ Frank; Cox	E.g., Gill, Hettne, Robinson, Arrighi	E.g., Persaud, Slater, Pasha, Gills, Frank, Gruffydd-Jones, Matin
EXPLICIT IMPERIALISM	ANTI-IMPERIALISM	ANTI-IMPERIALISM	ANTI-IMPERIALISM	ANTI-IMPERIALISM
PATERNALIST EUROCENTRISM	SUBLIMINAL ANTI-PATERNALIST EUROCENTRISM	SUBLIMINAL ANTI-PATERNALIST EUROCENTRISM	SUBLIMINAL ANTI-PATERNALIST EUROCENTRISM	NON-EUROCENTRISM

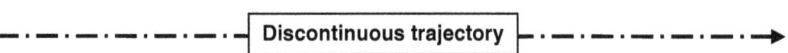

Figure 13.5 Alternative 'polymorphous/protean' career of Marxism

on one of the most taken-for-granted axioms of the discipline of IR. As I noted in Chapter 1, for many IR scholars it is an unreflexive axiom of the discipline that the concepts of anarchy and sovereignty are not merely twinned but that understanding the anarchic world of sovereign state relations constitutes the prime focus, or raison d'être, of IR theory. Zooming in a little further, it becomes apparent that from this general axiom three cardinal IR principles flow. The first principle is that sovereignty is an objective and fixed defining property of that which constitutes the state *qua* state. This largely entails a black-boxing of the state such that its social domestic properties as well as the wider international or global social context become extraneous to the discipline's remit (notwithstanding the Constructivist/Poststructuralist revolution that has disturbed this general axiom). The second cardinal principle is that sovereignty presupposes that all states are rational even if some are more powerful than others. And the third cardinal principle is that such a conception of world politics essentially rests on an anti-imperialist and cultural-pluralist base. That is, IR scholars take it as axiomatic not only that all states enjoy political self-determination but that they no less enjoy full *cultural* self-determination. Gerry Simpson refers to this latter dimension of sovereignty as *existential equality* (2004: ch. 2). More generally, this picture of the sovereignty discourse has usefully been termed an 'equalitarian regime' (Reus-Smit 2005). All in all, the assumption that IR theory enquires into the relations between fully self-determining and juridically-equal sovereign states under anarchy, coupled with its three underlying cardinal assumptions, leads many IR scholars to assume that their discipline cannot be, by definition, imperialist or Eurocentric.

But do these interconnected assumptions in fact capture the scope of international theoretical enquiry? Edward Keene thinks not. In his important text-book he begins with the assumption that international political thought has more often focused on communities and their inter-relations and that in turn such communities have been defined by the application of the social standard of civilization. As he rightly points out, many thinkers in the nineteenth century, especially international lawyers,[280] believed that *civilized* nations should behave differently in their dealings with uncivilized peoples than they should with regard to one another. And he concludes that 'the distinction between civilized and barbaric peoples was even more fundamental to [pre-1945] international political [and international legal] thought than the drawing of territorial boundaries between different sovereign states'.[281] While Keene believes that this bipolar or schizophrenic conception was critical to much of *historical* international political thought, my point is that it is precisely the civilizational definitions of sovereignty that have governed the vast majority of international theory throughout the 1760–2010 period. One of the principal claims that my book makes is that sovereignty never has been understood as an objective and universal fixed attribute of all states, but has always been constructed through an *inequalitarian* discourse depending on the particular Eurocentric/racial conception of civilization that underpins each theory. Moreover, these discourses focus principally on the domestic cultural/institutional or racial attributes of states at the domestic level, which is then carried over into the international realm to provide a picture of the social-civilizational or racial differences between Eastern and Western states.

While leading constructivists and poststructuralists have done much excellent work on revealing sovereignty as a discursive construct,[282] nevertheless I argue here that we need to go one step further by recognizing that within international theory sovereignty has been grounded in various Eurocentric metanarratives that place the standard of civilization

---

[280] For the imperial Eurocentrism of nineteenth-century international law see: Grovogui (1996); Simpson (2004); Anghie (2005); Kayaoglu (2010).
[281] Keene (2005: 11); see also Long and Schmidt (2005b).
[282] Most notably: Campbell (1992); Walker (1993); Weber (1995); Bartelson (1995); Doty (1996); Wendt (1999); Reus-Smit (1999); Malmvig (2006).

centre-stage.[283] And, no less importantly, because the various discourses of Eurocentrism/racism have changed through time so too has the discourse of sovereignty within international theory, thereby testifying to its highly protean and malleable nature. Accordingly we need to talk about the lineages, or changing discursive architecture, of 'graded sovereignty' – or what has been called 'stratified sovereignty' (Simpson 2004: 85) – as it chops and changes in a discontinuist non-linear time sequence. Moreover, it is no less important to note that different conceptions of sovereignty cut in both diachronically and synchronically.

If the equalitarian conception of sovereignty is the flip-side of the anarchy coin, then the logical upshot of my focus on 'gradated sovereignty' must be an inequalitarian conception of civilizational/racial hierarchy within international theory.[284] While there is now a growing literature on hierarchy in the international system,[285] this has for the most part been applied either to the empirical practice of world politics or, if it has been applied to IR theory at all, it has been to critique neorealism.[286] Here I complement my discussion of gradated sovereignty with two main conceptions of civilizational hierarchy that find their place across the gamut of international theory – formal/manifest hierarchy and informal/subliminal hierarchy (see Figure 13.6).

Formal or manifest hierarchy is found within the imperialist theories where the West gains *hyper-sovereignty* to intervene in Eastern states and where the latter have their sovereignty either withheld (i.e., prior to 1945) or are granted only *conditional* sovereignty (mainly after 1989). By contrast, given the non-interventionist stance of anti-imperialist Eurocentrism, so hierarchy takes on a subliminal/informal modality, issuing the constructs of *full* state sovereignty in the West and *qualified* sovereignty or sovereignty-by-*default* in the East. And to the obvious objection that anti-imperialism implies non-intervention and, therefore, self-determination for all, it needs to be appreciated that Eurocentrism/racism of all persuasions denies cultural pluralism and thereby rejects

---

[283] See also Simpson (2004); Kayaoglu (2010); Bowden (2009).
[284] For an excellent analysis of the practice of gradated or 'stratified' sovereignty as it has played out in the practice of international law in the last two centuries, and which complements my analysis of international theory, see Simpson (2004).
[285] See, for example: Onuf (1989); Buzan *et al.* (1993); Lake (1996); Wendt and Friedheim (1996); Deudney (1996); Paul (1999); Hobson and Sharman (2005); Shilliam (2006); Donnelly (2009); Kayaoglu (2010).
[286] Partial exceptions to this are found in Kaufman *et al.* (2007); Kayaoglu (2010); Simpson (2004); with the former two focusing in large part on the English School.

CHAPTER 13: CONSTRUCTING CIVILIZATION: 1760–2010

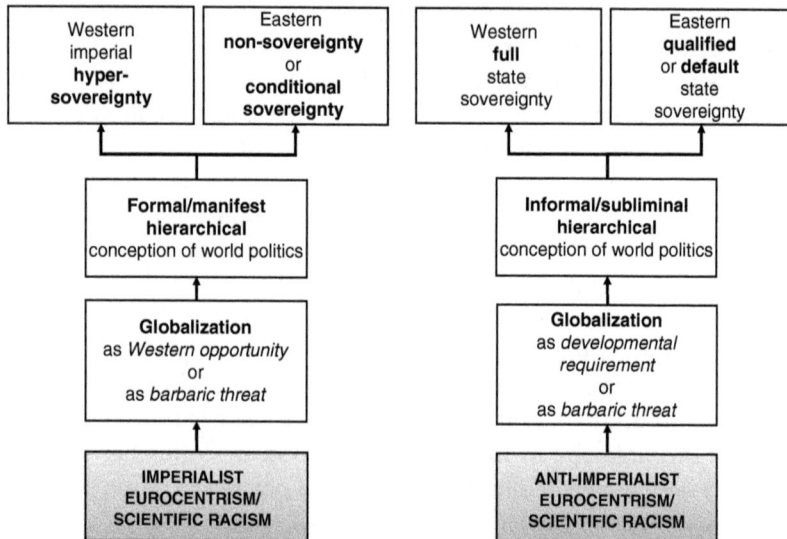

Figure 13.6 Civilizational hierarchies and gradated sovereignties in the Eurocentric and scientific racist mirrors

one of the key aspects of sovereignty – i.e., what Simpson (2004) calls 'existential equality'. Thus, like imperialist Eurocentrism, so anti-imperialist Eurocentrism works within differing degrees of gradated sovereignty.

In recent years many scholars have argued that the practice of world politics has often contradicted the theory of sovereignty that allegedly underpins IR theory. This, of course, has been conducted in a range of areas, the headlining examples of which are those concerning subsystems hierarchies under anarchy and, more frequently, the sovereignty-dissolving effects of globalization. These analyses in turn issue decrees to drop IR theory's apparent obsession with sovereignty, and to avoid the perils that are associated with 'Westphalian common-sense' (Grovogui 2002) or equally with the 'Westphalian blind alley' (Paul 1999), the 'Westphalian straitjacket' (Buzan and Little 2001), or even the 'Westphilian straitjacket' (Hobson 2009). More generally it has also led some to argue that there is a now a clear divorce or 'lack of fit' between the theory and practice of sovereignty (Cutler 2001).[287] But when viewed through a non-Eurocentric lens this common assumption becomes

---

[287] Or what has been described by my PhD student as a 'descriptive gap' (Mathieu 2010).

inverted. Thus by arguing that Eurocentric international theory never has embraced a uniform equalitarian conception of sovereignty we necessarily confront the counter-intuitive and deeply paradoxical point that international theorists have failed to recognize why, in the end, it turns out that there is little or no gap between the theory of sovereignty/ anarchy and the practice of gradated sovereignty/hierarchy. For this is precisely because all Eurocentric theories of sovereignty explicitly or implicitly invoke a hierarchical conception of world politics that entails the idea of gradated sovereignty. The purpose of the two following subsections is to reveal how and why this is the case.

Lastly, though, I want to argue that the apparent focus on anarchy and sovereign state relations within IR has served to obscure the process of globalization which, I argue, has underpinned much of international theory in the last 250 years. Such a claim, however, would appear to be counter-intuitive, if not perplexing, to many an IR reader. For it is, after all, an axiom of the discipline that the concern with globalization emerged initially with the rise of interdependence theory in the 1970s only to take off at the beginning of the 1990s when it became the buzz-word of the decade. But in what follows I shall discuss how globalization has not only been an important aspect of a great deal of international theory since 1760 but how it has taken two principal discursive forms: either 'globalization-as-Eastern barbaric threat' or 'globalization-as-Western opportunity' to exploit, or more often than not, to civilize the East. How then does all this play out within international theory?

Lineages of formal hierarchy, imperial hyper-sovereignty and globalization, 1760–2010

Focusing on the left-hand side of Figure 13.6 I want to begin by noting that many imperialist thinkers place a premium on global interdependence within their theories. It is well-known that Marx and Engels viewed the expansion of capitalism as akin to early globalization in *The Communist Manifesto* – even if they did not use the actual word – seeing in it a homogenizing process through which all societies would become attuned to the diktat and rhythm of modern Western capitalism. And as I argued in Chapter 2, globalization – or the global primitive accumulation of capital – is for Marx the handmaiden of colonialism. But the idea of global interdependence also found expression in liberal imperial theory, which views it as issuing the opportunity for Europe to remake the world along Western civilizational lines. Thus, for example, from the paternalist-Eurocentrism of J. A. Hobson's theory of sane imperialism to the offensive racism of Raymond Buell (1925), we encounter the paternalist assumption that under the 'strenuous conditions' of modern global interdependence it is impossible for even 'the most remote lands to escape the intrusion of "civilized" nations ... The contact with white races cannot be avoided' (Hobson 1938/1968: 230, also 231). This, of course, also formed the imperialist lynchpin of the League of Nations Mandate System (specifically Article 22 of the Covenant). And this in turn rests upon the imperialist idiom of 'social efficiency' (see also Angell 1937: 50–2), which dictates that Europeans must colonize backward lands on behalf of global humanity should their inhabitants fail to autonomously develop their own resources. For the world is now a single economic unit and all peoples now reside in a global community of shared economic fate.[288] And, of course, for many offensive racists, globalization represents a white racial opportunity to colonize and thereby develop the resources of the tropics in order to enhance (white) civilization, though this simultaneously benefited the world since it was the means by which civilization would be diffused across the globe (even if for some of these thinkers the weakest races were to be selected out either by nature or by the guns of the white colonial overlords in the process). The upshot of this, of course, is the point that such international theory advocates a formal hierarchic conception of world politics; no more clearly summarized at that time than by the paternalist-Eurocentric liberal, Gilbert Murray:

> With regard to the general hegemony of the white races, our Liberal position is clear. It is expressed in Article XXII of the Covenant. We do not believe in the equality of all nations; we believe rather in a certain hierarchy, no doubt a temporary hierarchy of races, or, at least, of civilizations.[289]

---

[288] One liberal even provides a definition of global interdependence in 1919 that bears an uncanny resemblance to the formulation that supposedly emerged first in the 1990s: 'On sea and land, distance has been annihilated and remote peoples are closer together today than were the various parts of a small kingdom a century ago ... Furthermore, the extension of [communications] and banking service to all parts of the world has made the whole earth an economic unit. Currents of trade set far beyond national boundaries. Capital goes wherever it sees a prospect of profit ... Information conveyed almost instantaneously around the world becomes common property ... The interrelations of financial adjustment give to the economic world a sort of sensory system. Whatever affects one part of it is instantly felt by all the others (Jordan 1919: 102–3).

[289] Murray, 1925, cited in Morefield (2005: 215).

There were also some, though clearly not all, racist-realists who emphasized the opportunity or perils that globalization issued. Both Mahan and Mackinder placed a great deal of emphasis on 'globalization-as-barbaric threat', with the latter re-issuing this fear in his 1919 book: 'We are now presented with a closed system ... Every shock, every disaster or superfluity, is now felt even to the antipodes ... Every deed of humanity will henceforth be echoed and reechoed in like manner all round the globe' (1919: 40). And in the context of military security threats associated with the shrinking of the world, the racist-realist, Nicholas Spykman, also emphasized the perils of globalization (see Spykman 1942: 165, 166, 448). Notable too is Adolf Hitler's construction of global economic interdependence as issuing a particular threat to Germany – specifically the flooding of the German economy with American imports. As he put it: 'Through modern technology and the communication it enables, international relations between peoples have become so effortless and intimate that the European – often without realizing it – takes the circumstances of the American life as the benchmark for his own life' (Hitler and Weinberg 2003: 21).[290]

I have concentrated largely on the pre-1945 situation to make my case, given that the place of globalization in various post-1945 theories is widely recognized. Even so, it is worth noting that the imperialist side of classical English School pluralism as well as neorealist hegemonic stability theory embraces the 'Eurocentric big-bang theory' of world politics, focusing on nineteenth-/early twentieth-century European imperialism as the vehicle that globalizes the world and seeks to remake the East in the image of the West. Moreover, with respect to Hedley Bull, it is noteworthy that while he is famous for his argument concerning the 'anarchical society of sovereign states', it turns out that for the period of the late-eighteenth century through to 1945, only European international society was constructed as anarchic whereas, by contrast, he envisaged on normative grounds Europe's relations with the non-European world in terms of formal hierarchy. That is, he in effect adhered to the notion of the 'hierarchical global international society' as it emerged in the nineteenth and twentieth centuries. And, of course, neoliberal institutionalism and interdependence theory obviously presuppose a globalized world. Indeed all these aforementioned post-1945 theories essentially view

---

[290] And for a wider discussion of this see Anievas (2011: 175–80).

globalization-as-Western opportunity to 'civilize the world'. This is a trope of the majority of post-1989 Western-liberal theories too, which contrast with the construct of globalization-as-barbaric threat that is invented within the neo-imperialist imaginary of most post-1989 Western-realists.

Lineages of informal hierarchy, qualified/default Eastern sovereignty and globalization, 1760–2010

While my conceptualization of formal hierarchy/gradated sovereignty might seem obvious and unproblematic in the context of imperialist/neo-imperialist international theory, nevertheless my reader might well have potential misgivings about extending this argument to the anti-imperialist literature. For one might well anticipate that the anti-imperialist thinkers would stand firmly for an equalitarian conception of sovereignty and would advocate self-determination as a universal principle. And this would be supported by the inter-related assumption that all states are equally rational, even if some are more powerful than others. The problem, though, is that in the racist and Eurocentric anti-imperialist conceptions of world politics the ideas of cultural pluralism and cultural self-determination simply fail to apply, while rationality is thought to be the monopolistic preserve of civilized Western states. It is for these reasons, I argue, that most of anti-imperialist theory turns out to invoke an *informal* hierarchical conception of world politics along with its associated idiom of gradated sovereignty.

While I argued in Chapter 3 that both Adam Smith and especially Immanuel Kant were strong critics of European imperialism, nevertheless I also argued that they exhibited an anti-paternalist Eurocentric monism rather than a cultural pluralism. That is, they both insisted that non-European economies not only will but *should* or *must* evolve into an idealized Western civilizational form. Moreover, they constructed global interdependence in terms that were similar to the liberal paternalists, viewing it as bringing all societies – civilized, barbaric and savage – into a global community of shared economic and political fate. And it is this which feeds into their argument that globalization unleashes the 'developmental imperative' or 'developmental requirement' upon savage and barbaric peoples. For as I also explained in that chapter, Kant viewed cultural pluralism and full self-determination as possible *only* in a *pre*-global/interdependent world, where savages can move away from civilized societies if they wished to maintain their uncivilized cultural autonomy. But under conditions of global interdependence that he observed in the second half of the eighteenth century, this exit option is no longer available. While he was unequivocal that Europeans *cannot* appropriate other peoples' lands through imperialism, nevertheless they *can* and *ought* to demand that savage and barbaric peoples become civilized by developing into an idealized Western civilizational form in the first instance precisely so that they could enter into the future cosmopolitan international legal state that would outlaw war in the last instance.[291] Accordingly, it is this 'inequalitarian formula' that issues a conception of informal hierarchy wherein European states enjoy *full* sovereignty while non-European polities are, in effect, awarded *qualified* sovereignty.

Much of defensive racism views emergent global interdependence as delivering the barbaric threat onto the doorstep of white civilization as, of course, it did for some offensive racists. Imperialism and global interdependence are particularly problematic because they create an open door for the non-white races to enter the white heartland; something that is greatly exacerbated by the pernicious effect of the Trojan Horse of liberal, multicultural politics within the Western citadel (as in the anti-imperialist racist cultural realism of the likes of Charles Pearson and Lothrop Stoddard). At first sight, defensive racism, which insists that Eastern races should be left alone and should be free of Western imperialist intervention, would appear to support an equalitarian regime of sovereignty and hence self-determination for all. But not much below the surface lurks the conception of 'residual sovereignty' or 'sovereignty-by-default'. For it is not that Eastern polities should be awarded sovereignty and be treated *on a par* with Western states, but rather that they are deemed to be unequal according to the application of the racial standard of civilization. Accordingly, defensive racism entails an informal civilizational hierarchical conception of racial apartheid such that the West *must* break off all direct contact with the East in large part so as to insulate the West from the contaminating effects that contact with the inferior races would inevitably bring. Thus anti-imperialism abroad coupled with strong immigration controls at home is the basis of their 'racial-apartheid conception of world politics'. Accordingly, sovereignty

[291] The development of global interdependence played a key part in Kant's theory of cosmopolitan right. Here he claims that '[t]he peoples of the earth have thus entered in varying degrees into a universal community, and it has developed to the point where a violation of rights in one part of the world is felt everywhere' (Kant 1970b: 107–8).

is not awarded to Eastern polities according to a cultural pluralist sensibility but is *derived through default*, as a contemptuous residue of this racist-apartheid politics that in turn implies an *inequalitarian* regime of gradated sovereignties.

But even if the reader accepts these arguments vis-à-vis pre-1945 Eurocentric and racist international theory, she might well question its salience in the post-1945 context. Indeed, she might cite the example of the English School, especially its pluralist wing, wherein one of its cardinal political values is precisely that of sovereign equality within international society. Two responses are pertinent here, both of which emanate from pluralism's Janus-faced, or schizophrenic, posture. Thus while I mentioned the imperialist side of pluralist thought in the last subsection, here I consider its anti-imperialist side. The critical point is that even this anti-imperialist position fails to embrace an equalitarian sovereignty regime. Here the issue at stake lies with Bull's belief that cultural self-determination for Eastern polities is the very cause of instability in modern global international society, precisely because these states lack the fully rational institutions of the West. Moreover, as with the anti-paternalist Eurocentrism of Smith and Kant, so Bull argued that global order and stability could only be achieved once the recalcitrant Eastern polities had undergone a full cultural conversion to the trappings of Western civilization. And Bull echoed their logic by refusing to countenance Western imperial/neo-imperial intervention in the East so as to effect this transformation in the post-1945 period, while advocating that the Eastern polities must conform to the 'developmental requirement'. Accordingly, because Bull denies full cultural self-determination to Eastern polities so he ends up by subscribing to an informal hierarchical conception of *qualified* sovereignty in the East and *full* sovereignty in the West.

But the reply might be that even if this is true for the classical pluralist wing of the English School, surely anti-imperialist realism and anti-imperialist Marxism are consistent with a fully developed universalist conception of sovereignty? Certainly the neo-Marxists would not hesitate in advocating sovereignty for all states.[292] But, I argue, the logic of their Eurocentrism leads them to adopt an *informal* civilizational hierarchical conception of world politics. In the first instance they judge or

---

[292] With the exception of Bill Warren (1980) who, like Marx and Engels, subscribes to a *formal* hierarchical vision of world politics.

read all societies according to a subliminal standard of civilization.[293] Thus world-systems theory views capitalist globalization as akin to the, albeit lamentable, triumph of the West and reconvenes the nineteenth-century three-worlds metageographical trope of civilized/barbaric/savage societies through its tripartite hierarchical vision of Western core, Eastern semi-periphery and Eastern periphery. Much the same is true of Gramscianism which views Anglo-Saxon hegemony and capitalist globalization as the, albeit lamentable, triumph of the West and reconvenes the tripartite metageography of the first world of advanced (civilized) Western capitalist states, the second world of Eastern (barbaric) neo-mercantilist states, and the third world of Eastern (savage) proto-states. And in the second instance, as explained in the first section of this chapter, they almost entirely deny agency to the East. Thus while this in no way returns us back to a hidden imperialist politics – even if it unwittingly naturalizes Western imperialism/neo-imperialism – nevertheless we encounter a conception of informal hierarchy and gradated sovereignty that creeps in through the subliminal Eurocentric backdoor. And moreover, their conception of globalization, which is grounded in the 'Eurocentric big-bang theory of world politics' that accords the West hyper-agency merely reinforces this problem. But what then of anti-imperialist realism?

It is certainly the case that neither Carr nor Morgenthau advocated an imperialist politics as part of their normative armoury.[294] However, Morgenthau's 'anti-imperialist' stance is to an important extent compromised by his desire to sanitize Western colonialism from the conceptual map of world politics, while also presenting decolonization as a gracious gift of the West. This forms an important prong of his deployment of the 'Eurocentric big-bang theory of world politics', in which the big bang of modernity explodes in Europe and then expands outwards to incorporate the rest of the world; or, what amounts to the standard Eurocentric trope of 'first the West, then the Rest' (cf. Chakrabarty 2000). And as was explained earlier, his reification of the West as the universal in world politics, coupled with his elision of Eastern agency means that he elevates the West to the highest normative referent in word politics, in effect awarding it full sovereignty and granting Eastern

---

[293] Notwithstanding those exceptional Marxists who draw on postcolonial or non-Eurocentric approaches (as mentioned earlier).
[294] And here I shall ignore Carr's approval of the nineteenth century Pax Britannica as a guarantor of order and progress (see especially Carr 1945: 13–17).

states 'qualified sovereignty'. As I also explained in Chapter 8, the same is true for E. H. Carr and Kenneth Waltz, notwithstanding the latter's residual paternalist-imperialist Eurocentric support for US hegemony at the very end of his book.

Finally, a softer test case for my argument lies with the defensive Eurocentric cultural realism of Huntington and Lind, who are explicit both in terms of their critique of imperialism and their celebration of Western civilization as the highest normative referent in world politics. Interestingly, their construct of 'globalization-as-barbaric threat' returns us directly to the arguments of the racist cultural realists, especially Stoddard and Charles Pearson. For these reasons it seems clear that they invoke an informal hierarchical conception that implies a sliding scale of gradated sovereignty.

Conclusion: 'To be or not to be a positivist – is that the question?'

All of which brings me to my final concluding point. For the upshot of the analysis of this book is that IR theory fails to deliver on one of its key promises – specifically to produce positivist, value-free analyses and universalist theories of world politics. Rather, it turns out that what we encounter in the vast majority of international theory is the provincial or parochial normative purpose of *defending and celebrating the ideal of the West in world politics*, whether this takes anti-imperialist or predominantly imperialist/neo-imperialist forms, expressed in either scientific racist or manifest/subliminal Eurocentric institutional guises. Accordingly, the message of this book provides a key dual challenge to the discipline of IR. First, we need to ascertain the extent to which IR scholars can concede the Eurocentric foundations of their discipline and, if so, we need to ascertain whether this is or is not a problem. For it may turn out that some Eurocentrics might wish to 'come out of the closet' and openly defend or even celebrate their Eurocentrism. If, however, the preference is to resist this manoeuvre then we need to work out how a non-Eurocentric foundation for IR theory might be reconstructed. But to those who wish to defend or celebrate their Eurocentrism the logical conclusion is that they have little choice but to accept that IR theory can no longer be represented as positivist, objective or value-free. In which case, the key question is no longer 'to be or not to be a positivist' but 'to be or not to be Eurocentric – that is the question'.

REFERENCES

Primary sources (pre-1945): Books, pamphlets, articles and dissertations

Angell, Norman 1913: *The Great Illusion* (London: G. P. Putnam & Sons).
Angell, Norman 1931: 'The New Imperialism and the Old Nationalism', *International Affairs* 10(1): 69–83.
Angell, Norman 1933: 'The International Anarchy', in Woolf (ed.): 19–66.
Angell, Norman 1937: *The Defence of the Empire* (London: Hamish Hamilton).
Bagehot, Walter 1872/2010: *Physics and Politics* (Whitefish, MT: Kessinger).
Bagehot, Walter 1974: *The Collected Works of Walter Bagehot*, VIII, ed. Norman St John-Stevas (London: The Economist).
Bernhardi, Friedrich von 1911/1914: *Germany and the Next War* (New York: Longmans, Green & Co.)
Bernhardi, Friedrich von 1912/1914: *Britain as Germany's Vassal* (London: W. M. Dawson & Sons).
Blair, James L. 1899: *Imperialism, Our New National Policy* (St Louis: Gottschalk).
Bloch, Jean de 1899: *The Future of War* (Boston, MA: Ginn & Co.).
Bowman, Isaiah 1922: *The New World Problems in Political Geography* (New York: World Book Company).
Bowman, Isaiah 1942: 'Geography versus Geopolitics', *Geographical Review* 32(4): 646–58.
Brailsford, H. N. 1915: *The War of Steel and Gold* (London: G. Bell & Sons).
Brigham, Albert Perry 1903: *Geographic Influences in American History* (New York: The Chautauqua Press).
Bright, John 1895: *The Public Letters of the Right Hon. John Bright*, (ed.) H. J. Leech (London: Sampson Low, Marston & Co.).
Brinton, Daniel G. 1901: *Races and Peoples* (Philadelphia: David McKay).
Buell, Raymond L. 1925: *International Relations* (New York: Henry Holt & Co.).
Bukharin, Nikolai 1929/2003: *Imperialism and World Economy* (London: Bookmarks).
Bunche, Ralph 1936: *A World View of Race* (Port Washington, NY: Kennikat Press).
Burgess, John W. 1890: *Political Science and Comparative Constitutional Law*, 2 vols (Boston, MA: Ginn & Co.).
Burgess, John W. 1895: 'The Ideal of the American Commonwealth', *Political Science Quarterly* 10(3): 404–25.

Burgess, John W. 1902: *Reconstruction and the Constitution 1865-1877* (New York: Charles Scribner & Sons).
Chamberlain, Houston Stewart 1910/1977: *Foundations of the Nineteenth Century*, I (London: Bodley Head).
Chamberlain, Houston Stewart 1912: *Foundations of the Nineteenth Century*, II (London: Bodley Head).
Cobden, Richard 1868a: *Political Writings*, I (London: William Ridgway).
Cobden, Richard 1868b: *Political Writings*, II (London: William Ridgway).
Commons, John R. 1907/1967: *Races and Immigrants in America* (New York: Augustus M. Kelly).
Davis, William Morris 1898: *Physical Geography* (Boston, MA: Ginn & Co.).
DeCourcy Ward, Robert, 1908: *Climate: Considered especially in Relation to Man* (London: G. P. Putnam & Sons).
Dickinson, G. Lowes 1918: *The European Anarchy* (London: Macmillan).
Dilke, Sir Charles 1868: *Greater Britain*, 2 vols (London: Macmillan).
Duncan, David 1911: *The Life and Letters of Herbert Spencer* (London: Williams & Norgate).
Du Bois, W. E. B. 1905: *The Souls of Black Folk* (London: Archibald Constable & Co.).
Du Bois, W. E. B. 1915: 'The African Roots of War', *The Atlantic Monthly* 115(5): 707–14. Posted at: www.webdubois.org/dbAfricanRWar.html
Ellis, Havelock 1911: *The Problem of Race Regeneration* (London: Cassell & Co.).
Fiske, John 1885: *American Political Ideas* (New York: Harper & Brothers).
Freeman, Edward 1879: *The Origin of the English Nation* (Michigan: University of Michigan Library).
Freeman, R. Austin 1921: *Social Decay and Regeneration* (London: Constable & Co.).
Freud, Sigmund 1930/1989: *Civilization and its Discontents* (New York: W. W. Norton).
Galton, Francis 1869: *Hereditary Genius* (London: Macmillan).
Galton, Francis 1883: *Inquiries into Human Faculty and its Development* (London: Macmillan).
Giddings, Franklin 1898: 'Imperialism?', *Political Science Quarterly* 13(4): 585–605.
Gobineau, Comte Arthur de 1853–5/1970: *Racial Inequality in Gobineau: Selected Political Writings*, (ed.) Michael D. Bidiss (London: Jonathan Cape).
Grant, Madison 1918: *The Passing of the Great Race Or the Racial Basis of European History* (New York: Charles Scribner & Sons).
Haldane, J. B. S. 1932: *The Inequality of Man and Other Essays* (London: Chatto & Windus).
Haldane, J. B. S. 1938: *Heredity and Politics* (London: Allen & Unwin).
Haushofer, Karl 1938/2002: *Geopolitics of the Pacific Ocean*, (ed.) Lewis A. Tambs (New York: Edwin Mellen Press).
Hegel, Georg W. F. 1837/2001: *The Philosophy of History* (Kitchener, Ontario: Batoche Books).

Hennig, Richard 1931: *Geopolitik* (Leipzig: B. G. Teubner).
Hilferding, Rudolf 1910/1985: *Finance Capital* (London: Routledge & Kegan Paul).
Hitler, Adolf 1939: *Mein Kampf* (London: Hurst & Blackett).
Hitler, Adolf, and Gerhard L. Weinberg 2003: *Hitler's Second Book: The Unpublished Sequel to Mein Kampf* (New York: Enigma Books).
Hoar, George F. 1900: *Our Duty to the Philippines* (New England: New England Anti-Imperialist League).
Hobhouse, Leonard T. 1904/1972: *Democracy and Reaction*, ed., Peter Clark (Brighton: Harvester).
Hobson, John A. 1898: 'Free Trade and Foreign Policy', *Contemporary Review* 74(2): 167–80.
Hobson, John A. 1901a: *The Psychology of Jingoism* (London: Grant Richards).
Hobson, John A. 1901b: *The Social Problem* (London: James Nisbet).
Hobson, John A. 1915a: *Towards International Government* (London: George Allen & Unwin).
Hobson, John A. 1915b: *A League of Nations* (London: Union of Democratic Control).
Hobson, John A. 1920: *The Morals of Economic Internationalism* (New York: Houghton).
Hobson, John A. 1921: *Problems of a New World* (London: George Allen & Unwin).
Hobson, John A. 1932: *The Recording Angel* (London: George Allen & Unwin).
Hobson, John A. 1934: *Democracy and a Changing Civilisation* (London: Bodley Head).
Hobson, John A. 1938/1968: *Imperialism: A Study* (London: George Allen & Unwin).
Hosmer, James 1903: *A Short History of Anglo-Saxon Freedom* (New York: Charles Scribner & Sons).
Huntington, Ellsworth 1915: *Climate and Civilization* (New Haven, CT: Yale University Press).
Huntington, Ellsworth 1919: *World-Power and Evolution* (New Haven, CT: Yale University Press).
Huntington, Ellsworth 1935: *Tomorrow's Children: The Goal of Eugenics* (New York: John Wiley).
Huxley, Julian 1926: 'The Case for Eugenics', *Sociological Review* 18: 279–90.
Hyndman, Henry Mayers 1919/2010: *The Awakening of Asia* (Memphis, TN: General Books).
Ireland, Alleyne 1905: *The Far Eastern Tropics* (Boston, MA: Houghton, Mifflin & Co.).
James, C. L. R. 1938/2001: *The Black Jacobins* (London: Penguin).
Jordan, David Starr 1901: *Imperial Democracy* (New York: D. Appleton & Co.).
Jordan, David Starr 1907: *The Human Harvest* (Boston, MA: American Unitarian Association).
Jordan, David Starr 1914/2009: *War and Waste* (Ithaca, NY: Cornell University Press).
Jordan, David Starr 1915: *War and the Breed* (Boston, MA: Beacon Press).
Jordan, David Starr 1919: *Democracy and World Relations* (New York: World Book Co.).

Kant, Immanuel 1970a: 'Idea for a universal history with a cosmopolitan purpose', in H. Reiss (ed.), *Kant's Political Writings* (Cambridge: Cambridge University Press), 41–53.
Kant, Immanuel 1970b: 'Perpetual peace: a philosophical sketch', in H. Reiss (ed.), 93–130.
Kant, Immanuel 1970c: 'The metaphysics of morals', in H. Reiss (ed.), 131–75.
Kant, Immanuel 1970d: 'Review of Herder's Ideas on the Philosophy of the History of Mankind', in H. Reiss (ed.), 201–20.
Kant, Immanuel 1997a: 'On the different races of man', in Emmanuel Chukwudi Eze (ed.), *Race and the Enlightenment* (Oxford: Blackwell), 38–48.
Kant, Immanuel 1997b: 'On National Characteristics', in E. C. Eze (ed.), 49–58.
Kant, Immanuel 1997c: 'Physical Geography', in E. C. Eze (ed.), 58–64.
Kant, Immanuel 2001a: 'On the use of teleological principles in philosophy (1788)', in Robert Bernasconi (ed.), *Race* (Oxford: Blackwell), 37–56.
Kant, Immanuel 2001b: *Kant: On History* (Upper Saddle River, NJ: Prentice Hall).
Kellogg, Vernon 1916: *Military Selection and Race Deterioration* (Oxford: Clarendon).
Kidd, Benjamin 1894: *Social Evolution* (London: Macmillan).
Kidd, Benjamin 1898: *The Control of the Tropics* (New York: Macmillan).
Kjellén, Rudolf 1917: *Der Staat als Lebensform* (Leipzig: Hirzel).
Knox, Robert 1850: *The Races of Men* (Philadelphia: Lea & Blanchard).
Lamarck, Jean-Baptiste 1809/2011: *Zoological Philosophy* (Cambridge: Cambridge University Press).
Laski, Harold J. 1910: 'The Scope of Eugenics', *Westminster Review* 174: 25–34.
Laski, Harold J. 1933: 'The Economic Foundations of Peace', in Woolf (ed.): 499–547.
Laski, Harold J. 1940: 'Nationalism and the Future of Civilization', in *The Danger of Being a Gentleman* (London: George Allen & Unwin): 189–225.
Lenin, Vladimir 1915/1975: 'On the Slogan for a United States of Europe', in Lenin, *Selected Works*, 629–32.
Lenin, Vladimir 1916/1973: *Imperialism, the Highest Stage of Capitalism* (Peking: Foreign Languages Press).
Lenin, Vladimir I. 1917/1975: 'The Military Programme of the Proletarian Revolution', in Lenin, *Selected Works*, 740–9.
Lenin, Vladimir 1975: *Selected Works*, I (Moscow: Progress Publishers).
List, Friedrich 1841/1909: *The National System of Political Economy* (London: Longmans, Green & Co.).
Locke, John 1689/2005: *Two Treatises of Government*, (ed.) Peter Laslett (Cambridge: Cambridge University Press).
Lodge, Henry Cabot 1899: *The War With Spain* (New York: Harper & Brothers).
Luxemburg, Rosa 1915/1951: *The Accumulation of Capital* (London: Routledge & Kegan Paul).
MacDonald, Ramsay 1907: *Labour and the Empire* (London: George Allen).
McLellan, David 1975: *Marx* (London: Fontana).

Mackinder, Halford J. 1904: 'The Geographical Pivot of History', *The Geographical Journal* 23(4): 421–37.
Mackinder, Halford J. 1919: *Democratic Ideals and Reality* (New York: Henry Holt & Co.)
Mahan, Alfred Thayer 1897: *The Influence of Seapower upon History* (London: Sampson, Law, Marston).
Malthus, Thomas Robert 1798/1971: *An Essay on the Principle of Population* (New York: Augustus Kelly).
Marx, Karl 1845/1965: *The German Ideology* (London: Lawrence & Wishart).
Marx, Karl 1867/1954: *Capital*, I (London: Lawrence & Wishart).
Marx, Karl 1867/1959: *Capital*, III (London: Lawrence & Wishart).
Marx, Karl 1843/1959: *A World Without Jews*, ed. Dagobert D. Runes (New York: Philosophical Library).
Marx, Karl 1969: *Karl Marx on Colonialism and Modernization*, ed. Shlomo Avineri (New York: Anchor).
Marx, Karl 1973a: *Surveys from Exile*, ed. David Fernbach (Harmondsworth: Penguin).
Marx, Karl 1973b: *Grundrisse* (New York: Vintage).
Marx, Karl, and Friedrich, Engels 1848/1967: *The Communist Manifesto* (Harmondsworth: Penguin).
Marx, Karl, and Friedrich Engels 1971: *Ireland and the Irish Question* (Moscow: Progress Publishers).
Mill, John Stuart 1836/1977: 'Civilization', in J. M. Robson (ed.), *Collected Works of John Stuart Mill*, XVIII (Toronto: University of Toronto Press), 119–47.
Mill, John Stuart 1859/1984: 'A Few Words on Non-Intervention', in J. M. Robson (ed.), *Collected Works of John Stuart Mill*, XXI (Toronto: Toronto University Press): 111–24.
Mill, John Stuart 1859/1998: 'On Liberty', in J. S. Mill, *On Liberty and Other Essays* (Oxford: Oxford University Press), 5–128.
Mill, John Stuart 1861/1998: *Considerations on Representative Government*, in Mill, *On Liberty and Other Essays*, 447–67.
Mitrany, David 1933: *The Progress of International Government* (London: George Allen & Unwin).
Money, Leo George Chiozza 1925: *The Peril of the White* (London: W. Collins).
Montesquieu, Baron Charles de 1748/1900: *The Spirit of Laws* (New York: The Colonial Press).
Muir, Ramsay 1917/2010: *The Expansion of Europe* (Memphis, TN: General Books).
Muirhead, John H. 1900/1997: 'What Imperialism Means', in Boucher (ed.): 237–52.
Nicolai, G. F. 1918: *The Biology of War* (New York: The Century Co.)
Novicow, Jacques 1911: *War and its Alleged Benefits* (New York: Henry Holt & Co.)
Osborn, Henry Fairfield 1918: 'Preface to the New Edition', in Grant: xi–xiii.
Pearson, Charles Henry 1894: *National Life and Character: A Forecast* (London: Macmillan).

Pearson, Karl 1905: *National Life from the Standpoint of Science* (London: Adam & Charles Black).
Powers, Harry H. 1898: 'The War as a Suggestion of Manifest Destiny', *Annals of the American Academy of Political and Social Science* 12: 1–20.
Putnam Weale, B. L. 1910: *The Conflict of Colour* (New York: Macmillan).
Ratzel, Friedrich 1898: 'Studies in Political Areas II: Intellectual, Political, and Economic Effects of Large Areas', *American Journal of Sociology* 3(4): 449–63.
Reade, W. Winwood 1864: *Savage Africa* (New York: Harper & Brothers).
Reid, Whitelaw 1900: *Problems of Expansion* (New York: The Century Co.).
Reinsch, Paul S. 1903: 'Review of *Imperialism: A Study*, by John A. Hobson', *Political Science Quarterly* 18(3): 531–3.
Reinsch, Paul S. 1905a: 'The Negro Race and European Civilization', *American Journal of Sociology* 11(2): 145–67.
Reinsch, Paul S. 1905b: *Colonial Administration* (New York: Macmillan).
Ricardo, David 1819: *On the Principles of Political Economy and Taxation* (Georgetown, DC: Joseph Milligan).
Richet, Charles 1906: *Peace and War* (London: J. M. Dent & Co.)
Ripley, William Z. 1900: *The Races of Europe* (London: Kegan Paul, Trench, Trübner & Co.).
Ritchie, David G. 1900: *Ethical Democracy*, ed. Stanton Coit (London: Grant Richards).
Robertson, J. M. 1900: *Patriotism and Empire* (London: Grant Richards).
Roosevelt, Theodore 1894/1897: 'National Life and Character', in Roosevelt, *American Ideals* (New York: G. P. Putnam & Sons), 289–320.
Roosevelt, Theodore 1905: *The Strenuous Life* (New York: The Century Co.)
Ross, Edward A. 1914: *The Old World in the New* (London: T. Fisher Unwin).
Sanger, Margaret 1932: 'A Plan for Peace', *Birth Control Review* 16(4): 107–8.
Seeley, John Robert 1883/1906: *The Expansion of England* (Leipzig: Velhagen & Klansing).
Semple, Ellen Churchill 1911: *Influences of Geographic Environment* (New York: Henry Holt & Co.).
Shaw, George Bernard (ed) 1900: *Fabianism and the Empire: A Manifesto by the Fabian Society* (London: Grant Richards).
Shaw, George Bernard 1903/2009: *Man and Superman* (New York: Classic Books International).
Sidgwick, Henry 1897: *The Elements of Politics* (London: Macmillan).
Smith, Adam 1759/1982: *The Theory of Moral Sentiments* (Indianapolis: Liberty Fund).
Smith, Adam 1762–3/1982: *Lectures on Jurisprudence* (Indianapolis: Liberty Fund).
Smith, Adam 1776/1937: *The Wealth of Nations* (New York: The Modern Library).
Snow, A. H. 1911: 'Review of *The Great Illusion* by Norman Angell', *American Journal of International Law* 5(2): 557–66.
Spencer, Herbert 1851/1864: *Social Statics* (New York: D. Appleton & Co.).
Spencer, Herbert 1881: *The Man Versus the State* (London: Williams & Norgate).

Spencer, Herbert 1893/1966: *The Principles of Ethics*, II (Osnabrück: Otto Zeller).
Spencer, Herbert 1896/2004: *Principles of Sociology*, I (Honolulu: University Press of the Pacific).
Spencer, Herbert 1902: *Facts and Comments* (New York: D. Appleton & Co.).
Spengler, Oswald 1919/1932: *The Decline of the West* (London: Allen & Unwin).
Spykman, Nicholas J. 1942: *America's Strategy in World Politics* (New York: Harcourt, Brace & Co.)
Stoddard, Lothrop 1920: *The Rising Tide of Color Against White World Supremacy* (New York: Charles Scribner & Sons).
Stoddard, Lothrop 1922a: *The New World of Islam* (London: Chapman & Hall).
Stoddard, Lothrop 1922b: *The Revolt Against Civilization* (London: Chapman & Hall).
Stoddard, Lothrop 1935: *Clashing Tides of Colour* (London: Charles Scribner & Sons).
Storey, Moorfield 1901: *Our New Departure* (Boston, MA: George Ellis).
Strong, Josiah 1885: *Our Country* (New York: The Baker & Taylor Co.).
Strong, Josiah 1889: *The United States and the Future of the Anglo-Saxon Race* (London: Saxon & Co.).
Stubbs, William 1874: *The Constitutional History of England* (Oxford: Clarendon).
Sumner, William Graham 1879/1969: *The Forgotten Man and Other Essays* (Manchester, NH: Ayer Publishing).
Sumner, William Graham 1883/2007: *What Social Classes Owe to Each Other* (Bel Air, CA: BiblioBazaar).
Sumner, William Graham 1911: *War and Other Essays* (New Haven, CT: Yale University Press).
Townshend, Meredith 1911/2010: *Asia and Europe* (Memphis, TN: General Books).
Treitschke, Heinrich von 1898/1916: *Politics* (New York: Macmillan).
Trotsky, Leon 1932-3/1967: *History of the Russian Revolution*, I (London: Sphere).
Vitoria, Francisco di 1539/1991: 'On the American Indians', in Anthony Pagden and Jeremy Lawrance (eds.), *Vitoria: Political Writings* (Cambridge: Cambridge University Press), 231-92.
Wallace, A. R. 1900: *Studies: Scientific and Social*, 2 vols (London: Macmillan).
Ward, Lester F. 1884: 'Review of William Graham Sumner's, *What Social Classes Owe Each Other*', *Man* 4: 100-1.
Ward, Lester F. 1903/2002: *Pure Sociology* (Honolulu: University Press of the Pacific).
Webb, Sidney 1907: *The Decline in the Birth-Rate* (London: Fabian Society).
Webb, Sidney 1910-11: 'Eugenics and the poor law: the minority report', *Eugenics Review* 11: 233-41.
Wells, H. G. 1902: *Anticipations of the Reaction of Mechanical and Scientific Progress upon Human Life and Thought* (London: Chapman & Hall).
Williams, Eric 1944: *Capitalism and Slavery* (London: Andre Deutsch).
Wilson, Woodrow 1901a: 'The Reconstruction of the Southern States', *Atlantic Monthly* 87(519): 2-11. Posted at: digital.library.cornell.edu/cache/c/a/7/ca711c6f64cfd0f3e922cbd63afa921e/atla008

Wilson, Woodrow 1901b: 'Democracy and Efficiency', *Atlantic Monthly* 87(521): 289–99. Posted at: www.theatlantic.com/ideastour/politics/wilson-full.mhtml

Wilson, Woodrow 1902a: *A History of the American People*, Vol. 5 (New York: Harper & Brothers).

Wilson, Woodrow 1902b: 'The Ideals of America', *Atlantic Monthly* 90(6): 721–34. Posted at: www.theatlantic.com/issues/02dec/wilson.htm

Wilson, Woodrow 1898/1918: *The State* (New York: D.C. Heath & Co.) (3rd ed. revised by Edward Elliott).

Woolf, Leonard 1916: *International Government* (London: George Allen & Unwin).

Woolf, Leonard 1920: *Empire and Commerce in Africa* (London: George Allen & Unwin).

Woolf, Leonard 1928/1933: *Imperialism and Civilization* (London: Hogarth Press).

Woolf, Leonard (ed) 1933a: *The Intelligent Man's Way to Prevent War* (London: Victor Gollancz).

Woolf, Leonard 1933b: 'Introduction', in Woolf (ed.): 7–18.

Zimmern, Alfred 1934: *The Third British Empire* (Oxford: Oxford University Press).

Zimmern, Alfred 1936: *The League of Nations and the Rule of Law* (London: Macmillan).

Primary sources (post-1945): Books, pamphlets, articles and dissertations

Alderson, Kai, and Andrew Hurrell (eds) 2000: *Hedley Bull on International Society* (London: Palgrave Macmillan).

Anderson, Perry 1974: *Lineages of the Absolutist State* (London: Verso).

Anievas, Alexander 2011: 'Capitals, States, and Conflict: International Political Economy and Crisis, 1919–1945', (Unpublished PhD thesis, Department of Politics and International Studies, University of Cambridge).

Archibugi, Daniele, David Held, and M. Köhler 1998: *Re-imagining Political Community* (Cambridge: Polity).

Arrighi, Giovanni 1994: *The Long Twentieth Century* (London: Verso).

Augelli, Enrico, and Craig N. Murphy 1988: *America's Quest for Supremacy* (London: Pinter).

Boot, Max 2001: 'The Case for American Empire', *The Weekly Standard* (15/10/2001). Posted at: www.drake.edu/artsci/PolSci/pols75/boot.pdf

Braudel, Fernand 1981: *Civilization and Capitalism, $15^{th}-18^{th}$ Century*, I (London: Collins).

Braudel, Fernand 1982/2002: *Civilization and Capitalism, $15^{th}-18^{th}$ Century*, II (London: Phoenix).

Braudel, Fernand 1992: *Civilization and Capitalism, $15^{th}-18^{th}$ Century*, III (Berkeley: University of California Press).

Brzezinski, Zbigniew 1993: *Out of Control* (New York: Scribner).

Brzezinski, Zbigniew 2004: *The Choice* (New York: Basic Books).

Bull, Hedley 1966: 'International Theory: The Case for a Classical Approach', *World Politics* 18(3): 361–77.
Bull, Hedley 1972/2000: 'International Relations as an Academic Pursuit', in Alderson and Hurrell (eds.): 246–64.
Bull, Hedley 1977: *The Anarchical Society* (London: Macmillan).
Bull, Hedley 1980/2000: 'The European International Order', in Alderson and Hurrell (eds): 170–87.
Bull, Hedley 1984/2000: 'Justice in International Relations: The 1983 Hagey Lectures', in Alderson and Hurrell (eds): 206–45.
Bull, Hedley 1984a: The Emergence of Universal International Society', in Bull and Watson (eds): 119–26.
Bull, Hedley 1984b: 'The Revolt against the West', in Bull and Watson (eds): 217–28.
Bull, Hedley and Adam Watson (eds) 1984a: *The Expansion of International Society* (Oxford: Oxford University Press).
Bull, Hedley and Adam Watson 1984b: 'Introduction', in Bull and Watson (eds.): 1–9.
Bull, Hedley and Adam Watson 1984c: 'Conclusion', in Bull and Watson (eds.): 425–35.
Caplan, Richard 2007: 'From Collapsing States to Neotrusteeship: The limits to solving the problem of "precarious statehood" in the 21st century', *Third World Quarterly* 28(2): 231–44.
Carr, E. H. 1945: *Nationalism and After* (London: Macmillan).
Carr, E. H. 1946/1981: *The Twenty Years' Crisis 1919–1939* (London: Macmillan).
Carr, E. H. 1951: *The New Society* (London: Macmillan).
Carr, E. H. 1964: *What is History?* (London: Pelican).
Carr-Saunders, Alexander 1926: *Eugenics* (London: Oxford University Press).
Cooper, Robert 2002: 'The New Liberal Imperialism', *The Observer* (7 April). Posted at: www/observer.guardian.co.uk/print/0,38584388912-102273,00.htm
Cooper, Robert 2004: *The Breaking of Nations* (London: Atlantic Books).
Cox, Robert W. 1981/1986: 'Social Forces, States and World Orders: Beyond International Relations Theory', in R. O. Keohane (ed.): 204–54.
Cox, Robert W. 1987: *Production, Power and World Order* (New York: Columbia University Press).
Cox, Robert W. 1996: *Approaches to World Order* (Cambridge: Cambridge University Press).
Cox, Robert W. 2001: 'Civilizations and the Twenty-First Century: Some theoretical considerations', *International Relations of the Asia-Pacific* 1(1): 105–30.
Davis, Horace B. 1967: *Nationalism and Socialism* (New York: Monthly Review Press).
Diamond, Larry 1992: 'Promoting Democracy', *Foreign Policy* 87 (Summer): 25–46.
Ferguson, Niall 2002: *Empire* (London: Allen Lane).
Ferguson, Niall 2004: *Colossus* (Harmondsworth: Penguin).
Feuer, Lewis 1986: *Imperialism and the Anti-Imperialist Mindset* (Buffalo, NY: Prometheus Books).

Finnemore, Martha 1996a: *National Interests in International Society* (Ithaca: Cornell University Press).
Finnemore, Martha 1996b: 'Norms, Culture, and World Politics: Insights from Sociology's Institutionalism', *International Organization* 50(2): 325–47.
Finnemore, Martha 2003a: *The Purpose of Intervention* (Ithaca: Cornell University Press).
Finnemore, Martha 2003b: 'Constructing Norms of Humanitarianism', in Katzenstein (ed.): 153–85.
Frank, Andre Gunder 1967: *Capitalism and Underdevelopment in Latin America* (London: Monthly Review Press).
Frank, Andre Gunder 1998: *ReOrient* (Berkeley: University of California Press).
Frank, Andre Gunder, and Barry K. Gills (eds) 1996: *The World System* (London: Routledge).
Friedman, Thomas 1999: *The Lexus and the Olive Tree* (London: Harper Collins).
Friedman, Thomas, and Robert Kaplan 2002: 'States of Discord', *Foreign Policy* 129 (March–April): 64–70.
Fukuyama, Francis 1989: 'The End of History?', *The National Interest* 16: 3–18. www.wesjones.com/eoh.htm#source
Fukuyama, Francis 1992: *The End of History and the Last Man* (London: Hamish Hamilton).
Fukuyama, Francis 2005: 'Building Democracy after Conflict: "Stateness First"', *Journal of Democracy* 16(1): 84–8.
Fukuyama, Francis 2006: *After the Neocons* (London: Profile Books).
Gill, Stephen 1990: *American Hegemony and the Trilateral Commission* (Cambridge: Cambridge University Press).
Gill, Stephen 1995a: 'Globalisation, Market Civilisation and Disciplinary Neoliberalism', *Millennium* 24(3): 399–423.
Gill, Stephen 1995b: 'Theorizing the Interregnum: The Double Movement and Global Politics in the 1990s', in Hettne (ed.): 65–99.
Gill, Stephen 1995c: 'The Global Panopticon? The Neoliberal State, Economic Life and Democratic Surveillance', *Alternatives* 20(1): 1–49.
Gills, Barry K. 1993: 'The Hegemonic Transition in East Asia: A Historical Perspective', in Stephen Gill (ed.), *Gramsci, Historical Materialism and International Relations* (Cambridge: Cambridge University Press), 186–212.
Gilpin, Robert 1975: *U. S. Power and the Multinational Corporation* (New York: Basic Books).
Gilpin, Robert 1981: *War and Change in World Politics* (Cambridge: Cambridge University Press).
Gilpin, Robert 1987: *The Political Economy of International Relations* (Princeton: Princeton University Press).
Gilpin, Robert 2001: *Global Political Economy* (Princeton: Princeton University Press).

Gong, Gerrit W. 1984: *The Standard of 'Civilisation' in International Society* (Oxford: Clarendon).
Held, David 1995: *Democracy and the Global Order* (Cambridge: Polity).
Held, David, Anthony McGrew, David Goldblatt, and Jonathan Perraton 1999: *Global Transformations* (Cambridge: Polity).
Held, David, and Heikki Patomäki 2006: 'Problems of Global Democracy: A Dialogue', *Theory, Culture & Society* 23(5): 115–33.
Helman, G. B., and S. R. Ratner 1992-3: 'Saving Failed States', *Foreign Policy* 89: 3–20.
Herbst, Jeffrey 2004: 'Let Them Fail: State Failure in theory and practice – implications for policy', in R. I. Rotberg (ed.), *When States Fail* (Princeton: Princeton University Press).
Hettne, Bjorn (ed) 1995: *International Political Economy: Understanding Global Disorder* (London: Zed).
Hirst, Paul, and Barry Hindess 1977: *Modes of Production and Social Formation* (London: Routledge & Kegan Paul).
Holzgrefe, J. L., and R. O. Keohane (eds) *Humanitarian Intervention* (Cambridge: Cambridge University Press).
Huntington, Samuel P. 1993: 'The Clash of Civilizations?', *Foreign Affairs* 72(3): 22–49.
Huntington, Samuel P. 1996: *The Clash of Civilizations and the Remaking of World Order* (London: Touchstone).
Huntington, Samuel P. 2004: *Who are We?* (New York: Simon & Schuster).
Ignatieff, Michael 2003a: 'The Burden', *New York Times Magazine* (5 January). Posted at: www.nytimes.com/2003/01/05magazine/the-american-empire-the-burden.html?pagewanted=all&5cr=pm.
Ignatieff, Michael 2003b: 'Empire Lite', *Prospect* 83 (February). Posted at: www.prospectmagazine.co.uk/2003/02/empirelite/
Ignatieff, Michael 2005: 'Introduction: American Exceptionalism and Human Rights', in M. Ignatieff (ed.), *American Exceptionalism and Human Rights* (Princeton: Princeton University Press), 1–26.
Ikenberry, G. John 2004: 'Liberalism and Empire: Logics of Order in the American Unipolar Age', *Review of International Studies* 30(4): 609–30.
Ikenberry, G. John, and Anne-Marie Slaughter 2006: 'Forging a World of Liberty Under Law: U.S. National Security in the 21st Century', *The Princeton Project on National Security* (Woodrow Wilson School of Public and International Affairs, Princeton University): www.princeton.edu/~ppns/report/FinalReport.pdf
Kagan, Robert 1998: 'The Benevolent Empire', *Foreign Policy* 111 (Summer): 24–35.
Kagan, Robert 2004: *Paradise and Power* (London: Atlantic Books).
Kagan, Robert 2008: *The Return of History and the End of Dreams* (London: Atlantic Books).
Kagan, Robert, and William Kristol (eds) 2000: *Present Dangers* (San Francisco: Encounter).
Kaplan, Robert D. 1994: 'The Coming Anarchy', *Atlantic Monthly* (February): www.TheAtlantic.com/atlantic/election/connection/foreign/anarcf.htm

Kaplan, Robert D. 2003: *Warrior Politics* (New York: Vintage).
Kaplan, Robert D. 2006: *Imperial Grunts* (New York: Random House).
Keck, Margaret E., and Kathryn Sikkink 1998: *Activists Beyond Borders* (Cambridge: Cambridge University Press).
Kennedy, Paul M. 1988: *The Rise and Fall of the Great Powers* (London: Unwin Hyman).
Kennedy, Paul M. 1993: *Preparing for the Twenty-First Century* (New York: Random House).
Keohane, Robert O. 1984: *After Hegemony* (Princeton, NJ: Princeton University Press).
Keohane, Robert O. (ed) 1986: *Neorealism and its Critics* (New York: Columbia University Press).
Keohane, Robert O. 1989: *International Institutions and State Power* (Boulder, CO: Westview Press).
Keohane, Robert O. 1993: 'Institutional Theory and the Realist Challenge after the Cold War', in D. Baldwin (ed.): 269–300.
Keohane, Robert O. 1998: 'Beyond Dichotomy: Conversations Between International Relations and Feminist Theory', *International Studies Quarterly* 42: 193–8.
Keohane, Robert O. 2003: 'Political Authority after Intervention: Gradations in Sovereignty', in Holzgrefe and Keohane (eds.): 275–98.
Kindleberger, Charles P. 1973: *The World in Depression 1929–1939* (Berkeley: University of California Press).
Kindleberger, Charles P. 1996: *World Economic Primacy, 1500–1990* (Oxford: Oxford University Press).
King, Gary, Robert O. Keohane, and Sidney Verba 1994: *Designing Social Inquiry* (Princeton: Princeton University Press).
Klotz, Audie 1995: *Norms in International Relations* (Ithaca: Cornell University Press).
Knutsen, Torbjørn 1997: *A History of International Relations Theory* (Manchester, Manchester University Press).
Knutsen, Torbjørn 2008: 'A Lost Generation? IR Scholarship before World War I', *International Politics* 45(6): 650–74.
Krasner, Stephen D. 1978: *Defending the National Interest* (Princeton: Princeton University Press).
Krasner, Stephen D. 1992: 'Realism, Imperialism, and Democracy: A Response to Gilbert', *Political Theory* 20(1): 38–52.
Krasner, Stephen D. 2004: 'Sharing Sovereignty: New institutions for collapsed and failing states', *International Security* 29(2): 85–120.
Krauthammer, Charles 1990–91: 'The Unipolar Moment', *Foreign Affairs* 70(1): 23–33.
Krauthammer, Charles 2004: 'Democratic Realism: An American Foreign Policy for a Unipolar World', (American Enterprise Institute Short Publications Series).
Kristol, William, and Robert Kagan 1996: 'Toward a Neo-Reaganite Foreign Policy', *Foreign Affairs* 75(4): 18–32.
Kurth, James 1994: 'The Real Clash', *The National Interest*. Posted at: findarticles.com/p/articles/mi_m2751/is_n37/ai_16315038?tag=artBody;col1

Kurtz, Stanley 2003: 'Democratic Imperialism: A Blueprint', *Policy Review* 118. Posted at: www.hoover.org/publications/policy-review/article/6426

Laclau, Ernesto 1971: 'Feudalism and Capitalism in Latin America', *New Left Review* 67: 19–38.

Layne, Christopher 1989: 'Realism Redux: Strategic Independence in a Multipolar World', *SAIS Review* 9(2): 19–44.

Lind, William S. 1991: 'Defending Western Culture', *Foreign Policy* 84: 40–50.

Lyon, Peter 1993: 'The Rise and Fall and Possible Revival of International Trusteeship', *Journal of Commonwealth & Comparative Politics* 31(1): 96–110.

Mallaby, Sebastian 2002: 'The Reluctant Imperialist: Terrorism, Failed States, and the Case for American Empire', *Foreign Affairs* 81(2): 2–7.

Mathieu, Xavier 2010: 'Re-assessing Sovereignty in International Politics: The Complex Relationship between Concept and Reality', MA Research thesis (Institute of Political Science, University of Bordeaux).

Mearsheimer, John J. 1995: 'The False Promise of International Institutions', *International Security* 19(3): 5–49.

Mearsheimer, John J. 2001: *The Tragedy of Great Power Politics* (New York: W.W. Norton).

Morgenthau, Hans 1948/1967: *Politics Among Nations* (New York: Alfred A. Knopf).

Moynihan, Daniel Patrick 1993: *Pandaemonium* (Oxford: Oxford University Press).

Mueller, John 1990: *Retreat From Doomsday* (New York: Basic Books).

Munck, Ronaldo 1984: *Politics and Dependency in the Third World* (London: Zed).

Murphy, Craig N., and Roger Tooze (eds) 1991: *The New International Political Economy* (Boulder, CO: Lynne Rienner).

Nussbaum, Martha C. 1995: 'Introduction', in M. C. Nussbaum and Jonathan Glover (eds.), *Women, Culture and Development* (Oxford: Clarendon): 1–34.

Owen, John 1994: 'How Liberalism produces Democratic Peace', *International Security* 19(2): 87–125.

Pfaff, William 1993: *The Wrath of Nations* (New York: Simon & Schuster).

Pipes, Daniel 1990: 'The Muslims are Coming! The Muslims are Coming!', *National Review* (November). Posted at www.danielpipes.org/article.php/198

Rawls, John 1999: *The Law of Peoples* (London: Harvard University Press).

Rieff, David 1999: 'A New Age of Liberal Imperialism?', *World Policy Journal* 16(2): 1–10.

Risse, Thomas, Steven C. Ropp, and Kathryn Sikkink (eds) 1999: *The Power of Human Rights* (Cambridge: Cambridge University Press).

Robinson, William I. 2004: *A Theory of Global Capitalism* (Baltimore: Johns Hopkins University Press).

Rostow, Walt W. 1960: *The Stages of Economic Growth* (Cambridge: Cambridge University Press).

Russett, Bruce 1990: *Controlling the Sword* (Cambridge, MA: Harvard University Press).

Sakomoto, Yoshikazu 1995: 'Democratization, Social Movements and World Order', in Hettne (ed.): 129–43.
Särkkä, Timo 2009: 'Hobson's Imperialism: A Study in Late-Victorian Political Thought', PhD thesis (University of Jyväskylä, Finland: Jyväskylä Studies in Humanities 118).
Slater, David 2004: *Geopolitics and the Post-Colonial* (Oxford: Blackwell).
Slaughter, Ann-Marie 1995: 'International Law in a World of Liberal States', *European Journal of International Law* 6(4): 503–38.
Slaughter, Anne-Marie, and Lee Feinstein 2004: 'The Duty to Prevent', *Foreign Affairs* 83(1): 136–50.
Søbjerg, Lene Mosegaard 2007: 'Trusteeship and the Concept of Freedom', *Review of International Studies* 33(3): 457–88.
Téson, Fernando 2003: 'The Liberal Case for Humanitarian Intervention', in Holzgrefe and Keohane (eds.): 93–129.
Van der Pijl, Kees 2007: *Nomads, Empire, State*, I (London: Pluto).
Van der Pijl, Kees 2010: *The Foreign Encounter in Myth and Religion*, II (London: Pluto).
Vincent, R. John 1984: 'Racial Equality', in Bull and Watson (eds.): 239–54.
Wallerstein, Immanuel 1974a: *The Modern World-System*, I (London: Academic Press).
Wallerstein, Immanuel 1974b: 'The Rise and Future Demise of the World Capitalist System: Concepts for Comparative Analysis', *Comparative Studies in Society and History* 16(4): 387–415.
Wallerstein, Immanuel 1974c: 'Dependence in an Interdependent World: The Limited Possibilities of Transformation within the Capitalist World Order', *African Studies Review* 17(1): 1–26.
Wallerstein, Immanuel 1984: *The Politics of the World-Economy* (Cambridge: Cambridge University Press).
Wallerstein, Immanuel 1996: 'World System versus World-Systems', in Frank and Gills (eds.): 292–6.
Waltz, Kenneth N. 1979: *Theory of International Politics* (New York: McGraw Hill).
Waltz, Kenneth N. 1986: 'Reflections on *Theory of International Politics*: A Response to my Critics', in R. O. Keohane (ed.): 322–45.
Waltz, Kenneth N. 1993a: 'The New World Order', *Millennium* 22(2): 187–95.
Waltz, Kenneth N. 1993b: 'The Emerging Structure of International Politics', *International Security* 18(2): 44–79.
Waltz, Kenneth N. 1999: 'Globalization and Governance', *PS: Political Science and Politics* 32(4): 693–700.
Warren, Bill 1980: *Imperialism: Pioneer of Capitalism* (London: Verso).
Watson, Adam 1984: 'European International Society and its Expansion', in Bull and Watson (eds.): 13–32.
Watson, Adam 1992/2009: *The Evolution of International Society* (London: Routledge).

Wheeler, Nicholas J. 1992: 'Pluralist or Solidarist Conceptions of International Society: Bull and Vincent on Humanitarian Intervention', *Millennium* 21(3): 463–87.
Wheeler, Nicholas J. 2000: *Saving Strangers* (Oxford: Oxford University Press).
Wight, Martin 1977: *Systems of States* (Leicester: Leicester University Press).
Wight, Martin 1992: *International Theory* (New York: Holmes & Meier).
Wolf, Martin 2005: *Why Globalization Works* (London: Yale Nota Bene).
Zakaria, Fareed 2002: 'Our Way', *The New Yorker* (October 14). Available at: www.fareedzakaria.com/articles/nyer/101402.html
Zakaria, Fareed 2003: 'The Arrogant Empire', *Newsweek* (March 24). Available at: www.fareedzakaria.com/articles/newsweek/032403.html

Secondary sources (post-1945): Books and articles

Abernethy, David B. 2000: *The Dynamics of Global Dominance* (New Haven, CT: Yale University Press).
Abu-Lughod, Janet L. 1989: *Before European Hegemony* (Oxford: Oxford University Press).
Acharya, Amitav 1997: 'The Periphery as the Core: The Third World and Security Studies', in K. Krause and Michael C. Williams, *Critical Security Studies* (London: Routledge): 299–328.
Adib-Moghaddam, Arshin 2011: *A Metahistory of the Clash of Civilisations* (London: Hurst).
Agathangelou, Anna M., and L. H. M. Ling 2009: *Transforming World Politics* (London: Routledge).
Ahmad, Aijaz 2008: *In Theory* (London: Verso).
Alexandrowicz, Charles H. 1967: *An Introduction to the History of the Law of Nations in the East Indies* (Oxford: Clarendon).
Alexandrowicz, Charles H. 1971: 'The Juridical Expression of the Sacred Trust of Civilization', *The American Journal of International Law* 65(1): 149–59.
Allerfeldt, Kristofer 2004: 'Wilsonian Pragmatism? Woodrow Wilson, Japanese Immigration, and the Paris Peace Conference', *Diplomacy & Statecraft* 15(3): 545–72.
Allett, John 1981: *New Liberalism* (Toronto: University of Toronto Press).
Al-Rodhan, Nayef R. F. 2009: *Sustainable History and the Dignity of Man* (London: Transaction Publishers).
Ambrosius, Lloyd E. 1987: *Woodrow Wilson and the American Diplomatic Tradition* (Cambridge: Cambridge University Press).
Ambrosius, Lloyd E. 2002: *Wilsonianism* (Houndmills: Palgrave Macmillan).
Amin, Samir 1989: *Eurocentrism* (London: Zed Books).
Amos, Valerie, and Pratibha Parmar 1984: 'Challenging Imperial Feminism', *Feminist Review* 17: 3–19.
Anghie, Antony 2005: *Imperialism, Sovereignty and the Making of International Law* (Cambridge: Cambridge University Press).

Anievas, Alexander (ed) 2010: *Marxism and World Politics* (London: Routledge).
Apel, Karl-Otto 1997: 'Kant's Toward Perpetual Peace as Historical Prognosis from the Point of View of Moral Duty', in J. Bohman and M. Lutz-Bachmann (eds.), *Perpetual Peace* (Cambridge, MA: MIT Press), 79–110.
Ashworth, Lucian M. 2002: 'Did the Realist-Idealist Debate Really Happen? A Revisionist History of International Relations', *International Relations* 16(1): 33–51.
Ashworth, Lucian M. 2006: 'Where are the idealists in interwar International Relations?', *Review of International Studies* 32(2): 291–308.
Ashworth, Lucian M. 2011: 'Realism and the Spirit of 1919: Halford Mackinder, Geopolitics and the Reality of the League of Nations', *European Journal of International Relations* 17(2): 279–302.
Ashworth, Lucian M. 2012: 'Mapping a New World: Geography and the Interwar Study of International Relations', *International Studies Quarterly* 56(2).
Bain, William 2003: *Between Anarchy and Society* (Oxford: Oxford University Press).
Bala, Arun 2006: *The Dialogue of Civilizations in the Birth of Modern Science* (Houndmills: Palgrave Macmillan).
Baldwin, David (ed) 1993: *Neorealism and Neoliberalism* (New York: Columbia University Press).
Balibar, Etienne 1991: 'Is There a Neo-Racism?', in Etienne Balibar and Immanuel Wallerstein, *Race, Nation, Class* (London: Verso): 17–28.
Bannister, Robert C. 1979: *Social Darwinism: Science and Myth in Anglo-American Thought* (Philadelphia: Temple University Press).
Banton, Michael 1977: *The Idea of Race* (London: Tavistock).
Banton, Michael 2002: *The International Politics of Race* (Cambridge: Polity).
Barendse, R. J. 2002: *The Arabian Seas* (London: M. E. Sharpe).
Barkan, Elazar 1992: *The Retreat of Scientific Racism* (Cambridge: Cambridge University Press).
Barkawi, Tarak 2001: 'War Inside the Free World: The Democratic Peace and the Cold War in the Third World', in Barkawi and Laffey (eds.): 107–28.
Barkawi, Tarak 2005: *Globalization and War* (Lanham: Rowman & Littlefield).
Barkawi, Tarak, and Mark Laffey (eds) 2001: *Democracy, Liberalism, and War* (London: Lynne Rienner).
Barkawi, Tarak and Mark Laffey 2006: 'The Postcolonial Moment in Security Studies', *Review of International Studies* 32(2): 329–52.
Barker, Martin 1981: *The New Racism* (London: Junction Books).
Bartelson, Jens 1995: *A Genealogy of Sovereignty* (Cambridge: Cambridge University Press).
Bassin, Mark 1987: 'Race contra Space: the conflict between German *Geopolitik* and National Socialism', *Political Geography Quarterly* 6(2): 115–34.

Bell, Duncan S. A. 2001: 'International relations: the dawn of a historiographical turn?', *British Journal of Politics & International Relations* 3(1): 115-26.
Bell, Duncan S. A. 2009: 'Writing the World: Disciplinary History and Beyond', *International Affairs* 85(1): 3-22.
Belloni, Robert 2007: 'The Trouble with Humanitarianism', *Review of International Studies* 33(3): 451-74.
Bernal, Martin 1991: *Black Athena*, I (London: Vintage).
Bernasconi, Robert 2001: 'Who Invented the Concept of Race? Kant's Role in the Enlightenment Construction of Race', in R. Bernasconi, *Race* (Oxford: Blackwell): 11-36.
Bernasconi, Robert, and Tommy L. Lott 2000: 'Introduction', in Bernasconi and Lott (eds.), *The Idea of Race* (Indianapolis: Hackett Publishing Co.): xii-xviii.
Bhabha, Homi K. 1994: *The Location of Culture* (London: Routledge).
Bhambra, Gurminder 2011: 'Talking Among Themselves? Weberian and Marxist Historical Sociologies as Dialogues Without "Others"', *Millennium* 39(3): 667-81.
Bieler, Andreas, and Adam David Morton (eds) 2006: *Images of Gramsci* (London: Routledge).
Bieler, Andreas, and Adam David Morton 2008: 'The deficits of discourse in IPE: turning base metal into gold?', *International Studies Quarterly* 52(1): 103-28.
Blaney, David L. 2001: 'Realist Spaces/Liberal Bellicosities: Reading the Democratic Peace as World Democratic Theory', in Barkawi and Laffey (eds.): 25-44.
Blaney, David L., and Naeem Inayatullah 2008: 'International Relations from Below', in C. Reus-Smit and Duncan Snidal (eds.), *The Oxford Handbook of International Relations* (Oxford: Oxford University Press): 663-74.
Blaney, David L., and Naeem Inayatullah 2010: *Savage Economics* (London: Routledge).
Bodelsen, C. A. 1960: *Studies in Mid-Victorian Imperialism* (London: Heinemann).
Boli, J. W., and G. M. Thomas (eds.) 1998: *Constructing World Culture* (Stanford: Stanford University Press).
Bonnett, Alistair 2004: *The Idea of the West* (London: Palgrave Macmillan).
Boucher, David (ed) 1997a: *The British Idealists* (Cambridge: Cambridge University Press).
Boucher, David 1997b: 'Introduction', in Boucher (ed.): viii-xxxiii.
Bowden, Brett 2009: *The Empire of Civilization* (Chicago: University of Chicago Press).
Bowden, Brett, and Leonard Seabrooke (eds) 2006: *Global Standards of Market Civilization* (London: Routledge).
Brenner, Robert 1977: 'The Origins of Capitalist Development: a Critique of Neo-Smithian Marxism', *New Left Review* 104: 25-92.
Brenner, Robert 1982: 'The Agrarian Roots of European Capitalism', *Past & Present* 97 (Nov.): 16-113.

Brewer, Anthony 1980: *Marxist Theories of Imperialism* (London: Routledge & Kegan Paul).
Brown, Chris 2000: 'International Political Theory–A British Social Science?', *British Journal of Politics and International Relations* 2(1): 114–23.
Brown, Garrett W. 2008: 'The Laws of Hospitality, Asylum Seekers and Cosmopolitan Right: A Kantian Response to Jacques Derrida', *European Journal of Political Theory* 9(3): 308–27.
Brown, Garrett W. 2009: *Grounding Cosmopolitanism* (Edinburgh: Edinburgh University Press).
Bruff, Ian 2008: *Culture and Consensus in European Varieties of Capitalism* (Houndmills: Palgrave Macmillan).
Burchill, Scott, and Andrew Linklater (eds) 2009: *Theories of International Relations* (Houndmills: Palgrave Macmillan).
Bulbeck, Chilla 1998: *Re-Orienting Western Feminisms* (Cambridge: Cambridge University Press).
Buzan, Barry 2004: *From International to World Society?* (Cambridge: Cambridge University Press).
Buzan, Barry 2010: 'Culture and International Society', *International Affairs* 86(1): 1–26.
Buzan, Barry, Charles A. Jones, and Richard Little 1993: *The Logic of Anarchy* (Columbia: Columbia University Press).
Buzan, Barry, and Richard Little 2000: *International Systems in World History* (Oxford: Oxford University Press).
Buzan, Barry, and Richard Little 2001: 'Why International Relations has Failed as an Intellectual Project and What to do about It', *Millennium* 30(1): 19–39.
Cain, Peter J. 2002: *Hobson and Imperialism* (Oxford: Oxford University Press).
Callahan, William A. 2004: 'Nationalising International Theory: Race, Class, and the English School', *Global Society* 18(4): 305–23.
Callinicos, Alex 2009: *Imperialism and Global Political Economy* (Cambridge: Polity).
Campbell, David 1992: *Writing Security* (Manchester: Manchester University Press).
Campbell, J. A., and D. N. Livingstone 1983: 'Neo-Lamarckism and the Development of Geography in the United States and Great Britain', *Transactions of the Institutes of British Geographers* 8(3): 267–94.
Carvalho, Benjamin de, Halvard Leira, and John M. Hobson 2011: 'The Big Bangs of IR: The Myths that your teachers still tell you about 1648 and 1919', *Millennium* 39(3): 735–58.
Chakrabarty, Dipesh 2000: *Provincializing Europe* (Princeton: Princeton University Press).
Chandler, David 2004: '*The Responsibility to Protect*? Imposing the "Liberal Peace"', *International Peacekeeping* 11(1): 59–81.

Chang, Ha-Joon 2002: *Kicking Away the Ladder* (London: Anthem).
Chowdhry, Geeta, and Sheila Nair (eds.) 2002: *Power, Postcolonialism and International Relations* (London: Routledge).
Colás, Alejandro 2002: 'The Class Politics of Globalization', in Mark Rupert and Hazel Smith (eds.), *Historical Materialism and Globalization* (London: Routledge): 191–209.
Conrad, Sebastian, and Dominic Sachsenmaier (eds) 2007: *Competing Visions of World Order* (Houndmills: Palgrave Macmillan).
Cox, Michael 2004: 'Empire, Imperialism and the Bush Doctrine', *Review of International Studies* 30(4): 585–608.
Crawford, R. M. A., and D. S. L. Jarvis (eds) 2001: *International Relations–Still an American Social Science?* (Albany: SUNY Press).
Crook, Paul 1994: *Darwinism, War and History* (Cambridge: Cambridge University Press).
Cumings, Bruce 1992: 'The Wicked Witch of the West is Dead: Long Live the Wicked Witch of the East', in M. J. Hogan (ed.), *The End of the Cold War* (Cambridge: Cambridge University Press): 87–102.
Cutler, A. Claire 2001: 'Critical Reflections on the Westphalian Assumptions of International Law and Organization: A Crisis of Legitimacy', *Review of International Studies* 27(2): 133–50.
Dawson, Grant 2002: 'Preventing "a great moral evil": Jean de Bloch's *The Future of War* as anti-revolutionary pacifism', *Journal of Contemporary History* 37(1): 5–19.
Denemark, Robert A., J. Friedman, B. K. Gills, and G. Modelski (eds) 2000: *World System History* (New York: Routledge).
Derrida, Jacques 2000: 'Foreign Question', in Anne Dufourmantelle (ed.), *Of Hospitality* (Stanford: Stanford University Press): 3–75.
Deudney, Daniel 1996: 'Binding Sovereigns: Authorities, Structures, and Geopolitics in Philadelphian Systems', in Biersteker and Weber (eds.): 190–239.
Donnelly, Jack 1998: 'Human Rights: A new standard of civilization?', *International Affairs* 74(1): 1–24.
Donnelly, Jack 2009: Rethinking Political Structures: From "ordering principles" to "vertical differentiation"–and beyond', *International Theory* 1(1): 49–86.
Doty, Roxanne Lynn 1996: *Imperial Encounters* (Minneapolis: University of Minnesota Press).
Doyle, Michael W. 1983a: 'Kant, Liberal Legacies, and Foreign Affairs', *Philosophy and Public Affairs* 12(3): 205–35.
Doyle, Michael W. 1983b: 'Kant, Liberal Legacies, and Foreign Affairs, Part 2', *Philosophy and Public Affairs* 12(4): 323–53.
Drinnon, Richard 1980: *Facing West* (Minneapolis: University of Minnesota Press).
Dryzek, John, and Stephen T. Leonard 1988: 'History and Discipline in Political Science', *American Political Science Review* 82(4): 1245–60.

Dunne, Timothy J. 1997: 'Colonial Encounters in International Relations: Reading Wight, Writing Australia', *Australian Journal of International Affairs* 51(3): 309–23.
Dunne, Timothy J. 1998: *Inventing International Society* (London: Macmillan).
Dunne, Timothy J., and Nicholas J. Wheeler 1996: 'Hedley Bull's Pluralism of the Intellect and Solidarism of the Will', *International Affairs* 72(1): 91–107.
Etherington, Norman 1984: *Theories of Imperialism* (London: Croom Helm).
Eze, Emmanuel Chukwudi (ed.) 1997: *Race and the Enlightenment* (Oxford: Blackwell).
Fearon, James D., and David D. Laitin 2004: 'Failed States and Protectorates', *International Security* 28(4): 5–43.
Fidler, David P. 2000: 'A Kinder, Gentler System of Capitulation? International Law, Structural Adjustment, and the Standard of Liberal, Globalized Civilization', *Texas International Law Journal* 35(3): 387–413.
Freeden, Michael 1979: 'Eugenics and Progressive Thought: A Study in Ideological Affinity', *Historical Journal* 22(3): 745–71.
Füredi, Frank 1994: *The New Ideology of Imperialism* (London: Pluto).
Füredi, Frank 1998a: *The Silent War* (London: Pluto).
Füredi, Frank 1998b: *Colonial Wars and the Politics of Third World Nationalism* (London: I. B. Tauris).
Füredi, Frank 2007: *Invitation to Terror* (London: Continuum).
Gabriel, Jürg-Martin 1994: *Worldviews and Theories of International Relations* (London: Macmillan).
Gallagher, John, and Ronald Robinson 1953: 'The Imperialism of Free Trade', *Economic History Review* 6(1): 1–15.
Gasman, Daniel 1971/2004: *The Scientific Origins of National Socialism* (London: Transaction Publishers).
Gerschenkron, Alexander 1962: *Economic Backwardness in Historical Perspective* (Cambridge, MA: Harvard University Press).
Geulen, Christian 2007: 'The Common Grounds of Conflict: Racial Visions of World Order 1880–1940', in Conrad and Sachsenmaier (eds.): 69–96.
Ghazanfar, S. M. 2006: *Islamic Civilization* (Lanham, Maryland: Scarecrow Press).
Giddens, Anthony 1985: *The Nation-State and Violence* (Cambridge: Polity).
Goody, Jack 2004: *Islam in Europe* (Cambridge: Polity).
Goonatilake, Susantha 1998: *Toward a Global Science* (New Delhi: Vistaar Publications).
Gossett, Thomas F. 1963/1997: *Race: The History of an Idea in America* (Oxford: Oxford University Press).
Gould, Stephen J. 1992: *The Mismeasure of Man* (London: Penguin).
Grieco, Joseph M. 1993: 'Anarchy and the Limits of Cooperation: A Realist Critique of the Newest Liberal Institutionalism', in Baldwin (ed.): 116–42.
Griffiths, Martin 1992: *Realism, Idealism, and International Politics* (London: Routledge).

Grovogui, Siba N. 1996: *Sovereigns, Quasi Sovereigns and Africans* (Minneapolis: University of Minnesota Press).
Grovogui, Siba N. 2002: 'Regimes of Sovereignty: International Morality and the African Condition', *European Journal of International Relations* 8(3): 315-38.
Gruffydd-Jones, Branwen (ed) 2006: *Decolonizing International Relations* (Lanham: Rowman & Littlefield).
Grunberg, Isabelle 1990: 'Exploring the "myth" of hegemonic stability', *International Organization* 44(4): 431-77.
Guilhot, Nicolas 2008: 'The Realist Gambit: Postwar American Political Science and the Birth of IR Theory', *International Political Sociology* 2(4): 281-304.
Hall, Martin, and John M. Hobson 2010: 'Liberal International Theory: Eurocentric but not always Imperialist?', *International Theory* 2(2): 210-45.
Hall, Martin, and Patrick T. Jackson (eds) 2007: *Civilizational Identity* (London: Routledge).
Hannaford, Ivan 1996: *Race: The History of an Idea in the West* (Baltimore: Johns Hopkins University Press).
Hannerz, Ulf 1991: 'Scenarios for Peripheral Cultures', in Anthony D. King (ed.), *Culture, Globalization and the World-System* (London: Macmillan).
Harding, Sandra 1998: *Is Science Multicultural?* (Bloomington: Indiana University Press).
Hasenclever, Andreas, Peter Mayer, and Volker Rittberger 1997: *Theories of International Regimes* (Cambridge: Cambridge University Press).
Hawkins, Mike 1997: *Social Darwinism in European and American Thought 1860-1945* (Cambridge: Cambridge University Press).
Hehir, Aidan 2008: 'The Myth of the Failed State and the War on Terror', *Journal of Intervention and State-Building* 1(3): 307-32.
Heske, Henning 1987: 'Karl Haushofer: His role in German geopolitics and in Nazi politics', *Political Geography Quarterly* 6(2): 125-44.
Higgott, Richard 1991: 'Toward a non-hegemonic IPE: An Antipodean Perspective', in Murphy and Tooze (eds.): 97-128.
Hindess, Barry 2001: 'Not at Home in the Empire', *Social Identities* 7(3): 363-77.
Hirson, Baruch 1991: 'Colonialism and Imperialism', *New Interventions* 2(1). Posted at: www.whatnexjournal.co.uk/pages/Newint/Baruch.html
Hobson, John M. 1997: *The Wealth of States* (Cambridge: Cambridge University Press).
Hobson, John M. 2000: *The State and International Relations* (Cambridge: Cambridge University Press).
Hobson, John M. 2002: 'What's at Stake in "Bringing Historical Sociology *Back* into International Relations"? Transcending "Chronofetishism" and Tempocentrism" in International Relations', in Stephen Hobden and J.M. Hobson (eds.), *Historical Sociology of International Relations* (Cambridge: Cambridge University Press): 3-41.

Hobson, John M. 2004: *The Eastern Origins of Western Civilisation* (Cambridge: Cambridge University Press).

Hobson, John M. 2007: 'Deconstructing the Eurocentric Clash of Civilizations: De-Westernizing the West by Acknowledging the Dialogue of Civilizations', in Hall and Jackson (eds.), 149–65.

Hobson, John M. 2009: 'Provincializing Westphalia: Eastern origins of sovereignty in the Oriental global age', *International Politics* 46(6): 671–90.

Hobson, John M. 2011a: 'Introduction. John A. Hobson, the International Man: A Report from Earth', in J. A. Hobson, *Selected Writings of John A. Hobson 1932-1938: The Struggle for the International Mind*, eds. J. M. Hobson and C. Tyler (London: Routledge): 1–78.

Hobson, John M. 2011b: 'What's at stake in the neo-Trotskyist debate? Towards a non-Eurocentric historical sociology of uneven and combined development', *Millennium* 40(1): 147–66.

Hobson, John M., and J. C. Sharman 2005: 'The Enduring Place of Hierarchy in World Politics: Tracing the Social Logics of Hierarchy and Political Change', *European Journal of International Relations* 11(1): 63–98.

Hobson, John M., and Leonard Seabrooke (eds) 2007: *Everyday Politics of the World Economy* (Cambridge: Cambridge University Press).

Hoffmann, Stanley 1977/2001: 'An American Social Science: International Relations', in Crawford and Jarvis (eds.): 27–51.

Hofstadter, Michael 1968/1992: *Social Darwinism in American Thought* (New York: Beacon Press).

Hunt, Michael H. 1987: *Ideology and US Foreign Policy* (London: Yale University Press).

Hutchings, Kimberly 2011: 'Dialogue between Whom? The Role of the West/Non-West Distinction in Promoting Global Dialogue in IR', *Millennium* 39(3): 639–47.

Inayatullah, Naeem, and David L. Blaney 2004: *International Relations and the Problem of Difference* (London: Routledge).

Iriye, Akira 1997: 'The Second Clash: Huntington, Mahan, and Civilizations', *Harvard International Review* 19(2): 44–5, 70.

Ishihara, Shintaro 1991: *The Japan That Can Say No* (New York: Simon & Schuster).

Jackson, Robert H. 1990: *Quasi-States* (Cambridge: Cambridge University Press).

Jackson, Robert H. 2000: *The Global Covenant* (New York: Oxford University Press).

Jahn, Beate 2000: *The Cultural Construction of International Relations* (Houndmills: Palgrave).

Jahn, Beate 2005: 'Barbarian Thoughts: imperialism in the philosophy of John Stuart Mill', *Review of International Studies* 31(3): 599–618.

Jahn, Beate (ed) 2006a: *Classical Theory in International Relations* (Cambridge: Cambridge University Press).

Jahn, Beate 2006b: 'Classical Smoke, Classical Mirror: Kant and Mill in liberal international relations theory', in Jahn (ed.): 178–203.
Jones, Greta 1980: *Social Darwinism and English Thought* (Atlantic Highlands, NJ: Humanities Press).
Kang, David C. 2007: *China Rising* (New York: Columbia University Press).
Katzenstein, Peter J. (ed) 2003: *The Culture of National Security* (New York: Columbia University Press).
Katzenstein, Peter J. 2009: 'A World of Plural and Pluralist Civilizations: Multiple Actors, Traditions, and Practices', in Katzenstein (ed.), *Civilizations in World Politics* (London: Routledge): 1–40.
Kaufman, Stuart J., Richard Little, and William C. Wohlforth (eds) 2007: *The Balance of Power in World History* (London: Palgrave).
Kayaoglu, Turan 2010: *Legal Imperialism* (Cambridge: Cambridge University Press).
Keal, Paul 2003: *European Conquest and the Rights of Indigenous Peoples* (Cambridge: Cambridge University Press).
Kearns, Gerry 2004: 'The Political Pivot of Geography', *The Geographical Journal* 170(4): 337–46.
Keene, Edward 2002: *Beyond the Anarchical Society* (Cambridge: Cambridge University Press).
Keene, Edward 2005: *International Political Thought* (Cambridge: Polity).
Kelly, Alfred 1971: *The Descent of Darwin* (Chapel Hill: University of North Carolina Press).
Kevles, Daniel J. 1985: *In the Name of Eugenics* (Berkeley: University of California Press).
Krenn, Michael L. (ed) 1999: *The African American Voice in U.S. Foreign Policy since World War II* (London: Garland).
Kwon, Heonik 2010: *The Other Cold War* (New York: Columbia University Press).
Laffey, Mark, and Jutta Weldes 2008: 'Decolonizing the Cuban Missile Crisis', *International Studies Quarterly* 52(3): 555–77.
Lake, David A. 1996: 'Anarchy, Hierarchy, and the Variety of International Relations, *International Organization* 50(1): 1–33.
Lake, David A. 2009: 'TRIPS across the Atlantic: Theory and Epistemology in IPE', *Review of International Political Economy* 16(1): 47–57.
Lake, Marilyn, and Henry Reynolds 2008: *Drawing the Global Colour Line* (Cambridge: Cambridge University Press).
Larrain, Jorge 1991: 'Classical Political Economists and Marx on Colonialism and "Backward" Nations', *World Development* 19(2/3): 225–43.
Lasch, Christopher 1958: 'The Anti-Imperialists, the Philippines, and the Inequality of Man', *The Journal of Southern History* 24(3): 319–31.
Lauren, Paul Gordon 1996: *Power and Prejudice* (Boulder, CO: Westview Press).

Lawson, George 2008: 'A Realistic Utopia? Nancy Fraser, Cosmopolitanism and the Making of a Just World Order', *Political Studies* 56(4): 881–906.
Leonard, Thomas C. 2005: 'Mistaking Eugenics for Social Darwinism: Why Eugenics is Missing from the History of American Economics', *History of Political Economy* 37: 200–33.
Leuchtenburg, William E. 1952: 'Progressivism and Imperialism: The Progressive Movement and American Foreign Policy, 1898–1916', *The Mississippi Valley Historical Review* 39(3): 483–504.
Levin, N. Gordon 1973: *Woodrow Wilson and World Politics* (Oxford: Oxford University Press).
Lindqvist, Sven 2002: *Exterminate all the Brutes* (London: Granta).
Ling, L. H. M. 2002: *Postcolonial International Relations* (Houndmills: Palgrave Macmillan).
Linklater, Andrew 1998: *The Transformation of Political Community* (Cambridge: Polity).
Linklater, Andrew 2009: 'The English School', in Burchill and Linklater (eds.): 86–110.
Linklater, Andrew, and Hidemi Suganami 2006: *The English School of International Relations* (Cambridge: Cambridge University Press).
Livingstone, David N. 1992: *The Geographical Tradition* (Oxford: Blackwell).
Long, David 1996: *Towards a New Liberal Internationalism* (Cambridge: Cambridge University Press).
Long, David 2005: 'Paternalism and the Internationalization of Imperialism: J. A. Hobson on the International Government of the "Lower Races"', in Long and Schmidt (eds.): 71–91.
Long, David, and Brian C. Schmidt (eds) 2005a: *Imperialism and Internationalism in the Discipline of International Relations* (New York: SUNY).
Long, David, and Brian C. Schmidt 2005b: 'Introduction', in Long and Schmidt (eds.): 1–21.
Long, David, and Peter Wilson (eds) 1995: *Thinkers of the Twenty Years' Crisis* (Oxford: Clarendon).
Loomba, Ania 1998: *Colonialism/Postcolonialism* (New York: Routledge).
MacMaster, Neil 2001: *Racism in Europe* (Houndmills: Palgrave).
Magnusson, Lars 1994: 'Hobson and Imperialism: An Appraisal', in J. Pheby (ed.) *J. A. Hobson After Fifty Years* (London: St Martin's Press): 143–62.
Malik, Kenan 1996: *The Meaning of Race* (New York: Palgrave).
Malmvig, Helle 2006: *State Sovereignty and Intervention* (London: Routledge).
Mann, Michael 2004: *Fascists* (Cambridge: Cambridge University Press).
Matin, Kamran 2007: 'Uneven and Combined Development in World History: The International Relations of State-Formation in Premodern Iran', *European Journal of International Relations* 13(3): 419–47.
Matin, Kamran 2012: 'Redeeming the Universal: Postcolonialism and the Inner Life of Eurocentrism', *European Journal of International Relations* 18.

Mazrui, Ali 1984: 'Africa Entrapped: Between the Protestant Ethic and the Legacy of Westphalia', in Bull and Watson (eds.): 289–308.
McCarthy, Thomas 2009: *Race, Empire, and the Idea of Human Development* (Cambridge: Cambridge University Press).
Meek, Ronald L. 1976: *Social Science and the Ignoble Savage* (Cambridge: Cambridge University Press).
Mehta, Uday Singh 1999: *Liberalism and Empire* (Chicago: University of Chicago Press).
Meyer, J. W., J. Boli, and G. M. Thomas 1997: 'World Society and the Nation-State', *American Journal of Sociology* 103: 144–81.
Miles, Robert 1993: *Racism after 'Race Relations'* (London: Routledge).
Millennium 2011: 'Dialogue in International Relations', *Millennium* 39(3) (Special Issue): 607–803.
Miller, J. D. B. 1995: 'Norman Angell and Rationality in International Relations', in Long and Wilson (eds.): 100–21.
Miller, Richard W. 2003: 'Respectable Oppressors, Hypocritical Liberators: Morality, Intervention, and Reality', in D. K. Chaterjee and D. E. Scheid (eds.), *Ethics and Foreign Intervention* (Cambridge: Cambridge University Press): 215–50.
Mitchell, Harvey 1965: 'Hobson Revisited', *Journal of the History of Ideas* 26(3): 397–416.
Mohanty, C. T. 1986: 'Under Western Eyes: Feminist Scholarship and Colonial Discourses', *Boundary 2* 12(3): 333–58.
Mohanty, C. T. 2003: '"Under Western Eyes" Revisited: Feminist Solidarity through Anticapitalist Struggles', *Signs* 28(2): 499–535.
Morefield, Jeanne 2005: *Covenants Without Swords* (Princeton: Princeton University Press).
Mori, K. 1978: '"Marx and Underdevelopment": His Thesis on the "Historical Roles of British Free Trade" Revisited', *Annals of the Institute of Social Science* (University of Tokyo): 19: 35–61.
Morton, Adam David 2007: *Unravelling Gramsci* (London: Pluto).
Muthu, Sankar 2003: *Enlightenment Against Empire* (Princeton: Princeton University Press).
Muthu, Sankar 2008: 'Adam Smith's Critique of International Trading Companies: Theorizing "Globalization" in the Age of Enlightenment', *Political Theory* 36(2): 185–212.
Nair, Sheila (ed) 2007: 'Forum: Edward W. Said and International Relations', *Millennium* 36(1): 77–145.
Nandy, Ashis 1983: *The Intimate Enemy* (Delhi: Oxford University Press).
Neocleous, Mark 2011: 'The Police of Civilization: The War on Terror as Civilizing Offensive', *International Political Sociology* 5(2): 144–59.
Neumann, Iver 1998: *Uses of the Other* (Minneapolis: University of Minnesota Press).

Nossal, Kim Richard 2001: 'Tales That Textbooks Tell: Ethnocentricity and Diversity in American Introductions to International Relations', in Crawford and Jarvis (eds.): 167–86.
O'Brien, Peter 2009: *European Perceptions of Islam and America from Saladin to George W. Bush* (New York: Palgrave Macmillan).
O'Hagan, Jacinta 2007: 'Discourses of Civilizational Identity', in Hall and Jackson (eds.): 15–31.
O'Leary, Brendan 1989: *The Asiatic Mode of Production* (Oxford: Blackwell).
Olson, Mancur 1965: *The Logic of Collective Action* (Cambridge, MA: Harvard University Press).
Olson, Mancur, and Richard J., Zeckhauser 1966: 'An Economic Theory of Alliances', *Review of Economics and Statistic* 48(3): 266–79.
Onuf, Nicholas G. 1989: *World of Our Making* (Columbia, SC: University of South Carolina Press).
Oren, Ido 2003: *Our Enemies and US* (Ithaca: Cornell University Press).
Osiander, Andreas 1998: 'Rereading Early Twentieth-Century IR Theory: Idealism Revisited', *International Studies Quarterly* 42(3): 409–32.
Pagden, Anthony 1995: *Lords of All the World* (London: Yale University Press).
Parekh, Bhikhu 1997: 'The West and its Others', in Keith Ansell-Pearson, Benita Parry, and Judith Squires (eds.), *Cultural Readings of Imperialism* (London: Lawrence & Wishart): 173–93.
Pasha, Mustapha Kamal 2006: 'Islam, "Soft" Orientalism and Hegemony: A Gramscian Rereading', in Andreas Bieler and Adam David Morton (eds.), *Images of Gramsci* (London: Routledge): 149–64.
Pateman, Carole 2007: 'The Settler Contract', in Carole Pateman and Charles W. Mills, 35–78.
Pateman, Carole, and Charles W. Mills 2007: *Contract and Domination* (Cambridge: Polity).
Paterson, J. H. 1987: 'German Geopolitics Reassessed', *Political Geography Quarterly* 6(2): 107–14.
Patomäki, Heikki 2003: 'Problems of Democratizing Global Governance: Time, Space and the Emancipatory Process', *European Journal of International Relations* 9(3): 347–76.
Paul, Darel E. (1999) 'Sovereignty, Survival and the Westphalian Blind Alley in International Relations', *Review of International Studies* 25(2): 217–31.
Paul, Diane 1984: 'Eugenics and the Left', *Journal of the History of Ideas* 45(4): 567–90.
Peet, Richard 1985: 'The Social Origins of Environmental Determinism', *Annals of the Association of American Geographers* 75(3): 309–33.
Perry, Richard J. 2007: *'Race' and Racism* (New York: Palgrave Macmillan).
Persaud, Randolph B. 2001: *Counter-Hegemony and Foreign Policy* (New York: SUNY Press).

Scott, James C. 1993: 'Everyday Forms of Resistance', *PRIME*: Occasional Papers Series, No. 15, International Peace Research Institute Meigaku, Yokohama.
Sebestyen, Victor 2009: *Revolution 1989: The Fall of the Soviet Empire* (New York: Pantheon).
Seth, Sanjay (ed) 2011a: *Postcolonial Theory and International Relations* (London: Routledge).
Seth, Sanjay 2011b: 'Postcolonial Theory and the Critique of International Relations', *Millennium* 40(1): 167–83.
Sewell, Dennis 2009: *The Political Gene* (London: Picador).
Shields, Stuart 2009: *The International Political Economy of Transition* (London: Routledge).
Shilliam, Robbie 2006: 'What about Marcus Garvey? Race and the Transformation of Sovereignty Debate', *Review of International Studies* 32(3): 379–400.
Shilliam, Robbie 2009: 'The Atlantic as a Vector of Uneven and Combined Development', *Cambridge Review of International Affairs* 22(1): 69–88.
Shilliam, Robbie (ed) 2011: *International Relations and Non-Western Thought* (London: Routledge).
Simons, Anna, and David Tucker 2007: 'The Misleading Problem of Failed States: A "Socio-Geography" of Terrorism in the Post-9/11 Era', *Third World Quarterly* 28(2): 387–401.
Simpson, Gerry 2004: *Great Powers and Outlaw States* (Cambridge: Cambridge University Press).
Skocpol, Theda 1977: 'Wallerstein's World Capitalist System: A Theoretical and Historical Critique', *American Journal of Sociology* 82(5): 1075–90.
Slotkin, Richard 1973: *Regeneration Through Violence* (Middleton: Weslyan University Press).
Smith, Michael J. 1986: *Realist Thought from Weber to Kissinger* (London: Louisiana University Press).
Smith, Steve 1995: 'The Self Images of a Discipline: A Genealogy of International Relations Theory', in Ken Booth and Steve Smith (eds.), *International Relations Theory Today* (Cambridge: Polity): 1–37.
Soloway, Richard 1995: *Demography and Degeneration* (Chapel Hill: University of North Carolina Press).
Stocking, George W. 1982: *Race, Culture and Evolution* (Chicago: University of Chicago Press).
Sullivan, Eileen P. 1983: 'Liberalism and Imperialism: J. S. Mill's Defense of the British Empire', *Journal of the History of Ideas* 44(4): 599–617.
Suzuki, Shogo 2009: *Civilization and Empire* (London: Routledge).
Sylvest, Caspar 2009: *British Liberal Internationalism, 1880–1913* (Manchester: Manchester University Press).
Teschke, Benno 2003: *The Myth of 1648* (London: Verso).

Thies, Cameron G. 2002: 'Progress, History and Identity in International Relations Theory: The Case of the Idealist-Realist Debate', *European Journal of International Relations* 8(2): 147–85.
Tickner, Arlene B., and Ole Wæver (eds) 2009: *International Relations Scholarship Around the World* (Oxford: Routledge).
Tickner, J. Ann 1992: *Gender in International Relations* (New York: Columbia University Press).
Tickner, J. Ann 2001: *Gendering World Politics* (New York: Columbia University Press).
Tickner, J. Ann 2011: 'Retelling IR's Foundational Stories: Some Feminist and Postcolonial Perspectives', *Global Change, Peace & Security* 23(1): 5–13.
Tilly, Charles 1990: *Coercion, Capital, and European States, AD 990–1990* (Oxford: Blackwell).
Tinker, Hugh 1977: *Race, Conflict and the International Order* (London: Macmillan).
Todorov, Tzvetan 1984: *The Conquest of America* (New York: Harper and Row).
Townshend, Jules 1990: *J. A. Hobson* (Manchester: Manchester University Press).
Trivedi, Parita 1984: 'To Deny Our Fullness: Asian Women in the Making of History', *Feminist Review* 17: 37–50.
Tuathail, Gearóid Ó. 1994: 'The Critical Reading/Writing of Geopolitics: Re-reading/writing Wittfogel, Bowman and Lacoste', *Progress in Human Geography* 18(3): 313–32.
Tuathail, Gearóid Ó. 1996: *Critical Geopolitics* (London: Routledge).
Tuck, Richard 1999: *The Rights of War and Peace* (Oxford: Oxford University Press).
Tully, James 1995: *Strange Multiplicity* (Cambridge: Cambridge University Press).
Tully, James 2002: 'The Kantian Idea of Europe: Critical and Cosmopolitan Perspectives', in Anthony Pagden (ed.), *The Idea of Europe* (Cambridge: Cambridge University Press): 331–58.
Turner, Bryan S. 1978: *Marx and the End of Orientalism* (Sydney: Allen & Unwin).
Viner, Jacob 1948: 'Power Versus Plenty as Objectives of Foreign Policy in the Seventeenth and Eighteenth Centuries', *World Politics* 1(1): 1–29.
Vitalis, Robert 2000: 'The Graceful and Generous Liberal Gesture: Making Racism Invisible in American International Relations', *Millennium* 29(2): 331–56.
Vitalis, Robert 2002: 'International Studies in America', *Items & Issues* (Social Science Research Council) 3(3–4): 1–2, 12–16.
Vitalis, Robert 2005: 'Birth of a Discipline', in Long and Schmidt (eds.): 159–81.
Vitalis, Robert 2010: 'The Noble American Science of Imperial Relations and Its Laws of Race Development', *Comparative Studies in Society and History* 52(4): 909–38.
Vitalis, Robert (forthcoming): *The End of Empire in American Political Science* (unpublished book manuscript).

Walker, R. B. J. 1993: *Inside/Outside* (Cambridge: Cambridge University Press).
Watson, Matthew 2012: 'The Eighteenth-Century Historiographic Tradition and Contemporary "Everyday IPE"', *Review of International Studies* 38.
Weikart, Richard 2003: 'Progress through Racial Extermination: Social Darwinism, Eugenics, and Pacifism in Germany, 1860–1918', *German Studies Review* 26(2): 273–94.
Weikart, Richard 2004: *From Darwin to Hitler* (Houndmills: Palgrave Macmillan).
Weikart, Richard 2011: *Hitler's Ethic* (Houndmills: Palgrave Macmillan).
Weinstein, Jay, and Nico Stehr 1999: 'The Power of Knowledge: Race Science, Race Policy, and the Holocaust'. Posted at: www://soziologie.uni-duisburg. de/personen/material/stehr/stehr2.pdf
Weiss, Linda, and John M. Hobson 1995: *States and Economic Development* (Cambridge: Polity).
Wendt, Alexander 1987: 'The agent-structure problem in international relations theory', *International Organization* 41(3): 335–70.
Wendt, Alexander 1999: *Social Theory of International Politics* (Cambridge: Cambridge University Press).
Wendt, Alexander, and Daniel Friedheim 1996: 'Hierarchy under Anarchy: Informal Empire and the East German State', in T. J. Biersteker and C. Weber (eds.), *State Sovereignty as Social Construct* (Cambridge: Cambridge University Press) 240–77.
Westad, Odd Arne 2007: *The Global Cold War* (Cambridge: Cambridge University Press).
Whelan, Frederick 2009: *Enlightenment Political Thought and Non-Western Societies* (London: Routledge).
Whitfield, Peter 1994: *The Image of the World* (London: The British Library).
Williams, John 2005: 'Pluralism, Solidarism and the Emergence of World Society in English School Theory', *International Relations* 19(1): 19–38.
Wilson, Peter 1998: 'The Myth of the "First Great Debate"', *Review of International Studies* 24: 1–15.
Wilson, Peter 2005: 'Fabian Paternalism and Radical Dissent: Leonard Woolf's Theory of Economic Imperialism', in Long and Schmidt (eds.): 117–40.
Wink, André 1990: *Al-Hind: The Making of the Indo-Islamic World*, I (Leiden: E. J. Brill).
Wittfogel, Karl 1963: *Oriental Despotism* (New Haven, CT: Yale University Press).
Wolf, Eric R. 1982: *Europe and the People Without History* (Berkeley: University of California Press).
Wood, Allen W. 2006: 'Kant's Philosophy of History', in P. Kleingeld (ed.), *Toward Perpetual Peace and Other Writings on Politics, Peace and History* (New Haven, CT: Yale University Press), 243–63.
Young, Robert J. C. 1995: *Colonial Desire* (London: Routledge).

Zarakol, Ayşe 2011: *After Defeat: How the East Learned to Live with the West* (Cambridge: Cambridge University Press).

Zhang, Yongjin 2001: 'System, empire and state in Chinese international relations', in Michael Cox, Ken Booth and Tim Dunne (eds.), *Empires, Systems and States* (Cambridge: Cambridge University Press): 43–63.

INDEX

Abu-Lughod, Janet L., 65, 225, 236, 238
Acharya, Amitav, 17, 206
Adib-Moghaddam, Arshin, 12, 74
Agathangelou, Anna, 14
Ahmad, Aijaz, 52, 55
Albright, Madeleine, 195, 272
Al-Rodhan, Nayef, 225
Ambrosius, Lloyd, 167, 169
America
   original stage of development, 80
Amin, Samir, 4, 236
Amos, Valerie, 14
Anderson, Perry, 58
Angell, Norman, 17, 40–45, 134, 135, 274, 315, 317, 318, 337
   conditional Eastern agency, 43
   critique of the League, 167
   critique of racist-realism, 43, 44
   globalization as Western opportunity, 20
   links to Hobson's theory, 50
   pro-British Empire, 43–44, 178
   paternalist conception of imperialism, 25, 42–44
Anghie, Antony, 3, 12, 63, 220, 315, 333
Anievas, Alexander, 254, 338
anti-imperialism, 6, 59–66, 74–78, 84–88, 95–104, 139–147, 228–232, 238–240, 244–247, 279–284, 339–343
   definition, 1–2, 28–30
anti-paternalist Eurocentrism, 6, 28, 59–83, 228–232, 317, 319, See also paternalist Eurocentrism, Eurocentric institutionalism, anti-imperialism
   contrasted with paternalist Eurocentrism, 6, 317

anti-Semitism. See Adolf Hitler, Eugenics, Jewish 'peril'
Archibugi, Daniele, 295
Ashworth, Lucian, 124, 133, 150
Augelli, Enrico, 254

Bagehot, Walter, 41, 107, 111, 330
Bain, William, 309, 310
Bala, Arun, 225
Balibar, Etienne, 13, 322
Bannister, Robert, 11, 85
Banton, Michael, 11, 12
barbaric peril, 8, 87, 108, 124, 269, 279–284, See also yellow peril
Barendse, R. J., 238
Barkawi, Tarak, 206, 209
Barker, Martin, 13, 322
Bartelson, Jens, 334
Bassin, Mark, 160, 161
Bell, Duncan, 15
Belloni, Robert, 302
Benga, Ota, 324
Bernal, Martin, 4
Bernasconi, Robert, 67, 73
Bernhardi, Friedrich von, 155, 158, 315, 318
Beveridge, William, 108
Bhambra, Gurminder, 17, 138
Bieler, Andreas, 249, 254
big-bang theory of world politics. See Eurocentric institutionalism
Bin Laden, Osama, 209
Blair, James L., 8, 99–103, 179
Blaney, David, 3, 12, 63, 80, 242, 308, 315
Bloch, Jean de
   precursor to Norman Angell, 41
Bonnett, Alistair, 111, 143, 267

Boot, Max, 276, 277
Boucher, David, 46, 92
Bowden, Brett, 3, 12, 14, 35, 59, 63, 66, 67, 257, 261, 315
Bowman, Isaiah, 155, 161
Brailsford, H. N., 134, 136, 177, 319
Braudel, Fernand, 236
Brenner, Robert, 234, 242
Brewer, Anthony, 138
Brigham, Albert, 161
Bright, John, 35, 315, 329
  critique of Oriental despotism, 37
  pro-British Empire in India, 39
Brinton, Daniel, 86, 161, 317
British Empire, 26, 30, 45, 135, 157, 167, 177, 178, 179, 180, 181, 199, 351, 371
Brown, Garrett W., 64, 71
Bruff, Ian, 254
Brzezinski, Zbigniew, 26, 266, 271
Buell, Raymond, 134, 166, 167, 303, 318, 324, 338
  benign-racist conception of imperialism, 25
Buffon, Comte de, 324
Bukharin, Nikolai, 136, 142, 319
Bulbeck, Chilla, 14
Bull, Hedley
  Eastern developmental requirement, 342
  anarchical (European) society, 226–228, 339
  anti-imperialist politics, 228–232, 342
  'Eastern problem', 229–232, 342
  Eurocentric ahistoricism, 232
  flirtation with solidarism, 231
  hierarchical (global) society, 226–228, 339
  pro-imperialist politics, 226–227, 339
  'revolt against the West', 228–232
  'whitewashing' of imperialism, 320
Bunche, Ralph, 17
Burgess, John W., 129, 169, 171, 172, 175, 282
Bush, President George W., 272

Buzan, Barry, 205, 222, 223, 231, 232, 335, 336

Cabot Lodge, Henry, 9
Cain, Peter J., 46
Callahan, William, 222, 227, 228
Callinicos, Alex, 51
Campbell, David, 334
Caplan, Richard, 309
Carnegie, Andrew, 84
Carr, E. H., 15, 133, 135, 150–151, 188, 318, 344
  Eurocentric theory of international change, 192–193
  intra-Western politics as the universal, 192–193
  myths of 1919, 133–136, 150–151
  Pax Britannica as world stabilizer, 343
Carr-Saunders, Alexander, 108
Carvalho, Benjamin de, 17, 133
Cecil, Lord Robert, 174
Chakrabarty, Dipesh, 9, 167, 343
Chamberlain, Houston Stewart, 9, 147, 163, 164, 165
Chamberlain, Joseph, 273
Chandler, David, 305
Chowdhry, Geeta, 14, 17
civilizing mission. *See* imperialism
Cobden, Richard, 35–40, 274, 315, 329
  Eurocentric critique of Ottoman Empire, 36–37
  'Irish peril', 38
  paternalist conception of imperialism, 25
  pro-civilizing mission (in Ireland), 38–39
  pro-civilizing mission (in the Ottoman Empire), 37–38
  pro-English nationalism, 38
Colás, Alex, 252
colonial-racist guilt syndrome
  end of empire, 320
  end of scientific racism, 320
  decline of (post-1989), 326
Commons, John R., 103
Concert of Democracies, 306–307
constructivism

constructivism (cont.)
  Eurocentrism, 302–305
  'temporal othering', 303
Cooper, Robert, 261, 264, 269, 271, 274–275
cosmopolitan democracy. *See* liberalism (Western liberalism, post-1989), David Held
cosmopolitanism. *See* liberalism (Western-liberalism, post-1989)
Cox, Michael, 271
Cox, Robert W., 16, 17, 242–248, 251–253, 254
  critical versus problem-solving theory, 243
  elision of Eastern agency, 250, 251
  Eurocentric 'big-bang theory', 247
  Eurocentric conception of globalization, 247–249
  Eurocentric conception of hegemony, 243–246
critical race theory, 13, 322–324
Crook, Paul, 11, 12, 43, 84, 92, 107, 110
cultural realism. *See* realism (cultural-realism)
Cumings, Bruce, 206

Davis, William Morris, 161
decolonization
  end of scientific racism, 319
DeCourcy Ward, Robert, 161
default/qualified sovereignty. *See* sovereignty
defensive racism, 8, 84–105, 142–149, 316–317, *See also* scientific racism, offensive racism
  anti-imperialism, 95–105, 147
  derivative Eastern agency, 93
  globalization as barbaric threat, 88, 143, 341
  informal hierarchy, 87
  miscegenation as racial contamination, 86, 97, 148, 149, 317
  parallels with Hitler's Eugenics, 318
  qualified/default (Eastern state) sovereignty, 87, 342

  racial apartheid conception of world politics, 99
  'relativism' differentiated from 'universalism', 85–87
  'relativist' variant, 99–104
  tropical climatic threat to the white race, 86, 88, 89, 148, 317
  'universalist' variant, 87–99
  yellow peril, 8, 87–89, 142–149
democratic peace theory
  Eurocentric foundations, 308–310
  parallels with John Stuart Mill, 307
  problematic links to Immanuel Kant, 307
Denemark, Robert A., 236, 254
Derrida, Jacques, 64
Deudney, Daniel, 335
Dickinson, G. Lowes, 134
Dilke, Sir Charles, 79, 107, 111, 274, 316
Donnelly, Jack, 133, 261, 310, 335
Doty, Roxanne Lynn, 334
Doyle, Michael, 64, 307, 308
Drinnon, Richard, 125
Du Bois, W. E. B., 17, 89
Dunne, Timothy, 222, 223
duty to prevent
  Eurocentric foundations, 305–307
  parallels with the 2002 Bush doctrine, 306

East
  ideational construct, 22
Eastern agency
  conditional, 6, 33, 43, 56–57, 60, 93, 138, 168, 176, 180, 214, 228, 315, 317
  derivative, 6, 60, 83, 93, 316, 317, 322
  extremely high predatory, 8, 87, 88, 145–148, 201–203, 279–282
  predatory, 9, 108, 126–130, 186, 229, 263–270, 315
  very low/none, 8, 9, 100, 110, 114, 139, 141, 319
Eastern false consciousness, 271
Ellis, Havelock, 108
Empire-lite, 26, 220, 274, *See also* Michael Ignatieff

English School theory, 222
  anarchical (European) society 288
  anti-imperialist politics of (anti-paternalist Eurocentrism), 228–232, 342
  Eastern conditional agency, 214
  'Eastern problem', 228
  Eurocentric 'big-bang theory', 223–228
  Eurocentric bipolar conception of the international, 228
  Eurocentric logic of immanence, 224, 225
  'full' Western sovereignty, 342
  globalization as Western opportunity, 339
  hierarchical (global) society, 342
  links with racist cultural-realism, 229
  non-Eurocentrism, 329
  parallels with racist-realism, 229, 230
  predatory Eastern agency, 215
  pro-imperialist politics of (paternalist Eurocentrism), 226–228
  'qualified' Eastern sovereignty, 342
  'revolt against the West', 228–232
  'whitewashing' of imperialism, 320
Enlightenment
  partly Eurocentric, 3, 82
  partly imperialist, 60
  partly non-Eurocentric, 60
Etherington, Norman, 51
Eugenics
  anti-imperialism, 103–104, 142–147
  definition, 117
  demographic threat, 144
  demographic threat to the white race, 146
  extreme racial anxiety, 162–164
  extreme white racial anxiety, 142–149
  historical climax, 143
  imperialism, 104–105, 116–119, 158–159
  Jewish 'peril', 162–164
  'negative', 117
  'pacifist Eugenics', 103–105, 107, 112, 113, 142–149
  perils of miscegenation, 117, 148, 159
  'positive', 117
  racial hygiene, 148
  socialist variant, 108
  war as dysgenic, 103–105, 146, 148
  white proletarian threat to the white race, 110, 146
  yellow peril, 143–146, 147–148
Eurocentric institutionalism
  American interest as the universal, 271
  'big-bang theory', 139–142, 186, 190, 196, 215, 223–228, 236–240, 244–246, 247, 296–298, 339, 343, See also paternalist Eurocentrism, anti-paternalist Eurocentrism
  critique of 'social efficiency', 60, 62, 63
  differences within anti-paternalism, 319
  differentiated from scientific racism, 3–9, 322–324
  double standards, 262–263, 288–290
  Eastern false consciousness, 271
  generic properties of 'subliminal' Eurocentrism (post-1945), 319
  international imperialism, 50, 166, 175–177, 317, 318
  its changing architecture (1760–2010), 313–327
  logic of immanence, 34, 57, 139, 140, 196, 215, 223, 224, 225, 236, 244, 247, 253, 296
  'manifest' differentiated from 'subliminal', 10, 185–187, 214–216
  return of 'manifest' Eurocentrism (post-1989), 325–327
  rise of 'subliminal' Eurocentrism, 185–186, 319–320
  role of climate, 5
  'social efficiency', 35, 48, 49, 231, 274, 338

380   INDEX

Eurocentric institutionalism (cont.)
  three worlds construct, 33–35,
    59–62, 229–231, 236–238,
    240–242, 246, 260–262,
    287–288
  trope of European exceptionalism,
    139, 186, 225, 233, 236, 237, 296
  Western triumphalism, 189, 286,
    291, 302
Eurocentrism
  changing architecture (1760–2010),
    313–327
  four key internal variants, 3–10, See
    also Eurocentric
    institutionalism
Europe
  exceptional, 6, 34, 139, 186, 224, 225,
    233, 236, 237, 296, 297
Eze, Emmanuel Chukwudi, 67

Fabianism
  imperialism, 51
failed states. See states (Eastern)
Feinstein, Lee, 305
Feminism, 14
Ferguson, Niall, 26, 27, 199, 270, 272,
  277–278
Fidler, David, 220, 261, 304
Final Solution. See Adolf Hitler
Finnemore, Martha, 216, 302, 303–304,
  319
Fiske, John, 79, 107, 113, 129, 169,
  274, 316
Fool's Cap map of the world, 21–22
Frank, Andre Gunder, 65, 197, 225,
  236, 238
Freeden, Michael, 51, 107, 110
Freeman, Austin, 110
Freeman, Edward, 169
Freud, Sigmund, 135
Friedman, Thomas, 77, 290, 291
Fukuyama, Francis, 20, 258, 308
Füredi, Frank, 13, 206, 231, 257, 270,
  320, 322, 327

Gallagher, John, 27
Galton, Francis, 111, 117
Gasman, Daniel, 11, 104, 112, 163

Gentili, Albert, 63
geopolitical theory, 123–130, 151–161,
  318, See also realism (racist-
  realism)
  Columbian epoch, 125
  critique of direct racial exterminism,
    159
  differentiated from Hitler's
    Eugenics, 155, 164–165, 318
  environmentalist racism, 155
  'geographical pivot', 128
  'heartland', 128, 270
  imperialism, 128–130, 156–159
  indirect racial exterminism, 156
  Lamarckian social Darwinism,
    159, 160
  land-power, 128
  'Lebensraum', 155, 156
  post-Columbian epoch, 126, 128
  pre-Columbian epoch, 126, 127–128
  state as an organism, 155
  similarities with Hitler, 155
  social Darwinism, 155
  war as biological necessity, 155
  'yellow peril', 123–130, 157
Gerschenkron, Alexander, 201
Giddings, Franklin, 47, 120, 124, 129,
  262, 265, 274, 278, 315, 317
Gill, Stephen, 248, 249, 251, 254
Gills, Barry K., 225, 236, 242, 244
Gilpin, Robert, 25, 26, 30, 193–203,
  273, 321
  drawing on Karl Marx's paternalist
    imperial politics, 198, 201
  Eurocentric foundations of the
    decline of hegemony, 199–203
  Eurocentric foundations of the rise
    and exercise of hegemony, 196–199
Global hierarchy. See hierarchy,
  globalization (construct),
  sovereignty
Globalization (construct)
  anti-imperialist construction,
    340–343
  barbaric threat, 20, 88, 108,
    124–127, 143, 263–270, 280, 339,
    341–342, 344
  developmental requirement, 340

imperialist construction, 337–340
Western opportunity, 20, 35, 48–50, 53–55, 66, 110, 117, 290–291, 337–338
Gobineau, Comte de, 86, 93, 161, 165, 317
Gong, Gerrit, 227, 319
Goody, Jack, 225
Goonatilake, Susantha, 225
Gossett, Thomas, 11, 12
Gould, Stephen J., 11
gradated sovereignty. *See* sovereignty
Gramscianism, 242–254
  ahistorical Eurocentrism, 252–253
  elision of Eastern agency, 249–252
  Eurocentric 'big-bang theory', 244, 247
  Eurocentric conception of globalization, 247–249
  Eurocentric conception of hegemony, 243–246
  Eurocentric logic of immanence, 244, 247, 253
  Eurocentric overlaps with hegemonic stability theory, 243, 244
  Eurocentric overlaps with world-systems theory, 244, 246, 252–254
  Eurofetishism, 252
  globalization as the triumph of the West, 343
  informal (global) hierarchy, 343
  naturalizing Western imperialism, 252
  'problem-solving' theory, 253–254
  structural-Eurofunctionalism, 246, 252
  three-worlds Eurocentric construction, 246
Grant, Madison, 86, 93, 117, 135, 179, 282, 318, 324
  inspiration to Hitler, 149, 165
Grieco, Joseph M., 197
Griffiths, Martin, 190
Grotius, Hugo, 63
Grovogui, Siba N., 12, 63, 334, 336
Gruffydd-Jones, Branwen, 17, 254

Grunberg, Isabelle, 194, 197, 203
Gumplowicz, Ludwig, 110, 111, 120, 159, 324

Haeckel, Ernst, 104, 108, 112, 163
Haldane, J. B. S., 108
Hall, Martin, 17
Hannaford, Ivan, 11
Hannerz, Ulf, 247, 248
Harding, Sandra, 14, 225
Haushofer, Albrecht, 160
Haushofer, Karl, 155, 157, 158, 318
  differences with Hitler, 160
Hawkins, Mike, 11, 12, 110, 112
Hegel, G. W. F., 291
  issue of climate, 5
  Eurocentrism, 52, 53, 56, 57
hegemony. *See* realism (hegemonic stability theory), Gramscianism, world-systems theory, 26
Hehir, Aidan, 270
Held, David, 295–299, 306
  Eurocentric account of globalization, 297
  Eurocentric account of state-formation, 297
  Eurocentric big bang theory, 296–297
Hennig, Richard, 160, 318
Herbst, Jeffrey, 308, 309
Herder, Johann Gottfried, 72–73
hierarchy
  Eurocentric bipolar conception of the international, 37, 42, 228, 262, 275, 288, 308
  formal, 19, 33, 37, 41, 42, 55, 205, 218, 228, 262, 275, 288, 326, 337–340
  informal, 19, 62, 72, 83, 85, 87, 105
  the changing discursive architecture of formal hierarchy, 337–340
  the changing discursive architecture of informal hierarchy, 340–344
Hilferding, Rudolf, 136, 319
Hindess, Barry, 35, 58, 59
Hirst, Paul, 58

Hitler, Adolf, 9, 93, 112, 117, 339
  admirer of Madison Grant, 149, 165
  Aryan race, 163
  differences with Ernst Haeckel, 164
  differences with geopolitical theory, 155, 318
  differences with Karl Haushofer, 158, 160
  differences with Lamarckianism, 164
  Final Solution, 163
  German imperialism, 158, 318
  'Jewish peril', 162–164, 318
  limited role of climate in race-formation, 162
  overlaps with von Treitschke, 164
  parallels with Houston Stewart Chamberlain, 164
  perils of miscegenation, 159
  similarities with geopolitical theory, 155
Hoar, George, 100
Hobhouse, Leonard, 51
Hobson, John A., 17, 45–51, 315, 318
  critique of *insane* imperialism, 48
  critique of the League, 167
  critique of scientific racism, 47
  differences with Lenin, 46
  globalization as Western opportunity, 20, 48, 338
  Hobson's theory as precursor to the Mandate System, 50
  League of Nations Mandate System, 166
  non-economic focus of *Imperialism*, 46
  precursor to classical Marxist IR theory, 136
  sane imperialism, 25, 47–51, 317
  similarities with Marx, 51
  social efficiency, 48–49
  theory of international government, 50
Hoffmann, Stanley, 190, 195
Hofstadter, Richard, 11
Hosmer, James, 129, 169
Hottentot (Khoikhoi). *See* races (black)
House, Colonel Edward, 174
Hughes, Billy, 174

humanitarian intervention
  imperialist, 17, 25–26, 293, 299–305, 326
Hume, David, 275
Hunt, Michael, 11, 13, 125, 320, 322
Huntington, Ellsworth, 86, 161, 317
Huntington, Samuel, 279–284, 323, 344, *See also* Realism (Cultural-realism), Lothrop Stoddard, Charles Pearson
  critique of imperialism, 282–284
  extreme Western angst, 258
  fundamental East–West divide, 284
  globalization as barbaric threat, 264, 280
  parallels with post-1889 scientific racist-realism and racist cultural-realism, 279–284
Hutchings, Kimberly, 14, 17
Huxley, Julian, 108
hyper-sovereignty. *See* sovereignty

Ignatieff, Michael, 26, 264, 271, 272, 277, 303
ignoble savage (discourse of). *See* noble savage
Ikenberry, G. John, 271, 306
imperialism, *See also* civilizing mission, international paternalism
  civilizing mission, 5, 6, 7, 23, 25, 26, 27, 29, 33–34, 35, 36, 38, 40, 42–44, 47, 49, 50, 52–56, 60, 61, 63, 82, 86, 88, 93, 96, 100, 107, 121, 122, 159, 175, 187, 198–199, 200, 201, 221, 226, 274, 302, 303, 304, 305, 315, 316, 317, 321, 325, 326
  cultural conversion, 6, 23, 25, 27, 30, 33, 77, 122, 199, 216, 220, 289, 290, 292–295, 301, 321, 326
  definition, 23–27
  humanitarianism, 17, 25, 222, 293–294, 299–303
  informal, 27, 28
  'international imperialism', 50, 175–177, 317, 318
  regressive, 6, 8, 62–66, 74–78, 86–87, 95–105

Inayatullah, Naeem, 3, 12, 63, 80, 242, 315
international financial institutions, 199, 220, 246, 290, 325
  parallels with the nineteenth century 'unequal treaties', 220, 293, 326
  structural adjustment/conditionality, 17, 199, 220, 221, 326
international paternalism, 25–27, 33–35, 36–39, 41–45, 47–50, 52–58, 121–123, 172–174, 176–177, 179–181, 198–199, 220, 226–228, 288–290, 293–294, 299–304
International Relations (discipline)
  1919 and the East–West clash, 134
  1919 and the European identity-crisis, 134
  conventional account of the birth of IR, 133
  defender of Western civilization, 1–2, 14–21
  liberal Western-imperial anxiety, 135
  myth of the first great debate, 15–16, 135
  myth of the great debates, 18
  (partial) myth of 1919, 133–136, 150–151
  positivist myth, 16, 344
  sovereignty/anarchy myth, 19–20, 331–344
  study of hierarchy and gradated sovereignty, 19
  thirty years' crisis, 133
international theory
  defender of the idea of Western civilization, 1–2, 15–23, 344
  formal hierarchy, 337–340
  globalization as a central concept of, 340–344
  informal hierarchy, 340–344
  non-Eurocentric scholars, 16
  mythical clash of theories, 20–21
  polymorphous career of liberalism, 329–329

polymorphous career of Marxism, 331
  polymorphous career of realism, 331–333
  positivist myth, 16–18, 344
  promiscuous/polymorphous, 20, 327–331
  sovereignty/anarchy myth, 19–20, 331–344
international trusteeship (post-1989)
  Eurocentric foundations, 308
  parallels with the League of Nations Mandate System, 309
Ireland, Alleyne, 20, 111, 122, 123, 274, 316, 324
  benign-racist conception of imperialism, 25
Iriye, Akira, 279
Islam
  progressive, 225
  regressive, 37, 145, 262, 264, 269, 270, 280

Jackson, Patrick T., 17
Jackson, Robert H., 230, 302
Jahn, Beate, 3, 17, 35, 64, 80, 307, 315
James, C. L. R., 17
Jewish 'peril', 162–165, 318
Jordan, David Starr, 8, 99–104, 107, 167, 180, 318, 338

Kagan, Robert, 26, 258, 269, 271, 275–276, 306
Kang, David, 207
Kant, Immanuel, 59–74, 340
  anti-paternalist Eurocentrism, 66
  cosmopolitan right as critique of imperialism, 63
  critique of imperialism, 28–29, 62–66
  critique of 'primitive/savage' societies, 68–70
  critique of 'social efficiency', 62
  critique of unequal trade, 64
  'developmental requirement', 62, 340

Kant, Immanuel (cont.)
  differentiated from critical anti-paternalist Eurocentrism, 319
  Eurocentric theory of the pacific federation of republican states, 69–72
  globalization, 66, 340, 341
  informal hierarchy, 72
  Kant–Herder debate, 72–73
  links with Adam Smith's theory, 68, 69
  'near-imperialist' argument, 65–66
  parallels with Spencer's defensive racism, 316
  postcolonial critique, 64
  scientific racism, 67, 73
  state of nature (domestic), 69–70
  teleological stagist model, 67–72
  'unsocial sociability', 68
Kaplan, Robert, 266, 269, 270, 276
Katzenstein, Peter J., 303
Kaufman, Stuart, 335
Kavaphes, Konstantinos, 265
Kayaoglu, Turan, 222, 334, 335
Keal, Paul, 223
Keck, Margaret, 302
Keene, Edward, 12, 19, 20, 84, 125, 223, 227, 228, 327, 334, 334
Kellogg, Vernon, 104, 107
Kennedy, Paul M., 196, 198, 266–269
Keohane, Robert O., 17, 77, 216–222, 308
  neo-imperialist politics, 214–221
  parallels with Norman Angell, 218, 221
  withholding of Eastern sovereignty, 309
Kevles, Daniel, 11, 107, 112
Keynes, John Maynard, 108
Kidd, Benjamin, 8, 47, 108, 110, 111–112, 114–116, 118, 277, 316, 317
  critique of Pearson's 'dire prophecy', 114
  globalization as Western opportunity, 20
  liberal 'imperial guilt syndrome', 114, 116
  offensive racist imperial theory, 115–116
Kindleberger, Charles P., 193, 196, 200
Kipling, Rudyard, 200
Kjellén, Rudolf, 155, 160
Klotz, Audie, 319
Knox, Robert, 39, 86, 93, 161, 317
Knutsen, Torbjørn, 16, 124, 133, 134
Krasner, Stephen, 194, 195, 200, 278, 308
Krauthammer, Charles, 26, 269, 271
Kristol, William, 258, 275
Kurth, James, 281
Kurtz, Stanley, 272
Kwon, Heonik, 206

Laclau, Ernesto, 234, 242
Laffey, Mark, 209
Lake, David A., 15, 16, 335
Lake, Marilyn, 12, 87
Lamarck, Jean-Baptiste, 6, 7–8, 91, *See also* Lamarckianism
Lamarckianism, 6–8, 91–94, 122, 159–161, 164–165, 166, 168, 173, 282
  anti-imperialism, 95–99
  'benign' civilizing mission, 119
  differences with Darwinism, 91, 92
  differentiated from Hitler's Eugenics, 159–165
  direct racial exterminism, 119
  imperialism, 121–123, 156–158, 159–161, 172–174
  multivalent, 6–8, 92, 121, 166
Larrain, Jorge, 55, 57, 58
Laski, Harold, 108, 134, 136, 318, 319
Lauren, Paul Gordon, 305
Lawson, George, 205
Layne, Christopher, 261
League of Democracies, 306
League of Nations, 167, 177
  1884 Berlin Conference, 166
  Article 22, 173
  British Empire as preserver of the League, 180, 318
  Mandate System, 50, 166, 167, 169, 173, 177, 179, 220, 295, 317, 338

Leira, Halvard, 133
Lenin, Vladimir, 138–142, 319
  critique of globalization, 139
  defence of Western civilization, 142
  denial of Eastern agency, 142
  differences with Marx, 141
  Eurocentric logic of immanence, 140
  fetishization of the West, 142
  Western hyper-imperial agency, 141
Levin, Gordon, 174
liberalism
  conventional ahistorical narrative, 327
  polymorphous/protean career, 328–329
liberalism (classical liberal internationalism), 33–45, 59–83
  anti-imperialism, 59–62, 74–78
  anti-paternalist Eurocentrism, 66–74
  paternalist Eurocentrism, 33–45
  pro-imperialism, 37–40, 41–45
liberalism (neoliberal institutionalism), 216–222
  imperialism, 220–222
  problems with the constructivist interpretation, 216–217
liberalism (new liberalism), 45–51, 110, See also John A. Hobson
liberalism (racist-liberalism), 89–105, 107, 119–123, 167–175, 316
  anti-imperialism, 95–104, 105
  direct racial exterminism, 119–121, 316
  imperialism, 111, 114–116, 119–123, 172–174
  indirect racial exterminism, 114–116, 316
  paternalist civilizing mission, 121–123
  white racial anxiety, 151
Liberalism (Western-liberalism, post-1989)
  Concert of Democracies, 306–307
  conditional Eastern sovereignty, 288–290
  cultural conversion of the East, 289, 290, 293–294, 300–303, 308–310
  democratic peace theory, 307–308
  differentiated from Western-realism, 286
  Eurocentric big-bang theory, 296–297
  Eurocentric conception of the bipolar international, 295
  Eurocentric double standards, 288–290, 294
  Eurocentric logic of immanence, 296
  Eurocentric three-worlds construct, 287–288
  globalization as Western opportunity, 290–291
  hierarchical conception of world politics, 288–290
  international trusteeship, 308–310
  paternalist Eurocentrism, 285–286, 287–292
  paternalist imperialism, 286, 292–295, 299–303
  'progressive' Western optimism/triumphalism, 257, 286
  realist-liberalism, 258, 259, 271–273, 274, 305–307
  standard of civilization, 287
  standard of statehood, 287
  'temporal othering', 285, 303, 325
Lind, William S., 270, 280, 281, 282, 283, 344
Lindqvist, Sven, 112
Ling, L. H. M., 14, 216, 217, 303
Linklater, Andrew, 193, 222
List, Friedrich, 5, 73, 197, 219, 323
Little, Richard, 232, 336
Livingstone, David N., 12, 165
Locke, John, 63
Lodge, Henry Cabot, 106, 124, 129
London, Jack, 107
Long, David, 12, 19, 46, 50, 51, 133, 135, 334
Long, Edward, 324
Loomba, Ania, 14
Lugard, Sir Frederick, 309
Luxemburg, Rosa, 319
Lyon, Peter, 308

MacDonald, Ramsay, 51, 315, 316
Mackinder, Halford, 9, 108, 124–126, 127–128, 154, 160, 162, 202, 262, 263, 265, 270, 274, 278, 315, 322
  globalization as barbaric threat, 124–126, 339
  predatory Eastern agency, 126–127
  pro-League of Nations, 318
  yellow peril, 127–128
MacMaster, Neil, 13, 322
Magnusson, Lars, 46
Mahan, Alfred, 9, 108, 126–127, 160, 162, 202, 262, 263, 265, 274, 279, 280, 315, 322
  globalization as barbaric threat, 124–125
  imperialism, 128–130
  predatory Eastern agency, 126
Malik, Kenan, 13, 322
Mallaby, Sebastian, 26, 277, 278
Malmvig, Helle, 334
Malthus, Thomas, 267
  Eurocentric approach, 267
Manchester School, 329
Mann, Michael, 164
Marx, Karl, 52–58
  Asiatic mode of production, 56
  China as rotting semi-civilization, 53
  conditional Eastern agency, 56, 57
  differences with Lenin, 138
  Eurocentric logic of immanence, 57
  Europe as the progressive driver of world history, 56–57
  European hyper-sovereignty, 55
  formal hierarchical conception of world politics, 55
  globalization and imperialism as global primitive accumulation, 54
  globalization as Western opportunity, 20, 337
  India as backward and 'history-less', 53
  issue of climate, 5
  moral disgust of imperialism, 56–57
  neo-Marxist defence against the imperialist charge, 55
  opium wars as emancipatory, 53
  paternalist-Eurocentric conception of imperialism, 25, 35, 52–57, 315
  paternalist-Eurocentric theory of history, 56–57
  political necessity of imperialism, 53, 56–57
Marxism
  polymorphous career, 331
Marxism (classical), 52–58, 136–142
Marxism (neo-Marxism). *See* Gramscianism, world-systems theory
Matin, Kamran, 138, 254
McCarthy, Thomas, 12, 13, 35, 73, 74, 272, 322, 323
McLellan, David, 55
Mearsheimer, John, 197
Meek, Ronald, 80, 81
Mehta, Uday Singh, 12, 14, 35, 59
Mendel, Gregor Johann, 7
Miles, Robert, 13, 322
Mill, John Stuart, 25, 35, 78, 79, 81, 272, 274, 275, 289, 315
Mills, Charles, 12, 59, 63, 315
Mitrany, David, 166
modernization theory
  Eurocentrism, 321
Mohanty, Chandra Talpade, 14
Money, Leo Chiozza, 108, 111
Monist League (Germany), 104, 107, 163
Montesquieu, Baron de, 5, 60, 80, 82, 323
Morefield, Jeanne, 14, 135, 178, 180, 181
Morgenthau, Hans J.
  eliding Western imperialism, 188–190, 320
  Eurocentric big-bang theory, 190, 343
  Eurocentric theory of international change, 190–192
  intra-Western politics as the universal, 190–192
  naturalization of Western imperialism, 188–190
  qualified Eastern sovereignty, 343
  whitewashing of Western imperialism, 343

Morton, Adam David, 248, 249, 252, 254
Moynihan, Daniel Patrick, 266
Mueller, John, 261, 307
Muir, Ramsay, 26, 317, 318
Muirhead, John, 51
Murphy, Craig N., 251, 254
Murray, Gilbert, 25, 135, 178, 317, 338
Muthu, Sankar, 14, 59, 62, 63, 64, 66, 67–74, 75

Nair, Sheila, 14, 17
Nandy, Ashis, 9
Nazism. *See* Adolf Hitler, Eugenics
Neocleous, Mark, 325
neorealism. *See* realism (hegemonic stability theory), realism (Waltzian neorealism)
Neumann, Iver, 270
Nicolai, G. F., 104, 107, 112
Nkrumah, Kwame, 308
noble savage (discourse of), 80
Nossal, Kim Richard, 194, 195, 200
Novicow, Jacques, 43, 104
Nussbaum, Martha, 20, 300

O'Hagan, Jacinta, 272
O'Leary, Brendan, 56
offensive Eurocentrism, 258. *See* realism (Western-realism, post-1989)
offensive racism, 8–9, 111, 315–317
  Anglo-Saxon racial alliance, 108
  direct (genocidal) racial exterminism, 9, 110, 112, 117, 118–119, 121, 164, 262
  globalization as barbaric threat, 108, 124–125
  globalization as Western opportunity, 117, 338
  imperialism, 111–113, 115–116, 118–123, 156–160, 172–174
  indirect racial exterminism, 104, 110, 112–113, 156, 164
  multiple conceptions of imperialism, 315–316
  overlaps with paternalist Eurocentric conception of imperialism, 166, 315, 318
  positive miscegenation, 119
  white triumphalism, 121
Olson, Mancur, 200, 202, 213
Onuf, Nicolas, 335
Oren, Ido, 172
Oriental despotism. *See* states (Eastern)
Orientalism, 3
  reductive conception, 1, 3–6
Osiander, Andreas, 133
Owen, John, 307, 308

pacifist Eugenics. *See* Eugenics
Pagden, Anthony, 3, 12, 59, 63
Parekh, Bhikhu, 12, 35, 78
Paris Peace Conference, 173
Parmar, Pratibha, 14
Pasha, Mustapha Kamal, 17, 242, 250, 254
Pateman, Carole, 12, 59, 63, 315
paternalism. *See* international paternalism, imperialism (civilizing mission), humanitarian intervention
paternalist Eurocentrism, 6, 25, 33–58, 193–203, 211–213, 226–228, 257, 285–310, 315, 317
  contrasted with anti-paternalist Eurocentrism, 6, 317
  contrasted with offensive racism, 315–316
  optimistic, 257
  'progressive' optimism, 313
  parallels with offensive Eurocentrism, 111
  parallels with offensive racism, 166, 315, 318
Patomäki, Heikki, 296
Paul, Darel, 335, 336
Pearson, Charles Henry, 8, 87–89, 108, 114, 117, 118, 124, 146, 203, 229, 263, 265, 279, 280, 317, 341
  compared with Karl Pearson, 117
  globalization as barbaric threat, 88
  supreme white racial anxiety, 87
Pearson, Karl, 8, 47, 84, 108, 110, 111, 116–119, 180, 262, 316, 317

Pearson, Karl (cont.)
  compared with Charles Henry
    Pearson, 117
Perry, Richard, 13, 322, 323
Persaud, Randolph, 17, 242, 250, 254
Peters/Gall world map, 22
Petito, Fabio, 17
Pieterse, Jan Nederveen, 11, 12,
    254, 315
Pitts, Jennifer, 14, 35, 59, 78–80
Porter, Bernard, 46
postcolonialism, 6, 59, 60, 64, 77–78
  definition of imperialism, 23,
    28–29
Powers, Harry, 120, 129, 262, 265,
    274, 315
Price, Richard, 303
Putnam Weale, B. L., 263, 270, 279

race suicide, 318
races
  Anglo-Saxon racial alliance, 108,
    124, 129, 278, 315
  black, 89, 94, 102, 119, 123, 144, 148,
    176, 275, 324
  brown, 144, 146
  red, 118, 144
  white, 87, 89, 94, 115, 121, 144, 146,
    163, 172
  yellow, 8, 9, 87, 100, 105, 106, 108,
    128, 129, 143, 144, 146, 147, 315
racial exterminism, 8, 9
  direct (genocidal), 9, 110, 112, 117,
    118–119, 121, 164, 262
  indirect, 110, 112–113, 156, 164
racial-hygiene (German school of), 165
racism. *See* scientific racism
Rainbow Circle, 51
Raju, C. K., 225
Ratzel, Friedrich, 155, 156, 159, 160, 318
Ratzenhofer, Gustav, 110, 111, 120,
    159, 324
Rawls, John, 27, 77, 292–295, 306, 307
  Eurocentric double standards, 294
  Eurocentric three-worlds construct,
    287–288
  globalization as Western
    opportunity, 20

Reade, Winwood, 113
realism
  conventional ahistorical narrative,
    331
  polymorphous career, 164–165, 331
realism (classical realism), 187–193
  eliding Western imperialism,
    188–190
  Eurocentric big bang theory, 190
  'full' Western sovereignty, 343
  intra-Western politics as the
    universal, 190–193
  Western hyper-agency, 321
realism (cultural-realism, post-1989),
    279–284, See also Samuel
    Huntington, William Lind,
    Lothrop Stoddard, Charles Henry
    Pearson
  'barbaric peril', 279–282
  critique of imperialism, 282–284
  critique of multiculturalism, 281
  fundamental East–West
    divide, 284
  neo-Malthusianism, 279
realism (hegemonic stability theory),
    10, 193–203
  Eurocentric foundations of the
    decline of hegemony, 199–203
  Eurocentric foundations of the rise
    and exercise of hegemony, 196–199
  Eurocentric logic of immanence, 196
  extremely high predatory Eastern
    agency, 201–203
  globalization, 339
  imperialism, 25, 198–199, 321
  parallels with racist cultural-realism,
    203
  parallels with racist-realism,
    202, 203
  yellow peril, 8, 106, 201–203
realism (racist-realism), 8–9, 123–130,
    151–165, 318, See also geopolitical
    theory
realism (Waltzian neorealism),
    203–213
  eliding Eastern agency, 188
  eliding Western imperial hierarchy,
    205

INDEX 389

Eurocentric foundations of key concepts, 210
naturalizing Western imperialism, 189
residual paternalist Eurocentrism, 211
similarities and differences with racist-realism, 154–156
'tempocentric' ahistoricism, 206
Western hyper-agency, 320
realism (Western-realism, post-1989)
differentiated from Western-liberalism, 286
Eastern barbaric threat, 260–271
Eurocentric bipolar conception of the international, 275
Eurocentric double standards, 288–290
Eurocentric three-worlds construct, 260
high degree of Western angst, 258
imperialist politics, 270–278
international trusteeship, 308–310
Islamic threat, 270
liberal-realism, 258, 289
neo-Malthusianism, 266–269
offensive Eurocentrism, 258, 259, 260, 263, 270, 278
parallels with post-1889 racist-liberalism, 277
parallels with post-1889 racist-realism, 262, 263–264, 269, 270, 274
predatory Eastern agency, 263–270
Sino-Islamic threat, 269
standard of civilization, 261
standard of statehood, 261
Western hyper-sovereignty, 263
Western liberal-realism, 258
Reid, Whitelaw, 106, 124, 129
Reinsch, Paul, 111, 121–123, 166, 274, 303, 316, 324
benign-racist conception of imperialism, 25
globalization as Western opportunity, 20
Lamarckianism, 121

similarities with Alleyne Ireland, 122, 123
similarities with J. A. Hobson, 122, 123
Reus-Smit, Christian, 216, 333, 334
Reynolds, Henry, 12, 87
Ricardo, David, 77, 78
Richet, Charles, 104
Rieff, David, 271
Ripley, William Z., 86, 161, 317
Risse, Thomas, 302
Ritchie, David, 107, 111
social Darwinian imperialism, 51
Robertson, J. M., 315
Robertson, William, 51
Robinson, Ronald, 27
Robinson, William, 248
rogue states. *See* states (Eastern)
Roosevelt, Theodore, 9, 106, 113, 124, 315
Rosenberg, Justin, 138, 254
Ross, Edward A., 103, 146, 179, 318
Rothkopf, David, 271, 273
Russett, Bruce, 307

Sabaratnam, Meera, 17
Said, Edward W., 1, 2, 3, 4, 10, 52, 242
Sakamoto, Yoshikazu, 251
Salter, Mark, 12, 189, 257, 264, 265, 272
Sanger, Margaret, 107
Särkkä, Timo, 46, 51
Schmidt, Brian C., 12, 14, 16, 19, 20, 21, 133, 134, 327, 334
scientific racism. *See also* defensive racism, offensive racism, Eugenics, Lamarckianism, social Darwinism, Eastern agency, racial exterminism
anti-imperialism, 87–89
brown imperialism, 148
common misconceptions, 6–8, 121
definition, 28–29
demographic threat to the white race, 144
differentiated from Eurocentric institutionalism, 3–10, 322–324

scientific racism (cont.)
  extreme white racial anxiety, 87, 124–130
  germ-plasm theory, 6
  inter-war climax, 134
  internally fractured, 9
  links with Thomas Malthus, 267
  miscegenation threat to the white race, 8, 73, 86, 97, 110, 117, 118, 144, 148, 149, 159, 163, 282, 317
  positive miscegenation, 119, 120, 159, 326
  race science (*Rassenwissenschaft*), 112
  race suicide, 146
  role of climate, 6, 115
  social efficiency, 47, 115, 118, 120, 121, 130, 156
  socialism, 20, 107–108, 116–119
  the end of (post-1945), 319–320
  the Russo-Japanese war as an omen, 145
  tropical climatic threat to the white race, 89, 99, 101, 103, 110, 115, 148, 317
  unfit white proletariat, 89
  white proletarian threat to the white race, 110, 146
  white racial anxiety, 9, 106, 142–149
  white racial triumphalism, 9, 106, 107, 121, 315
  yellow imperialism, 87
Seabrooke, Leonard, 251, 261
Seeley, John Robert, 79, 107, 111, 316
Semple, Ellen Churchill, 160
Seth, Sanjay, 17, 222, 254
Sewell, Dennis, 107
Sharman, Jason C., 205, 335
Shaw, George Bernard, 51, 108
Shields, Stuart, 254
Shilliam, Robbie, 17, 138, 254, 335
Sidgwick, Henry, 20, 111, 122, 159, 166, 274, 316, 324, 349
  benign-racist conception of imperialism, 25
Sikkink, Kathryn, 302
Simpson, Gerry, 333, 334, 335, 336
Slater, David, 242, 254

Slaughter, Anne-Marie, 305–307
Slotkin, Richard, 125
Smith, Adam,
  anti-paternalist Eurocentric theory of development, 78–83
  compared with J. S. Mill, 78, 79, 81
  critique of imperialism, 28–29, 74–78
  'derivative' Eastern agency, 83
  'developmental requirement', 62
  differentiated from critical anti-paternalist Eurocentrism, 319
  free trade, 28, 77
  informal hierarchy, 83
  Jean-Jaques Rousseau, 81
  occasional signs of Western triumphalism, 79
  parallels with Herbert Spencer's defensive racism, 84, 93, 316
  postcolonial critique, 77–78
  qualified sovereignty, 83
Smith, N. Woodruff, 159
Smith, Steve, 190
Smuts, Jan, 174
Søbjerg, Lene, 308
social Darwinism, 12, 84, 119
  anti-imperialism, 87–89, 95–99
  imperialism, 114–116, 119–121, 123–130, 151–158
  indirect racial exterminism, 112
  laissez-faire state, 90–91
  left-liberal direct racial exterminism, 119
  optimistic approach, 84
  'pacifist Darwinism', 84, 112
  positive state intervention, 119
social efficiency, 35, 47, 115, 118, 120, 121, 231, 262, 338
  'terra nullius', 274
socialist-Eurocentrism, 51, 175–177
socialist-racism, 107–108, 116–119, 316
sovereignty
  conditional, 6, 19, 33, 43, 205, 258, 262, 263, 288, 289, 290, 295, 301, 308, 309, 321, 326, 335
  conventional interpretation, 333
  full, 19, 62, 83, 341
  founded on an inequalitarian discourse, 334

founded on the standard of
  civilization, 334
gradated, 19, 33, 41, 327, 331–344
hierarchy, 334–337
hyper, 19, 33, 39, 55, 60, 72, 86, 151,
  263, 288, 289, 295, 301, 308, 326,
  327, 335
its changing discursive architecture
  (1760–2010), 337–344
myth of 'existential equality', 336
qualified, 19, 62, 83, 86, 340–344
shared, 278
Spencer, Herbert, 8, 89–99, 119, 179
  anti-determinist conception of
    historical progress, 92
  anti-imperialism, 28–29, 84,
    95–99
  anti-paternalist theory of the state,
    90–91
  'coming slavery', 90, 96
  contrasts with anti-paternalist
    Eurocentrism, 316
  critique of miscegenation, 97
  derivative Eastern agency,
    93, 316
  laissez-faire and 'survival of the
    fittest', 90–91
  Lamarckianism, 8, 91–94
  optimistic conception of history, 84
  overlaps with anti-paternalist
    Eurocentrism, 84, 93, 316
  racist conception of history,
    91–94
  'rebarbarization of civilization', 8,
    96–97
  the 'whitewashing', 322
Spengler, Oswald, 135
Spykman, Nicholas, 154, 158, 160, 318,
  339
stadial models (as Eurocentric), 67–72,
  80–82
standard of civilization, 3, 19, 30, 80,
  81, 166, 204, 226, 227, 228, 229,
  261, 263, 287, 307, 310, 325, 334,
  341, 343
standard of statehood, 263, 307, 310
states (Eastern)
  axis of evil, 325
  failed, 64, 80, 185, 211, 222, 229, 240,
    245, 250, 262, 266, 270, 287, 290,
    293, 295, 301, 309, 325, 337
  Oriental despotism, 5, 37, 56, 57,
    198, 230, 237, 262, 268, 269, 287,
    293, 301, 306, 308, 325
  quasi, 229
  rogue/pariah, 325
Stöcker, Helene, 104
Stoddard, Lothrop, 8, 108, 117, 135,
  142–149, 179, 203, 229, 263, 265,
  279, 280, 281, 283, 284, 317, 318,
  341
  coloured immigration peril, 144
  contrasts with Nazism, 149, 318
  critique of imperialism, 147
  extremely high predatory Eastern
    agency, 145–146
  globalization as barbaric threat,
    143–146
  links with B. L. Putnam-Weale, 143
  links with Charles Henry Pearson, 143
  overlaps with Hitler's Eugenics,
    149, 165
  'pacifist Eugenics', 143
  precursor to Samuel Huntington,
    143
  racial apartheid conception of the
    world, 144
  racial hierarchical conception of
    world politics, 144
  yellow peril, 143–146, 147–148
Storey, Moorfield, 100
stratified sovereignty. See sovereignty
  (gradated)
Strong, Josiah, 20, 79, 107, 129, 169,
  274, 316
Stubbs, William, 169
subliminal Eurocentrism. See
  Eurocentric institutionalism
Sumner, William Graham, 8, 89, 91, 96,
  98–99, 119, 161
  critique of imperialism, 96, 98–99
  laissez-faire and 'survival of the
    fittest', 91
Suttner, Bertha von, 108, 112
Suzuki, Shogo, 223
Sylvest, Caspar, 46, 93

Tannenwald, Nina, 303
Teschke, Benno, 254
Téson, Fernando, 20, 300–301
Thies, Cameron, 133
three worlds Eurocentric construct. *See* Eurocentric institutionalism
Tickner, J. Ann, 14, 17
Tinker, Hugh, 12, 320
Titmuss, Richard, 108
Todorov, Tzvetan, 9
Tooze, Roger, 251, 254
Townshend, Jules, 46
Townshend, Meredith, 146
Treitschke, Heinrich von, 154, 156, 164, 165, 315, 318
Trivedi, Parita, 14
Trotsky, Leon, 136, 137, 201, 319
Tuathail, Gearóid, 124, 125
Tuck, Richard, 12, 14
Tully, James, 12, 59, 62, 67, 72

United States of America
  imperialism, 271–274, 276–278
  the national interest as the universal, 271
  trope of American exceptionalism, 196, 198, 213, 271
  trope of manifest destiny, 198, 271

Van der Pijl, Kees, 254
Vattel, Emmerich de, 63
Vincent, R. J., 319
Vitalis, Robert, 12, 16, 17, 124, 133, 134, 135
Vitoria, Francisco di, 63

Walker, R. B. J., 17, 334
Wallace, A. R., 108
Wallerstein, Immanuel, 236–243
  eliding Eastern agency, 240–242
  endogenous Eurocentric logic of immanence, 237–238
  Eurocentric ahistoricism, 253–254
  Eurofetishism, 240, 252
  parallels with Robert Brenner, 237–238
  structural Eurofunctionalism, 240–242
  three worlds Eurocentric construct, 240–242
Waltz, Kenneth N.
  eliding Eastern agency, 208–210
  eliding Western imperial hierarchy, 205
  Eurocentric foundations of key concepts, 210–211
  naturalizing Western imperialism, 204–208
  residual paternalist Eurocentrism, 211–213
  'tempocentric' ahistoricism, 206, 210
  Western hyper-agency, 321
Ward, Lester, 8, 84, 108, 110, 111, 119–121, 277, 316, 324
  critic of laissez-faire social Darwinism, 92, 119
  critic of liberal altruistic doctrine, 120
  Lamarckianism, 8
Warren, Bill, 140, 234, 342
Watson, Adam, 223–225, 226, 227, 229, 230, 232
Watson, Matthew, 81
Webb, Sidney, 108, 316
Weber, Cynthia, 334
Weber, Max, 52
Weikart, Richard, 12, 104, 105, 110, 112, 163, 165
Weismann, August, 6, 111
Weiss, Linda, 219
Weldes, Jutta, 209
Wells, H. G., 108, 316
Weltpolitik, 159
Wendt, Alexander, 207, 216, 240, 334, 335
West
  ideational construct, 22
Westad, Odd Arne, 206
Wheeler, Nicholas, 222
Whelan, Frederick, 56, 60, 80, 275, 291
white man's burden, 27, 35, 180, 198, 200, 315
Wight, Martin, 224, 232
Williams, Eric, 17
Wilson, Peter, 133, 176

Wilson, Woodrow, 167–175, 274, 303, 316, 318, 324
 'character' as pre-requisite for democracy, 172
 containment of Negroes, 169, 170–172
 critique of Southern Reconstruction, 170–172
 denial of Eastern self-determination, 173
 globalization-as-Western opportunity, 20
 imperialism, 25, 172–174
 implicit links to J. A. Hobson's theory, 50
 Lamarckianism, 166, 168, 172, 173
 nurturing 'character' through imperialism, 172
 parallels with John W. Burgess, 170, 172
 qualified conception of democracy, 172
 racist policies/actions, 168
 rejection of non-white immigration, 169, 175
 rejecting the Japanese racial equality clause, 168, 174–175
 Teutonic race theory of the state, 169
 the 'whitewashing', 322
Wittfogel, Karl A., 5
Wolf, Eric R., 236
Wolf, Martin, 290
Woolf, Leonard, 17, 134, 175–177, 317, 318
 commitment to 'sane' international imperialism, 176
 critique of 'insane' imperialism, 175
 critique of scientific racism, 176
 critique of the League, 167
 globalization as Western opportunity, 20
 overlaps with J. A. Hobson's theory, 50, 175, 177
 paternalist conception of imperialism, 25, 175–177
 Western hyper-agency, 176

world-polity theory, 304
world-systems theory, 236–242
 compared with scientific racism, 319
 differentiated from orthodox anti-paternalist Eurocentrism, 322
 eliding Eastern agency, 238, 240–242
 endogenous Eurocentric logic of immanence, 236–238
 Eurocentric ahistoricism, 253–254
 Eurocentric 'big bang theory', 236–240
 Eurocentric overlaps with Gramscianism, 252–253
 Eurofetishism, 240, 252
 globalization as the triumph of the West, 343
 hegemony, 239
 naturalizing Western imperialism, 234
 structural Eurofunctionalism, 238–240, 241–242, 252
 three worlds Eurocentric construct, 236–240

yellow peril, 8, 88, 89, 104, 106, 107, 108, 127, 145, 147, 157, 201, 202, 265, 270, 278, 315, *See also* barbaric peril
Young, Robert J. C., 286

Zakaria, Fareed, 271
Zarakol, Ayşe, 222, 303
Zhang, Yongjin, 207
Zimmern, Alfred, 50, 134, 135, 177–181, 317, 318
 globalization as Western opportunity, 20
 imperial angst, 178–179
 paternalist conception of imperialism, 25, 179
 'second' British Empire, 179
 'third' British Empire, 181
 the British Empire as preserver of the League, 180

Persaud, Randolph B., and R. B. J. Walker (eds) 2001: 'Race in International Relations', (special issue) *Alternatives* 26: 373–543.
Pick, Daniel 1989: *Faces of Degeneration* (Cambridge: Cambridge University Press).
Pieterse, Jan Nederveen 1991: 'Dilemmas of Development Discourse: The crisis of developmentalism and the comparative method', *Development and Change* 22(1): 5–29.
Pieterse, Jan Nederveen 1992: *White on Black* (London: Yale University Press).
Pitts, Jennifer 2005: *A Turn to Empire* (Princeton: Princeton University Press).
Porter, Bernard 1968: *Critics of Empire* (London: Macmillan).
Price, Richard, and Nina Tannenwald 2003: 'Norms and Deterrence: The Nuclear Weapons Taboo', in Katzenstein (ed.): 114–52.
Quirk, Joel, and Darshan Vigneswaran 2005: 'The Construction of an Edifice: The Story of a First Great Debate', *Review of International Studies* 31(1): 89–107.
Raju, C. K. 2007: *Cultural Foundation of Mathematics* (New Delhi: Pearson Education).
Reus-Smit, Christian 1999: *The Moral Purpose of the State* (Princeton: Princeton University Press).
Reus-Smit, Christian 2005: 'Liberal Hierarchy and the License to use Force', *Review of International Studies* 31(SI): 71–92.
Rich, Paul 2002: 'Reinventing Peace: David Davies, Alfred Zimmern and Liberal Internationalism in Interwar Britain', *International Relations* 16(1): 117–33.
Rosenberg, Justin 2008: 'Uneven and Combined Development: The Social-Relational Substratum of "the International"?', *Cambridge Review of International Affairs*, 21(1): 77–112.
Rothkopf, David 1997: 'In Praise of Cultural Imperialism?', *Foreign Policy* 107 (Summer): 38–53.
Said, Edward W. 1978/2003: *Orientalism* (Harmondsworth: Penguin).
Salter, Mark B. 2002: *Barbarians & Civilization in International Relations* (London: Pluto).
Salter, Mark B. 2007: 'Not Waiting for the Barbarians', in Hall and Jackson (eds.): 81–93.
Sandbrook, Dominic 2010: 'Stop Saying Sorry for our History', *Daily Mail* (31 July): 16–17.
Schmidt, Brian C. 1998a: *The Political Discourse of Anarchy* (New York: SUNY Press).
Schmidt, Brian C. 1998b: 'Lessons from the Past: Reassessing the Interwar Disciplinary History of International Relations', *International Studies Quarterly* 42(3): 433–59.
Schmidt, Brian C. 2002: 'Anarchy, World Politics and the Birth of a Discipline: American International Relations, Pluralist Theory and the Myth of Interwar Idealism', *International Relations* 16(1): 9–31.
Schmidt, Brian C. 2008: 'Political Science and the American Empire: A Disciplinary History of the "Politics" Section and the Discourse of Imperialism and Colonialism', *International Politics* 45(6): 675–87.

Lightning Source UK Ltd.
Milton Keynes UK
UKHW020948120819
347814UK00009B/61/P